GENERATION
AND DEGENERATION

GENERATION

AND DEGENERATION

Tropes of Reproduction in

Literature and History from Antiquity

through Early Modern Europe

EDITED BY VALERIA FINUCCI

& KEVIN BROWNLEE

Duke University Press   Durham and London 2001

An earlier version of "Menstruating Men" was published in
Italian as "Uomini menstruanti: Somiglianza e differenza
fra i sessi in Europa in etá moderna," *Quaderni Storici* 27,
no. 1 (1992): 51–103.

CONTENTS

ACKNOWLEDGMENTS

This book was born out of weekly dinner conversations held a few years ago in Philadelphia. Each Thursday we alternated between two different seating arrangements at the Brownlees' table: at 6:00, we participated in the children's activities; and at 8:00, we turned conversation into adult concerns. Generation and genealogy were more than fortuitous issues for us in those days, as Kevin and I, each for different existential reasons, started to contest biology and retest time. Soon our project turned into a collaborative process. Bringing colleagues on board became an occasion for creating friendships and renewing cooperation, and we relied on the efficiency of electronic mail to keep conversations going, no matter the miles. A visit by Dale Martin in Florence enlarged the original time frame of our inquiry, and a conference at Duke University on the body brought in Nancy Siraisi's voice. We have stories (and memories) for each of our friends in the volume—their intellectual interests are spread all over these pages just as their wit has brightened our endeavor.

We are happy to acknowledge the good will of Reynolds Smith of Duke University Press for his interest in the project and for shepherding it to the end; the anonymous readers contacted by the press for their generous suggestions, enthusiastic assessments, and a new turn at the title; Giuseppe Gerbino for his humor and expert skills at indexing; Maura High for her patience at each shift of our collective syntax; Patricia Mickelberry for her professional handling of the manuscript; and Sharon Torian for her sunny disposition.

Marina Brownlee provided the most cheerful friendship and love. Elizabeth Clark was there, as always. To them we—the lucky ones—dedicate this book.

Introduction
Genealogical Pleasures, Genealogical Disruptions

VALERIA FINUCCI

This book is about the discourses that inform constructions of genealogies, whether we speak of genealogy in the biological sense of procreation and reproduction or in the metaphorical sense of heritage and cultural patrimony. It retraces generational fantasies and generational discords in a variety of related contexts, from the medical to the theological, and from the literary to the historical. It moves through a number of centuries, from Greco-Roman times to our more recent past. It reflects on topics as varied as what makes men manly to who is Christ's father, and from what kinds of erotic practices went on among women in sixteenth-century Turkish seraglios to how men's hemorrhoids can be variously labeled.

Such discourses necessarily bring to the forefront concepts of sexual identity and gender politics. For many centuries generation—and thus genealogy—has been understood as men's business. So much has been written by physicians, theologians, philosophers, anthropologists, cultural critics, and writers of literature on why men and engendering are linked, that the point hardly seems in need of elaboration here. Women do not generate, Augustine reminds us, following the scripture. They conceive.[1] But can any man generate, and is marriage only for the generating kind? Unlike Roman law, the church did not take a position until a brief of Pope Sixtus V, "Cum frequenter" (1588), was interpreted as declaring that eunuchs, castrati, and *spadones* (that is, men with damaged sexual organs) were not real men because they could not offer intergenerational continuity, no matter their heterosexual affections, if any, and therefore could not legally

---

1. Augustine, *Opus imperfectum* 3.85.4. See also Clark's essay in this volume.

enter marriage.[2] The ability to perform sexually (*potentia coeundi*) may have made a man look like one, but the ability to generate (*potentia generandi*) alone guaranteed that he was one in the eyes of the legal and ecclesiastical system. Thus not only masculinity needed to be learned through rites of passage and practices of acculturation, but manhood also had to be a performance to register on the body of the next generation.

Womanhood has been so historically and socially related to reproduction that the obsession of physicians of the past with menstruation and amenorrhea can be easily understood. Less known is their preoccupation with the effects of the female mind on the generative process. Yet what kinds of genealogies do women create when only fathers have blood ties to children, as in Roman law? "Blood is the best of sauces, the food and pasture of life," Levino Lennio wrote, but there is blood and blood.[3] The blood concocted by women to help in generation, according to Galen, was not good enough, and the law held uterine ties less binding than blood ties.[4] A concerned philosopher and doctor, Marsilio Ficino, had a recipe for regeneration of old men that used blood as a reconstituent. Men between sixty-three and seventy years old who felt the burden of aging in their members could drink the blood of an energetic, healthy, and good-natured youth, he advised, taking care to enter this cure with the moon rising. Alternately, they could "ravenously" apply their mouths to the breasts of a healthy, happy, temperate, and beautiful maiden and suck ("pongi gamelico la bocca alle tette, e sugane il latte"), taking care to add powdered fennel and sugar to their diet to avoid putrefaction of her milk.[5] In Ficino's

2. Sixtus V, "Cum frequenter," Archivum Secretum Vaticanum, Fondo Secretariatus Brevium, Spagna, vol. 129, fol. 82.

3. Levino Lennio (Levinus Lemnius), *Della complessione del corpo humano* (Venice: Domenico Nicolino, 1564), 70r. My translation.

4. For a reading of blood ties and consanguinity in Roman law in this context (a child had blood ties with his father, since paternal semen was refined blood, and uterine ties with his mother, since the maternal uterus made him grow), see Gianna Pomata, "Legami di sangue, legami di seme: Consanguineità e agnazione nel diritto romano," *Quaderni storici* 86 (1994): 299–333.

5. Marsilio Ficino (1433–1499), *De le tre vite; cioè a qual guisa si possono le persone letterate mantenere in sanità* (Venice: Tramezzino, 1548), bk. 2, chap. 11, 44r–v. As for old women (called "witches" here), they too regenerated themselves by sucking the blood of children ("fantolini") on Thursday nights. In late medieval iconography, Christ too was represented as lactating blood to offer another kind of regeneration. See Caroline Walker Bynum, *Jesus as*

Galenic system, blood is not an equal-opportunity resource; when one uses women's liquids for regeneration, it is better to drink their milk, which is concocted from blood, than their blood, given the more rudimentary construction of female physiology and the excremental, moon-governed nature of most female fluids.

Generation inevitably evokes its opposite, degeneration. In the premodern world, degeneration was present everywhere, as a way of life and as a philosophy. People from all classes, but especially the poor, lived sorry lives tormented by scabies, leeches, fistulae, and malaria; they fed themselves so poorly that they routinely had scurvy and pellagra; rarely did they have the opportunity or even the medical recommendation to bathe; and their sanitary arrangements consisted of open-air cesspools. Money made little difference, in any case, in a philosophical system where all matter in nature degenerates even when seemingly in a healthy state, where women are most of the time intrinsically polluted by *immunditia menstruorum*, and where men's hot blood needs to undergo routine phlebotomies to avoid tumors.[6] The body, whether human or animal, was visualized as generating a legion of worms that needed to be managed through the widest array of herbal concoctions or by using one's bodily refuse as a cure. Urine, feces, menstrual blood, semen, smegma, sweat, saliva, earwax, even dried-out human flesh (*mummia*) were made into pessaries and electuaries to cure anything from gonorrhea to rheumatism, from lust to convulsions. In a humor-based system unaware of the role of ova in generation and of microbes in the propagation of disease, the mechanisms for engendering life were just as obscure as those put in place for curing its endless corruption.

On the psychoanalytical side too, generation has been rendered as a business involving men: the foundational myth of Saturn and Zeus, or that of Laius and Oedipus, involve a rebellion, a death and a growth. Any son, the myth promises, can take the place of his father and eventually acquire his authority. No wonder that *patria potestas* has so often been represented as castrating. The genealogy of male writers, Harold Bloom has suggested,

Mother: Studies in the Spirituality of the High Middle Ages (Berkeley: University of California Press, 1982), 112–13.

6. See, for example, Giambattista Della Porta, *Della fisionomia dell'huomo* (Vicenza: Tozzi, 1615), 11. Most at risk were fat men with red hair.

follows somewhat the same trajectory. All literary sons have to deal with the ghost of established bards in a dynamics of desire and jealousy, acceptance and refusal, imitation and alienation that at best fosters the necessary anxiety of authorship leading to creativity, and at worst cripples the young writers and leads them into hysterical isolation and brooding defeatism. But let us put gender into the equation. Do daughters suffer from an anxiety of influence vis-à-vis their mothers, just as sons do for their fathers? And why would a lack of proper paternal sponsorship, even a literary one, be worked through by sisters the same way as by brothers?[7] To subsume genealogy to male lineage—and to equate literary heritage across genders—is just as questionable as confusing heterosexuality with paternal and maternal reproductive desires.

A search for origin, identity, and authorization informs the first section of this book, "Theories of Reproduction." In Latin *genitus* (past participle of *gignere*, to be born) is the one who generates, the genitor, and the one who works toward reproduction through genitals. That is, a living being is created in the presence of two genitors (more or less actively involved, depending on whether one uses Aristotelian or Hippocratic/Galenic categories) and through the use of organs made to engender. Until the discovery by Francesco Redi in 1688 that there is no spontaneous generation in nature, this process was not thought to apply to inferior beings such as lizards, toads, and bees, which were formed through putrefaction and therefore needed no genitor.[8] A still current exception is the generation of Christ. In her essay "Generation, Degeneration, Regeneration: Original Sin and the Conception of Jesus in the Polemic between Augustine and Julian of Eclanum," Elizabeth A. Clark demonstrates that even highly theological debates, such as those concerning Christ's lineage, can be grounded in culturally bound and historically determined biological understandings of reproduction. Clark retraces the development of the debate over original sin

---

7. Harold Bloom, *The Anxiety of Influence* (New York: Oxford University Press, 1973). For a classic feminist response to Bloom, see Sandra Gilbert and Susan Gubar, *The Madwoman in the Attic: The Woman Writer and the Nineteenth-Century Literary Imagination* (New Haven: Yale University Press, 1979).
8. Francesco Redi, *Esperienze intorno alla generazione degli insetti*, in *Scienziati del Seicento*, ed. Maria Luisa Altieri Biagi (Milan: Rizzoli, 1969), 314–463. See also Howard Adelmann, *Marcello Malpighi and the Evolution of Embryology* (Ithaca: Cornell University Press, 1966).

between Julian of Eclanum, a Pelagian bishop, and Augustine. This polemic soon moved beyond theology to touch issues related to sexuality, marriage, and generation. For the Pelagian, Adam's seed was formed through sexual desire, as the doctors of the time were saying; thus procreation was the result not of human sinfulness but of a natural human function. In this view, children are born innocent of sin. Augustine argued otherwise. He used what we could call a genetic insight in claiming that children are born with original sin although their parents may have already been redeemed through baptism, just as parents can transmit defects to their offsprings that they themselves do not carry.

The controversy was important, Clark demonstrates, because it directly involved the issue of the marriage of Mary and Joseph and the birth of Christ. Augustine reasoned that Mary and Joseph had a regular marriage but never engaged in sexual intercourse. Working from the premises that man, not woman, gives seed to generate, and that no man was involved in the engendering of Jesus, Augustine concluded that Jesus was free of original sin. He was not conceived through sex. Mary's contribution was not seed but matter. True, being born of man, she was under the shadow of original sin, but God's grace had redeemed her. The theory of man's seed and woman's matter was central to the medical pronouncements of the Roman doctor Soranus who certified woman's inferiority in generation. Clark shows that Augustine used this theory to bend the issue of Jesus's genealogy in his favor, that is, to prove that he was without original sin. And so a long-lasting theological tenet was underpinned by medical theory.

The role of women in the generative process, although inferior to that of man, was of course necessary. Aristotle had famously argued that women contributed nothing to generation other than the womb in which the fetus develops, but the Renaissance sided with Galen and gave women an active role vis-à-vis men, albeit inferior because the female humoral system was insufficiently refined to reach a hot-and-dry optimum. Lack of proper male participation, deemed possible among some animal species like the hyena, which was considered bisexual and able to engender by itself in alternate years when it was female, would only make women generate monsters.[9] That is, the possession of organs of generation was sufficient to filiate, but

9. Pliny the Elder, *Natural History*, trans. H. Rackham (Cambridge: Cambridge University Press, 1942), 8.44.77.

only fathers could make the whole process right through their capacity to give a form and a soul to a fetus with their semen. How to account then for monstrous offsprings? By postulating a too-active female imagination.[10] Such is the case explored in the essay "Maternal Imagination and Monstrous Birth: Tasso's *Gerusalemme liberata*," where I look at the effects of uncontrolled maternal fantasy. In Tasso's *Gerusalemme*, the woman warrior Clorinda bears no somatic relation to her parents, in that she is white and her genitors are black. The explanation given for this siring gone awry is that Clorinda's pregnant Ethiopian mother looked so much at the pious image of a white virgin saved by Saint George that her child's features were indelibly impressed with her hysterical desire. I examine fifteenth- and sixteenth-century books on monstrosity, especially African monstrosity, medical treatises on the effects and ills of maternal imagination, and the cultural fashion among rich Venetians of placing paintings of heroes and virginal saints hanging on bedchambers' walls, to reconstruct the appeal of such a fantasy of generation/degeneration in Renaissance culture.

This hidden blackness of Clorinda's—of which the woman warrior was totally unaware as she was growing up—constitutes the indelible mark that allows Tasso to construct a woman so impossible to assimilate that she needs *a priori* to die. In order to accomplish this goal Tasso engineers a masterful, if overly teary, scene of soul cleansing and martyrdom that has remained famous in Italian literature and music for centuries: Clorinda is not only unwittingly killed by the man (Tancredi) who loves her but she also declares herself happy to be dead, when she later appears to him in a dream, because he made her Christian. Her baptism by Tancredi *in extremis* authenticates her as white (not that blacks couldn't be Christian, but the Ethiopian Church was suspect because of its Anabaptist practices) and pacifies an author equally obsessed with Counter-Reformation orthodoxy and the desire for an authorizing paternal figure, a heavenly, all-forgiving, and (it was supposed) white Father.

In the second section of this book, "Boundaries of Sex and Gender," the issue of reproduction is problematized further as fathers turn out to be precarious engenderers, male bodies leak like humor-challenged female

---

10. Monstrosity was also a sign from heaven or the result of devilish interventions, but by the sixteenth century causes were mostly attributed to human faults.

bodies, and lesbians bypass accepted strategies of heterosexuality and re-production altogether. Dale Martin's essay, "Contradictions of Masculinity: Ascetic Inseminators and Menstruating Men in Greco-Roman Culture," shows how ideology can accommodate deviations from what is considered normal, so that it was possible for Greek and Roman doctors to believe that masculinity was revealed both through indulgence in sex and through abstention from sex. The same could be said of the many recorded cases of "menstruating" men, whose corporeal bleeding, hemorrhoids, and nose-bleeds showed that some male bodies were inadequately male—without doctors necessarily inferring that such male menstruation was a sign of effeminacy or of lack of masculinity.

Thus for Martin the cultural constructions of masculinity are unstable; any man, at any given time, may not live up to the standards for the male sex. To be male and to be manly are not necessarily linked. But it is pre-cisely this postulated inadequacy that makes constructions of masculinity more ideologically serviceable, Martin argues, for it ensures that mascu-linity is controlled, or at times restored, by the many physicians who cared for upper-class men (doctors rarely concerned themselves with slaves or the poor) and wrote about what makes men manly. Maleness, in this sense, becomes valuable precisely because contradictions within masculinity are culturally accommodated.

A typically feminine function, menstruation, is at the center of the next essay, which considers male menstruation from a different perspective. Gianna Pomata's "Menstruating Men: Similarity and Difference of the Sexes in Early Modern Medicine" looks at so-called menstruating men from the sixteenth through the nineteenth century in Europe and provides a surprising number of instances in which this phenomenon is recorded in medical opinions and treatises. Pomata argues that our idea that there is something negative, abnormal, or pathological in menstruation is perhaps more in tune with a view of nature as constituted by a set of mechanical laws (a view that came into fashion after the second half of the seventeenth cen-tury), rather than as a providential and curative force, which was the case from the Hippocratics through Galen. It was only in the nineteenth cen-tury, she argues, that menstruating men were connected to cases of herma-phroditism as science medicalized and pathologized the condition. Earlier, menstruating men were thought to be sexually normal, or even sexually well endowed. The fact that the male body menstruated was seen positively as a way for nature to respect its laws, which meant that the human organism naturally evacuated whatever was superfluous. In this sense, the female body was considered more efficient than the male.

The result of this line of thinking is that Pomata is able to put a hole in the assumption among historians of science that until the late seventeenth century there existed a homology between the male and the female body, with the latter being considered inferior but not dissimilar to the former. If such was the case, she asks, why was no negative opinion expressed in recorded cases of male menstruation? Why was this form of bodily discharge encouraged as an outlet for superfluous humors and thought to follow a distinct monthly or lunar female pattern? Finally, why would a man want to replicate the functions of female bodies when these bodies were considered inferior?

Pomata's emphasis on the specificity of menstruation as a signifying female position is echoed in the next essay, where a claim is made for a distinct female space in erotic practices. In "The Psychomorphology of the Clitoris, or The Reemergence of the *Tribade* in English Culture," Valerie Traub argues that lesbianism is not an infantile stage of female desire en route to heterosexuality (Freud's story), but a transgressive strategy that disrupts heterosexuality. The discourse on lesbianism, she writes, was born in the sixteenth century with the "rediscovery" of the clitoris by Falloppio and Colombo and the writing down of fantasies about what tribadism meant. By moving a few centuries back, she challenges Foucauldian accounts that same-sex eroticism became articulated and intelligible only after modern discourses of identity were formulated, and Thomas Laqueur's social constructionist view that only after the emergence of a differentiated biological construction of the male and female body (which he placed in the eighteenth century) did a truly homoerotic discourse become possible.

Traub retraces the genealogy of the tribade and of the clitoris in the travel narratives of the sixteenth century, which located lesbian forms of sexual desire in Turkish baths or among fortune-tellers in Fez. She then moves to England and to the medical treatises that fantasized on the shape and the uses and abuses of the clitoris and offered recommendations on what techniques worked to curb disruptions of same-sex pleasures. Traub's task is not to privilege the clitoris as the prime source of lesbian sexuality nor to depathologize Freudian narratives of lesbianism, but to disrupt the logic of anatomical essentialism that—by making desires commensurate—restricts erotic practices and dictates identities.

When one adds a history to generation, we have a genealogy, that is, a *genitus* and a *logos*. Philosophically and culturally speaking, women and men have never related equally to the *logos;* this has meant that socially women have been constructed with impunity as inferior to men and legally they have been unable to transmit titles or have jurisdiction over their children. Still, women have been just as active as men, although less vocal, in fashioning their own genealogy. In the third section, "Female Genealogies," the term "genealogy" is used metaphorically as a way for women to create a literary and political lineage and break out of the strictures of their worlds without exorcizing their mothers. Focusing on Spain, Marina Scordilis Brownlee shows how women writers carefully set about creating genealogies that run counter to official state discourses on identity politics, family, and reproduction. In her essay, "Genealogies in Crisis: Maria de Zayas in Seventeenth-Century Spain," Brownlee argues that Maria de Zayas uses narratives of the family and domestic details to comment on the state of decay of the Spanish empire. In her short stories and in the construction of her literary persona (made by herself and by others), Zayas provides intriguing examples of the intrusion of class issues and race relations—history—into everyday life. Rather than being branded as a "whore" for leaving the domestic space to become a public figure with her writing, she is hailed as the tenth muse, and the laudatory remarks made about her conform to her representation as a neuter being, neither male nor female.[11] What sets Zayas apart is her constant exposé of colonial discourses regarding relations of race, blood purity, and gender norms, and her focus on the imbalances and chaos of the empire.

The way Zayas achieves her extended critique of the family romance is by offering human relationships that do not conform to the heterosexual paradigms of marriage and procreation. Zayas first eliminates children and then offers alternatives to the nuclear family that have the effect of commenting on the officially sanctioned myths of male/female relations, such

---

11. On the tenth muse, see Stephanie Jed, "The Tenth Muse: Gender, Rationality, and the Marketing of Knowledge," in *Women, "Race," and Writing in the Early Modern Period,* ed. Margo Kendricks and Patricia Parker (New York: Routledge, 1994), 195–208.

as the story of the woman sexually involved with her black slave or that of the wife who walks in on her husband's homoerotic liaison. Marina Brownlee argues that such fascination with "bizarre," ungenerative models of human behavior is, in part, a function of the unprecedented "tabloid" craze that took over Spain in the seventeenth century as an expression of "scientific" inquiry and discourse — of the untold (often monstrous) wonders of the New World being transmitted for the first time to the museums, salons, and street corners of Europe. Yet, at the same time, Zayas's unsanctioned couplings irreparably question and disrupt the hallowed genealogies of state power itself.

Taking a different route toward the construction of female agency and descent in the absence of a generating man and of children, Maureen Quilligan's piece, "Incest and Agency: The Case of Elizabeth I," centers on Elizabeth I's translation of Marguerite de Navarre's poem *Le Miroir de l'ame pecheresse* (1548), a text banned in France at the time because of its incestuous connotations. Quilligan argues that the then eleven-year-old English princess may have chosen the work to empower herself by connecting two royal females, a ghostly literary one, Marguerite — she too a would-be queen without the legal means to qualify for a throne, given French laws of succession — and a real woman, her stepmother, Katherine Parr, to whom she presented the translation. In doing so, Elizabeth appropriated for herself a fantasized incestuous genealogy. In the French work, the soul's relationship to God is rendered in gendered terms so that a kind of "holy incest" is staged: the love of God is equated with the male line of love — that is, father, brother, spouse, and son — while the soul is equated with the female line: sister, mother, spouse, and child. Connecting this work to the story of Elizabeth's life and her family, Quilligan demonstrates how intimately tied to incest this royal life was, given that her father had broken with the Catholic Church over an issue of incest and that her mother was executed because, among other things, she was accused of having slept with her brother. Elizabeth was thus the product of a publicly incestuous mother, whose death made her a bastard, and of a privately incest-oriented father. If these twin problems of incest and illegitimacy on the one hand complicated marriage arrangements, on the other hand they enabled female agency. Thus Elizabeth's acceptance and fantastic reworking of an incestuous family lineage allowed her to "stop" the marriage traffic in women.

Quilligan gives a close material analysis of Elizabeth's text, in the literal sense of looking at the covers, inscriptions, and prefaces of its various editions from 1548 to 1569, 1582 and 1590. She argues that Elizabeth's discourse of incest, rather than figuring anxiety, served different, multiple purposes: it gratified the fantasized erotics of a prospective husband, it linked her to the church as spouse and to the people as mother, and it valorized the eloquence of other prayerful women. In the end, Elizabeth made an incestuous story of origins serve the purposes of the state as well as her own need to control her self-image and public role.

The last section, "The Politics of Inheritance," offers another metaphorical genealogy, one that involves men rather than women; specifically, sons who further their political and economic motivations by inventing a scientific, social, and literary ancestry. In declaring their emancipation from fathers, these male writers solipsistically create their precursors. In "In Search of the Origins of Medicine: Egyptian Wisdom and Some Renaissance Physicians," Nancy G. Siraisi examines the construction of a genealogy of medicine in the sixteenth century that links this branch of knowledge and practice to Egyptian rather than Greek fathers. She concentrates on discussions among physicians at the University of Padua and on the reactions that thoughts on the subject generated. Doctors who supported the Egyptian origins of medicine held that some medical techniques, such as bloodletting and the clyster, came from Egypt because they were naturally observed in Egyptian animals, such as the hippopotamus and the ibis. They noted that some human or semidivine names of discoverers of medicine were Egyptian, such as Mercury/Hermes, and that the first pseudo-Galenic text gave Egypt as much authority in medical practice as Greece. The intent of the two Paduan doctors most linked to this search, Prospero Alpino and his teacher Guilandinus, was primarily pharmacological and botanical in that they identified specifically Egyptian medical ingredients, although there was a difference in their views of what was being found. The same material spoke differently, however, to Girolamo Mercuriale, who reduced the discoveries of Egyptian doctors to the invention of *ars cosmetica*. What downgraded Egyptian medicine in his eyes and in those of a number of historicizing experts was its link to magic and superstition. Greek medicine, on the other hand, provided a role for understanding the human body through various theories of humors and temperaments. Thus when Paracelsus claimed the origin of the alchemical tradition in Hermes, the response from Mercuriale and his colleagues could only be narrow: in their need to discredit alchemy they had to doom Egyptian medicine altogether.

The search for a father—Greek or Egyptian—was considered not only a humanistic search for origins, Siraisi posits, but also a political and economic drive, in that the commercial interests of the Venetian Republic—and thus of Paduan professors—overdetermined the attitude of physicians and philosophers of medicine toward the near East.

The issue of paternal authorization, and the fear that an overly dominant father engenders in a son determined to find his place, informs the essay by Kevin Brownlee. In "The Conflicted Genealogy of Cultural Authority: Italian Responses to French Cultural Dominance in *Il Tesoretto, Il Fiore,* and *La Commedia,*" Brownlee examines how three Italian medieval authors—Brunetto Latini, Durante, and Dante—dealt with the hegemony of French literature in European culture while trying to establish the worth and merit of their vernacular Italian output. By focusing on representations of the *locus amoenus* and of the god of love in these texts, Brownlee shows that the Italians chose to bypass, and programmatically suppress, French models in their writings by claiming instead a direct genealogy with classical authors, specifically (given the context) Ovid. This correction took many shapes: it was at times a deconstruction and a marginalization, while at others it became an omission or an outright dismissal of the *Roman de la rose* as father text.

Thus Brunetto, the writer of *Il Fiore,* and Dante could assert their own linguistic supremacy and authority through two enabling techniques; by harking back to prestigious French literary works without explicit acknowledgment, they could use a format that would guarantee them a readership, and by reinscribing themselves in the Western tradition through specific imitation of classical models, they could appropriate a literary lineage for themselves. And so through idiosyncratic misreadings, they also became fathers: Brunetto is today Dante's acknowledged literary mentor ("la cara e buona imagine paterna"), and Dante is recognized, then as now, as the patriarch of Italian literature.[12]

Kevin Brownlee's literary sons were able to fashion a genealogy for themselves without paternal *fiat.* But can a seemingly void, nongenerative figure of generation, like the ghost, activate identities and lineage as well? In "Hauntings: The Materiality of Memory on the Renaissance Stage," Peter Stallybrass concentrates on the most famous ghost on stage, Hamlet's father, and the clothes he wore in different versions of Shakespeare's

12. Dante, *Inferno,* 15.83.

play—mostly armor, but at times a sort of "spirit drapery"—to show that in the Renaissance ghosts were very material figures, while later they became somewhat invisible as our belief in them diminished. Thus the question, What clothes do ghosts wear? For Hamlet's father, armor marks his status and gives away his genealogy. The costumed king demands his son to right his legacy, and what legacy he wants remembered is written all over his armor. This ghost haunts because he "wears," so to speak, names, duties, and memories. Stallybrass argues that the material identity supplied by armor contrasts with the slow disintegration of identity of the physical body in sheets. The cloth wrapping the dead body subsumes both body and identity to decay, but armor works to display the continuity of aristocratic identities.

The father's death here signifies little, since his identity, and thus his patriarchal authority, survives, body or no body. The person wearing his armor can occupy that identity as well as bestow it to somebody else. But Stallybrass also notices that armor rusts, just as cloth decays, and it too is transferred from body to body. This detachability runs counter to the idea that armor confers name and fame, and therefore it makes armor alienable. The ghost may disappear after all.

Thus we have come full circle: Stallybrass's paternal ghosts defy biological paternity just as much as Clark's "superfluous" father of Christ. As new theological systems were devised by church fathers to reconcile christological beliefs and "scientific" evidence, new ways of accommodating sexual choices have lately redirected in more ways than one legal debates about *consanguinitas*. Sixtus V's pronouncement against the marriage of nonprocreative men, a decision that surprisingly stood for almost four centuries, was repealed by the Catholic Church in 1966. In 1977, the church's Sacred Congregation for the Doctrine of the Faith, the legislative branch that once was called the Inquisition, legislated that all men can marry if they wish so, whether or not they can emit *verum semen* in copulation (that is, semen produced in the testicles), as long as they choose a heterosexual partner.[13] But the social anxieties that blamed maternal imagination for fetal abnormalities in the early modern period have not disappeared. They get restaged

---

13. Thus not only vasectomized men but also those lacking both testicles because of accidents or congenital conditions can contract marriage. As late as 1946 the marriages of men who voluntarily chose surgical sterilization were annulled. Ecclesiastic jurisprudence recurred specifically to eunuchs for comparison: "Eum qui duplicem vasectomiam passus

today through the claim that addicted mothers, never fathers, are vectors of fetal risk. The cultural construction of procreation, biology, degeneration, masculinity, femininity, legacy, and lineage only ensures that, now as in our common "Western" past, genealogical pleasures are fully matched by genealogical disruptions.

---

est censemus omnino impotentem et inhabilem ad matrimonium, quippe omnino aequiparandum eunucho." In Francesco Saverio Wernz and Pedro Vidal, *Ius matrimoniale* in *Ius canonicum* (Rome: Pontificia Università Gregoriana, 1946). vol. 5, n. 233. I examine some of these issues in my forthcoming book, *The Politics of the Body in the Italian Renaissance*.

I
THEORIES
OF REPRODUCTION

Generation, Degeneration, Regeneration: Original Sin and the Conception of Jesus in the Polemic between Augustine and Julian of Eclanum

ELIZABETH A. CLARK

While he was still speaking to the people, behold, his mother and
his brothers stood outside, asking to speak to him. But he replied to the
man who told him, "Who is my mother, and who are my brothers?" And
stretching out his hand toward his disciples, he said, "Here are my
mother and my brothers! For whoever does the will of my
Father in heaven is my brother, and sister, and mother."
—Matt. 12:46–50

... the father of Joseph, the husband of Mary, of whom Jesus was born,
who is called Christ. — Matt. 1:16

Jesus, when he began his ministry, was about thirty years of age,
being the son (as was supposed) of Joseph. — Luke 3:23

Who can declare his generation? — Isaiah 53:8

I

Who, indeed, were Jesus' father and mother? Most early Catholic Christians answered "God" and "Mary," the latter deemed a virgin at the time she conceived Jesus, but whose sexual and marital status after Jesus' birth was a

Abbreviations used in the notes: CCL *Corpus Christianorum,* Series Latina (Turnhout: Brepols, 1953–); CSEL *Corpus Scriptorum Ecclesiasticorum Latinorum* (Vienna: C. Gerodi, et al., 1866–); *Ep. Epistula;* PL *Patrologia Latina,* ed. J.-P. Migne (Paris: Migne, 1844–1865); TU *Texte und Untersuchungen zur Geschichte des altchristlichen Literatur* (Berlin: Akademie-Verlag, 1883–).

matter of considerable debate.[1] The decade-long polemic between Augustine of Hippo and his Pelagian opponent, Julian of Eclanum,[2] in the early fifth century proved important in defining for the later Latin West *why* Jesus' "father" was divine and his mother, human but virginal. Although Elizabeth Cady Stanton (and doubtless many other moderns) have expressed dissatisfaction with the incoherence of the Gospel accounts of Jesus' genealogy and birth ("If a Heavenly Father was necessary, why not a Heavenly Mother? If an earthly Mother was admirable, why not an earthly Father? . . . These Biblical mysteries and inconsistencies are a great strain on the credulity of the ordinary mind."),[3] the Christian confession of divine paternity and human maternity was in Augustine's view not only founded on scriptural revelation but was also in accord with ideas concerning human generation and degeneration implied in his theory of original sin.

The earliest Christian writings we possess—Paul's letters—testify to the author's preoccupation with sin and its origin. Particularly in his letter to the Romans, Paul noted the seeming universality of sinfulness, the "war in the members" that pits the "flesh" against the "spirit" of all humans. In Romans 5, Paul wrote that "sin came into the world through one man and death through sin, and so death spread to all men because all men sinned"—words that could be interpreted to mean that all men followed Adam in sinning and brought death upon themselves as a punishment for their sins. Yet Paul used the phrases "if many died through one man's trespass" and "if, because of one man's trespass, death reigned through that

---

1. For example, debate over whether or not Mary and Joseph's relation constituted a marriage; whether the brothers and sisters of Jesus mentioned in the Gospels were blood-brothers and sisters, or "relatives." See discussion at 33–34.

2. Pelagianism (named after its founder, Pelagius) was a Christian movement arising in the early fifth century that stressed the goodness of creation and humans' ability to keep the biblical commandments. It was condemned as a heresy from the second decade of the fifth century onward for its alleged failure to emphasize human sinfulness and the necessity of God's forgiving grace; opponents of Pelagianism believed that the movement preached a message of "self-help." Pelagians, for their part, thought that Augustine's theory of original sin implied that God was unjust in creating humans as morally weak, but nonetheless requiring them to keep the biblical commandments, and in condemning unbaptized infants to hell. Julian, bishop of Eclanum in southern Italy, was a "second-generation" Pelagian who extended the original Pelagian argument to center on issues of marriage and reproduction, as this essay details.

3. Elizabeth Cady Stanton, *The Woman's Bible* (Seattle, Wash.: Coalition Task Force on Women and Religion, 1992), 113.

one man" — words that could be interpreted to mean that there was a *causal* effect between Adam's sin and that of later humans (Rom. 5:12, 15, 17). The latter interpretation was bolstered by an early Latin translation implying that death came to all not "because" or "in that" all humans sinned, but because of the sin of him "in whom" we all sinned (i.e., Adam).[4] Although Paul does not so much highlight the responsibility of Adam for all future human sin in contrast to the divine gift of forgiveness with human waywardness, his authoritative words set the stage for discussions by various church fathers that connected our sinfulness and our deaths, somewhat vaguely, with Adam's. Within the Latin patristic tradition, Cyprian and Ambrose stand as two precursors whose reflections on the topic were to influence Augustine,[5] yet neither theologian tightly tied the notion of original sin to a biological process. This task was left to Augustine, whose developed theory was refined in the process of debate with Pelagius and his followers after 412 C.E.

This essay details the development of the polemic between Augustine and the "second-generation" Pelagian bishop, Julian of Eclanum, against the background of religious and ethical issues of the late fourth and early fifth century — issues that could prompt accusations of heresy. In the course of the debate over original sin and its implications for the evaluation of marriage and reproduction, questions of anthropology, late ancient biology, and the status of Jesus were raised and contested. Although these debates are little known outside the rather narrow circle of scholars who study late ancient Christianity, they were formative for all later Christian teaching on sexuality, reproduction, and the confession of Jesus' sinlessness.

II

Long before Augustine encountered Pelagius, however, he had done battle with a form of Manicheanism[6] that flourished among small circles of the

4. See Gerald Bonner, "Augustine on Romans 5, 12," *Studia evangelica* 2 (1968): 242–47, for a brief discussion of the issue.

5. Augustine appeals to Cyprian in *Opus imperfectum* 1.50; 1.72; and cites Ambrose on original sin in *Opus imperfectum* 1.2; 1.48; 1.72; 1.114; 2.1; 2.113; 2.163–64; 2.202; 2.208; 2.228 (among many other places).

6. Manicheanism (named after its founder, Mani) was a syncretist religion that developed from a Jewish baptismal sect in mid-third-century Persia. The movement taught that the material world (and everything in it, including human bodies) had been formed as the result

intellectual elite in the Latin West. Augustine's early, postconversion years as a Christian were marked by his opposition to Manichean determinism. Himself a former Manichean, Augustine wished as a Catholic to distance himself from the Manichean assignment of human wrongdoing to the power of darkness that allegedly overtook the human person: thus the Manichean "I" was not responsible.[7] Augustine's first writings as a Catholic Christian, by contrast, stressed the power of human free will and individual responsibility for one's actions: his early treatise that proclaimed this message, *On Free Will,* would in later decades be thrown in his face by his Pelagian opponents who cited it to oppose his mature predestinarian theory.[8] In the mid-390s, however, Augustine began to study the Pauline writings more closely. Once he had appropriated Paul's notion of universal human sinfulness, he was on his way to constructing a theory of predestination that emerged in fully developed form only in the second decade of the fifth century.[9]

The first stage of Augustine's conflict with Pelagians centered on the interpretation of God's goodness and justice in relation to human sin, on "free will" and "grace," for short. Nonetheless, even in Augustine's first anti-Pelagian treatise, *On the Merits and Remission of Sins,* dated to 412 C.E., the

---

of a battle between the original powers of light and darkness. All matter was thus tainted. Members of the Manichean sect were taught to refrain from procreation, which only further trapped particles of light in evil matter. The movement spread rapidly throughout the Near East and reached Egypt and then North Africa by the early fourth century. Augustine was a member of the Manichean sect from his adolescence until his middle twenties. To accuse a Christian of being a "Manichean" — as Julian of Eclanum accused Augustine in his later years — was to charge that the person had adopted overly ascetic theories or practices out of hatred for the created order and the God who made it. Roman emperors declared strict sanctions against Manicheans in the fourth century.

7. For a good discussion of this issue, see Robert A. Markus, "Augustine's *Confessions* and the Controversy with Julian of Eclanum: Manicheism Revisited," in *Collectanea Augustiniana: Mélanges T. J. Bavel,* ed. B. Bruning, M. Lamberigts, and J. Van Houtem (Leuven: Leuven University Press, 1990), 913–25.

8. Pelagius cites *On Free Will* against Augustine; see Augustine, *De natura et gratia* 81; *De dono perseverantiae* 27; 30; *Retractiones* 1.9.

9. For Augustine's exploration of Paul in the 390s, see Peter Brown, *Augustine of Hippo: A Biography* (Berkeley: University of California Press, 1969), 151–57, and Paula Fredriksen, "Paul and Augustine: Conversion Narratives, Orthodox Traditions, and the Retrospective Self," *Journal of Theological Studies,* n.s. 37 (1986): 3–34.

themes of his later debate with Julian of Eclanum—sexuality, marriage, and generation—are present. Augustine here claims that original sin is manifested in the "disobedient excitation of the members" that ensures all children will be born with "concupiscence," [10] that an "injury" is transferred to infants through the "sinful flesh" of those who produce them.[11] We infer from this treatise that already by 412, Pelagians had posed the questions with which Augustine would wrestle in his debate with Julian: Why do regenerated Christians not produce regenerated children? [12] Why do humans still die (on Augustine's theory, a punishment for original sin) if we have remission of sins through Christ? [13] Is the soul propagated with the body or not—and if not, how is sin, which pertains to the soul, transmitted? [14]

During the next few years, Augustine had much opportunity to reflect on the sin committed in the Garden of Eden. His most famous statement of the matter from this period is found in book 14 of the *City of God*. Here, Augustine posits that if Adam and Eve had not sinned, no unruly lust would have disturbed their peace and clouded their mental functions. The couple would have engaged in sexual intercourse in Eden to produce children, but they would not have been disturbed by the tussle between spirit and flesh. The genital organs of Adam and Eve would have moved at the bidding of the will, just as do our other bodily parts.[15] Defloration and labor pains would have remained unknown, since no injury could mar the happiness of Eden.[16] Our unruly sexual members and our feeling of shame at naked-

---

10. Augustine, *De peccatorum meritis et remissione* 1.57 (29); 2.4 (4) (CSEL 60, 56, 73).

11. *De peccatorum meritis* 3.2 (2) (CSEL 60, 130).

12. *De peccatorum meritis* 2.39 (25) (CSEL 60, 111): If Hebrews 7:9–10 testifies that Levi paid tithes in the loins of Abraham, the Pelagians ask why should we not think that regeneration is received by those still in the loins of baptized and regenerated fathers?

13. *De peccatorum meritis* 2.53 (33) (CSEL 60, 123).

14. *De peccatorum meritis* 2.59 (36) (CSEL 60, 127–28). Augustine responds with the answer to which he will forever adhere: we don't know, since Scripture gives no "certain and clear proofs." Augustine even rallies Pelagius's support for his caution: 3.18 (10) (CSEL 60, 144). On this point, it is useful to recall that Augustine was well aware of the theological difficulties that theological positions about the soul might entail: see *Epistula* 73.6 (3) (CSEL 34, 270–71) for his acknowledgment of reading Jerome's *Contra Rufinum*, a central document of the origenist debate. Also see Augustine's *Ep.* 143.6–11; 164.19–20 (7); 166; 180.2 (CSEL 44, 255–61, 538–39, 545–85, 698) for further reflections on the origin of the soul.

15. Augustine, *De civitate Dei* 14.23–24 (CCL 48, 444–48).

16. *De civitate Dei* 14.10; 14.15–16; 14.23; 14.26 (CCL 48, 430–31, 437–39, 444–46, 449–50).

ness and at sexual intercourse, Augustine posits, are among the latter-day signs that the sin of Adam and Eve affected all later generations.[17]

Although Augustine stands as a theologian, not as a scientist, the images he uses to describe Edenic and post-Edenic sex slide him toward the realms of biology and "genetics."[18] One such image he borrowed from Virgil's *Georgics*: Adam in a sinless Eden, preparing to engage in a reproductive sexual act, might be compared to a farmer who prepares his mares for the seed to be sown "on the field of generation."[19] Indeed, fructifying and "genetic" allusions play an increasing role in Augustine's discussion during these years. By 417, he had found his preferred metaphor to describe the transmission of sin: from the cultivated olive tree are produced only wild olive trees, not cultivated ones. This dendrological example bolsters the principle that regenerated (i.e., baptized Christian) parents do not transmit to their children the state of their "rebirth," but their old "carnal" natures.[20] Thus Augustine began to explain the "biology" of original sin by 419, the year in which Julian most likely composed his first attack upon him.

In 418, Julian and other Pelagian bishops were condemned by both religious and imperial authorities.[21] In response, Julian and his confreres ap-

---

17. *De civitate Dei* 14.18–20 (CCL 48, 440–43). Augustine in chap. 20 (unlike elsewhere) denies that Diogenes the Cynic could have had sexual intercourse in public: the act would not have been pleasurable.

18. "Genetics" must be kept in quotation marks, to distinguish modern understandings from those of the ancients; *pace* Philip A. Barclift, who goes so far as to discuss Jesus' reception of Mary's DNA ("In Controversy with Saint Augustine: Julian of Eclanum on the Nature of Sin," *Recherches de théologie ancienne et médiévale* 58 [1991]: 5–20).

19. *De civitate Dei* 14.23 (CCL 48, 446), citing *Georgics* 3.136—although Virgil's horses are far lustier than Augustine's ideal first couple.

20. *Ep.* 184A.3 (1) (CSEL 44, 734). In *De nuptiis et concupiscentia,* the image occurs at 1.21 (19); 1.37 (32); 1.38 (33); 2.58 (34). Hereafter abbreviated *De nuptiis.* The image of the wild and the cultivated olive trees comes from Romans 11:17–24, in which Paul envisions the Gentiles being "grafted in" to the original (Jewish) olive tree.

21. For a detailed account of events, see Otto Wermelinger, *Rom und Pelagius: Die theologische Position der römischer Bishöfe im pelagianischen Streit in den Jahren 411–432,* Päpste und Papstum 7 (Stuttgart: Anton Hiersemann, 1975), pts. 3 and 4. Pelagius himself had been considered in Rome (where he lived from about 395 to 408) a bulwark of orthodoxy against Arianism and Manicheanism (Wermelinger, pp. 122–23). When Pope Innocent I in 417 proved somewhat conciliatory to Pelagius and his supporters, and his successor, Zosimus, also originally took a mediating stand, North African churchmen appealed directly to the imperial court at Ravenna, which issued a rescript against Pelagius and his followers on April 30, 418. Zosi-

parently solicited support in Rome for their cause. Julian also wrote to a certain Count Valerius at the imperial court, alleging that the views of Augustine and his supporters were Manichean, that is, that they denigrated God's good creation, including the reproductive process.[22] Julian himself had been married[23] (we have the epithalamium composed by Paulinus of Nola upon the occasion of his wedding),[24] and he approached Valerius, also married, to signal the danger that Augustine's overly ascetic theories posed. Valerius was, as Peter Brown has put it, "just the man" for Julian, someone calculated to be sympathetic to the allegedly heretical threat emanating from Hippo Regius.[25] In 419, Augustine composed the first book of his treatise *On Marriage and Concupiscence,* and sent it to Count Valerius, no doubt hoping to convince him that it was Pelagians like Julian, not Augus-

---

mus issued a similar condemnation in his *Tractoria* during the summer of 418. Those who refused to subscribe to Zosimus's decree (including Julian and eighteen other bishops) were excommunicated. Although the *Tractoria* exists only in fragments, reports of it suggest that among the points of Pelagian theology condemned were that Adam was mortal and would have died anyway (i.e., that death is not a punishment for sin); that Adam's sin affected only himself, not others; that newborn infants are in the condition of Adam before the Fall (i.e., infants do not inherit "original sin"); that unbaptized children who die can have eternal life; and that the human race does not die because of Adam's death nor do all humans rise through Christ. See Wermelinger, *Rom und Pelagius,* pt. 4, for elaboration; for a shorter account in English, see Brown, *Augustine,* chaps. 29-30. Augustine's role in the condemnation is explored by J. Patout Burns, "Augustine's Role in the Imperial Action against Pelagius," *Journal of Theological Studies* 29 (1978): 67-83.

22. Julian, in Augustine, *Contra duas epistolas Pelagianorum* 1.3 (1); 1.4 (2) (CSEL 60, 424-25). On the history of the quarrel between Julian and Augustine, see Albert Bruckner, *Julian von Eclanum: Sein Leben und seine Lehre. Ein Beitrag zur Geschichte des Pelagianismus* (TU 15, 3; Leipzig: J. C. Hinrichs, 1897); Yves de Montcheuil, "La Polémique de Saint Augustin contre Julien d'Eclane d'après *l'Opus imperfectum,*" *Recherches de science religieuse* 44 (1956): 193-218; François Refoulé, "Julien d'Eclane, théologien et philosophe," *Recherches de science religieuse* 52 (1964): 42-84, 233-47; shorter summaries in Michel Meslin, "Sainteté et mariage au cours de la seconde querelle pélagienne," *Mystique et continence: Travaux scientifiques du VIIᵉ Congrès International d'Avon,* Les Etudes Carmélitaines (Paris: Desclée de Brouwer, 1952), 294-95; Brown, *Augustine,* chap. 32; Emile Schmitt, *Le Mariage chrétien dans l'oeuvre de Saint Augustin: Une théologie baptismale de la vie conjugale* (Paris: Etudes Augustiniennes, 1983), 56-61.

23. See discussion in Peter Brown, "Sexuality and Society in the Fifth Century A.D.: Augustine and Julian of Eclanum," in *Tria corda: Scritti in onore di Arnaldo Momigliano,* ed. E. Gabba. Biblioteca di Athenaeum 1 (Como: New Press, 1983), 54.

24. Paulinus of Nola, *Carmen* 25 (CSEL 30, 238-45).

25. Brown, "Sexuality and Society," 58.

tine himself, who constituted the real threat to Christian ethical teaching.[26] Probably Augustine did not know the full details of Julian's attack upon him when he wrote the first book of this treatise, for he poses no arguments beyond those he had previously elaborated. Rising to the bait, Julian composed a response in the form of a treatise *To Turbantius,* gave a copy to Valerius, who in turn sent it to Augustine; Augustine responded with book 2 of *On Marriage and Concupiscence.*[27] In the next years, Augustine and Julian engaged in a protracted literary debate. Near the time of his death in 430, Augustine was still at work on his huge *Contra secundam Juliani responsionem opus imperfectum.*[28]

Once attacked by Julian, Augustine could no longer rest his entire case on appeals to Scripture and Christian tradition: Julian argued that Augustine's theory of original sin was based on a highly dubious biological substructure. Julian intended to raise up these underpinnings for public inspection, to force Augustine's response to the charge against him of Manicheanism, that is, that Augustine's theory implied that human sinfulness was predetermined and innate. Augustine doubtless would have preferred to argue on theological grounds, but the terms of the debate were set for him by his opponent. Julian wished to make Augustine's views seem unscientific, ridiculous—and deeply unchristian. From book 2 of *On Marriage and Concupiscence,* through the *Against Julian,* to the *Opus imperfectum,* Augustine labored to answer Julian, attempting to shift the grounds of argument from biology to theology. He was not, I shall suggest, entirely successful.

---

26. Augustine, *De nuptiis* 1.1 (1) (CSEL 42, 211).

27. *De nuptiis* 2.1 (1); 2 (2) (CSEL 42, 253, 254); *Opus imperfectum,* praefatio (CSEL 85¹, 3); *Retractiones* 2.53.1 (CCL 57, 131). See also Albert Bruckner, *Die vier Bücher Julians von Aeclanum an Turbantius: Ein Beitrag zur Charakteristik Julians und Augustins,* Neue Studien zur Geschichte der Theologie unde der Kirche 8 (Berlin: Trowitzsch and Sohn, 1910), for a discussion of the treatise that prompted *De nuptiis* 2, with a reconstruction of the fragments contained in Augustine's work.

28. *Opus imperfectum,* preface (CSEL 85¹, 3-4). I have elaborated the details of the controversy at greater length in "Vitiated Seeds and Holy Vessels: Augustine's Manichean Past," in Clark, *Ascetic Piety and Women's Faith: Essays on Late Ancient Christianity* (Lewiston: Edwin Mellen Press, 1986), 291–349; also printed in *Images of the Feminine in Gnosticism,* ed. Karen L. King (Philadelphia, Penn.: Fortress Press, 1988), 367–401. A highly readable account of the controversy's main points can be found in Elaine Pagels, *Adam, Eve, and the Serpent* (New York: Random House, 1988), chap. 6 ("The Nature of Nature").

Julian was nothing if not pointed in his objections to Augustine's views. Just what is it about marriage, he asks, that the devil can claim its offspring as his own? It can't be the difference between the sexes, for God so made us. It can't be the union of male and female, for God blessed this union in Genesis 1:28 and 2:24. It can't be human fecundity, for reproduction was the reason why marriage was originally instituted.[29] Augustine's response—"None of the above, but carnal concupiscence"[30]—spurs Julian to argue that Augustine's understanding of concupiscence is not properly scientific.

Indeed, although Augustine had previously claimed that there could be a lust or concupiscence for vengeance, money, victory, and domination,[31] his most common use of the word was in a sexual (and negative) sense.[32] Throughout the debate, Augustine expressed annoyance that Julian substituted phrases such as "the natural appetite"[33] or "the vigor of the members"[34] for "concupiscence," in an attempt to shift the word's meaning away from the realm of moral and religious discourse and toward that of "science."[35] Julian's handling of several scriptural passages indeed reveals this interest. When, for example, Genesis 4:25 states that Seth was the seed God

---

29. *De nuptiis* 2.13 (4) (CSEL 42, 264–65).

30. *De nuptiis* 2.14 (5) (CSEL 42, 265).

31. *De civitate Dei* 14.15 (CCL 48, 438). For discussion of the meaning of "concupiscence" for Augustine, and differences between his view and that of Julian, see Meslin, "Sainteté," 298–99, 300–301, 303; Refoulé, "Julien," 70–71; Schmitt, *Le Mariage,* 95–105; G. I. Bonner, "*Libido* and *Concupiscentia* in St. Augustine," *Studia Patristica* 6 (TU 81) (Berlin: Akademie-Verlag, 1962), 303–14; François-Joseph Thonnard, "La Notion de concupiscence en philosophie augustinienne," *Recherches augustiniennes* 3 (1965): 59–105, esp. 80–95; Athanase Sage, "Le Péché originel dans la pensée de saint Augustin, 412 à 430," *Revue des études augustiniennes* 15 (1969): 75–112, esp. 91–97; Emanuele Samek Lodovici, "Sessualità, matrimonio e concupiscenza in sant'Agostino," in *Etica sessuale e matrimonio nel cristianesimo delle origini,* ed. Raniero Cantalamessa, Studia Patristica Mediolanensia 5 (Milan: Università Cattolica del Sacro Cuore, 1976), esp. 251–62. For a modern reflection on concupiscence as "anxious grasping," see Margaret R. Miles, "The Body and Human Values in Augustine of Hippo," in *Grace, Politics and Desire: Essays on Augustine,* ed. Hugo A. Meynell (Calgary: University of Calgary Press, 1990), 57–59.

32. Made clear already in *De civitate Dei* 14.16 (CCL 48, 438–39).

33. *De nuptiis* 2.17 (7) (CSEL 42, 269).

34. *De nuptiis* 2.59 (35) (CSEL 42, 317).

35. *De nuptiis* 2.17 (7) (CSEL 42, 269–70).

raised up from Adam, Julian interprets the verse to mean that God stirred up sexual desire in Adam, through which the seed was "raised" in order to be "poured" into Eve's womb:[36] following medical theory of his day, Julian believed that the seed was "formed" through sexual desire.[37] Using another agricultural metaphor, Julian reminds Augustine that the crop is not affected if the seeds are "stolen": that is, children produced by an adulterous relationship are no different from those born in legitimate marriage.[38] Seed is simply a biological phenomenon, whatever the morality of human agents.

As the debate proceeded—and as we perceive it from Augustine's *Contra Julianum* and his *Opus imperfectum*—seeds became an increasingly important topic. Augustine agrees with Julian that God makes all humans from seed, but (unlike Julian) he believes that the seed is already condemned and vitiated through Adam's sin.[39] Moreover, Augustine argues that the seed is created by God directly and does not receive its formation (as Julian thought) from lust[40]—for to admit the latter would both remove procreation from divine agency and allow sin, of which lust is a manifestation, to be responsible for human generation.[41] Since Augustine did not, at this early stage of the debate, concede that lust could have been present in the Garden of Eden, how could Adam and Eve have procreated, if (as on Julian's—and medical—theory) lust were necessary for the creation of the generative seed? On Augustine's theory, the seed was in essence good, but the devil had "sowed the tares" of evil in it.[42]

For Julian, in contrast, lust—or natural appetite—is simply one of the bodily senses that we are given as part of our human endowment;[43]

---

36. *De nuptiis* 2.19 (8) (CSEL 42, 271). Augustine's response: the author means only that God gave him a son.

37. *De nuptiis* 2.25 (12) (CSEL 42, 277).

38. *De nuptiis* 2.40 (25) (CSEL 42, 293–94).

39. Augustine, *Contra Julianum* 3.33 (17) (PL 44, 719).

40. *Contra Julianum* 4.12 (2) (PL 44, 742).

41. *Contra Julianum* 5.34 (8) (PL 44, 804).

42. *Contra Julianum* 3.51 (22) (PL 44, 728); cf. Matt. 13:24–30. Late in the debate, Augustine conceded that there *might* have been a kind of "concupiscence" in the sinless Garden of Eden, but it would not have operated as does the raging, unruly "lust" that we know in the post-Fall world: see *Opus imperfectum* 1.68 and *Epistula* 6*.3; 5.

43. *Contra Julianum* 4.65 (14) (PL 44, 769–70). Augustine believes that libido is natural in animals but a penalty in human beings: *Contra Julianum* 4.56 (10) (PL 44, 765).

hence, we cannot believe that it originated from human sinfulness. Against Augustine's view that all human nature was ever after changed by Adam's sin,[44] Julian argues that human nature (including sexual appetite) does not change, since God bestows our essential human constitution and neither sin nor grace has the power to alter it.[45] Augustine's list of the penalties for sin derived from Genesis 3 — labor pains, sweat, work, the submission of women to men — are, in Julian's view, all part of the natural order and thus unchangeable.[46] Although Julian believes that an "excess" of lust leading humans to intemperate fornication is blameworthy,[47] sexual desire of a "moderate" sort is one of God's good creations.

In addition to arguing that sexual appetite was part of our original (and good) human constitution, Julian also appealed to "genetics." Here, Julian relied on Aristotle's discussion of accidents inhering in subjects: "That which inheres in a subject cannot exist without the thing which is the subject of its inherence." Julian concludes, "Therefore, the evil which inheres in a subject cannot transmit its guilt to something else to which it does not extend, that is to say, to the offspring."[48] Acquired characteristics such as sin cannot "wander off" from their proper subject to attach themselves to another.[49] Two points of Augustine's position are touched by this argument. First, Julian argues against Augustine, "natural things cannot be transformed by an accident"; hence, human nature cannot be changed forever by one person's act of will.[50] Second, if parents no longer have a property (namely, sin) they can't transmit it; if on the other hand, they do transmit it to their children, as Augustine holds, they must never have lost it (through regenerating baptism).[51] Augustine's image of the cultivated olive tree producing wild olives is of no use for the discussion; illustrations can-

---

44. *Opus imperfectum* 6.37 (PL 45, 1596).

45. *Opus imperfectum* 3.142 (CSEL 85¹, 447–48). In 1.71, 2 (CSEL 85¹, 81), concupiscence is called a "natural and innocent *affectio*." Also see *Opus imperfectum* 1.96; 2.94; 3.109.2–3; 3.142.2; 4.120; 5.46 (CSEL 85¹, 111, 227, 429, 447; PL 45, 1414, 1482).

46. *Opus imperfectum* 6.26; 6.27; 6.29 (PL 45, 1561–62, 1566–68, 1577).

47. *Contra Julianum* 3.26 (13) (PL 44, 715).

48. *Contra Julianum* 5.51 (14) (PL 44, 812).

49. *Contra Julianum* 5.51 (14) (PL 44, 813). Besides, says Julian, even if infants contract evil, a merciful God would cleanse them of it (5.53 [15] [PL 44, 813]). Cf. Aristotle, *Categories* 2, 1a 23–29. I thank Michael Ferejohn for assistance with this reference.

50. *Contra Julianum* 6.16 (6) (PL 44, 831–32).

51. *Contra Julianum* 6.18 (7) (PL 44, 833).

not shore up indefensible points.[52] If Augustine seeks a horticultural image from Scripture, why doesn't he turn to Matthew 7:17–18, the good tree that bears good fruit, an example that illustrates the goodness of human nature and of its offshoots?[53]

Augustine in response postulates a different version of "genetic theory." Although he agrees with Julian (and Aristotle) that qualities inhere in a subject, that they do not wander off, he *also* holds that qualities can be transmitted by "affection." Thus the Ethiopians beget black children because the parents' blackness affects the children's bodies; similarly, the color of Jacob's rods affected the color of the lambs produced.[54] A medical writer (whom he later identifies as Soranus) testifies that an ugly king had his wife gaze at a portrait of a handsome man while they engaged in intercourse so that the child would be affected.[55] Morever, Augustine argues, parents *can* transmit accidental properties to their children: a man who had lost the sight of one eye produced a son with sight in one eye, so that what had been an "accident" in the parent became "natural" in the child. And parents can also transmit what they *don't* themselves have, as is proved by the same father's producing a fully sighted son[56] and by circumcised fathers begetting sons with foreskins![57] With so much scientific evidence, why can't we believe that original sin affects an offspring?[58] Augustine also appeals to the concept of "contagion" to describe the same phenomenon: in contagion, "another quality of the same kind is produced," as when diseased parents transmit their illness to their children.[59]

Julian also argues, especially in the treatise Augustine cites in the *Opus*

52. *Contra Julianum* 6.15 (6) (PL 44, 831).

53. *Contra Julianum* 1.38 (8) (PL 44, 667).

54. *Contra Julianum* 5.51 (14) (PL 44, 812). For the story of Jacob and the rods, see Genesis 30:25–43.

55. *Contra Julianum* 5.51 (14) (PL 44, 812). In *Retractiones* 2.62.2 (CSEL 57, 139), Augustine reports that he mistakenly wrote that Soranus had given the king's name (Dionysius); he had not, and Augustine must have gotten the name from elsewhere. Augustine's reference is important because it shows he knew something of Soranus's works: see n. 122 below.

56. *Contra Julianum* 6.16 (6) (PL 44, 832). The belief in the inheritance of acquired characteristics, to be sure, was again championed in the early nineteenth century by Lamarck and his followers.

57. *Contra Julianum* 6.18 (7); 6.20 (7) (PL 44, 833, 834).

58. Julian, of course, believes in sin "by imitation." See his interpretation of Romans 5:12, given toward the end of section IV.

59. *Contra Julianum* 5.51 (14); 6.55 (18) (PL 44, 813, 855).

imperfectum, that Augustine's theory of original sin implies a certain view of the origin of the soul. To the end of his life, Augustine professed ignorance on this issue: he was unable to decide on scriptural or theological grounds what view of the soul's origin was "correct."[60] Should we believe that the soul became corrupted simultaneously with the body's conception (a corrupt soul then being transmitted by the parents along with the body); or was the soul vitiated *after* having been created by God, and was then placed in a corrupted body "as in a faulty vessel"?[61] The manifest problem was to remove God from culpability in human creation, yet affirm the presence of original sin from the time of the soul's union with the body. Augustine's theory of the transmission of original sin would work best on the view that the soul was transmitted along with the body — a view known as traducianism — but he never explicitly adopts this position, perhaps because the process seemed too material for his Platonizing tastes.[62]

Julian, however, firmly held to the "creationist" view of the soul's origin, that is, that each soul was a new creation by God. The soul, for Julian, does not come down through bodily seed — and hence parents could not, in any event, pass sin to their children in this manner.[63] If Augustine believes that sin became mixed with seed and makes the *conceptus* guilty, he is, in Julian's eyes, a traducian, and traducians are to be equated with Manicheans in their view of innate human evil.[64]

Julian also employs arguments derived from what we would call anthropology. Anthropological data were useful to Julian in subverting Augustine's appeal to the allegedly universal shame surrounding nudity and sexual intercourse as evidence for original sin. For Julian, the use of clothing was not related to sin's entrance to the world and the desire to cover unruly genitals, as Augustine would have it.[65] Rather, clothing was simply an aspect of "human inventiveness" that the first couple developed over time.[66]

---

60. See n. 14 above.

61. *Contra Julianum* 5.17 (4) (PL 44, 794).

62. See discussion in my *The Origenist Controversy: The Cultural Construction of an Early Christian Debate* (Princeton, N.J.: Princeton University Press, 1992), 232–36.

63. *Opus imperfectum* 2.24.1 (CSEL 85¹, 178).

64. *Opus imperfectum* 1.6; 1.27; 1.66; 2.8; 2.14; 2.27.2; 2.202; 3.10 (CSEL 85¹, 9, 23, 64, 168, 172, 181, 314, 355).

65. See especially *De civitate Dei* 14.17 (CCL 48, 439–40).

66. *Contra Julianum* 4.81 (16) (PL 44, 780). Augustine responds, was it sin that made us so clever? Julian also apparently argued that the parts Adam and Eve covered were their "sides,"

Besides, Julian argues, even today we do not shun nudity in some circumstances: we don't blame artisans, athletes, or sailors (witness Peter in John 21:7) for their state of undress since their activities require it. Moreover, Scots and other barbarians go naked without shame. Augustine's teaching that universal shame accompanies nudity is "destroyed" by such evidence, Julian asserts:[67] Augustine has tried to universalize the sensation of shame whose manifestations are in truth culturally conditioned.

A second piece of anthropological evidence to which Julian appeals concerns birthing pains. Against Augustine's view that labor pains are a punishment on women for Eve's role in the first sin, Julian suggests that such pains are natural to the human and animal condition and hence are not to be associated with sin.[68] Besides, he argues, the experience of labor pains varies widely among women: rich women, accustomed to a life of indolence, suffer more than the poor, who have by necessity been more physically active; barbarian and nomadic women give birth with ease, scarcely interrupting their travels to bear children. How, on this evidence, can Augustine say that labor pains are universal and a penalty for sin?[69] Once again, Augustine is faulted for not taking a properly scientific view of the issue.

To be sure, Julian can also appeal to more strictly religious arguments in his debate with Augustine. For example, Julian holds that God's power and goodness are called into question on Augustine's theory, for how could a powerful and benevolent deity allow "in the womb of a baptized woman, whose body is the temple of God," to be formed a child under the power of the devil?[70] Augustine's entire understanding of sin is askew. As Julian

---

not their genital organs. Augustine faults both Julian's Greek and his shamelessness: is he raising the *perizomata* up to their shoulders and leaving the turbulent members in full view? *Contra Julianum* 5.7 (2) (PL 44, 785–86).

67. *Opus imperfectum* 4.44 (PL 44, 1363–64). Augustine responds (1364–65) that we should look to the "parents of all nations," Adam and Eve, not just to a particular group like the Scots. The first couple were not originally corrupted with evil doctrine, as were the Cynics, nor did they have to perform manual labor (as Peter did; his nudity is excused).

68. *Opus imperfectum* 6.26 (PL 45, 1562). Augustine responds (1563) that we do not know what animals feel when they give birth. Do their sounds portend joyous song or grief? Perhaps they feel pleasure, not pain? Cf. *De Genesi contra Manichaeos* 2.29 (19) (PL 34, 210).

69. *Opus imperfectum* 6.29 (PL 45, 1577). Augustine responds (1578), so what if the pain varies? *All* women still suffer; hence all are affected by original sin.

70. *Contra Julianum* 6.43 (14) (PL 44, 846). For a discussion that links Julian's understanding of the "naturalness" of concupiscence with the justice and goodness of God, see Mathijs

archly puts it, "How could a matter of will be mixed with the creation of seeds?"[71] From Julian's perspective, Augustine has confused a matter of morals (the will's determination of good and evil acts) with an issue of biology (the creation of sperm).

Moreover, Augustine's biotheology had definite consequences for his reflection on Jesus — and Mary and Joseph. It was not just human procreation in general that was affected by the theory of original sin, but the generation of Jesus in particular. A wider range of theological issues, it appears — especially the definition of marriage and Christological formulations — were related to the theory of original sin. To these issues we next turn.

IV

Augustine's views on sexuality and marriage changed significantly throughout his life, in response to the controversies in which he engaged and to the stimulus of his own scriptural study and theological reflection.[72] Although he had early held a spiritualized view of Adam and Eve's relation in the Garden of Eden ("increase and multiply" meant "spiritual increase," not "physical union"),[73] in the opening years of the fifth century his views on Eden became more grounded in the physical. Now Augustine struggles to mediate the positions elaborated a decade earlier by the Latin-writing theologians Jerome and Jovinian in their debate over virginity: Jerome had so exalted virginity that he often seemed to denigrate marriage, while Jovinian, in contrast, had argued that once they were baptized, there was no difference between the married and the celibate, other moral qualities being comparable.[74] Responding to this debate, Augustine in two treatises, *On the Good of Marriage* and *On Holy Virginity*, composed in about 401, sketched out a

---

Lamberigts, "Julian of Aeclanum: A Plea for a Good Creator," *Augustiniana* 38 (1988), esp. 17–22.

71. *Contra Julianum* 6.24 (9) (PL 44, 837): "Qui fieri potest ut res arbitrii conditioni seminum misceatur?"

72. See my "'Adam's Only Companion': Augustine and the Early Christian Debate on Marriage," *Recherches augustiniennes* 21 (1986): 139–62, and Peter Brown, *The Body and Society: Men, Women, and Sexual Renunciation in Early Christianity* (New York: Columbia University Press, 1988), chap. 19.

73. Augustine, *De Genesi contra Manichaeos* 1.19.30 (PL 34, 187).

74. See the exposition in David G. Hunter, "Resistance to the Virginal Ideal in Late-Fourth-Century Rome: The Case of Jovinian," *Theological Studies* 48 (1987): 45–64.

theory of marriage that was to sustain him for many years—and one that accommodated his theory of original sin, fully elaborated only in the second decade of the fifth century.

In these treatises, Augustine attempted to show that virginity could be praised without denigrating marriage. He hints that "some" champions of virginity (clearly Jerome) had so implicated marriage that they had lent plausibility to Jovinian's charges of Manicheanism (that is, the denigration of God's created order) against Jerome's position.[75] For Augustine marriage and reproduction are goods.[76] He now posits, tentatively, that Adam and Eve could have had sexual intercourse in Eden even if they had not sinned. Reproduction would have been part of God's plan for the first couple, even though, as sinless, they would not have grown old or died;[77] Augustine thus implicitly rejects the traditional argument that reproduction's purpose is to fill up the ranks of the dead. Augustine here names the "three goods" of marriage—offspring, fidelity, and the sacramental bond[78]—which would be more fully elaborated in such later works as *On Marriage and Concupiscence.*[79] The third "good," the "sacramental bond," somewhat ill defined in Augustine's writings, constituted the link between the partners that rendered divorce impossible. Even if a couple produced no children or if one of the partners committed adultery—that is, even if the first and second "goods" were not upheld—the third "good," the sacramental bond, remained: the couple was truly married. The promise of the Christian couple to each other infrangibly cemented this bond.[80]

The question of what constituted a true marriage, of the essence of marriage, had gained greater prominence in late-fourth-century Christian discussions. Although Roman law was more concerned with the effects

75. So Augustine states in *Retractiones* 2.48 (= 22).1 (CCL 57, 107–108).

76. Augustine, *De bono coniugali,* passim (CSEL 41, 187–231); *De sancta virginitate* 10 (9); 12 (12); 18 (18); 21 (21) (CSEL 41, 243, 244, 251, 254–55). In addition to works already cited on Augustine's marital ethic, see François-Joseph Thonnard, "La Morale conjugale selon saint Augustin," *Revue des études augustiniennes* 15 (1969): 113–31.

77. *De bono coniugali* 2 (2) (CSEL 41, 188–90).

78. *De bono coniugali* 32 (24) (CSEL 41, 226–27).

79. *De nuptiis* 1.19 (17) (CSEL 42, 231).

80. Ibid. A recent discussion of the "sacramental bond" can be found in Eugenio Scalco, " 'Sacramentum Connubii' et institution nuptiale: Une lecture du 'De bono coniugali' et du 'De sancta virginitate' de S. Augustin," *Ephemerides theologicae lovanienses* 69 (1993): 27–47.

brought about by marriage than in defining of marriage's essence,[81] Christians had a particular case about which they must worry: the relationship of Joseph and Mary. Around 383, Jerome had conducted a literary debate with a certain Helvidius. Helvidius took the view that although Mary was a virgin at the time she conceived Jesus, she and Joseph had sexual relations subsequently—hence the brothers and sisters of Jesus mentioned in the Gospels. Jerome, in contrast, argued vigorously for the perpetual virginity of Mary, whom he deemed exemplary for women making (or contemplating) vows of virginity.[82] In Jerome's interpretation, the brothers and sisters of Jesus became cousins,[83] while Joseph himself (in correction of earlier traditions)[84] was transformed into a lifelong celibate to serve as a model for Christian men.[85] For Jerome, Joseph was Mary's guardian, not her husband;[86] the relation was not a marriage, which for Jerome implied sex.[87] The position of Ambrose, writing within a few years of Jerome, is somewhat ambiguous on the issue: although Ambrose claims that it is the "conjugal pact," not defloration, that makes a marriage, he does not press the argument that Joseph and Mary were truly married despite their lack of sexual relation.[88] Augustine thus remains the first major Western theolo-

81. See my "'Adam's Only Companion,'" 158–61, for discussion and copious references on Roman marriage law.

82. Jerome, *Adversus Helvidium* 4–16 (PL 23, 195–211).

83. *Adversus Helvidium* 11–15 (PL 23, 203–209).

84. *Protevangelium Jacobi* 8.2–9.1 (*Evangelia Apocrypha*, ed. K. Von Tischendorf [reprint; Hildesheim: Georg Olms Verlagsbuchhandlung, 1966], 17–18): Joseph is a widower.

85. Jerome, *Adversus Helvidium* 19 (PL 23, 213).

86. *Adversus Helvidium* 4; 19 (PL 23, 196, 213); see Walter Delius, *Geschichte der Marienverehrung* (Munich: Ernst Reinhardt Verlag, 1963), 134–35.

87. Sexual intercourse is described as the *res nuptiarum* in *Adversus Helvidium* 4 (PL 23, 196). Jerome describes the relationship as a *virginale coniugium* (*Adversus Helvidium* 19 [PL 23, 213]). For a summary of Jerome's position (though pressing Jerome closer to Augustine's "correct" view), see Johannes Niessen, *Die Mariologie des heiligen Hieronymus: Ihre Quellen und ihre Kritik* (Münster in Westfalen: Aschendorffsche Verlagsbuchhandlung, 1913), 88–96.

88. Ambrose, *De institutione virginis* 6.41 (PL 16, 316). His ambivalence emerges in his early *Expositio Evangelii secundum Lucam* 2.7 (CSEL 32 ³, 45): there he compares Mary to the Church in these words, "Bene desponsata, sed virgo, quia est ecclesiae typus, quae est immaculata, sed nupta." But against a true marriage of Joseph and Mary, see Ambrose, *Ep. de causa Bonosi* 4–5 (PL 16, 1224) and *De institutione virginis* 7.47–48 (PL 16, 332–33). See Neumann, *Virgin Mary*, 85–86.

gian to argue that Joseph and Mary had a genuine marriage although they never engaged in sexual intercourse.

It was, interestingly, against Manichean opponents that Augustine first elaborated this view. In his treatise *Against Faustus the Manichean*, composed in 397–398,[89] Augustine sought to refute Faustus's charge that the Gospel genealogies should be discarded since Jesus was not born from a human mother—birth, to Faustus, was a disgusting process in which the deity would not involve himself. Faustus points out various discrepancies between the genealogical accounts in Matthew and in Luke, and cites such verses attributed to Jesus as "I am not of this world" (John 8:23) and "Who is my mother? Who are my brothers?" (Matt. 12:48 = Mark 3:33) to establish that Jesus did not have physical relatives.[90] Augustine in reply admits that the genealogies do not square with each other and seeks to resolve the discrepancies.[91] In doing so, he attempts to answer the question why Joseph is there called the "father" of Jesus, and why the genealogies come down through him, when he was not responsible for the physical conception of Jesus. Augustine argues that because Joseph acted in the social role of Jesus' father, he deserves the title. Joseph also can be called Mary's husband, despite their lack of sexual relation: they are named husband and wife because "intercourse of the mind is more intimate than that of the body." Fleshly intercourse is not the chief aspect of marriage, Augustine asserts; a couple can be husband and wife without it.[92] Thus, reflection on the genealogies of Jesus prepared the way for his discussion of marriage in *On the Good of Marriage*, written just a few years after *Against Faustus the Manichean*, and in *On Marriage and Concupiscence*, written two decades later.

89. Dating in Brown, *Augustine*, 184.

90. Augustine, *Contra Faustum* 7.1 (CSEL 25¹, 302–03).

91. *Contra Faustum* 3.2; 3.3; 3.5 (CSEL 25¹, 262–65, 266–67).

92. *Contra Faustum* 23.8 (CSEL 25¹, 713). Many of these points are reiterated in a work Augustine composed two or three years after the *Contra Faustum*, the *De consensu evangelistarum*; see especially 2.1.2; 2.1.3; 2.3.5. Augustine is the first Latin-writing church father to emphasize that Mary had taken a vow of virginity (*De sancta virginitate* 4.4 [CSEL 41, 238]). It is interesting to note that the only "sexual" dimension of Augustine's narration of Jesus' conception is purely metaphorical: he often employs Psalm 19:5 to claim that Jesus emerged from Mary's womb "like a bridegroom leaving his chamber." A "holy marriage" had taken place between Word and flesh in Mary's womb (*Sermo* 126.5–6 [PL 38, 701]); her womb was the "marriage chamber" where was consummated the holy union of Word and flesh (*Sermo* 291.6 [PL 38, 1319]).

By the time Augustine wrote *On Marriage and Concupiscence,* he was deeply engaged in the struggle against the Pelagian celebration of human free will to the detriment (so Augustine thought) of God's grace and the need for forgiveness of sin. With his theory of original sin in place, the controversy with Julian of Eclanum sharpened Augustine's view of the "biology" of original sin: the guilt of Adam and Eve passed to all their descendants — we are all "in Adam" — and the mechanism by which this transfer takes place is through the sexual intercourse that leads to the creation of the fetus. In particular, lust is the issue: it is both a result of Adam and Eve's sin and the aspect of the sexual act that transfers the guilt.[93] That this view might have strong implications for notions concerning the conception of Jesus is evident.

For Augustine, Jesus is born free from "sinful fault" because he was not born from the sexual union of Joseph and Mary, through "the concupiscence of sexual intercourse."[94] Although likewise an advocate of the Virgin birth, Julian disapproved of Augustine's use of the example of Joseph and Mary to suggest that sexual union was not necessary for a true marriage. "Show me any bodily marriage without sexual union!" he demands of Augustine;[95] "marriage consists of nothing else than the union of bodies."[96] In Julian's opinion, since Joseph and Mary never engaged in sexual intercourse, they were not married.[97] On Augustine's view, he posits, we might imagine that Adam and Eve could have been "married" in Eden without sexual union.[98] Augustine's praise of sexless marriage hints of Manicheanism to Julian.

93. E.g., *De nuptiis* 2.15 (5); 2.20 (8); 2.55 (33) (CSEL 42, 266–67, 272–73, 312–13), to be further explicated in later works. For an extensive discussion of what being "in Adam" might mean, see Robert J. O'Connell, *The Origin of the Soul in St. Augustine's Writings* (New York: Fordham University Press, 1987).

94. *De nuptiis* 2.15 (5) (CSEL 42, 267); *Contra Julianum* 5.54 (15) (PL 44, 814). Jesus' conception thus differs from that of Jeremiah or John the Baptist, who although "sanctified" in their mothers' wombs, nonetheless had contracted original sin and would have been born "children of wrath" had they not been delivered by God's grace: *Opus imperfectum* 4.134 (PL 45, 1428–29).

95. *De nuptiis* 2.37 (22) (CSEL 42, 291).

96. *Contra Julianum* 5.62 (16) (PL 44, 818). Augustine fears that this definition would allow adultery and other sexual relationships to count as marriage.

97. *Contra Julianum* 5.46 (12) (PL 44, 810). Scripture calls Joseph Mary's husband because it follows the common view (5.47 [12] [PL 44, 810–11]).

98. *Contra Julianum* 5.48 (12) (PL 44, 811). Augustine denies the charge.

Julian puts some difficult questions to Augustine on these points. Even if Joseph were not involved in Jesus' conception, why did not Mary have "concupiscence" from her *own* birth that she transferred to her son? (Recall that for Julian, "concupiscence" was a natural quality, akin to the five senses.) [99] If Mary was descended from Adam, she must have given her son the same flesh that we all have — flesh that is *not* sinful, *contra* Augustine. [100] Or, if Augustine wishes to claim that Jesus did not possess one of the senses with which we are all endowed, then Augustine is guilty of Apollinarianism, [101] that is, he denies the full humanity of Christ. In fact, Julian argues, we could call Augustine Manichean for his refusal to admit that Christ's body was like ours, due to the lack of concupiscence in his conception. [102]

Here we return to the issue of "seeds." Although various medical authorities, such as Galen and Soranus, thought that women as well as men produced "seed," they also believed that the male seed was largely (wholly, in Soranus's view) responsible for the creation of a child. [103] Does this not mean, Julian asks, that Augustine, by connecting original sin with male seed, suggests that sin is a particularly "male" problem? [104] Did not Augustine assert that the generating seed was "vitiated by the father's sinfulness?" [105] When Augustine claimed that Jesus was born sinless because he was not born "of the seed of man," [106] did he not mean "male seed," quite

---

99. See earlier discussion at p. 26.

100. *Contra Julianum* 5.52 (15) (PL 44, 813): Paul in Romans 8:3 does not mean to imply that bodies are sinful.

101. *Contra Julianum* 5.55 (15) (PL 44, 814). Apollinaris, a fourth-century theologian who was condemned as a heretic, denied that Jesus had a human mind; the divine Logos took its place.

102. *Contra Julianum* 5.52 (15) (PL 44, 814–15).

103. See Galen, *Peri physikōn dynameōn* 2.3: the semen works like an artist (e.g., Phidias) on the woman's blood; it is the active principle, while the blood provides the "matter." According to Soranus (*Gynecology* 1.3.12), the "female seed" seems not to be used in generation, since it is excreted. Soranus's *Gynecology* was influential in the West by the late fourth century (Owsei Temkin, *Soranus' Gynecology* [Baltimore, Md.: The Johns Hopkins University Press, 1956], xxix). For Augustine, children are "poured off" (*transfunduntur*) from the man to the woman: *Opus imperfectum* 2.178.2 (CSEL 85¹, 299).

104. See page 26. Readers may rightly note that already in *De civitate Dei* 14.16, Augustine's description of original sin's manifestation utilized typically male examples (erection and impotence).

105. *Contra Julianum* 6.5 (2); cf. 6.26 (9) (PL 44, 823–24, 837–38).

106. *Contra Julianum* 2.8 (4) (PL 44, 678–79); Ambrose is cited as being in agreement (2.10 [5]; 2.15 [6] [PL 44, 681, 684]).

specifically? Julian argues his case against Augustine in two ways: from the interpretation of Romans 5:12 ("through one man sin entered the world") and from a discussion of the Virgin birth.

Since Romans 5:12 was one of Augustine's favorite texts, Julian easily located his opponent's extensive commentaries on it.[107] When Paul wrote that sin entered the world "through one man," Julian argues, he could not possibly have meant "through generation," for everyone — even Augustine — knows that reproduction takes two.[108] Rather, according to Julian, sin arose through *imitation* of the first man's evil deed, not by transmission[109] — a view Augustine found nonsensical. According to Augustine, if Paul had wished to teach that sin emerges through imitation of bad examples, he would have blamed Eve, not Adam, since she sinned first and set the pattern of sin for him.[110] Paul is correct in claiming that sin entered through the man, Augustine argues, because it comes through the "seed of generation," which is cast off from the male and through which the woman conceives.[111] Paul wrote as he did because it is "not from the seed that conceives and bears [i.e., the woman's seed] that generation takes its beginning, but from the male seed [*a viro seminante*]."[112] Besides, women don't "generate," they "conceive," a point confirmed by biblical language pertaining to begetting.[113] On Augustine's view, the offspring contract original

107. See Augustine's use of Romans 5:12 in *De perfectione iustitiae hominis* 39 (18); 44 (21); *De gratia Christi* 1.55 (5); 2.34 (29); *De nuptiis* 1.1 (1); 2.3 (2); 2.8 (3); 2.15 (5); 2.20 (8); 2.24 (11); 2.37 (22); 2.42 (26); 2.45 (27); 2.47 (27); *De peccatorum meritis* 1.8 (8); 1.9 (9); 1.10 (9); 1.11 (10); 3.8 (4); 3.14 (7); 3.19 (11); *De spiritu et littera* 47 (27); *De natura et gratia* 9 (8); 46 (39); 48 (41); *De anima et ejus origine* 1.28 (17); 2.20 (14); *Contra duas epistolas Pelagianorum* 4.7 (4); 4.8 (4); 4.21 (8).
108. *Opus imperfectum* 2.56.1; 2.75 (CSEL 85¹, 203, 218).
109. *Opus imperfectum* 2.56.1; 2.61; 2.194 (CSEL 85¹, 203, 207–208, 309).
110. *Opus imperfectum* 3.85.1 (CSEL 85¹, 411–12). Julian's explanation for why the man is named although the woman sinned first is that fathers have more *auctoritas* than women; possessing the *potestas* of the male sex, a man's example (Adam's) would carry more weight than a woman's (Eve's): *Opus imperfectum* 2.190 (CSEL 85¹, 307).
111. *Opus imperfectum* 2.56 (CSEL 85¹, 204–205). In 2.173.1 (CSEL 85¹, 293), Augustine asserts that readers have a choice of only two views: the one here espoused or that Eve is included with Adam in the phrase "one man." Augustine does not pursue the latter alternative.
112. *Opus imperfectum* 2.83 (CSEL 85¹, 221). Nonetheless, in *De nuptiis* 2.26 (13), Augustine mentions in passing that reproduction occurs through "the commingling of seminal elements of the two sexes in the womb" (CSEL 42, 279).
113. *Opus imperfectum* 3.85.4; 3.88.3–4 (CSEL 85¹, 413, 415–16).

sin from Adam's descendant, the male who engenders; the woman receives the already vitiated seed from him, conceives, and gives birth.[114]

The implications for Virgin birth theory are obvious: because Jesus is not conceived through the seed of a male, he is free of the concupiscence that carries original sin.[115] Christ does not share our "sinful flesh" because he alone was not born from the "commingling of the sexes."[116] Conceived rather by the Holy Spirit and free from the debilitating effects of sin, Jesus is able to release others from it. Thus Jesus acquires his saving function quite precisely because he is exempt from having been generated.[117]

Julian presses further: if, as Augustine claims, sin is a condition of human flesh since the time of Adam, should not have Jesus acquired sin from his mother?[118] Augustine admits that Mary contributed the *materia* of Jesus' fleshly body[119]—but would this have conveyed the sin? Augustine concedes that Mary, by condition of her own birth, would have been "submitted to the devil" (i.e., under the sway of original sin) if the grace of God had not loosed that condition.[120] This concession hints in the direction of the doctrine of the immaculate conception of Mary, proclaimed as Catholic dogma

114. *Opus imperfectum* 2.179 (CSEL 85¹, 299–300).

115. *Opus imperfectum* 4.104 (PL 45, 1401). Cf. other expressions of this idea in Augustine's sermons, such as that Jesus was "conceived in a womb no seed had entered" (*Sermo* 192 [Ben.]. 1 [PL 38, 1012]); that he was "conceived without the seed of man (*Sermo* 215.3–4 [PL 38, 1073–74]); and that he was "born of his Father without time, of his mother without seed" (*Sermo* 194 [Ben.].1 [PL 38, 1015]). Augustine's Christmas sermons in particular often mention the "seedless" conception of Jesus, but since the sermons are difficult to date, they are not useful in an historical argument, as are the treatises or letters that can be dated with some precision.

116. *Opus imperfectum* 4.79 (PL 45, 1384).

117. *Opus imperfectum* 6.22 (PL 45, 1553).

118. *Opus imperfectum* 4.51 (PL 45, 1369).

119. *Opus imperfectum* 6.22 (PL 45, 1553). It is because Jesus received "mortality" from his mother (otherwise, how could he have died?) that Paul writes in Romans 8:3 that Jesus had "the likeness of sinful flesh" (i.e., not our "sinful flesh" itself: *Contra Julianum* 5.54–55 (15) [PL 44, 814–15]).

120. *Opus imperfectum* 4.122 (PL 45, 1418). On Augustine's Mariological theory, see Joseph Huhn, "Ein Vergleich der Mariologie des Hl. Augustinus mit der Hl. Ambrosius in ihrer Abhängigkeit, Ähnlichkeit, in ihrem Unterschied," in *Augustinus Magister: Congrès international augustinien, Paris, 21–24 septembre, 1954* (Paris: Etudes augustiniennes, 1954), 1: 221–39; Henri Frévin, *Le Mariage de Saint Joseph et de la sainte Vierge: Etude de théologie positive de Saint Irénée à Saint Thomas* (Cahiers de Joséphologie 15, 2; Montréal: Centre de Recherche et de Documentation Oratoire Saint-Joseph, 1967), 239–67. For background, see Hugo Koch, *Virgo Eva-*

in 1850, according to which God intervened at the moment of Mary's conception to prevent the transfer of original sin to her soul.[121] The debate between Julian and Augustine can thus be seen as an early stage of the discussion that eventually led to the 1850 dogmatic proclamation.

There is yet another subtlety attending this issue, one that would have been suggested to Augustine by his reading of Soranus—at least if he had read very carefully. Soranus mentions, just in passing, that women's seed is not part of the reproductive process, for it passes through their seminal vessels to the bladder and is excreted outside the body, not into the uterus.[122] If Augustine registered this point and accepted it, he might have had the grounds for arguing that Mary did not contribute seed to the conception of Jesus because *no* woman contributed seed to conception. Since on Augustine's manifest view only males furnish the (vitiated) seed that is responsible for forming the fetus but also for marking it with original sin, then Jesus, as fatherless, is exempt from the latter. Augustine *could* have claimed that his understanding of Jesus' sinless conception rested on a scientific view of human reproduction propounded by an important medical authority of late antiquity, Soranus—but he did not.

Yet another of Augustine's unusual biological views is here worth mentioning. It was a commonplace among the medical experts of Augustine's era (and earlier) that the woman as well as the man must feel sexual desire in order for conception to take place. Soranus even argues that in the case of women who were "forced" (i.e., raped) and conceived as a result, there

---

Virgo Maria: Neue Untersuchungen über die Lehre von der Jungfrauschaft und der Ehe Mariens in der ältesten Kirche (Arbeiten zur Kirchengeschichte 25; Berlin: Verlag Walter de Gruyter, 1937).

121. The 1850 bull of Pius IX, *Ineffabilis Dei,* states: "We declare, pronounce and define that the Most Blessed Virgin Mary, at the first instant of her Conception was preserved immaculate from all stain of original sin, by the singular grace and privilege of the Omnipotent God, in virtue of the merits of Jesus Christ, the Savior of mankind, and that this doctrine was revealed by God, and therefore, must be believed firmly and constantly by all the faithful."

122. Soranus, *Gynecology* 1.3.12 (Temkin, *Soranus' Gynecology,* p. 12). Peter Brown ("Sexuality and Society," p. 61) follows Pierre Courcelle (*Les Lettres grecques en Occident* [Paris, 1948], pp. 181–82) in thinking that Augustine read Soranus in the Greek original. In the early fifth century, however, according to Owsei Temkin (introduction, *Soranus' Gynecology,* p. xliv), a Latin paraphrase of Soranus's *Gynecology* was available in Theodorus Priscianus's *Euporista* (originally in Greek, but translated by the author into Latin) and a Latin translation "not much later, probably," by Caelius Aurelianus. If Soranus *were* available in Latin translation in the second or third decade of the fifth century, it is much more likely that Augustine read the work in Latin, given the limited extent of his Greek.

must have been some element of sexual desire present, however masked it was by "mental elements" at the moment of the assault; otherwise, the woman could not have become pregnant.[123] Desire (Augustine's "concupiscence") was thus deemed necessary for the "concoction" of the seed into a fetus.[124] This manifestly is the view accepted by Julian: he writes that the seeds mix with *voluptas*.[125] God gives the seeds their "force" (*vis*) and blesses them,[126] but it appears that, according to Julian, the seeds themselves are concocted by physical processes. Moreover, Julian makes clear that women as well as men have lust.[127]

For Augustine, in contrast, the seeds are not produced through the process of sexual pleasure; God makes them directly.[128] This enables Augustine to claim both that reproduction is a good and that it could (and ideally, should) have occurred without lust both in the Garden of Eden and among Adam and Eve's descendants. Such an understanding of biology would allow Augustine to argue even more strongly that the sex act itself is not sinful; it is the lust that renders the act a venial sin.[129]

"Who can declare his generation?" (Isa. 53:8). Augustine tried, but found himself derisively labeled *physicus iste novus* — "that new-fangled scientist" — by Julian for his allegedly novel understanding of human biology.[130] To Julian, Augustine's biotheology prompted the embrace of faulty notions of Christology, marriage, and the fate of unbaptized infants. Yet if Augustine's biology was here proclaimed deficient, his theology, in modified form, triumphed over Julian's: Augustine's narrative of human degeneration and divine regeneration has fertilized the production of the Catholic sexual and marital ethic until our day.

123. Soranus, *Gynecology* 1.10, 37 (Temkin, *Soranus' Gynecology*, p. 36).
124. Soranus, *Gynecology* 1.10, 37 (Tempkin, *Soranus' Gynecology*, p. 36).
125. *De nuptiis* 2.26 (13) (CSEL 42, 278); *Opus imperfectum* 5.11 (PL 45, 1440), cf. 2.39 (CSEL 85¹, 191); *Contra Julianum* 4.12 (2) (PL 44, 742).
126. *Opus imperfectum* 2.41 (CSEL 85¹, 192).
127. *Contra Julianum* 3.37 (19) (PL 44, 721–22); but cf. 5.23 (5).
128. *De nuptiis* 2.26 (13) (CSEL 42, 278–79).
129. E.g., *De nuptiis* 1.16 (14); 1.17 (15) (CSEL 42, 228–29, 229–30).
130. *Opus imperfectum* 5.11 (PL 45, 1440).

Maternal Imagination and Monstrous Birth: Tasso's *Gerusalemme liberata*

VALERIA FINUCCI

Nera sì, ma sì bella, o di natura
fra le belle d'amor leggiadro mostro.
—G. Marino, "Amore"

Can the Ethiopian change his skin or the leopard his spots?
—Jeremiah 14:23–24

Desolate Afric! thou art lovely yet!! . . .
What though thy maidens are a blackish brown,
Does virtue dwell in whiter breasts alone?
—W. Makepeace Thackeray, "Timbuctoo"

I

"Pater semper incertus est, mater est certissima," Freud wrote, repeating a well-known saying.[1] For centuries, before the onset of embryology and genetics, fathers could only hope they engendered the fetuses their companions were carrying. Yet when sometimes in the middle of the sixteenth century property began no longer to be divided among brothers (*in fraterna*), according to the model of a divisible patrilinear succession, but followed more frequently the rules of primogeniture, men started to have plenty at stake in wanting to know which children precisely they fathered.[2] Resem-

---

1. Sigmund Freud, "Family Romances," *The Standard Edition of the Complete Psychological Works of Sigmund Freud* (hereafter SE), ed. and trans. James Strachey, 24 vols. (1909; London: Hogarth Press, 1953–74), 9:239.
2. The shift in inheritance practices from fraternal to "patrilinear indivisible," and therefore from a family asset classifiable as "horizontal multiple" to "vertical multiple," was pushed aside gradually only in the second half of the eighteenth century with the new system of "bilateral divisible," in which brothers and sisters took their fair share. The movement to primogeniture in any case was neither swift nor uniform throughout Italy. In Venice the

blance played a key role in linking them to the babies for whose physical and social well-being they were legally responsible, and it became an organizing "biological" principle that, as Michel Foucault has argued, constructed knowledge and made it representable.[3] Even today in Italian law the individual who declares himself the begetter of a child born out of wedlock needs to recognize him ("riconoscere"), to see a similarity between himself and the being he claims he has fathered.[4] For many, a baby in whom the parental stamp was effaced was not just a bastard—newborns not bearing a somatic identity with their fathers were at times cast away, together with their supposedly prodigal mothers—but a monster. Aristotle asserted that much: "Monstrosities come under the class of offspring which is unlike its parents."[5] Torquato Tasso (1544–1595) felt this way too in *Il mondo creato*:

E chiunque traligna, al propio padre
ed a la stirpe de' maggior antica
dissimil fatto, è quasi al mondo un mostro.

. . . . .

Ned uomo è più, ma d'odioso aspetto
del male sparso e mal concetto seme
un mal nato animal ci nasce e vive
ch'è detto mostro. E la natura istessa
lo schiva ed odia, e disdegnando abborre

---

custom was to entail the estate or to allow only one son to marry. For a study of how agnatic legislation affected women, see Thomas Kuen, *Law, Family, and Women: Toward a Legal Anthropology of Renaissance Italy* (Chicago: University of Chicago Press, 1991) and Stanley Chojnacki, *Women and Men in Renaissance Venice: Twelve Essays on Patrician Society* (Baltimore: Johns Hopkins University Press, 2000). For a look at family structures in Italy, see Marzio Barbagli, *Sotto lo stesso tetto: Mutamenti della famiglia in Italia dal XV al XX secolo* (Bologna: Mulino, 1984), chap. 4.

3. "Up to the end of the sixteenth century, resemblance played a constructive role in the knowledge of Western culture. It was resemblance that largely guided exegesis and the interpretation of texts; it was resemblance that organized the play of symbols, made possible knowledge of things visible and invisible, and controlled the art of representing them." In Michel Foucault, *The Order of Things: An Archeology of the Human Sciences* (New York: Random, 1970), 17. The other principles Foucault selected were convenience, emulation, analogy, and sympathy.

4. The same applies to French law. See Marie-Hélène Huet, *Monstrous Imagination* (Cambridge, Mass.: Harvard University Press, 1993).

5. Aristotle, *Generation of Animals* (hereafter *GA*), trans. A. L. Peck (Cambridge, Mass.: Harvard University Press, 1990), 4.4.770b.

(And man can often so degenerate from his illustrious progeny as to resemble none in all mankind. A man no longer, he's an ill-born beast, the fruit of an ill-scattered, hateful seed, and therefore as a living monster's known. Nature herself abhors and dreads his sight.)[6]

In *Gerusalemme liberata,* Tasso had also repeatedly called a child not resembling either parent a monster. Such was the case of Clorinda, a Saracen female knight, born white of black Ethiopian parents. Her own mother looked horrified when she first saw the baby and decided to cast her away for fear of being accused of adultery: "Si turba; e de gli insoliti colori, / quasi d'un novo mostro, / ha meraviglia" ("She is distraught, and marvels as much at the unusual color as at a strange monster").[7] I will use this famous story in the *Liberata* to focus on the historical and cultural tradition behind the construction of maternal and filial monstrosity in the Renaissance. I will chronicle in broad strokes how monsters were thought to be engendered and what the mother's imagination supposedly had to do with it, why Ethiopians were considered monstrous, what the role of Saint George was in the birth of an Ethiopian baby, and finally, why characters with undefined gender alignments were cast in culture as monstrous. I will use *Gerusalemme liberata* extensively — literature was, after all, one of the many discourses that together with medicine, philosophy, law, and religion assembled and systematized learning in the past — for insights on the ways people dealt with genealogical issues.[8] The female body, which constitutes the focal point of my inquiry, will be read not as the customary place of erotic investment but as a site illustrative of presumed pathologies that were at the time obsessively studied, medicalized, and denounced.

Tasso provides very little information about Clorinda until the day she

6. Torquato Tasso, *Il mondo creato,* in *Le opere,* vol. 4, ed. Bruno Maier (Milan: Rizzoli, 1964), canto 6:1344–54. Translation by Joseph Tusiani here and subsequently in Torquato Tasso, *Creation of the World* (Binghamton, N.Y.: Center for Medieval and Early Renaissance Studies, SUNY, 1982), 6:1322–28.

7. Torquato Tasso, *Gerusalemme liberata* (finished 1575, published 1581) (Milan: Feltrinelli, 1961), canto 12, octave 24. Hereafter cited parenthetically in the text. The translation by Ralph Nash, here and subsequently, is in Torquato Tasso, *Jerusalem Delivered* (Detroit, Mich.: Wayne State University Press, 1987).

8. For example, bridging the gap between scientific and aesthetic knowledge, Celsus declared the birth of medicine was the result of developments in the discipline of literature. See Aulus Cornelius Celsus, "Proemium," in *De medicina,* ed. and trans. W. G. Spenser (Cambridge, Mass.: Harvard University Press, 1935–38), 4.

dies. We know that she is beautiful and strong, and that the Christian hero Tancredi has fallen in love with her at first sight. Then, one evening, just before engaging in what will turn out to be her last act of bravery, Clorinda hears from her eunuch Arsete, who plays the role of a father, the true story of her origins. She was born in Ethiopia, Arsete tells her, the daughter of the black Christian king, Senapo, and an unnamed black queen of that land.[9] Her father's jealousy kept her pregnant and beautiful mother a virtual recluse in a tower with the limited company of a few maids and a trusted servant, Arsete himself. With nothing else to do, the mother spent her days looking at a picture hanging on the wall, that of Saint George saving a virginal princess from a monster. When her time for delivery came, the queen was astounded to see that she had given birth to a white girl resembling the maiden in the painting. Afraid of her husband's reaction, she decided to substitute the newborn with a more proper black one, born a few days earlier, and gave her to Arsete to take away from the claustrophobic paternal house ("chiuso loco," 12.22; "la torre, ove chius'era," 12.25) with instructions to baptize the child.[10] Arsete, an Egyptian by birth, brought Clorinda back to Egypt and raised her, but did not christen her, although he was reminded of his promise on more than one occasion by Saint George, appearing to him in dreams. Arsete also came to realize that Clorinda was protected by

9. "Black but beautiful" is how Tasso describes the queen, echoing words from the Song of Songs 1:4 ("bruna è sì, ma il bruno il bel non toglie"), 12:21. The father, Senapo, was renamed David in the *Gerusalemme conquistata* (1593). We do not know anything about the father's physical characteristics, but in "Il forno overo de la nobiltà," Tasso wrote that Ethiopian kings were often the most handsome among the citizens because Ethiopians correlated nobility and virtue with physical appearance and gave the reign to the most handsome: "[Q]uando io lessi che gli Etiopi concedevano il regno al più bello, giudicai ch'essi il facessero credendo che la bellezza fosse argomento di nobiltà e di virtù." See *Dialoghi* in *Le opere* 4:439.

10. According to the tradition of the Ethiopian church, female babies were baptized later than boys, forty days after birth, a custom that Tasso learned from the travel relations of Francisco Alvarez, *Voyage in Ethiopia* (chap. 22), as he writes in his *Dubbi e risposte intorno ad alcune cose e parole concernenti alla Gerusalemme liberata*, in *Appendice alle opere in prosa di Torquato Tasso*, ed. Angelo Solerti (Florence: Successori Le Monnier, 1892), 164–65. Probably the custom comes from the notion that girls rendered the mother impure for a longer time, according to levitical law. See also David Quint, *Epic and Empire: Politics and Generic Form from Virgil to Milton* (Princeton, N.J.: Princeton University Press, 1993), 237. For a somewhat similar belief shared by the Hippocratics, see the article by Dale Martin in this collection. Female fetuses also supposedly took longer to develop than male fetuses because of their cold nature.

this father figure. Once, for instance, a wild animal that should have attacked her, suckled her instead, a monstrous sight by all means ("io miro timido e confuso, / come uom faría nuovi prodigi orrendi," "I am all agaze, fearful and uncertain, as a man would be, seeing strange and chilling prodigies" [12.31]); on another occasion, she was miraculously saved from death while crossing a river. Just a few hours earlier that same night Saint George had appeared to Arsete to request his charge's baptism and to make him understand that Clorinda's life was coming to a close.

Clorinda listens to Arsete's story and shrugs it off. She gives no thought to her newly found parents and simply answers that she prefers to keep the Muslim religion of her childhood and adult life. That same night, after having burned in a momentous exploit the Christian tower menacing the safety of Jerusalem, she finds herself shut out of the city. She meets Tancredi, who is looking for enemies to show off his valor, is not recognized in the new armor she is wearing, and is fatally wounded in a duel. Feeling that the end is close, she unexpectedly asks him to baptize her. Upon removing her helmet to perform the ceremony, Tancredi recognizes his beloved and despairs: he has managed to eliminate the only enemy he wanted to save and have. Clorinda later appears to him in a dream when he is at his most melancholic and morose, forgives him for having killed her, and pronounces herself happy in heaven.

A white child born of black parents, a citizen of a part of the world often described by missionaries and travelers as inhabited by monstrous people, a baby brought up defiantly against the "laws" of nature and sex ("vincesti il sesso e la natura assai," 12.38) by a father figure without a sex—literally—and a woman warrior with manly abilities and castrating desires: can all this make Clorinda less than a "monster"? To be sure, there is nothing in Clorinda's physical description that would brand her as not normal, if we take white as the standard of normality. Following the literary tradition of the time (specifically, Ariosto, who had written out race from the description of the astounding beauty of his oriental Angelica in *Orlando furioso*), Tasso gives seemingly no importance to the fact that Clorinda is black. As beauty goes, Clorinda is the best example, in fact, of white female perfection. If Armida, the other major female character in the *Liberata,* had consistently to construct her outward appearance, Clorinda's looks are instead natural: she has lovely blond hair and is tall and slender. Her very name, Clorinda, etymologically echoes her whiteness (as in "pale," "yellow," "greenish-yellow") and metaphorically reiterates her being "fresh," "living," "young." Tancredi cannot keep her image out of his mind; and the Saracen hero Argante appears to be in love with her as well. Of course, Clorinda is totally unconscious of the effect she creates on others, for in making her white, Tasso puts aside the usual association of blacks in culture with excessive sexuality and promiscuity.[11] It is also true that Clorinda is hardly the personification of femininity. While growing up, we are told, she prefers the outdoors to closed spaces, and mastering beasts to embroidery. She even takes particular care in making her body and face strong and masculine ("armò d'orgoglio il volto, e si compiacque / rigido farlo," 2.39) and eventually appears so strange that men take her for a beast, and beasts take her for a man ("fèra a gli uomini parve, uomo a le belve," 2.40).

Unlike Bradamante in Ariosto, Clorinda actively looks in the *Liberata* for occasions in which to show her worth in the battlefield. Dressed in white armor, a typical color for women warriors (it was also Bradamante's color), and with a tiger in her crest, Clorinda is easily recognized and feared by her enemies. Her appearance in the field, or even at a distance as an archer, means continuous wounding, slicing, decapitating, and maiming of any enemy coming closer to her: she kills Guglielmo, heir to the English throne, with an arrow (11.42), and does the same to Stefano and Roberto (11.43); the bishop Ademaro is wounded on the forehead (11.44); Berlinghiero is stabbed from front to back (9.68); Albin is pierced in the stomach (9.68); Gerniero's right hand is cut off (9.69); Achille's head is severed (9.70); and the chief Christian warrior, Goffredo, receives a leg wound. Unlike Bradamante once more then, Clorinda is constructed as a woman warrior with no other self-made purpose than that of showing that she is as good or better than all other male warriors of either camp. We know that she has feelings too, but they do not seem to take the upper hand: she cries upon hearing the story of the doomed pair, Sofronia and Olindo, at her entrance in the *Liberata* in canto 2 and actively works to save them from the stake, but we are also repeatedly told that she is unresponsive to the love pangs of

11. To give an example along these lines beyond the obvious case of Shakespeare's *Othello*, let's take Ariosto. In the *Furioso* he has Judge Anselmo tempted by a black homosexual Ethiopian, thus coding male sexual "perversion" as other and black. See *Orlando furioso* (1532), ed. Marcello Turchi (Milan: Garzanti, 1974). The tradition is an old one. Epiphanius (fourth century) tells a story about Origen almost being forced to have sex with a black Ethiopian male. In the *Liberata*, there is an Ethiopian Saracen, Assimiro of Meroe, who will be killed and symbolically castrated in the last canto, when Rinaldo cuts off his black neck ("nero collo," 20.54).

the Christian hero Tancredi. To be sure, the woman warrior figure and the androgynous female were very much in vogue in Renaissance literature, but unlike Bradamante, whose posited androgyny rests only in her choice of clothes, given her engulfment in a fully sexualized career as future wife and mother of the state, Clorinda is described as sexually and psychologically unresponsive. She may be unconsciously masquerading as white, but she is consciously masquerading as male. She is monstrous, combining in her persona two antithetical views of women: very feminine in her beauty and very unfeminine in her chosen warrior role. No wonder that she does not seem to fit anywhere.

What can Tasso do with a woman who for narrative purposes cannot be made to behave like one? A happy ending for a lady warrior who wounds and maims Christian heroes with gusto is hardly acceptable. A happy ending for a white Ethiopian princess is also out of the question, because it could breed fears of miscegenation, since Tasso's outward purpose in the *Liberata* is to create a heroic genealogy for his patron, of the Este family of Ferrara. Were Clorinda just a Saracen, the problem could be easily solved: like Marfisa and Ruggiero in the *Furioso*, we know that Saracen heroes turn out to be Christian the very moment in which their destiny becomes important to the ideological purposes of the epic. But as a freakish white and violent lady knight Clorinda has no chance to be absorbed into the system; born without the marks of a properly stamped paternal identity, she has to remain utterly different. Her incorrect, out-of-bound breeding marked by her black/not-black background effectively precludes a happy ending.

We are all aware, of course, that the only way for an unredeemed woman warrior to fit in is to die, more so in the work of an author such as Tasso, who had problems of his own in granting women—any woman in fact—a meaningful continuous role in his romance epic.[12] That Clorinda has not only to be ritualistically killed (as Argante will say, "Ella morì di fatal morte," 12.103) but also normalized both before and after her death through a process of feminization and Oedipalization should not surprise us either, given the social constraints attending the representation of women in narrative. Here, however, I would like to focus on why Clorinda is monstrous

12. For Paul Larivaille, for example, "ogni tentativo delle donne o di equipararsi all'uomo, o di invertire o intaccare in qualche modo il rapporto da inferiori a superiori intercorrente fra loro e gli uomini, è considerato una trasgressione della natura femminile e immancabilmente destinato a fallire." See *Poesia e ideologia* (Naples: Liguori, 1987), 209.

and what the stakes—cultural, historical, literary, and personal—are for creating such a genealogy.

II

Let us begin at the beginning, with conception itself. For the different doctors in antiquity whose collected work has passed to us as the Hippocratic corpus, for Pliny, Soranus, Galen, and most everybody who wrote on the subject, apart from Aristotle, until the discovery of the woman's ovum in the seventeenth century, for conception to occur the male seed needed to mix with female seed.[13] Given men's "stronger" semen and "hotter" nature, children were supposed to resemble their fathers more than their mothers, especially, of course, boys, because like generates like. Paternal imagination was a plus in forming "perfect" offspring. As Tasso wrote in "Il messaggiero," thanks to the high quality of men's fantasy, children tend to reproduce the virtue and the beauty conveyed in their father's mind at the time of copulation.[14] In this reading the mother's role is both unrecognized and unrecognizable: she may provide her body for the child to develop, but does not know how to control either herself or the fetus growing inside her. The father rules: from the most biological element (a "proper" seed) to the most aesthetic or philosophical one (a "proper" mind), a normal fetus bears all over the imprint of the one whose presence at the time of engendering could, however, never be proved after the fact.

The view that fathers provided more than mothers did not go uncontested. Isidore of Seville wrote in *Etymologiae* that a very strong maternal seed caused the child to resemble its mother, a view that comes from Lucretius's *De rerum naturae* and influenced many Renaissance writers.[15] In his

13. For Aristotle, unconcocted female semen becomes menstrual blood: women do not contribute any semen to generation, because there is no creature that produces two seminal secretions at once, thus semen in males equals menstrual fluid in females. He believed that conception occurs when male seed mixes with menstrual blood. See GA 1.19.727a.
14. "[P]erchè la virtù de la fantasia è grandissima, quando gli uomini vengono a gli abbracciamenti d'amore, venendoci pieni di sì alta imaginazione, i figliuoli che poi son prodotti soglion nascer simili a quell'eccelente idea di valore e di bellezza ch'i padri ne la mente avean conceputa." Tasso, "Il messaggiero," in *Dialoghi,* ed. Bruno Basile (Milan: Mursia, 1986), 86. This is not true, however, for the ancients, who made no such distinction.
15. See Jane Bestor, "Ideas about Procreation and Their Influence on Ancient and Medieval

Quaderni d'anatomia, Leonardo da Vinci noted that the offspring of an Italian woman and of an Ethiopian man showed strong maternal features, a demonstration, he concluded, that the "seed of the female was as potent as that of the male in generation."[16] For Tommaso Campanella, resemblance varied according to circumstances: a child was similar to the mother if her spirit and affection were predominant, he wrote, and resembled the father if his strength and imagination prevailed. But the newborn could also resemble relatives if the parents thought of them, or even strange people, when there were similarities of disposition. This opinion has a long history, since for Aristotle too a "relapse of male seed" meant that a baby would take after its grandfather, while a mastery of some male faculty on the part of the female plus a relapse of the male seed would make it look like its grandmother or some other ancestor (GA 4.3.768b). For Campanella, likeness was less mechanistically determined than it was for Aristotle, since it could also come from other sources: the parents' yearning for a certain food, their longings, the places they inhabited, or the influence of planets.[17]

A weak male seed, whether it came from a father too young or too old, constituted a problem in all cases, since not only was it held responsible for engendering female babies, because the matter was insufficiently shaped — and in fact it may have impeded conception altogether — but also it could generate a monster. Too much seed could have the same results. Aristotle, of course, made no clear distinction between those two categories, woman and monster. As he famously stated, "Anyone who does not take after his parents is really in a way a monstrosity, since in these cases Nature has in a way strayed from the generic type. The first beginning of this deviation is when a female is formed instead of a male, though (a) this indeed is a necessity required by Nature, since the race of creatures which are separated into male and female has got to be kept in being; and (b) since it is possible for the male sometimes not to gain the mastery either on account

---

Views of Kinship," in *The Family in Italy from Antiquity to the Present,* ed. David Kerzner and Richard Saller (New Haven Conn.: Yale University Press, 1991), 150–67, esp. 157.

16. In Joseph Needham, *A History of Embryology,* 3 vols. (New York: Abelard-Schuman, 1959), 3:96.

17. In his words: "dalla disposizione insolita dei genitori per varii cibi, affetti, luoghi e stelle." See Tommaso Campanella, "Magia della generazione," in *Del senso delle cose e della magia,* ed. Antonio Bruers (Bari: Laterza, 1925), 308. The text was written in Latin in the early 1590s and subsequently lost; the Italian version is probably from 1604.

of youth or age or some other such cause."[18] In Aristotle's rationalizations, monstrosity is the result of deviation from male perfection. The monster is not only the newborn who fails to resemble its makers, but woman herself, the *mas occasionatus* of Aquinas, the only difference between the two monstrosities being that the female is necessary to the human race, while the physically defective child is not. Given this line of argument, a woman unlike her parents must have appeared doubly freakish. Tasso was well aware of the problem and put it in verse in *Il mondo creato*:

> E s'adivien giamai che 'l maschio seme
> debole e raro sia del veglio stanco
> o sparso dal fanciul, nè vincer possa
> con quella sua virtù ch'informa e move
> ne' chiostri occulti del femineo ventre
> l'indigesta materia umida e informe,
> femina nasce; e ch'ella nasca è d'uopo,
> e se non caro, è necessario il parto.
> Ma d'uopo già non è che sia prodotto
> orrido mostro al mondo. (6:1324-33)

("If the male semen of a weak old man, or of an adolescent, fails to win and fecundate, to rouse and therefore shape in the dark corners of a woman's womb its matter, shapeless, wet, and still impure, a female's born — a necessary birth if not a happy one. But it is not necessity that brings monstrosities to this our world.") 6:1299-1307

Choices made during the sexual act could also be dangerous to the well-being of a fetus. In *De secretis mulierum*, Albertus Magnus warned that violent coitus and coitus while standing were conducive to monstrosities because the seed would have been unable to properly attach itself to the womb.[19] Other doctors recommended against coitus with menstruating women to avoid birth defects, an interdiction already present in the Bible.[20]

---

18. GA 4.3.767b. Later Aristotle repeats it: "[W]e should look upon the female state as being as it were a deformity, though one which occurs in the ordinary course of nature" (GA 4.6.775a).

19. Albertus Magnus (Alberto Magno), *De secretis mulierum* (Lugduni: Apud A. De Marsy, 1595).

20. *Leviticus* 18:19. Only in the second half of the sixteenth century and with the Counter-Reformation's stress on morality and female purity did the belief that menstruating women

Acts against nature, such as sodomy and coitus with women on top, also were thought to produce monsters. A rebellious female seed was just as problematic as a weak male one, because at best it would be responsible for engendering a female child and at worst a monster, fifteenth-century doctor Antonio Guainerio wrote.[21] Too much concocted seed, stated French court physician Ambroise Paré, could engender twins in the best cases and a monstrous child with too many organs in the worst ones; vice versa, too little seed could breed a child missing body parts. Paré cited as causes for foetal malformations a narrow maternal womb, bestiality, problematic pregnancy, and hereditary diseases. Strange or even habitual positions of the maternal body could have horrifying effects as well: seamstresses holding their legs crossed while working or women wearing clothes that were too tight could give birth to "hunchbacked and misshapen" children, Paré warned, to say nothing of the dangers that would result if a pregnant woman fell or succumbed to an illness.[22] Monstrous sex, that is, monstrous behavior on the part of the mother—anything too active, too unconventional, or too lacking in caution—produced monstrous beings. This view, of course, is hardly new: women have often been accused of being responsible for whatever men would rather not be held accountable themselves.

The fate of monstrous children in history has been a dire one. The Romans used to drown or expose them; the act was not considered murderous. Early Christianity, however, followed the Jewish custom of repudi-

---

could produce monsters become, as Ottavia Niccoli puts it, "a precise historical fact." See " 'Menstruum quasi monstruum': Monstrous Births and Menstrual Taboo in the Sixteenth Century," in *Sex and Gender in Historical Perspective: Selections from* "Quaderni storici," ed. Edward Muir and Guido Ruggiero (Baltimore, Md.: Johns Hopkins University Press, 1990), 1–25, 19. For more on the turn from the positive view of menstruation to the negative, see Gianna Pomata, "Menstruating Men: Similarity and Difference of the Sexes in Early Modern Medicine," in this volume. Corrupt menstrual blood was also held responsible for pregnant women's longings. See Patricia Crawford, "Attitudes to Menstruation in Seventeenth-Century England," *Past and Present* 91 (1981): 47–73, esp. 52.

21. Antonio Guainerio, *Tractatus de matricibus* (Treatise on the Womb), in *Opera Omnia* (Pavia, 1481), f. 2z6vb.

22. Ambroise Paré (1517–1590), *On Monsters and Marvels,* trans. Janis Pallister (1573; Chicago: University of Chicago Press, 1982), chaps. 4, 8, 10, 11, 13. Paré also mentioned a category, that of artifices, which covers the case of pretenders or of children mutilated by their own parents for the sake of getting more money from begging. Like many other doctors and philosophers of the time, Paré attributed monstrous birth to God's will and wrath and to the intervention of demons, but he also took steps to naturalize monstrosity.

ating the killing of weak and deformed infants, and by 374 infanticide had officially become a crime.[23] This is not to say that it did not still happen. In the Middle Ages and the Renaissance malformed newborns were at times murdered in the delivery room by the very midwife who brought them to life; if they survived, their crippled, displaced, excrescent bodies were often shown for money at fairs and freak shows.[24] The church considered monsters human beings and legislated whether they should be baptized. How should Siamese twins be christened, for example? Were they supposed to be one body and one soul, and thus be baptized once, or did they constitute two bodies and two souls? Midwives were repeatedly instructed on the procedure to follow in such peculiar instances.[25] Cicero wrote in *De divinatione* that monsters are so called because they demonstrate that something has to take place. In *De civitate Dei* Augustine argued that monsters are not errors but prodigies of nature because they plainly show God's will. His tripartite argument was that there may be races of monsters that actually do not exist, that if they exist they may not be human, and that if they are human they are all children of Adam, and therefore man has no business in second-guessing God's intentions (16.80).[26] Following him, Isidore of Seville too saw monsters as signs from heaven: they tended to die soon after seeing the light, he explained, because their birth was sufficient to ful-

23. See Uta Ranke-Heinemann, *Eunuchs for the Kingdom of Heaven: Women, Sexuality and the Catholic Church* (New York: Doubleday, 1990), 68.

24. The spice merchant Luca Landucci, for example, describes in his diary the showing in Florence in 1513 of a Spanish man having another creature coming out of his body, with legs and genitals protruding, but no head. See *Diario Fiorentino: A Florentine Diary from 1450 to 1516* (New York: Dutton, 1927). Celio Malespini recollects a similar case in Rome late in the sixteenth century when a man with two heads, one of which was coming out of his stomach, was being shown for money. See *Giardino di fiori curiosi* (Venice: Ciotti, 1597), bk. 1, p. 16. The book is a translation of a Spanish text by Antonio Torquemada, which came out originally in 1590.

25. Niccoli reports the case of a midwife who baptized a deformed baby before its full emergence from the birth canal ("Menstruum," 21, n. 12). Extremely deformed babies were, however, judged nonhumans and were not baptized. Also christened immediately upon delivery were children born by cesarian section or those whose mother died during delivery. See Renate Blumenfeld-Kosinski, *Not of Woman Born: Representations of Caesarian Birth in Medieval and Renaissance Culture* (Ithaca, N.Y.: Cornell University Press, 1991), chap. 1.

26. Marcus Tullius Cicero, *De divinatione*, ed. Arthur Pease (Urbana: University of Illinois Press, 1920–1923), 1.42; Augustine, *De civitate Dei*, ed. J. E. C. Welldon (London: Macmillan, 1924), 21.8.

fill their purposes.[27] The birth of a monster in Ravenna in 1512 was taken as a premonitory sign of the forthcoming devastation of Italy on the part of the French troops of Louis XII; that of the monstrous pope-ass left to die in the Tiber in Rome in 1496 became for Philip Melanchton a demonstration that God was fed up with the corruption of the Church of Rome. The same conclusion was reached by Martin Luther in his examination of the monk-claf baby born in Freiburg in 1522.[28]

In time, Renaissance thought grew away from a reading of monstrosity as supernatural manifestation and secularized its approach to the subject through a number of philosophical, scientific, and literary pronouncements. No longer explained away as signs of God's intervention in human affairs, monsters became the field of inquiry of anatomists, geneticists, and pathologists.[29] One result of this shift is the great number of manuals on teratology, the classification of monsters, that became fashionable after 1550.[30] Descriptions of monstrosity in the period were often enhanced by

27. Isidore of Seville, *Etymologiae* 1.11.3, *Patrologia latina*, ed. Jacques Paul Migne (Alexandria, Va.: Chadwick-Healey Inc, 1995), 82, col. 420. Hereafter *PL*. See also Niccoli, "Menstruum," 3; and Jean Céard, *La Nature et les prodiges: L'insolite au XVIe siècle en France* (Geneva: Droz, 1977), 21–33. Pietro Pomponazzi will later attribute monstrosity to cosmographic influences. See *De naturalium effectuum admirandorum causis, seu de incantationibus liber, item de fato, libero arbitrio, praedestinatione, prouidentia Dei* (Basel: Ex Officina Henricpetrina, 1567).

28. Martin Luther and Phillip Melanchton, "Deuttung der czwo grewlichen Figuren, Bapstesels czu Rom und Munchkalbs zu Freijberg ijnn Meijsszen funden," in Martin Luther, *Werke,* 58 vols. (Weimar, 1883–1948), 11:370–85. Such fanciful nicknames were given to visually describe the appearance of these repugnant bodies. On the political use of monsters and the anxieties they fed, see Ottavia Niccoli, *Prophecy and People in Renaissance Italy* (Princeton, N.J.: Princeton University Press, 1990), chap. 2.

29. See Katherine Park and Lorraine Daston, "Unnatural Conceptions: The Study of Monsters in Sixteenth- and Seventeenth-Century France and England," *Past and Present* 91 (1981): 21–54, esp. 23–24; and Jacques Gélis, *History of Childbirth, Fertility, Pregnancy and Birth in Early Modern Europe,* trans. Rosemary Morris (Boston, Mass.: Northeastern University Press, 1991), 267.

30. The Flemish doctor Lievin Lemnes's (Levinus Lemnius) text on "miracles of nature" was translated into Italian as *De gli occulti miracoli, et varii ammaestramenti delle cose della natura* and published in Venice in 1560; Benedetto Varchi wrote a *Lezzione . . . sopra la generatione de' mostri e se sono intesi dalla natura o no* (1548) published in Florence; Sebastian Munster issued *Cosmographia universalis* in 1544 in German, soon translated into Italian; and Jacob Rueff wrote *De conceptu et generatione hominis* in 1554. A few years later Benedetto Sinibaldi published in Rome a much researched and scholarly text of more than a thousand folio columns, titled *Geneanthopeiae sive de hominis generatione decatheuchon;* Tommaso Garzoni

fantasy, as in reports of newborns with the head or body of cows, cats, dogs, and frogs. Approaching the topic, Tasso declined to read monsters with a superstitious agenda and wrote that they were the result of defects in nature ("difetto di materia"). Still, he thought that monsters functioned as God's sign that all men face pain and death.[31] A second result of the shift is that women—in particular women's imagination—became even more the cause of newborns' deficiencies. Many doctors, such as Marsilio Ficino, Paré, and Paracelsus, developing Aristotelian and Galenic views, remarked that the maternal imagination at the time of conception, be it influenced by something the mother dreamt or saw, had a peculiar importance in shaping the fetus. To start with, female imagination was stronger than male imagination, it was thought, because of women's cold and humid nature, and cold object are subject to metamorphosis.[32] Since Empedocles's remark that statues and paintings seen during pregnancy could bring changes to a fetus's bodily features, maternal imagination had constituted one of the inscrutable, uncontrollable incursions into one's yet unborn life. Galen advised hanging a picture of a handsome man or of a beautiful doll on the ceiling of the expectant mother's bedroom or at her bedpost to assure pleasant-looking features for the newborn, each choice coded around the preferred sex.[33] The custom became so common by the middle of the sixteenth century that Lodovico Domenichi declared it fashionable among Venetian nobles.[34]

---

wrote *Serraglio degli stupori del mondo* in the 1580s, although it was printed in 1613; Fortunii Liceti's contribution, *De monstrorum caussis, natura et differentiis* appeared in Padua in 1616, and Ulisse Aldrovandi's *Monstrorum historia* was printed almost forty years after his death in Bologna in 1642. For a most comprehensive study of teratology in five volumes, see Cesare Taruffi, *Storia della teratologia* (Bologna: Regia Tipografia, 1881), and Ernest Martin, *Histoire des monstres depuis l'antiquité jusqu'à nos jours* (Paris: Reinwald, 1880).

31. *Il mondo creato* 6:1443–50. Giuseppe Liceti also expresses similar views in *Il ceva overo dell'eccellenza et uso de' genitali. Dialogo di Gioseppe Liceti Medico Chirurgo genovese. Nel quale si tratta dell'essenza, et generatione del seme humano; delle somiglianze dell'Huomo, e lor cagioni; della differenza del sesso; della generatione de' mostri, e d'altre cose non meno utili; che dilettevoli* (Bologna: Heredi di Gio. Rossi, 1598).

32. See Ian Maclean, *The Renaissance Notion of Woman* (Cambridge: Cambridge University Press, 1980), 42.

33. See Gélis, *History of Childbirth,* 55. Francesco da Barberino (1264–1348) also tells pregnant women to look at good images in order not to generate monsters. See *Del reggimento e costumi di donna,* ed. Giuseppe Sansone (Rome: Zauli, 1995).

34. "[P]ar che hoggi sia nato il costume fra gran Signori di tener per le camere quadri nobilis-

Problems were always lurking. A story often reported was that of a baby girl covered with hair as the result of her mother having gazed at a portrait of Saint John in a bearskin hanging over her bed. Then there was the case of a baby girl born in 1517 with a frog-like face because her mother had held a frog for the sake of curing a fever and kept holding it during coitus.[35] For Paracelsus it was crucial to cheer up melancholic and angry pregnant women because their unbridled imagination could have bad effects. A woman dying in childbirth may wish the whole world to die with her, he wrote, and this volition could convert into a spirit that "by means of the ('menstrual') birth discharge . . . can generate an epidemic." A pregnant woman with lascivious imagination, likewise, by offending Venus, produced "the semen of contagion notably plague." In fact, whenever there was no complete concordance between man, woman, and heaven, the woman produced monsters, Paracelsus concluded.[36] In 1548, Benedetto Varchi strongly lamented the effect of the mother's imagination on the fetus, as Ulisse Aldrovandi and Benedetto Sinibaldi did soon after.[37] Likewise, in his treatise on sacred and profane images, Gabriele Paleotti argued that it is a theory commonly accepted by both philosophers and doctors that bodies can show the signs of what we fantasize.[38]

---

simi di pitture perchè da simili oggetti le donne prendano imaginazione bellisssima." Lodovico Domenichi, *Historia naturale di G. Plinio Secondo, . . . tradotta per m. L. Domenichi con le additioni in margine* (1561; Venice: G. Bizzardo, 1612), 156.

35. See Paré, *On Monsters*, chap. 9. Holding frogs in one's hand was the cure for an array of problems. Falloppio recommends it for women with heavy menstruation. See Gabriele Falloppio (1523–1562), *Secreti diversi e miracolosi* (Venice: Bonfad, 1658), bk. 1, 120.

36. Paracelsus (Theophrastus Bombastus von Hohenheim) (1493–1541), *De virtute imaginativa*, in Walter Pagel, *Paracelsus: An Introduction to Philosophical Medicine in the Era of the Renaissance* (New York: Karger, 1958), 122 and 124.

37. Benedetto Varchi, *Lezzione* (1548), in Luigi Carrer, *Descrizioni di cose naturali* (Venice, 1841), 1–72; Ulisse Aldrovandi, *Avvertimenti del Dottore Aldrovandi sopra le pitture mostrifiche e religiose* (1581), reprinted in *Osservazione della natura e raffigurazione in Ulisse Aldrovandi*, ed. G. Olmi, special issue of *Annali dell'Istituto Storico Italo-Germanico di Trento* 3 (1977): 177–80; J. Benedicti Sinibaldi, *Geneanthropeiae sivi de hominis generatione decatheuchon, ubi ex ordine quaecumque ad humanae generationis liturgiam, ejusdem principia, organa, tempus, usum, modum, occasionem, voluptatem . . . Adjecta est historia foetus mussipontani* (1642; Frankfurt: Petri Zubrodt, 1669).

38. "Secondo i varii concetti che apprende la nostra fantasia delle cose, si fanno in essa così salde impressioni, che da quelle ne derivano alterazioni e segni notabili nei corpi, di che chiaro testimonio ci rende l'esperienza stessa." Gabriele Paleotti (1522–1597), *Discorsi intorno*

Many cases of monstrosity dealt with racial intermixing. A white woman, a story went, delivered a nonwhite child because she often gazed at the picture of a dark-skinned man in the bedchamber during her pregnancy. Juan Huarte categorically denied that a child with a different skin color than the father or the mother could be engendered.[39] Yet the jurist Andrea Alciati defended a woman accused of adultery because she delivered a black child, although she and her husband were white, because there was a painting of an Ethiopian in her bedroom.[40] Some believed that women themselves were to blame for black features originating in the race born of Adam. The dark color of skin came about, Agostino Tornielli claimed, because maternal imagination focused on something very black that could not be satisfied during pregnancy and in due course a black baby was born.[41] Père Lafitau made a similar statement on the power of maternal introjection as late as 1724. Originally there was one color for all mankind, he argued, but some men painted themselves black or red and this left a remarkable impression on the imagination of pregnant women, with the perceived racial results.[42] Even after James Blondel published not one but two treatises (1727, 1729) denying in detail the possibility of any role for maternal imagination in the generative process, beliefs in its power went unabated.[43] More than thirty

alle immagini sacre e profane (Bologna: Alessandro Benacci, 1582), reprinted in *Trattati d'arte del cinquecento fra Manierismo e Controriforma,* ed. Paola Barocchi (Bologna: Laterza, 1961), 2:230.

39. Juan Huarte (1529?-1588), *Essamina de gl'ingegni de gli huomini accomodati ad apprendere qual si voglia scienza* (Venice: Barezzi e' compagni, 1600), 432-33 and 445. The original Spanish text, *Examen des ingenios para la ciencias,* was published in 1575; the first Italian edition in 1582. Huarte's book was placed in the Index after the Jesuit Antonio Possevino criticized its determinism.

40. Andrea Alciati (1492-1550), *De verborum et rerum significatione,* in *Opera omnia* (Basel: Thomas Guarinum, 1582), vol. 2, col. 1196.

41. Agostino Tornielli, *Annales sacri, et ex profanis praecipui, ad orbe condito ad eumdem Christi passione redemptum* (Antwerp: Moretum 1620), 2 vols. See also Giuliano Gliozzi, *Le teorie della razza nell'età moderna* (Turin: Einaudi, 1986), 131-32; and Massimo Angelini, "Il potere plastico dell'immaginazione nelle gestanti tra XVI e XVIII secolo: La fortuna d'una idea," *Intersezioni* 14 (1994): 53-69, 57.

42. Père Lafitau, *Moeurs des sauvages américains* (Paris, 1724), 67. On this, see also Pierre Darmon, *Le Mythe de la procréation à l'âge baroque* (Paris: Seuil, 1979), 161.

43. James Blondel, *The Strength of Imagination in Pregnant Women Examin'd and the Opinion that Marks and Deformities in Children Arise from these Demonstrated to be a Vulgar Error* (London, 1727), and *The Power of the Mother's Imagination over the Foetus Examin'd* (London, 1729).

years later, in his treatise on skin color, Nicolas Lecat gave an example of a white German woman who gave birth to a black infant because she had seen a black servant during her pregnancy.[44] Friedrich Hegel too kept fearing the maternal imagination. In *Philosophy of the Mind,* he wrote "of children being born with an injured arm because the mother had actually broken an arm or at least had knocked it so severely that she feared it was broken, or, again, because she had been frightened by the sight of someone's else broken arm."[45] In more modern times, the so-called Elephant Man got his name not from his misshapen head, we are told, but from the fact that before his birth his mother had witnessed a circus elephant gone mad and was extraordinarily impressed by the elephant's trunk.[46]

At the time Tasso wrote, mothers could not only determine the features of the fetus through their imagination and have hysterical pregnancies that they would later abort ("molae"); they could also determine skin pigmentation. Birthmarks ("voglie" or "envies" in French, that is, wants, desires) could take many shapes; usually they were thought to be fruits that the mother longed to taste during pregnancy, reminders of another fruit perhaps, the apple that the mother of all mankind desired, thus dooming all her children to a life of toil.[47] When the use of coffee became common, a number of newborns were identified as having coffee-colored pigment stains. Women were recommended not to touch themselves or, if needed, only to touch parts of the body hidden to sight, so that a mark would not disfigure the newborn.[48] In Boiardo's chivalric romance *Orlando innamorato* (1492),

44. Nicolas Lecat, *Traité de la couleur de la peau humaine en général, de celle des nègres en particulier et de la métamorphose d'une de ces couleurs en l'autre, soit de naissance, soit accidentellement* (Amsterdam, 1765), bk. 1, art. 2, p. 20. See also the story of the lady from Seville giving birth to a black infant because her black maid's baby was lying on the lady's bed while she was engaged in coitus, as narrated by Marina Brownlee in this volume.

45. Friedrich Hegel, *Hegel's Philosophy of Subjective Spirit,* trans. and ed. M. J. Petry, 3 vols. (Dordrecht: Reidel, 1978), 2:237.

46. See Arnold Davidson, "The Horror of Monsters," in *The Boundaries of Humanity: Humans, Animals, Machines,* ed. James Sheehan and Morton Sosna (Berkeley: University of California Press, 1991), 36–67, 53.

47. See Alain Grosrichard, "Le Cas polyphème: Un monstre et sa mère," *Ornicar?* 11-12 (Sept.–Dec. 1977): 19-35; 45-57.

48. It was also thought that birthmarks could be produced by excess menstrual discharge, although Lorenzo Gioberti (Laurent Joubert) denies it. Moreover, some women, he stated, specifically Brazilian women, never menstruate. See Lorenzo Gioberti (1529-1583), *La prima*

Fiordespina is described as having a birthmark because of her mother's wandering mind. Children, in short, bore the mark of their mother's hysterical or promiscuous desires. Thus, in the case of a newborn resembling a dog, the resemblance did not mean, Ulisse Aldrovandi wrote, that the child was the fruit of bestial copulation, because an animal cannot reproduce itself in a human being. Rather, it showed that the mother must have been so much obsessed by her transgression and bestiality during coitus that she engendered a child resembling what she was thinking at the time.[49] In short, the monstrous child needs to be born as a witness to a mother's monstrous nature.

There is therefore a palpable difference between paternal and maternal imagination vis-à-vis the formation of a fetus's features. The father, as we saw with Tasso, needs simply to think of something in order for the child to be a perfect or perfected image of what he thinks; the mother, however, can only manage a poor reproduction of what she is desiring or seeing and can be influenced by circumstances to do things properly or to botch them. The father's imagination can improve on a child's genetic baggage; the mother, by not controlling herself and letting biology rather than fantasy work, can make a seemingly normal fetus monstrous.[50]

---

parte degli errori popolari: Nella quale si contiene l'eccellenza della medicina e de medici, della concettione, e generatione, della gravidanza, del parto, e delle donne di parto, e del latte, e del nutrire i bambini (Florence: Giunta, 1592). An English translation by Gregory David de Rocher, Popular Errors (Tuscaloosa: University of Alabama Press, 1989) of the original French version Erreurs populaires (Bordeaux, 1579), is now available. See also Thomas Laqueur, Making Sex: Body and Gender from the Greeks to Freud (Cambridge: Harvard University Press, 1990), 104.

49. Aldrovandi, Monstrorum historia, fol. 1642. Popular thinking and even some learned minds, such as Pliny, thought that interbreeding could be possible, however. For examples of such births, see Valeria Finucci, "Immaculate Conceptions: Pregnancy and Imagination in Early Modern Italy," paper delivered at the annual meeting of the Renaissance Society of America, Vancouver, Canada, April 1997. For the case of the English woman Mary Taft, whose declaration that she had given birth to seventeen rabbits in 1726 was believed by doctors and citizens alike, see Dennis Todd, Imagining Monsters: Miscreations of the Self in Eighteenth-Century England (Chicago: University of Chicago Press, 1995). Recently David Cressy has examined the case of a woman who claimed to have given birth to a cat in Leicestershire in 1569. See his Travesties and Transgressions in Tudor and Stuart England: Tales of Discord and Dissention (Oxford: Oxford University Press, 2000), 9–28.

50. On having pregnant women desire something of a shape and color that will be apparent upon delivery, see Campanella, Del senso, 309. For Thomas Lupton, A Thousand Notable Things (1579), and Thomas Fienus (Thomas Feyens), De viribus imaginationis tractatus (1608),

The implications of maternal imagination were far-reaching. If a fetus is imprinted with the image of something that its mother saw or desired or was frightened by, that confers on the pregnant mother only a passive role vis-à-vis the shaping of her offspring. Some doctors and philosophers, however, felt that the imaginative mother could actually shape the child she was carrying into whatever she wanted. Giambattista Della Porta reported the case of a woman who had a marble reproduction made of her imagined offspring in order to conceive the exact copy of the son she desired. She kept looking at it during intercourse and throughout pregnancy, and the son was born with the wanted features.[51] Years later Campanella too was sure that women impress on children the image of what they desire, as long as they desire to engender a child with human and not bestial features.[52] To ensure that a child looked like his/her father, the Hippocratics and Soranus suggested, it was necessary that during coitus and especially before having an orgasm (the sine qua non for conception to occur, according to medical texts well into the eighteenth century) the mother concentrate on evoking in her mind a picture of her husband. This guaranteed

------

the power of maternal imagination was so great that a single bad thought was sufficient to imprint a malformation on the child. For more examples of maternal power through fantasy, see Darmon, *Le Mythe de la procréation*, 158–62. Only in the eighteenth century did doctors dismiss the view that maternal imagination was responsible for monstrosity. See Paul Gabriel Bouché, "Imagination, Pregnant Women, and Monsters in Eighteenth-Century England and France," in *Sexual Underworlds of the Enlightenment*, ed. G. S. Rousseau and Roy Porter (Chapel Hill: University of North Carolina Press, 1988), 86–100. For an analysis centered on Italy, see Angelini, "Il potere plastico dell'immaginazione." Even today in Italy pregnant women's cravings are very much accommodated, to avoid birthmarks. The idea that women's imagination could mark the fetus was still alive scientifically well into the nineteenth century. See, for example, F. Viparelli, *Sulla influenza che ha sul germe la fantasia d'una pregnante* (Naples, 1842). More generally, see Claudia Pancino, *Voglie materne: Storia di una credenza* (Bologna: Cluebb, 1966).

51. He was "as pale and as white, as if he had been very marble indeed." Giambattista Della Porta in *Natural Magick,* first published as *Magiae naturalis* (1558) (reprint, New York: Basic Books, 1957), 53–54.

52. "[L]e donne incinte esprimono nei loro parti l'imagine di quello che bramano, perchè il loro spirito così affetto si comunica al feto e esprime facilmente nel corpo tenero del bambino l'oggetto dell'immaginazione. Le cose tuttavia agiscono come sono disposte: perciò lo spirito del cane organizza un corpo canino, e lo spirito dell'uomo un corpo umano giacchè è legato a tale figura." In Tommaso Campanella, *De homine* (Rome: Centro internazionale di studi umanistici, 1960–1961), 159.

that the newborn would resemble him.[53] A number of medical treatises also carried information on how women committing adultery could try to make the child engendered from the affair look like their legal husband. For Antonio Persio, for example, an illegitimate child could resemble the mother's husband because she may have been so afraid of having her adulterous encounter discovered that she impressed in the child the feature of the man paramount in her imagination at the time of conception, not the actual father but the legal one, and not because she loved him but because she did not.[54] The doctors Giovanni Marinello and Paré argue along the same lines.[55]

While alternately enhancing or canceling maternal contribution, what these doctors argue—uncannily so—is interesting: the mother carries a fetus that will look like her husband not because he is the genetic father of the baby but because she chooses, among a number of possibilities, to have her child look like what she finds desirable for herself—like the husband this time, like somebody else in the future. But this means that the engendering of a physically similar child has suddenly been put outside the reach of fathers. A man was still needed for generation to occur of course, but any man would do. All that a legal husband could hope for in matters of paternity was that his pregnant wife would not make him a laughing stock by choosing to have a child not resembling him, whether or not he was the child's biological father. Philosophically minded intellectuals were most in danger of having a child not similar to them, but to their wives' lovers, Doctor Scipione Mercurio wrote, for intellectuals tended to be too much

53. See Ann Hanson, "The Medical Writers' Woman," in *Before Sexuality: The Construction of Erotic Experience in the Ancient Greek World*, ed. David Halperin, John Winkler, and Froma Zeitlin (Princeton, N.J.: Princeton University Press, 1990), 309–37.

54. Antonio Persio, *Dell'ingegno dell'huomo* (Venice: Manuzio, 1576), 97. Alain Grosrichard, "Le cas polyphème," sees a double identification at play on the part of the child: one with the mother, since the child desires what she desires, and one with the father, or at least with the father as he is imagined by the mother, in that he/she desires to be what the mother desires for the child to be (48).

55. "Per aventura ne viene che i bastardi più somigliano coloro che non sono padri veri, ma imaginati, percioché le moglie essendo in adulterio e temendo de' lor mariti, di continuo mentre dura quello atto gli hanno nella mente," in Giovanni Marinello, *Le medicine partenenti alle infermità delle donne* (Venice: G. Francesco de' Franceschi, 1563), bk. 3, chap. 3. See also Ambroise Paré, *Toutes les oeuvres* (1585), bk. 24, chap. 1, 925–26; and Darmon, *Le Mythe de la procréation*, 159.

distracted by their thoughts during coitus to keep their wives' attention focused on them. Their offspring ended up resembling those men more able to satisfy women in the act of Venus ("dilettando la donna nell'atto di Venere").[56] For Mercurio, educated men are often melancholic, a condition that women hate. This may push them to imagine making love to a joyous, and perhaps stupid, man with strange consequences for the embryo.[57] The same opinion is expressed by Persio, who asserts that because men of letters and businessmen tend to make love with their minds elsewhere, they generate stupid and uncouth children ("certi figlioli balordi, zotichi, et istupiditi").[58] Thus, at the very moment in which woman performs her most clear-cut role in society, and her most recommended one biologically — that of reproducing — she manages to set herself free from patriarchy. To mother turns out to be a pose, a masquerade, because woman can perform maternity as she can perform femininity: all for the sake of man. If the mask of femininity, in which a woman willingly appears as men would want her to appear (especially before marriage), is what keeps her desirable in her younger years, the mask of maternity keeps her stock high after marriage. One way or the other, she has learned to play the games she needs to play to her own advantage.[59]

It is clear that this mother is too dangerous. To punish her, her behavior is pathologized: the impostor she produces is called a monster, monstrous because the mother is monstrous or monstrous because the child is unstamped, that is, illegitimate, unfathered, unfinished, mismatched, misrelated, and miscegenated. Thus, the popularity in the sixteenth and seventeenth centuries of stories of monstrosity coming from maternal imagination and desire could be the outcome of the repression of maternity and concomitant reinscription of paternal law that, according to some

56. Girolamo Mercurio (Scipion Mercurii), *La comare o riccoglitrice* (Venice: Ciotti, 1596), bk. 1, chap. 12.

57. Mercurio, *Comare,* bk. 3, chap. 12.

58. Persio, *Dell'ingegno,* 93. For an extended discussion of the dangers encountered by intelligent fathers insufficiently diligent in matters of engendering to generate similarly intelligent children, see Huarte, *Essamina de gl'ingegni,* chap. 15.

59. For a study of the masquerade of femininity, see Valeria Finucci, "The Female Masquerade: Ariosto and the Game of Desire," in *Desire in the Renaissance: Psychoanalysis and Literature,* ed. Valeria Finucci and Regina Schwartz (Princeton, N.J.: Princeton University Press, 1994), 61–88.

critics, took place during the Renaissance.[60] Marie-Hélène Huet has recently linked the backlash against maternal imagination to the Reformation period. Given the widespread presence of Saint Mary in fourteenth- and fifteenth-century art and culture, it is no surprise, she argues, that the later move to "defeminize" the Church and deemphasize maternal power would take Mary as a specific target for disempowerment. The punishment of the mother's idolatry of an image (e.g., painting) at the expense of her husband through the birth of a monstrous child thus reinstated the importance of the father in procreation, just as the Reformation revived the role of God as Father and forbade adoration of Christ's mother in church worship.[61]

The fear of the possible cancellation of a father's signature is also what is in many ways behind the emphasis today on control of pregnancy and manipulation of mothering on the part of science and law. In our age of in vitro fertilization paternal participation has turned out to be not only highly controllable but also suitable to be chosen at random, deferred in time, achieved, even, without any heterosexual or paternal desire on the part of man. Woman at the same time has been freed from the law of reproduction with her access to contraception and safe abortion on demand. It comes as no surprise then that the New Right and the pro-life movements have rushed to defend not just the fetus but also the embryo. In this age of epidemics of sexual disease women are constantly reminded of the value of abstinence and safe sex, and made to understand that the fetus they carry is not their property, because it has the right to be born (against their wishes if needs be) and the right to aggressive medical interventions aimed to bringing it to maturity. The new interest on different ways to mother—by donating an egg (ovarian mothers), by providing the uterus

---

60. Julia Kristeva argues that in the Middle Ages maternity was instead not repressed: "Christianity celebrates maternal fecundity and offsets the morbid and murderous filial love of paternal reason with mother/son incest." See "The Father Love and Banishment," in *Literature and Psychoanalysis,* ed. Edith Kurzweil and William Phillips (New York: Columbia University Press, 1983), 396.

61. Huet, *Monstrous Imagination,* 28–29. Romanticism will also emphasize paternal right, Huet argues. For a reading of the reinscription of the father's law in political terms in the Renaissance from Castiglione's *Il libro del cortegiano* (1528, but elaborated earlier) to Tasso's *Il Malpiglio, overo della corte* (1585), see Valeria Finucci, "In the Name of the Brother: Male Rivalry and Social Order in B. Castiglione's *Il libro del cortegiano,*" *Exemplaria* 9, no. 1 (1997): 91–116.

(uterine mothers), and by raising the child (social mothers) — has also de-mythified the lore of motherhood as a unique, irreplaceable activity, one which instead needs now to be monitored, poked, timed, and controlled by science. Woman once more becomes the container, the vessel, as Aristotle famously put it, of a life which is not only better understood by science (pregnant women are routinely told by doctors the age of the fetus they carry, although they themselves can often pinpoint the precise moment in which impregnation occurred), but which she could easily endanger. Her womb is once more a feared tomb.[62]

III

In *Gerusalemme liberata,* Tasso makes Clorinda not only unlike her father but also unlike her mother, since she is said to resemble not her, but the white virgin Sabra in the painting of Saint George. What the mother's imagination cancels from the reproductive process is race: seeing the "white monster" she has given birth to, the black queen can only react with "maraviglia."[63] For Tasso and the people of his time, however, the Ethiopi-ans themselves were monstrous. Writing in those years, for example, Tom-maso Campanella argued that children of beautiful women could be born not only monstrous or bestial, thanks to their mother's imagination, but also as Ethiopians ("mostri et etiopi").[64] It was common knowledge, Iso-dore had written in *Aetymologiae,* that an entire people could be monstrous; their monstrosities were in fact often illustrated in the same books that

62. Thus the appeal of the aptly named Operation Rescue, whose members block abor-tion clinics. For the womb as an "inhospitable waste land at war with the 'innocent' person within," see Carol Stabile, "Shooting the Mother: Fetal Photography and the Politics of Dis-appearance," *Camera Obscura* 28 (1992): 179–205, at 179; and Valerie Hartouni, "Containing Women: Reproductive Discourse in the 1980s," in *Technoculture,* ed. Constance Penley and Andrew Ross (Minneapolis: University of Minnesota Press, 1991), 27–56, esp. 43.

63. What constitutes the marvelous? Tasso asked in a letter to Father Marco da Ferrara in 1581. Are there things that are always marvelous, or do marvelous things cease to be such once we know the reason for their happening? Are marvelous things only the impossible ones or the most miraculous? (*Lettere,* 2:158–60).

64. Campanella, *Del senso,* 272 and 305. For Aldrovandi, Egypt had more monsters than other countries because there men are more fertile and prone to intercourse, just like cats, dogs, pigs, birds, chickens, and doves; where there is too much matter, monsters can result. See "Avvertimenti," in "Appendice," 179.

catalogued malformed individuals. Monstrous races were those living at the hedge of the known world: the Indians in the east, for example, and the Ethiopians in the south (unless of course they were civilized by Christian faith). In the *Liberata,* the geographic space between the Nile and the Hercules' columns is said specifically to be the one most inhabited by monsters ("Ciò che di mostruoso e di feroce / erra fra 'l Nilo e i termini d'Atlante," "Whatever of monstrous or of fierce roams between Nile and the boundaries of Atlas" [15.51]).[65] In a sermon once attributed to Saint Augustine, the narrator, visiting Ethiopia to spread the Word, told of having seen monsters of both sexes without a head, others with eyes in their chest or with a single foot so large that it functioned as an umbrella to shield the individual from the scorching African sun (*sciapodes*); in the south there were men with one eye in their forehead. Aside from these peculiarities of nature, the narrator continued, these people were similar to all others. Thus, since they were humans, they could be Christianized.[66] Monstrous representations of Ethiopians can be found in church sculptures in twelfth-century France, Céard writes, where an Ethiopian is represented next to a martikhora (an animal with human head), a liocorn, a faun, a chimera, a camel, a lion, a bear, and a monkey (49). Monstrous races are also portrayed in the mosaic pavements of the medieval cathedral of Casale Monferrato in northern Italy and in bas-reliefs of the cathedrals of Modena and Ferrara.[67]

65. Tasso's geographical knowledge was in tune with the travel literature of his time: he seemed to know quite precisely the configuration of Italy, Greece, and the territory around Jerusalem, for instance, but had nebulous ideas about northern Europe, the Far East, and the West. His understanding of the heart of Africa came from the travel accounts of Portuguese explorers such as Francisco Alvarez's *Ho Prest Joam das Indias: Verdadera informaçam das terra do Presto Joam* (Lisbon, 1540). This book was translated from Portuguese into Italian and printed ten years later. See Giovanni Battista Ramusio, *Navigazioni e viaggi,* ed. Marica Milanesi, 6 vols. (Turin: Einaudi, 1978–1988), 2:79–385; and Quint, *Epic and Empire,* 234–36. For a study of Tasso's geographical expertise, see Bruno Basile, *Poeta melancholicus: Tradizione classica e follia nell'ultimo Tasso* (Pisa: Pacini, 1984), chap. 6. Tasso also made annotations on Ethiopia in the margins of a book on cosmography, Giovanni Lorenzo d'Anania's *L'universale fabbrica del mondo,* which he owned. His edition was published in Venice in 1582, but the book itself came out in 1573 and was published again in 1576, that is, before Tasso finished the *Liberata.* See Basile, *Poeta melancholicus,* 356–58. Tasso refers to monstrous animals, and to monkeys and baboons, which he links to the Gorgons.
66. "Ad frates in Eremo, sermo XXXVII," PL 40, col. 1304. See Céard, *La Nature et les prodiges,* 48.
67. Rudolph Wittkower, "Marvels of the East: A Study in the History of Monsters," *Journal*

The mythical figure of Prester John (Prete Gianni) is said to have seen men with eyes in the front and back of their heads during his missions in Africa, and others with one eye only. He also believed in the existence of Amazons, living, properly enough, in the land of Femmenie.[68] The tradition is extensive and consistent with the fact that in the teratological geography of the time Ethiopians were seen as subhumans, cannibals.[69]

In tune with this tradition, Ethiopians were also thought to be sexually overendowed and overactive, so much so in fact that they would even tempt hermits. Hence, Saint Anthony was lured by an ugly black youngster in the desert; and in the *Vitae patrum* there is the story of a young, smelly, and ugly Ethiopian woman engaged in seducing a hermit.[70] Ethiopian women were considered immune from venereal diseases; some Venetians believed that the use of their bodies by men affected by gonorrhea provided an instant and definitive cure. True, a cure for gonorrhea was also achievable by sleeping with a virgin, Ercole Sassonia wrote, but only in the case of "mulier Aethiope" would the woman resist the infection.[71] Ethiopian women were in theory so lustful that clitoridectomy had to be practiced on them: "[In] Ethiopia, especially in the Dominions of Prester John, they Circumcise women. These Abassines have added errour upon errour, and sin upon sin, for they cause their Females to be circumcised."[72] Aristotle, like the

of the Warburg and Courtauld Institutes 5 (1942): 159–97, esp. 177; Dario Franchini et al., eds., "Mostri e immagine," in *La scienza a corte: Collezionismo eclettico, natura e immagine a Mantova fra Rinascimento e Manierismo* (Rome: Bulzoni, 1979), 101–14, esp. 102; and John Friedman, *The Monstrous Races in Medieval Art and Thought* (Cambridge, Mass.: Harvard University Press, 1981).

68. From *Lettres du Prestes Jehans,* cited in Céard, *La Nature et les prodiges,* 56. See also Renato Lefevre, *L'Etiopia nella stampa del primo Cinquecento* (Como: Cairoli, 1966).

69. For the link of Ethiopians with cannibalism in the Middle Ages, see David Williams, *Deformed Discourse: The Function of the Monster in Mediaeval Thought and Literature* (Montreal: McGill-Queens's University Press, 1996), 149.

70. *Vitae patrum,* 5.23, PL 73, 879.

71. Ercole Sassonia, *Perfectissimus tractatus:* "Sciendum autem est. quod habui a quibusdam expertis Venetis: Dicunt se a Gonorrhaea statim curatos usu Veneris cum mulier Aethiope. . . . Haec quoque scio, si tamen literis consignam licet antiqua gonorrhaea plures fuisse liberatos, qui cum uxore Virgine rem habuerunt, sed tunc mulier inficitur" (chap. 37, fol. 40), cited in Wilfred Schleiner, "Infection and Cure Through Women: Renaissance Constructions of Syphilis," *Journal of Medieval and Renaissance Studies* 24, no. 3 (1994): 499–517, at 508–9.

72. John Bulwer, *Anthropometamorphoses: Man Transformed, or The Artificial Changeling* (Lon-

Hippocratics, had argued that Egyptian women (intended here in a large sense as comprising Libyans, for example, in the west and, one may assume, Ethiopians in the south), were too prolific and therefore more prone to engender monsters: "The occurrence of monstrosities is more common in those regions where the women are prolific — in Egypt, for instance."[73] Possession by devils — in the shape of foul-smelling black Ethiopian men — was also common, as in the case of a woman helped by Beate Bridget to get rid of the incubus destroying her psychospiritual health: when the devil was expelled, she saw a dirty Ethiopian coming out of her breasts.[74] Blacks, in short, had limited possibilities for recuperation or assimilation within the white, "civilized" world. In both Greece and Rome a useless task was described as an attempt "to wash an Ethiop white": no matter how much a black is scrubbed, he remains black to the core.[75]

Although they were often referred to as Moors, Ethiopians were Christians. In fact, the process of conversion was very successful in Ethiopia, even though that success came to be soon marred by fears that Ethiopians furthered Anabaptist practices (e.g., adult rebaptism).[76] Churches in Ethiopia abounded in portrayals of saints. The saint most ubiquitously represented from the fifteenth century onward, second only to Mary, was Saint George, according to Stanley Chojnacki.[77] Saint George was the saint whose portrait Clorinda's mother gazed at in her many solitary hours during pregnancy. He is usually portrayed as a Christ figure, an equestrian saint de-

---

don, 1653). See also Thomas Laqueur, "Amor Veneris, Vel Dulcedo Appeletur," in *Fragments for a History of the Human Body,* ed. Michel Feher (New York: Zone, 1989), 115.

73. GA 4.4.770a. Aristotle considered Ethiopian men cowards and identified frizzy hair with lack of manly worth: "Those with very wooly hair are cowardly; this applies to the Ethiopians." See Aristotle, *Minor Works,* ed. and trans. W. S. Hett (Cambridge, Mass.: Harvard University Press, 1936), 131. Hairy men had also abundant seed and desired intercourse more often (GA 4.5.774b). But then Aristotle found this true also of light-skinned people like the Germans.

74. See Isak Collijn, *Acta et processus canonizacionis beatae Birgittae* (Upsala, 1924–1931), 513; and Michael Goodich, "Sexuality, Family, and the Supernatural in the Fourteenth Century," *Journal of the History of Sexuality* 4 (1994): 493–516, 512.

75. In the sixteenth century, "Moors," "Negroes," and "Ethiopians" were used more or less interchangeably. See Charles Lyons, *To Wash an Aethiop White: British Ideas about Black African Educability* (New York: Teachers College, Columbia University, 1975), 3.

76. See Quint, *Epic and Empire,* 242–43.

77. Stanley Chojnacki, "The Iconography of Saint George in Ethiopia," *Journal of Ethiopian Studies* 11, no. 1 (1973): 57–73; 11, no. 2 (1973): 51–92; and 12 (1974): 71–132.

feating the dragon. Although for Catholics he stood as a tortured martyr, in paintings Saint George is usually depicted as a victorious knight on a white horse, spearing a monstrous animal, either a dragon or a snake. In the earliest paintings, the Virgin is holding the baby Jesus and a flower, while the saint has a bird in his hands. Before the fifteenth century Saint George was represented as a young man killing a serpent; the dragon was only introduced in the following century, along with the rescued maiden.[78] The story of Saint George and the dragon had been well known in the Middle East since the Middle Ages. Pilgrimages to the spot near Beirut where the dragon was slain and the virgin Birutawit, later called Sabra, was chained were also common.[79] Sabra is usually dressed in the paintings, but is occasionally portrayed unclothed; in later representations, she is depicted perched on a tree or clinging to branches.

Saint George's rescue of a fearful virgin princess from a monster is, of course, only the Christianized version of another mythical rescue favored in the pagan world, that of Andromeda in chains, being saved by the winged Perseus from a marine monster bent on eating her. Interestingly enough, the tradition had it that Andromeda was Ethiopian. Thus, it is not surprising to find a story such as that of Heliodorus in *Aethiopica,* which enjoyed wide circulation in the Renaissance after it was discovered in 1526, in which the black queen of Ethiopia, Persinna, wife of king Hydustes, gives birth to a child, Chariclea, very much unlike herself and her husband: she resembles Andromeda, whose portrait she had before her eyes during copulation. Like Clorinda's mother in the *Liberata,* also an Ethiopian queen, Chariclea's mother had looked at the representation of Andromeda being saved from the monster by Perseus.[80] Persinna tells her husband that the

78. The artist responsible for the addition was Venetian, Nicolao Brancaleone, who was also called Märquoryos the Foreigner, according to Francisco Alvarez, who wrote the history of the first Portuguese embassy in Ethiopia (1520–1523). See Chojnacki, "Iconography of Saint George," 11 (1973), 58; and C. F. Beckingham and G. W. B. Huntingford, *The Prester John of the Indies* (London, 1958), 332. Francisco Alvarez too mentions the popularity of Saint George in Ethiopia. See Ramusio, *Navigazioni,* 2:146. For a study of Saint George in Italy, see Paolo Toschi, *La leggenda di San Giorgio nei canti popolari italiani* (Florence: Olschki, 1964).
79. Chojnacki, "Iconography of Saint George," 11 (1973): 57.
80. Heliodorus, *An Aethiopian Romance,* ed. F. A. Wright (London: Routledge, n.d.). As Dante Della Terza remarks, the story was discovered in the library of Matthias Corvinus, translated in Latin, and printed in Basel in 1534 ("History and the Epic Discourse: Remarks on the Narrative Structure of Tasso's *Gerusalemme liberata,*" *Quaderni d'italianistica* 1, no. 1

baby has died, but actually she has been sent away, in a basket. An old man rescues her, has shepherds take care of her, and raises her as a woman warrior priestess of Apollo.[81] In commenting on the Heliodorus story, Dante Della Terza notices that there is no mention in Heliodorus of the princess's color; we know that in Ariosto she — in the shape first of Angelica and then of Olimpia, the two women who replayed in the *Furioso* the Andromeda story — is white and blond, just like Clorinda.

In a previous study, I read the Andromeda story as a myth of domestication of femininity: saved by Perseus after her mother's foolishness put her life in jeopardy, Andromeda gladly accepts his offer of marriage. The myth tells us that a woman will always be rewarded if she remains passively in her place.[82] A white Christian princess is also clearly better qualified to embody the story of female submission than a black pagan from a faraway land. As if to underline the point, the princess rescued by Saint George is often represented in the tradition not naked, as Andromeda is in the classical rendering, but dressed in a white wedding dress, the perfectly subjugated daughter of Western patriarchy. The monster, be it the viscid serpentine one with which Orlando and Ruggiero in the *Furioso* fight or the serpent portrayed in representations of Saint George, represents uncontrollable sexual nature and also paradoxically, given the fact that it is not usually gendered, undifferentiated sexuality.[83] Thus the story of the vir-

---

[1980]: 30–45, 45 n. 5). Walter Stephens argues that Tasso may have read the story in Italian in the translation of Leonardo Ghini, which was first published in 1556. See "Tasso's Heliodorus and the World of Romance," in *The Search for the Ancient Novel*, ed. James Tatum (Baltimore, Md.: Johns Hopkins University Press, 1994), 67–87, esp. 67.

81. For sources of this episode, see Salvatore Martineddu, *Le fonti della Gerusalemme liberata* (Turin: Clausen, 1895), 128–30.

82. See Valeria Finucci, *The Lady Vanishes: Subjectivity and Representation in Castiglione and Ariosto* (Stanford, Calif.: Stanford University Press, 1992), chap. 5.

83. In this sense Arsete too is a monster, neither male nor female, as eunuchs were thought to be. When he dreams of Saint George reproaching him for not having baptized Clorinda, he is, as Migiel notices, in the position of the dragon ("[v]idi in sogno un guerrier che minacciando / a me su 'l volto il ferro ignudo pose," 12, 36). See Marilyn Migiel, "Clorinda's Father," *Stanford Italian Review* 10 (1991): 93–121, esp. 106. On the coincidence of dragon and virgin in this scene, see Paolo Braghieri, *Il testo come soluzione rituale: Gerusalemme liberata* (Bologna: Patron, 1978), 131. On the myth of Andromeda, see Adrienne Munich, *Andromeda's Chains: Gender and Interpretation in Victorian Literature and Art* (New York: Columbia University Press, 1989). For another take of this story, see the rendering of Redcross knight (Saint George) killing the monster Errour in Spenser's *Fairie Queene*.

gin Andromeda/Sabra achieves two purposes: to punish woman's surplus sexuality by displacing it on to the monster who will be killed by a patriarchal father figure, and to reward woman's passivity by having the patient virgin marry her savior after he has rescued her from danger, a move that allows her to enter the social order. The killing of the monster establishes, in short, the importance of a properly gendered man and a properly gendered woman in social relations and the value of controlling the anticipated disruptions generated by female sexuality.

The problem with Clorinda is that she can be thought of as monstrous in yet another way: her mother's *vis imaginativa* created her not only unlike her husband and unlike herself, but also, it turns out, unlike the image of the Caucasian woman she was thought to be copying, because she got the color right, but not the personality. Like Sabra, Clorinda is white; unlike Sabra, she is far from the picture of femininity and submissiveness that her model purportedly represents. The mother, in short, has been able to reproduce in her uncanny offspring the image, but not the meaning: the daughter is a living lie, a fraud. Thus, although seemingly feminine, Clorinda is made to fret at the limitations imposed on women: "Dunque sol tanto a donna e più non lice?" ("Is then a woman allowed to do only this much and no more?" [12.3]). When Belzebú creates a simulacrum of Clorinda, he appropriately opts to make it in the shape of a man, a marvelous monster, as Tasso parenthetically interjects:

> Questi di cava nube ombra leggiera
> (mirabil mostro) in forma d'uom compose;
> e la sembianza di Clorinda altera
> gli finse.

(He from a hollow cloud composed an insubstantial shade [marvellous monster] in a human shape; and counterfeited for it the face of the proud Clorinda.) (7.99)

Years later Aphra Behn will celebrate Clorinda as both woman and man, a "fair lovely lady" and a "lovely charming youth" about whom to fantasize in a lesbian relationship.[84]

---

84. Aphra Behn, "To the Fair Clarinda, Who Made Love to Me, Imagined More than Woman" (1688), in *The Norton Anthology of Literature by Women,* ed. Sandra Gilbert and Susan Gubar (New York: Norton, 1985), 94.

It will take a life of exile from the "correct" religion and civilization for Clorinda to become, in death, what she could have been in life—passive, meek, and properly gendered—if the process of mirroring like and like had not run amok. No wonder that the story of Saint George resurfaces at the end. Since the saint who saved Sabra from the monster is none other than a patriarchal father killing the monster in woman so that she can be reunited with her true, more feminine self, Tasso's Tancredi is another incarnation of the law of the father in his killing that uncivilized, castrating, manly, and unresponsive masquerade of femininity that is the pagan Clorinda. Then, like Saint George, he proceeds to recuperate her to his world through baptism, although, given the author's preferences, Clorinda can be present only as an uncorporeal, angelical form, coming in dream to thank her savior for having saved her, when, paradoxically, he has killed her. In the end, the figure of this woman warrior sadistically pierced and killed and ultimately projected as an angel becomes the personification of the image of orthodox femininity that Renaissance culture liked to foster. Only then does Tasso mark Clorinda as nonmonstrous: feminine (she is described as seductively revealing a golden and embroidered vest), virginal and Christian, an image, as Giovanni Getto put it, of immaculate luminosity ("immacolata luminosità").[85] Only after death does Tasso make Clorinda outline a newly found feminine identity: she is beautiful, she tells Tancredi in a dream, and happy ("Mira come son bella e come lieta," "Mark how happy I am and how well" [12.91]). She even invites him to admire her beauty in heaven, together with that of God ("vagheggerai le sue bellezze e mie," "you shall gaze upon [his] loveliness and mine" [12.92]). Having become perfectly beautiful and perfectly feminine, the *femme* as Lacan would say, Clorinda can now hide her castration and become an object of adoration rather than aggression. In short, to cancel out the fantasy figure that Tancredi had created for himself, it was necessary that *Woman* be made, narratively speaking, into a woman (that is, feminine) impossible to have (that is, dead and not-white). Clorinda's narrative recuperation through elimination of the body is now complete.

Yet why not think of maternal imagination in more powerful terms? Why would the lonely queen immerse herself in the fantasy scenario of virgin, saint, and monster? Why would she desire her baby to be what she

85. Giovanni Getto, *Nel mondo della Gerusalemme* (Florence: Vallecchi, 1968), 142.

should not be? "If . . . day-dreams are carefully examined," Freud wrote, "they are found to serve as the fulfillment of wishes and as a correction of actual life. They have two principal aims, an erotic and an ambitious one—though an erotic aim is usually concealed behind the latter too."[86] What ambitious and erotic dreams would the Ethiopian wife want gratified? A reading of the scene shows that by staging the fantasy of being loved as an event in which she takes the place of a virgin sufficiently valuable to be saved, Clorinda's mother makes herself worthy of consideration as an object of desire on the part of her husband. On the other hand, she also hides the wish to be Sabra, who was perhaps only desired as white or because she was white, by displacing it on to her daughter, whom she would like to be desired and white, like Sabra. But this desire is transgressive, hence the punishment through what she believes is a monstrous offspring. Lynda Boose has argued that the sexual relationship of a black male/white female could be culturally accommodated in the early modern period because the resulting black offspring, by canceling once more maternal input, would reinforce paternal primacy in generation; a white male/black female union, on the other hand, remained utterly unrepresentable.[87] In fact, Tasso's queen pays a worse penance, because such disobedience against the law of the father means that she will be killed by her own daughter, suffering either a social death—in which, by keeping Clorinda, the mother may be cast away—or a physical one—in which, by not keeping her, she may not outlive the pain: "Qui tacque; e 'l cor si rinchiuse e strinse / e di pallida morte si dipinse" ("Here she fell silent; and her heart closed up and shrank within itself, and she was the color of pale death" [12.28]).[88]

That female children kill their mothers is not new in Tasso. For one, Armida's mother dies in childbirth:

86. Sigmund Freud, "Family Romances," 238.

87. Lynda Boose, " 'The Getting of a 'Lawful Race': Racial Discourse in Early Modern England and the Unrepresentable Black Woman," in *Women, 'Race,' and Writing in the Early Modern Period,* ed. Margo Hendricks and Patricia Parker (New York: Routledge, 1994), 35–54. Boose refers to England, but the same could be argued about Italy.

88. For some critics it is unclear whether the mother dies or simply swoons. For the monster as scapegoat, see René Girard, *Violence and the Sacred* (Baltimore, Md.: Johns Hopkins University Press, 1977), 143–68.

Costei co'l suo morire quasi prevenne
il nascer mio, ch'in tempo estinta giacque
ch'io fuori uscia de l'alvo, e fu il fatale
giorno ch'a lei dié morte, a me natale.

(She with her death almost anticipated my birth, for she lay dead at the moment I issued from the womb, and the fatal day that brought her death was the day of my birth.) (4.43)[89]

Armida's mother is called Carichia, that is, she has the same name as the baby girl resembling Andromeda, whose birth story, as I have shown, Clorinda mirrors. (Tasso drops the mother's name in the *Conquistata*.) Armida, like Clorinda, is "monstrous," and explicitly described as such, as in her celebrated Medusan transformation in front of Rinaldo: "ma colei si trasmuta (oh novi mostri!)," ("she is transformed [O new monstrosities!]" [18.35]). For both women, conversion to Christianity is the way out of monstrosity. Armida will turn into a maternal and disempowered Virgin Mary at the end (" 'Ecco l'ancilla tua; d'essa a tuo senno / dispon,' gli disse 'e le fia legge il cenno,' " "Behold your handmaid; dispose of her at your discretion [she said], and your command shall be her law" [20:136]); as for Clorinda, having abjected her mother for good, she is made to embrace the symbolic order by asking for baptism. In finding the One, the Law, and the father no longer "incertus," she also ceases to be monstrous, because it was said that Ethiopians were monstrous only until civilized by religion.

IV

What are the personal and literary reasons that Tasso created Clorinda as he did? I would like to establish some connections at this point between the fictional narrative of Clorinda, that of her mythical predecessor—the lady warrior Camilla—and Tasso's own biography. Clorinda, it has been noticed many times, is drawn from Virgil's Camilla in *Aeneid* 11.[90] Their fictional life stories and even their deaths by wounds to their breasts, Amazon-like, are similar. Virgil had Latona protect Camilla; Tasso has Saint George

---

89. Erminia, the other major female figure in the *Liberata*, has a mother who, however, dies just before the action begins. She is therefore newly orphaned (6.59).

90. On sources for Clorinda's characterization as Amazon (Latin Camilla as well as Greek Penthesilea), see Quint, *Epic and Empire*, 238–39.

look over Clorinda. The two babies are raised away from civilization by men (her father Metabus in the case of Camilla; a father figure in that of Clorinda); both are fed on animal milk (a mare in Virgil; a tiger in Tasso); both are recommended to their protectors when they have to cross a river to escape enemies; both grow as unsurpassed warriors. In what perhaps is his most autobiographical writing, "Canzone al Metauro" (also called "O del grand'Apennino," 1578), Tasso compares his own forced exile from his mother, Porzia de' Rossi, to that of Camilla: "e seguii con mal sicure piante, / qual Ascanio o Camilla il padre errante."[91] A reading of the scene of Clorinda's departure from her mother and of the scene of nine-year-old Tasso's departure from his mother offer surprisingly close intertextual echoes: in the "Canzone," the mother wet her boy with doleful tears ("bagnò di lagrime dolenti"), in the Liberata the mother wet her kisses with tears ("bagnò i baci di pianto," 12.26). In bidding farewell to her newborn, she metaphorically baptizes Clorinda, as Porzia did Torquato, initiating her into a life of exile.[92] The young Torquato follows his father with uncertain steps and an ambivalent heart; Arsete, the unreliable father, reports the same for Clorinda ("incerte orme," 12.32). Neither man offers real protection: one is always on the run ("errante"), the other, while running, abandons his charge twice. References to captivity, reminding the readers of the captivity in Egypt of the children of Israel, also abound in Arsete's recounting of his journey with the outcast baby to Egypt.[93] Juliana Schiesari has brilliantly linked the son's loss of the mother, an Oedipal trauma, to Tasso's pervasive espousal of a melancholic attitude as a way of retaining his identification with the lost object of love. This loss is then expressed (mourned) through a discourse of victimization that acquires depth as it is repeated. Such a stance allows for the son's rivalry with the father to be denied.[94] In

91. "And I followed my wandering father with uncertain steps, like Ascanio and Camilla" (trans. mine). Italian text in Angelo Solerti, Le rime di Torquato Tasso (Bologna: Romanoli Dall'Acqua, 1900), 3:104–5.
92. Margaret Ferguson writes that Clorinda could be associated to Tasso's mother, she too lost "in part on the 'confusion' of his father's political career." See Trials of Desire: Renaissance Defenses of Poetry (New Haven, Conn.: Yale University Press, 1983), 62.
93. As in "ascosa," "ti celai da ciascun," "celatamente," "vita errante e pellegrina."
94. Juliana Schiesari, "The Victim's Discourse: Torquato Tasso's 'Canzone al Metauro,'" Stanford Italian Review 5 (1985): 189–203. See also her The Gendering of Melancholia: Feminism, Psychoanalysis, and the Symbolics of Loss in Renaissance Literature (Ithaca, N.Y.: Cornell University Press, 1992).

the case of Clorinda, she is unaware that she has lost her mother, and thus she is the farthest, I think, from being able to restage this loss through self-victimization. The only mother she wishes to claim is not her birth mother, Tasso makes her tell Arsete, but the social mother who gave her milk and faith at the same time.

Arsete, a eunuch, a man-made not-man, cannot function as a mother because he is unable to either feed Clorinda or save her from drowning, although he can cry abundantly for her. He is therefore incapable of being protective in the two places that are most connected to the maternal in these octaves: the woods and the whirling waters. On the first occasion, the maternal womb comes close to becoming a tomb for Clorinda, as a tiger appears from nowhere and Arsete abandons her. The animal turns into an unexpected savior and feeds the baby (12.31).[95] On the second occasion, a father figure, Saint George, substitutes for the ineffective Arsete and makes the water keep the toddler afloat. Clorinda is at this point sixteen months old and starting to talk ("tu con lingua di latte anco snodavi / voci indistinte," "You with your baby speech were still pronouncing indistinct words" [12.32]). Entry into language is entry into desire, and therefore into lack. Thus, at the moment of symbolic castration, which marks the male or female's first coming to terms with lack, a paternal figure saves a female child from being lost in maternal flux. That this figure stands for the law is clear; and it is because he is not seen but heard in a later dream in which he is cast as a warrior, a sword in his hand, that Saint George in fact becomes the phallus.[96] The subsequent ushering in of the Oedipus complex, in which

95. Tasso too in "Canzone" went back to the woods for maternal protection, to a tall oak tree inside which he hoped to hide. Thus this womb also foreshadows death. Tigers are animals with strong maternal connotations, but when Armida attempts to define Rinaldo as monstrous, she accuses him of having been fed by tigers: "e le mamme allattar di tigre ircana" (16.57). Goffredo too, when he shows himself unmoved by Armida, gets the same treatment from his companions: "[B]en fu rabbiosa a lui nutrice" (4.77). Animal milk was considered unhealthy for babies; moreover, it was inappropriate, since there could be some beastly transmigrations from the animal to the human being. As an adult, Clorinda will wear a tiger emblem on her helmet.

96. As Kaja Silverman remarks on the male voice-over in film, "We could say that the male subject finds his most ideal realization when he is heard but not seen; when the body . . . drops away, leaving the phallus in unchallenged possession of the scene. Thus, . . . the disembodied voice can be seen as 'exemplary' for male subjectivity, attesting to an achieved

the female child identifies with the mother and takes the father as a love object (Freud's argument in "Femininity"), does not lead Clorinda, who never had a chance to experience more than passing unity with her mother or even to register the other's self-devaluation, to assume the other's lack and thus experience melancholia.[97]

Instead, Tasso makes Clorinda incorporate the pre-Oedipal mother and feel no real attachment to any parent. Bound to no law, Clorinda makes her own laws. Born as doubly lacking and cast away because of her non-marking mark—the absence of an identifying skin color that would give her an identity and an origin—she is slowly constructed into a character that lacks nothing. To play with this illusion, which is fundamental to her fictional being, Clorinda is given a monstrous mask for herself and is made to challenge aggressively every purported enemy. Her inability to acknowledge the other without immediately wanting to cancel him out to prove that she does not lack (does not need anybody) and her description as tall and impenetrable, constantly seen from below, towerlike, make clear that Tasso wants to show her as self-centered.[98] Clorinda kills and wounds, especially aiming, it seems, at father figures. Since the father she knows, Arsete, is hardly a figure of desire, rather than loving the father, as in the classic version of the passage through Oedipus, Clorinda is made to want to "be" the father, hence her masculine behavior. The manly mask constructed for her body ("vincesti il sesso e la natura assai," "in palestra indurò i membri," "allenogli al corso"), the trenchant word that defines her ("feroce"), and the boastful and insulting ways with which she is made to address her

---

invisibility, omniscience, and discursive power." See *The Acoustic Mirror: The Female Voice in Psychoanalysis and Cinema* (Bloomington: Indiana University Press, 1988), 163–64.

97. Sigmund Freud, "Femininity," SE 22 (1964), 112–35. In the *Liberata,* the mother (but not the daughter) seems to personify the melancholic subject as described by Freud: "The patient represents [her] ego to us as worthless, incapable of any achievement and morally despicable; [she] reproaches [herself], vilifies [herself] and expects to be cast out and punished." See "Mourning and Melancholia," SE 14 (1957), 242–58 at 246.

98. On Clorinda's linkage with towers, see Georges Güntert, *L'epos dell'ideologia regnante e il romanzo delle passioni: Saggio sulla Gerusalemme liberata* (Pisa: Pacini, 1989), 150–52. Elisabeth Bellamy has suggested that what Tancredi loves in Clorinda is not her feminine side, but her aggressive one, because it better reflects his narcissistic investment in himself. See *Translations of Power: Narcissism and the Unconscious in Epic History* (Ithaca, N.Y.: Cornell University Press, 1992), 160.

enemies are ways intended to dominate "the identifications through which refusals of love are resolved," as Lacan suggests in "The Meaning of the Phallus."[99] Unloved, Clorinda is unloving; unsure of her origins, she refuses all possible lineage, African or other, and chooses to enter the narrative as Persian: "Viene or costei da le contrade perse" ("She is come now from the Persian regions," 2:41).[100] Not surprisingly, it is only in the context of Christianity that Clorinda will appear feminine and beautiful, that is, after death. As Saracen, she is other, strange, nonwomanly, and linked mostly to animals.[101]

Thus the imposing of Christianity on Clorinda—which Tasso frames as a request coming from her—becomes a way of belonging, a desire for legitimization. This desire to have an authorized, legitimate self is endemic in the author. Feeling often, in some way, an outcast, Tasso displayed it in his own repeated requests to have the theological apparatus of the *Liberata* checked by the Inquisitors; even more clearly he showed it in his autobiographical work, such as "O magnanimo figlio" in which he asked the father as ruler, Duke Alfonso as symbolic father, to protect and author(ize) him. Like Tasso, Clorinda too is made to look at the end for paternal authorization. Julia Kristeva describes this desire, which could hardly be labeled as feminine, in a stream-of-consciousness style: "The impossibility of existing without repeated legitimation (without books, map, family). Impossibility—depressing possibility—of 'transgression' . . . Or this murmur of emptiness, this open wound in my heart which means that I exist only in purgatory. I desire the law. And since it is not made for me alone, I run the

99. Jacques Lacan, "The Meaning of the Phallus," in *Feminine Sexuality: Jacques Lacan and the Ecole Freudienne,* ed. Juliet Mitchell and Jacqueline Rose (New York: Norton, 1982), 74–85.

100. According to Taviani, Asia was for Tasso a disturbance ("perturbamento") of gender, nature, race, nationality, and parentage: "Sembra, infatti, che Tasso associasse all'Asia l'idea di una fragile armonia di principi opposti: una delicatezza guerriera, una femminilità feroce, un turbamento della natura, della razza. La perdita d'una sicura appartenenza a un paese, ad un sesso ed a una casa." See Ferdinando Taviani, "Bella d'Asia: Torquato Tasso, gli attori e l'immortalità," *Paragone* 408–10 (1984): 5–76, esp. 55.

101. In chivalric romances, the Christian hero is traditionally handsome, while the pagan, his specular other, is ugly; if a pagan hero happens to be handsome, he either is made Christian (as Ruggiero and Marfisa in the *Furioso*) or is killed, since his handsomeness is out of place. This will be Clorinda's fate. See Hans Robert Jauss, "Giustificazione del brutto," in *Alterità e modernità della letteratura medievale* (Turin: Bollati Beringhieri, 1989), 285. Even as a Saracen, in any case, Clorinda is other: too magnanimous, for example, if we consider the behavior of her companions, Argante and Solimano, and too chivalric.

risk of desiring outside the law." [102] For Clorinda, desiring outside the law ends the moment she wears her new black armor, which substitutes the white one stolen by Erminia and is more befitting, narratively speaking, to the other woman. Her black armor does not embody for me her self-destructive ways and loss of identity, to reread Sergio Zatti, but precisely her discovery of an identity—Clorinda as black Ethiopian princess—that proves her own only the moment that she is bound to lose her life. [103] Since this is an identity that denies the one constructed previously, the Clorinda who came into the epic by declaring her name (" 'Io son Clorinda': disse 'hai forse intesa talor nomarmi,' " "I am Clorinda [she said]: you have perhaps heard my name some time" [2.46]) can only exit it by refusing to give herself an origin ("Indarno chiedi / quel ch'ho per uso di non far palese," "Vainly you ask what I by custom do not make known" [12.61]). In the passage from Clorinda the foundling to Clorinda the docile Christian, a father is found, and a daughter is finally recognized and welcomed "home."

As for Tancredi, Tasso's choice of keeping him enthralled in a vision of Clorinda as the sublime, impossible object of his desire is fraught with problems, because if, on the one hand, it allows him to have her the only way he can—in fantasy—on the other, it makes him lose his place in the order of the epic. This place will be filled now by his fellow knight Rinaldo, who, having accepted the losses of the real through the usual diminishment/renunciation of woman after his departure from Armida, is ready to become the true hero of the *Liberata* and true follower of the other father, the earthly, but no less serene, and no less *certus* Goffredo.

102. Julia Kristeva, "Stabat Mater," in *The Female Body in Western Culture: Contemporary Perspectives,* ed. Susan Rubin Suleiman (Cambridge, Mass.: Harvard University Press, 1986), 99–118, 109.
103. Sergio Zatti, *L'uniforme cristiano e il multiforme pagano: Saggio sulla Gerusalemme liberata* (Milan: Saggiatore, 1983), 111. For a powerful argument on the ability of armor to confer genealogical identity, even to ghosts, see the article by Stallybrass in this volume.

II

BOUNDARIES OF SEX
AND GENDER

Contradictions of Masculinity: Ascetic Inseminators and Menstruating Men in Greco-Roman Culture

DALE B. MARTIN

One might think that there was little chance for confusion about how to be a man in Greco-Roman culture. At first glance, the construction of masculinity appears consistent, monolithic, and ideologically secure. Physiognomies give directions about how to distinguish unmanly men from manly men, even when the usual signifiers are ambiguous. We are instructed, for instance, that though a man may talk tough or walk rough, though he may be married and with numerous progeny, though he may present a hard body and calloused hands — all signs of maleness — his real lack of masculinity is revealed when he scratches his head with one finger, walks with out-turned feet, or sneezes in a certain manner.[1] Teachers of rhetoric used

I would like to thank Elizabeth Clark and Bart Ehrman for their suggestions toward the improvement of this essay.

1. Scratching one's head with one finger was taken sometimes to be effeminate: Seneca the Elder, *Controversiae* 7.4.7; Juvenal, *Satires* 9.130–33; Plutarch, *Pompey* 48.7; *How to Profit by One's Enemies* (*De capienda ex inimicis utilitate*) 89E; Lucian, *Professor of Public Speaking* 11; Julian, *The Caesars* 323B. Elsewhere it is taken as a sign of lechery in general: Seneca, *Moral Epistles* 52.12; Ammianus Marcellinus, 17.11.4. But these two things are not so different, since being too given to love was generally considered a sign of effeminacy. On this combination, as well as other signs of effeminacy in the Greco-Roman world, see my "*Arsenokoitês* and *Malakos:* Meanings and Consequences," in *Biblical Ethics and Homosexuality: Listening to Scripture,* ed. Robert L. Brawley (Louisville, Ky.: Westminster/John Knox, 1996), 117–36. Out-turned feet: (pseudo-)Aristotle, *Physiognomics* 6, 813a14–16; see chap. 6 *passim* for other marks of effeminacy. Sneezing: Diogenes Laertius, *Lives* 7.173. See also H. Herter, "Effeminatus," *Reallexikon für Antike und Christentum* (Stuttgart: Hiersemann, 1959), 4.620–50. The collection of essays in *Roman Sexualities,* ed. Judith P. Hallett and Marilyn B. Skinner (Princeton, N.J.: Princeton University Press, 1997) came to my attention too late to be used for my study, but it should certainly now be consulted for the analysis of the construction of Roman masculinity.

such physiognomies to train their students to project the appropriate signals of true masculinity: strong voice, proper gestures, manly gait, firm eye.[2] And medical texts are full of overt and covert assumptions about what defines the true male. Galen's treatise *On Hygiene*, for example, is in part a handbook on how to take a boy and gradually mold his body to reflect the upper-class ideal male. Other medical texts teach doctors how to conduct girls through the precarious time of puberty, ensuring that they attain the proper level of heat and compactness while avoiding "masculinization."[3]

As several scholars have pointed out, the ideal male occupied the high end of a hierarchical spectrum whose low end was occupied by the female.[4] Heat is generally considered male, and cold female. The male body is dry; the female moist. The male is compact and dense; the female porous.[5] The male body is efficient; it properly uses up its fuel and so has no need to expel any excess on a regular basis. In contrast, the female body is a location of surfeit and excess, signified in its need to slough off excess blood and semen each month. There are differences of opinion about some of these attributes: some theorists, for example, hold that women's bodies are actually warmer than men's, but then the assumption is that women are *too* warm.[6] Nonetheless, there exists in all sorts of ancient texts a remarkable consensus about the construction of masculinity.

Ideological systems, however, contain contradictions. So too the ideology of masculinity in Greco-Roman authors is sometimes at odds with

2. Elizabeth C. Evans, *Physiognomics in the Ancient World* (Philadelphia, Pa.: American Philosophical Society, 1967), 12–13, 40–41, 59; Dale B. Martin, *The Corinthian Body* (New Haven, Conn.: Yale University Press, 1995), 18–19, 34–35.

3. See Martin, *The Corinthian Body*, 27–29, 32–34, 224–25. For the text of Rufus, the medical writer who prescribed a "regimen for virgins" to keep them from becoming masculinized, see Oribasius, *Libri incerti* 18.1–2, found in Oribasius, *Collectionum medicarum reliquiae*, ed. Ioannes Raeder (Amsterdam: Adolf M. Hakkert, 1964), 4.106–9.

4. Thomas Laqueur, *Making Sex: Body and Gender from the Greeks to Freud* (Cambridge, Mass.: Harvard University Press, 1990), 5–6; Maryanne Cline Horowitz, "Aristotle and Women," *Journal of the History of Biology* 9 (1976): 183–214; Prudence Allen, *The Concept of Woman: The Aristotelian Revolution 750 B.C.–A.D. 1250* (Montreal: Eden Press, 1985), 95–97; Hippocrates, *Regimen* 1.34; Clement of Alexandria, *Paedagogus* 3.3.

5. G. E. R. Lloyd, "The Hot and the Cold, the Dry and the Wet in Greek Philosophy," *Journal of Hellenic Studies* 84 (1964): 92–106; Lesley Dean-Jones, "The Cultural Construct of the Female Body in Classical Greek Science," in *Women's History and Ancient History*, ed. Sarah B. Pomeroy (Chapel Hill: University of North Carolina Press, 1991), 111–37.

6. Lloyd, "Hot and Cold," 102; Dean-Jones, "Cultural Construct," 134 n. 31.

itself. Indeed, it was precisely the contradictions of masculinity in ancient patriarchal culture that enabled that ideology to function so efficiently. In this essay, I analyze only two locations of corporeal interpretation and control, mainly in Greek and Roman medical texts, that illuminate the contradictions of masculinity in antiquity. First, I examine the role of sexual intercourse in defining the male. Does having sex make someone a man or endanger his masculinity? Confusingly, ancient persons seem to have believed it did both. Second, I examine the role of menstruation in defining the female. Asking the question "Why do women menstruate?" elicits the corresponding "Why don't men?" But again, ancient culture actually believed that men *did,* on occasion and by alternative means, menstruate. Thus, although men by definition don't menstruate, some men do. By considering how the ancient theorists placed such men on the gender map (are they feminized by bleeding? or is their masculinity strong enough to overcome this particular feminine signifier?), I hope to illustrate certain contradictions of masculinity. I also hope thereby to illuminate in a more complex way the efficiency of the ideological system of masculinity in the ancient world.

Asceticism or Insemination?

As in many cultures, ancient notions of masculinity were to some extent defined by the male act of insemination. A male could prove his masculinity by begetting, or at least by demonstrating his capacity to. The ability to impregnate or ejaculate, and in some cases the actual deed, was a signifier of manhood. Thus, in professional texts as well as popular conceptions, it seems, a boy's first emission of semen carries the same liminal significance as a girl's first menstruation: it marks the move into adulthood. Pliny the Elder passes on the common notion that several diseases are cured by either first intercourse, in the case of a young man, or first menstruation, in the case of a woman.[7] The youth's flow of semen functions for him precisely as the maiden's flow of blood for her: it makes him a man, as menarche makes her a woman.[8]

This cultural assumption is seldom spelled out, but it underwrites certain practices by which some people in the society attempt to control the

7. Pliny the Elder, *Natural History* 28.44.
8. See also Aristotle, *Historia animalium* 9.7.581b29–582a5.

masculinization of others. Aristotle, for example, is no doubt simply stating common sense when he points out that for men sexual intercourse lowers the voice — and the more sexual intercourse, the lower the voice.[9] So singers who wanted to maintain a high, youthful, bright quality to their voices often tried their best to avoid sex. Celsus, a first-century C.E. medical writer, gives instructions for an operation that was used to keep men from having sex. Their foreskins were pierced and the wound gradually allowed to heal so that a lockable pin (a "fibula") could be easily inserted through the foreskin.[10] As long as the pin was in place, the singer or slave would be able to achieve a full erection only painfully and with great difficulty; and he would not be able to penetrate anyone with his penis at all. By avoiding ejaculation, he avoided "becoming a man," with the ensuing change in voice. There were other, less drastic, methods to achieve nearly the same goal — diet, for instance. Democritus apparently taught that radishes were an aphrodisiac, which was why, he supposed, people who didn't want to damage their voices avoided them.[11]

The notion that generation is especially the prerogative of the male — that is, that generation is masculine and it is masculine to generate — is reflected in the way semen was seen to function in impregnation. Aristotle went so far as to assign semen solely to men, going against what was apparently the majority opinion, among philosophers and scientists as well as (probably) popular opinion, that both men and women produce semen. For Aristotle, the mother's body provided merely the "matter" of the embryo by means of the blood; the "form" of the resulting child was due entirely to the energizing and enlivening semen implanted by the man in the womb of the woman, like seed in a field.[12] Other theorists rejected this one-

9. Aristotle, *Historia animalium* 581a21.

10. Celsus, *De medicina* 7.25.2; Martial, *Epigrams* 7.82.1; 11.75.8; 14.215.2; Juvenal, *Satires* 6.379; *Priapea* 77.17; *Oxford Latin Dictionary,* s.v. "fibula."

11. Pliny, *Natural History* 20.28.

12. In *Historia animalium,* however, Aristotle repeatedly refers to the "female emission," and he even talks of the "female seed" in *Generation of Animals* (725b3; 728a26; 728b22; 737a28, etc.). According to Balme, the contradictions between the two works, and that between statements by Aristotle implying the existence of female semen/seed and his general theory, which denies it, are only apparent. See pp. 487–89 note c, to *Historia animalium* 10.634b29 (in the Loeb edition [1991]). See also Galen's discussion, and refutations, of Aristotle's view: Galen, *On Semen,* ed., trans., and comm. Phillip de Lacy (Berlin: Akademie, 1992), 1.3–4, 1.5.9, 1.9.15, 2.1, 2.4.5.

sided view, but they had other means of signifying the greater faculty of the male semen in procreation. Galen, for instance, argued that both the man's and the woman's semen were necessary for pregnancy, but that the weaker, colder, thinner female semen served merely as "a kind of nutriment for the male semen." It is the *male* semen that is the *archê drastikê* (meaning something like the "efficient origin" or "principal force or cause").[13] It seems it was important to these male doctors to argue that women had either no semen (and thus did not contribute any important substance to the formation of the fetus, for the doctors knew nothing of a female ovum) or genetically ineffectual semen; otherwise women's bodies would have everything they needed—blood, semen, and womb—to generate without men, and that certainly could not be allowed.[14]

The ancient world even provided myths to portray the disasters that result when females attempt to generate alone. In a Gnostic myth, datable probably to the second century C.E., the evil (or at least bumbling) creator god is a divine monster generated when a female deity, Sophia, attempts to procreate without her corresponding male consort.[15] Monsters happen when males are left out of the process. In folklore, too, we find similar assumptions. According to Columella's agricultural manual, mares, which are especially concupiscent creatures, become so lustful that they get themselves pregnant from the wind, without intercourse with a stallion. Such

13. Galen, *On Semen* 1.7.5; see also comment (to p. 86, 24–25) by de Lacy on p. 216. Soranus also believes that women, along with men, produce semen (*Gynecology* 1.9.34); while not as clear as Galen about the predominant role still played by the male semen, Soranus's language and images nevertheless consistently seem to portray the male semen as the more important and the female role as passive and receptive. Greek text: Johannes Ilberg, ed., *Sorani gynaeciorum libri IV*, Corpus Medicorum Graecorum 4 (Leipzig: Teubner, 1927); Valentino Rose, ed., *Sorani gynaeciorum* (Leipzig: Teubner, 1882). English translation: Soranus, *Gynecology*, trans. Owsei Temkin (Baltimore, Md.: Johns Hopkins University Press, 1956). Even the Hippocratic *On Semen*, which generally ascribes a greater role to female semen than many other texts, has other mechanisms to assure the more powerful role of the male semen. Male semen is said to be stronger than female, for instance (*On Semen* 6). And we are told that in the generation of twins, the one formed by the first spurt of semen is more likely to be male because the earlier spurts are generally of stronger semen (31). See also Diogenes Laertius, *Lives of the Philosophers* 7.159.

14. Galen reports the concern explicitly in *On Semen* 2.3.2 and 2.3.19.

15. *The Apocryphon of John* ("The Secret Book According to John") 9:25–10:6; *Hypostasis of the Archons* ("Reality of the Rulers") 93. See Bentley Layton, *The Gnostic Scriptures* (Garden City, N.Y.: Doubleday, 1987), 35, 74; see also pp. 16, 283.

"wind eggs," though, produce weak offspring that die within three years.[16] Apparently, men knew *they* could not generate without the other sex; these myths assured them that women couldn't either. Impregnation was thus an important sign of masculinity.

Contradiction comes into play, though, in the conflicting notion that it is particularly masculine to *avoid* sexual intercourse. And this also is a notion we find in popular as well as scientific contexts. As the following analysis will make clear, sexual asceticism in the ancient world was not limited to men. But the ancient ideology of sexual control was deeply embedded in ancient notions of masculinity. In order to see more particularly how ancient sexual control was implicated in masculinity, though, we will need to pay some attention to the broader context of the control of sex.

The popular notion that Christianity invented asceticism has been thoroughly disproved.[17] The ancient world provides much evidence that sex was being seen, well before any possible influence from Christianity, as something that should be avoided or severely controlled. All sorts of texts, magical and popular as well as medical, portray love as a dangerous disease that one would be wise to avoid. And both magic and popular folklore regularly held abstinence from food and sex to be important prerequisites for certain activities.[18] According to Columella, a landowner should choose for farm managers only a man and wife who are both quite self-controlled when it comes to sex. People handling food preparation must avoid sexual intercourse. Even dogs should be restrained from sex while they are young, lest sexual indulgence sap their strength.[19] Then there is the popular be-

16. Columella, *On Agriculture* 6.27.4; Galen relates similar beliefs about birds: *On Semen* 2.3.3.

17. See Michel Foucault, *The Care of the Self* (New York: Pantheon Books, 1986); Aline Rousselle, *Porneia: On Desire and the Body in Antiquity* (Oxford: Basil Blackwell, 1988); Laqueur, *Making Sex;* David Halperin et al., eds., *Before Sexuality: The Construction of Erotic Experience in the Ancient Greek World* (Princeton, N.J.: Princeton University Press, 1990); James A. Francis, *Subversive Virtue: Asceticism and Authority in the Second-Century Pagan World* (University Park: Pennsylvania State University Press, 1995); Dale B. Martin, *The Corinthian Body*, 200–205. Vincent L. Wimbush, ed., *Ascetic Behavior in Greco-Roman Antiquity: A Sourcebook* (Minneapolis, Minn.: Fortress, 1990); Vincent L. Wimbush and Richard Valentasis, *Asceticism* (New York: Oxford University Press, 1995).

18. David Martinez, " 'May She neither Eat nor Drink': Love Magic and Vows of Abstinence," in *Ancient Magic and Ritual Power*, ed. Marvin Meyer and Paul Mirecki (Leiden: Brill, 1995), 353–59; see esp. 356 for abstention from food and sex.

19. Columella, *On Agriculture* 11.1.14; 12.4.3; 7.12.11.

lief that bees will attack adulterers, or in another version, anyone who has recently had sex, evidently because bees are especially pure animals and appreciate purity in others.[20]

Ancient writers do pass along recipes for aphrodisiacs, but it seems that there are almost as many for *ant*aphrodisiacs. Pliny the Elder tells us, for example, that the soft root of the "cynosorchis" plant taken in goat's milk is an aphrodisiac, but the hard root of the same plant is an antaphrodisiac.[21] Hide from the left side of a hippopotamus's forehead worn on the groin also will serve as an antaphrodisiac.[22] Other antaphrodisiacs mentioned by Pliny include snails, pigeon dung taken with oil and wine, wearing a fighting cock's testicles that have been rubbed with goose grease and wrapped in ram's skin, and cock's blood and testicles placed under the bed. We are informed that a man who urinates on a dog's urine will be less driven sexually. The ash of a spotted lizard wrapped in linen works as an aphrodisiac if held in the left hand and an antaphrodisiac if held in the right. Dust in which a she-mule has wallowed lessens desire when sprinkled over the body. Because people seem to have believed that sexual desire was caused by excessive heat and moisture, especially in and around the genitals, they would place cold lead plates on the groin and kidneys to lessen desire and wet dreams.[23] Some doctors apparently also injected cold liquids up the urethra or, perhaps more mercifully, simply instructed their patients to follow a cold, dry diet.[24] Obviously, many men felt the need to quench their desires, probably so they could avoid sex.

20. Columella, *On Agriculture* 9.14.3; Plutarch, *Quaestiones naturales* 36; *Coniugalis praecepta* 144D; *Geoponica* [*Geoponika sive Cassiani Bassi scholastici de re rustica eclogae* (Leipzig: Teubner, 1895)] 15.2.15.

21. Pliny, *Natural History* 27.42.65. For a similar case in which different parts of the same plant work as an aphrodisiac or antaphrodisiac, see Theophrastus, *Enquiry into Plants* 9.18.3; this section, omitted in the Loeb edition, may be found in Greek in F. Wimmer, ed., *Theophrasti Erasii, Opera Omnia* (Paris: Didot, 1866; reprint Frankfurt am Main: Minerva, 1964); and in English translation in Chalmers L. Gemmill, "The Missing Passage in Hort's Translation of Theophrastus," *Bulletin of the New York Academy of Medicine* 49 (1973): 127–29.

22. Pliny, *Natural History* 27.42.65; 28.31.121.

23. Pliny, *Natural History* 30.49.141–43; 30.53.148; 34.50.166.

24. Caelius Aurelianus, *On Chronic Diseases* 5.7 (*On Acute Diseases, and On Chronic Diseases,* ed. and trans. I. E. Drabkin [Chicago, Ill.: University of Chicago Press, 1950], 958); David Brakke, "The Problematization of Nocturnal Emissions in Early Christian Syria, Egypt, and Gaul," *Journal of Early Christian Studies* 3 (1995): 419–60, at 424. See further Theodor

Besides the singers mentioned above, who wanted to avoid intercourse so their voices would not be "masculinized," athletes also were concerned with asceticism. Indeed, the concerns of athletes to avoid ejaculation highlight the close connection in the ancient ideology between asceticism and masculinity. According to Galen, athletes were so concerned to retain their semen, and thereby their strength, that they would have submitted to castration if that would not also have deprived them of strength itself:

Anyone who has no thought of children but has striven to win victory crowns in the games or has entered on some other undertaking of that kind, because of which he has determined that sexual indulgence is not good, would find nothing more beneficial than the excision of the testicles. It is time therefore for us to excise the testicles of the Olympic athletes on the grounds that not only do they have no thought of begetting children, but they are ready to deliver up any part of their body at all in order to win. But the excision is not safe, since along with the testicles it cuts out the strength of the entire body.[25]

The cultural common sense the athletes embody is that people can be more masculine (strong) by avoiding sex and retaining semen.[26] But this sensibility was not limited to athletes. The Emperor Augustus himself, according to his biographer, Nicolas of Damascus, abstained from sex as a young man for one whole year in order to increase his strength and demonstrate his powers of self-control.[27]

Philosophers and medical writers contributed theories to support these

Hopfner, *Das Sexualleben der Griechen und Römer von den Anfängen bis ins 6. Jahrhundert nach Christus* (Prague: J. G. Calve [R. Lerche], 1938), vol. 1, pt. 1, 314; Hugh Parry, *Thelxis: Magic and Imagination in Greek Myth and Poetry* (Lanham, Md.: University Press of America, 1992), 263. See also Alexander Trallian 11.7 [*Alexander von Tralles: Original-Text und Übersetzung nebst einer einleitenden Abhandlung: Ein Beitrag zur Geschichte der Medicin*, ed. and trans. Theodor Puschmann (Amsterdam: A. M. Hakkert, 1963), 2.494–499]; Galen, *Hygiene* 6.14. See also the essay in this volume by Gianna Pomata.

25. Galen, *On Semen* 1.15.34–38, trans. de Lacy.

26. But note the opposite point, made by Pliny, who says, citing Democritus in support, that whereas normally the less indulgence in sex the better, athletes sometimes regain their energy and strength *by means of* sexual intercourse. Sex also sometimes, he says, clears a husky voice, cures pain in the genital region, dullness of vision, mental illness, and melancholy (*Natural History* 28.16).

27. *Fragmenta Historicorum Graecorum*, ed. Carolus Müllerus (Paris: Didot, 1883), 3.434, frag. 100, 15.

notions. The Hippocratic texts, for their part, generally teach moderation and the control of sex, but not absolute avoidance. A man should be careful, for he could get a fever from sexual intercourse and drinking.[28] Since semen, for the Hippocratic writers, is usually understood as the potent distillation of the different liquids of the body, deriving its strength from theirs, the emission of semen, even in small amounts, weakens the body. For the Hippocratic writers, however, sexual intercourse may be enjoyed in moderation. Aristotle basically agrees. Sex is permissible but precarious. Therefore, even though young people and animals are especially desirous around the time of puberty, since their bodies are then in an aroused state of heat and surfeit, they should be prohibited from having sex lest it harm their delicate constitutions. If they indulge, the pores in their body will become wide and eager for even more sexual expenditure: "For the channels become dilated and make an easy passage for fluids in this part of the body; and at the same time their old memory of the accompanying pleasure creates desire for the intercourse that then took place." Aristotle also notes that the bodies of men who have too much sex develop "less completely" and age faster.[29]

The valuation of continence becomes even stronger in the early Empire. Soranus teaches that the only really healthy regimen is to avoid sexual intercourse entirely.[30] But for those who simply must indulge, he prescribes regimens of control that will make avoidance of sex easier and its control more dependable. Celsus (first century) and Galen (second century) agree with the more moderate idea that sexual desires may be somewhat indulged, but with care and moderation. They both interpret sex as something of a crisis of the body's constitution. It is one of several things that can "upset" the body. So especially during periods of pestilence, weakness, or fatigue it should be avoided, along with other corporeal crises like indigestion, cold, heat, vomiting, and loose bowels. Certain diseases, moreover, are particularly aggravated by sexual intercourse; thus, for people with pains in their feet and hands, "sex is always unhealthy" (venus semper inimica est).[31]

Doubtless, the various motivations for and understandings of sexual avoidance differed among these varied concerns to restrict sex, in some

28. Hippocrates, Epidemics 3.10.
29. Historia animalium 581b19–21, 582a22.
30. Soranus, Gynecology 1.7.30.
31. Celsus, De medicina 1.10.1 and 1.9.2; see also 4.31.1; Galen, On Semen 1.16.23.

cases reflecting an interest, perhaps, in cultic purity, in others an interest in managerial discipline, in still others an interest in retaining strength that might be squandered in the sexual act. My goal here is simply to point out that sexual control and avoidance were concerns in a wide range of social locations and among people with probably very different interpretations of *why* they were restricting sex. In a great variety of ways, ancient culture linked sexual indulgence to impurity or weakness and valued its avoidance or control. And in the ancient currency of self-control, the masculinization of sexual asceticism and the asceticizing of masculinity were two sides of the same coin. All people *might* be encouraged to control their sexual activities, but that encouragement was always understood within a larger structure in which self-control was basically a male characteristic. Thus, women might attempt—indeed, they *should* make *some* attempt—to control their urges and passions, but it was recognized that they were probably too weak to endure a strenuous regimen.[32] Stronger persons on the other hand, both masculine men and even some women, should be able to attain a height of health by corporeal control and, according to some systems, even the complete avoidance of sex.

There are several ways of understanding the logic of asceticism in the ancient ideology, which we can discern by analyzing discussions of the scientists, medical writers, and philosophers. To start with, we must continually remember the extent to which ancient society was hierarchical and the body was construed as a hierarchical society. All of the different elements and forces of the body are assigned by "the justice of the Creator" (which, for Galen, the author of these words, is "Nature") to their appropriate places. "Thus in all things Nature has been most just, distributing strength and weakness, thickness and thinness, and all other qualities according to merit."[33] Galen describes the process by which food is cooked and refined inside the body so that the substance changes from food to

32. See my *Corinthian Body,* especially pp. 222–26, for the different expectations concerning regimen and strength when related to gender.
33. Galen, *On the Usefulness of the Parts of the Body (De usu partium),* trans. and comm. Margaret Tallmadge May (Ithaca, N.Y.: Cornell University Press, 1968) 14.13, p. 649 (hereafter *De usu partium*). (The first numerals refer to book and chapter of *De usu partium* (Greek text: Georg Helmreich [Leipzig: Teubner, 1907 and 1909]). I also give the page numbers for May's translation; I do not list the volume number of May's translation and commentary, which is in two volumes, because she conveniently numbers the pages sequentially through the two volumes.

chyle (a form of nutritious matter) to blood. "When the liver has received the nutriment already prepared by its servants [i.e., the stomach and blood vessels] and having the crude outline, as it were, and indistinct semblance of blood, it provides the final elaboration itself so that the nutriment becomes actual blood."[34] Blood may be further refined to render milk or, in an even superior form, semen.

As long as sexual intercourse is associated with those parts of the body (genitals, liver, belly) lower than the ruling part (head or heart), the deprecation of sex and the valuation of asceticism can be seen to be not only possible but necessary for maintaining the system of "honor" implicated in the societal-corporeal hierarchy. Intellect and reason are placed at the top of the body, sexual desire below. Desire is linked to sexual objects such as women, boys, or slaves. "Reason" is associated with rule, management, the avoidance of manual labor or production, and the control of passions, those forces below.[35] Note that generally the sexual desire is not *excluded* but only *controlled* (with the exception of some Stoic theory).[36] The presence of desire is indispensable for the equilibrated hierarchy of society, nature, and body: desire must be present so that the "ruling part" will have something to rule. In this system, asceticism is a logical corollary of hierarchy.[37]

Within the hierarchy of bodily fluids, semen rises to the top. In the refinery process, speaking now of Galen's system in particular, food is changed into nourishing matter in the stomach and then, via the liver, into blood. For the production of semen, we are told, Nature uses only "perfectly concocted blood."[38] High-quality blood is refined (mixed with

---

34. Galen, *De usu partium* 4.3, p. 205 (trans. May).

35. Some of the classic instances of these assumptions, of course, come from Plato. See, e.g., *Phaedrus* 237E–241D; *Phaedo* 94B–D.

36. For the difference in positions among philosophers, along with the case that it was particularly the Stoics who argued for the complete extirpation of desire, see Martha C. Nussbaum, *The Therapy of Desire: Theory and Practice in Hellenistic Ethics* (Princeton, N.J.: Princeton University Press, 1994); see also my "Paul without Passion: On Paul's Rejection of Desire in Sex and Marriage," in *Constructing Early Christian Families: Family as Social Reality and Metaphor,* ed. Halvor Moxnes (London: Routledge, 1997), 201–15.

37. In a study of the construction of masculinity among the rabbis, Michael Satlow shows how self-restraint and control are the salient factors of masculinity also in rabbinic texts: " 'Try to Be a Man': The Rabbinic Construction of Masculinity," *Harvard Theological Review* 89 (1996): 19–40.

38. Galen, *De usu partium* 16.10, p. 712 (trans. May).

pneuma, the most energetic and intelligent material of the body) to become milk or semen.[39] And according to Galen, semen is higher than milk in the hierarchy. Semen is produced from blood by means of convoluted vessels and the testicles rather than being produced, like milk, purely in the vessels because greater refinement necessitates longer, more involved vascular and organic structures: "Since the semen needs a more perfect elaboration, the length of the interval alone was not enough for it, as it was for the milk. For in that case Nature would be unjust, bestowing equal parts, similar in every respect, on things that are unequal and dissimilar."[40] This is traditional antidemocratic rhetoric: just as conservative rhetoricians and philosophers claim that democracy is unjust since it treats people as equals who clearly are not equal, so Galen assumes that Nature will produce (superior) semen by a more careful process than (inferior) milk. Nature produces semen differently than it does milk because semen is superior to milk.[41]

Besides treating bodily substances like citizens in a polis, Galen seems also to be thinking of them the way a modern economist would of commodities: processing adds value to raw materials; and the more processing, the more value. The body spends more time refining semen than any other substance, so it is the most valuable, the strongest, most powerful substance. This valuation of semen is seen in common assumptions of other ancient theorists—the idea, for example, that semen is a product of the brain.[42] Furthermore, since semen is associated with the brain, strength,

39. Galen is no innovator here. For other examples of the belief that semen and milk are produced from refined blood, see *Herophilus: The Art of Medicine in Alexandria,* ed. and trans. Heinrich von Staden (Cambridge: Cambridge University Press, 1989), frag. 104, p. 213. See also von Staden's discussion of the various theories of where semen comes from, 290–96, 364, 536. See also Galen, *De placitis Hippocratis et Platonis (On the Doctrines of Hippocrates and Plato)* 7.3.29; Aristotle, *Generation of Animals* 4.8, 776a15–777a27.

40. Galen, *De usu partium* 16.10, p. 712 (trans. May).

41. For the antidemocratic argument that unequal men must not be treated equally, see Plato, *Laws* 5.744C, 6.767B; *Republic* 8.558C; Isocrates 3(*Nicocles*).14–16, 7 (*Areopagiticus*) 21–22; Aristotle, *Politics* 1280a7–25, 1301a26–b4, 1301b27–1302a8, 1317b2–10, 1318a3–8; Cicero, *Republic* 1.27.43, 1.34.53; Plutarch, *Moralia* 719b–c (*Table Talk* 8.2.2); de Ste. Croix, *Class Struggle* 413–414; F. D. Harvey, "Two Kinds of Equality," *Classica et Mediaevalia* 26 (1965): 101–46, and addenda in 27 (1966): 99–100; Elaine Fantham, "*Aequabilitas* in Cicero's Political Theory and the Greek Tradition of Proportional Justice," *Classical Quarterly* n.s. 23 (1973): 285–90.

42. Hippocrates, *Airs, Waters, Places* 22.20; Claudius Ptolemy, "On the *Kriterion* and *Hegemonikon*," 15.3; text and trans. in *The Criterion of Truth: Essays Written in Honour of George Kerford Together with a Text and Translation (with Annotations) of Ptolemy's* On the Kriterion

and power, but also danger (its activities are hard to predict or control), it becomes connected to insanity. For some theorists, an excess of semen may cause insanity; for others, its ejaculation prefigures insanity.[43] In any case, semen is recognized as the most potent, energetic, valuable corporeal substance. Its very value endows it with an aura of peril and a need for control.

In recognizing the higher valuation of semen in the corporeal hierarchy, we should keep in mind that women, according to most ancient theorists, also produced semen. The ancient system did not *simplistically* equate semen with men. If it did, it would have had to exclude women entirely from the structures of power and control that made up ancient asceticism. Since asceticism was based on a control of semen—along with the materials and forces that surrounded and constituted it—absolute lack of semen might have placed women's bodies out of the reach of asceticism. Since female bodies *did* have *some* semen (or semen of a weaker nature), women could be factored into the control of ancient asceticism. On the other hand, although semen existed in female bodies, it was nevertheless quintessentially a *male* fluid. Men had more and stronger semen. Thus women's bodies, by possessing semen, were included in the power structures of asceticism, but the position of women's bodies, because of the weaker nature of their semen, was maintained at a lower point in the hierarchy.

Another avenue by which we may understand the rationality of ancient medical asceticism is by recognizing it as an expression of the dominant "zero-sum" presupposition of ancient economics. Ancient social and economic theory almost always construed society as possessing a fixed amount of wealth. If the lower classes wanted to get richer, the upper class would

---

and Hegemonikon, ed. Pamela Huby and Gordon Neal (Liverpool, England: Liverpool University Press, 1989), 179–230. For different theories of the source of semen (from the brain, from blood, from all over the body, or from some combination of these), see *Herophilus,* ed. von Staden, 290–96, 364, 536.

43. On the potency of semen, see Aristotle, *Generation of Animals* 2.3,736b35–737a1. In the Hippocratic *On Generation,* nocturnal emissions are taken to be a precursor of madness (1.3). See comments and references by Iain M. Lonie, *The Hippocratic Treatises "On Generation," "On the Nature of the Child," "Diseases IV": A Commentary* (Berlin: de Gruyter, 1981), pp. 109–10. See also Caelius Aurelianus, *On Chronic Diseases* 5.7 (Drabkin ed., p. 958); and the discussion by David Brakke on the use of these theories by early Christian ascetics: "Nocturnal Emissions," 423–24.

have to become poorer.[44] One person's credit was necessarily another person's debit. So equality was always portrayed, by conservative writers and speakers, as lower-class "envy" of upper-class wealth. The body operates by the same dynamics. Thus Galen explains why women cease menstruating when they are pregnant. Nature has, in its typically wise, teleological foresight, connected the uterus to the breasts by means of special vessels so that the nutriment that normally would collect in the lower region may be drawn off first by the fetus for food and later by the breasts for milk: "For the parts [the uterus and breasts] that I mentioned earlier are the only ones needing to be connected by vessels, in order that whenever an embryo is being formed and is growing in the uteri, it alone may be flooded with nutriment from both parts by the common veins, and in order that when the child has been born, all the nutriment may in turn flow to the breasts. This is the reason why the female cannot menstruate properly and give suck at the same time; for one part is always dried up when the blood turns toward the other."[45] The human being is a social body of limited goods, a predetermined balance of constituents.

This is also seen in the role food is assumed to play in producing sexual desire and the role ejaculation is assumed to play in weakness. Practically all the medical theorists believe that satiety in food will automatically lead to excess of desire. Celsus instructs the patient who is submitting to an operation that will restore his foreskin to fast for a few days beforehand. Otherwise, while his penis is healing from the surgery, he will experience desire and have an erection, which, besides being quite painful, will ruin

44. For a discussion of "the perception of limited good" in the ancient Mediterranean in general, see Bruce J. Malina, *The New Testament World: Insights from Cultural Anthropology*, rev. ed. (Louisville: Westminster/John Knox, 1993), 94–96, 103–12. For zero-sum assumptions in political theory, see Aristotle, *Politics* 1.3.23, 1258b2; 2.42, 1266b1–8. The "zero-sum game" also played itself out in the economics of honor and shame: see Alvin W. Gouldner, *Enter Plato: Classical Greece and the Origins of Social Theory* (New York: Basic Books, 1965), 49–60; John Winkler, *The Constraints of Desire: The Anthropology of Sex and Gender in Ancient Greece* (New York: Routledge, 1990), 47 and passim; David Cohen, *Law, Sexuality, and Society: The Enforcement of Morals in Classical Athens* (Cambridge: Cambridge University Press, 1992), 35–69; Cohen, *Law, Violence, and Community in Classical Athens* (Cambridge: Cambridge University Press, 1995), 26, 63; Josiah Ober, *The Athenian Revolution: Essays on Ancient Greek Democracy and Political Theory* (Princeton, N.J.: Princeton University Press, 1996), 101.
45. Galen, *De usu partium* 14.8, p. 638 (trans. May).

the plastic surgery just completed.[46] Ingested food fills the body up and turns into blood, thus providing material for semen and heat. But then, of course, this surfeit must be taken care of in some way. Ejaculation is an expenditure of abundance, nature's way of getting rid of excess. Just as the political body gets into trouble when there is too much wealth and luxury among certain members of the body politic, so the human body gets into trouble by taking in too much food.[47] And just as a social crisis is usually the means by which social and political stability is restored (with the unfortunate but necessary "expenditure" of excess—in some cases, excess citizens), so a corporeal crisis like ejaculation, wet dreams, hemorrhage, or nosebleed "takes care of" surfeit. Of course, the optimum situation would be to avoid the need for crisis at all, and thus by controlling the intake of food and drink to avoid the internal excess that prompts sexual desire. The zero-sum economy of the body encourages asceticism.[48]

Ancient economic assumptions tended to encourage conservatism and preservation, not investment or risk taking, and this also expressed itself in the rationality of ancient asceticism. Moderation should always be sought. As Celsus instructs:

> Indeed, one should not desire sexual intercourse too much, nor be too afraid of it. If done rarely, it energizes the body; if frequently, it dissolves it. But "frequency" should be measured by nature, not number, taking account of the age and (kind of) body. One should recognize that it is not harmful if neither weakness nor pain of the body follows. It is worse if indulged during the day, and better at night. Those who have sex during the day, though, should not eat immediately afterward. Those who indulge at night should not stay awake or work following sex. These observations will keep people healthy, though they should beware lest in favorable health their defenses against adverse [influences] are used up.[49]

46. Celsus, *De medicina* 7.25.1; see also Plutarch, *Quaestiones naturales* 21, 917b; 30, 919c.

47. For an excess of wealth and luxury leading to *stasis* or political crisis, see Plato, *Republic* 2.373E; Aristotle, *Politics* 5.2.8, 1303a11; Plutarch, *Advice about Keeping Well (De tuenda sanitate praecepta)* 125F; C. Bradford Welles, "The Economic Background of Plato's Communism," *Journal of Economic History* 8 (1948): 101–14, esp. 108.

48. For the recurrence, again, of these medical and cultural assumptions in early Christian asceticism, see Brakke, "Nocturnal Emissions," 426, 440, 441.

49. Celsus, *De medicina* 1.1.4.

Sex is here seen as the expenditure of reserves, reserves that may be needed at any time for energetic living or staving off other disease-causing factors such as heat, cold, fatigue, surfeit. Sexual intercourse is always risky. What happens if a man has sex one day only to find that the next is extremely hot and that he now needs that previously spent strength in order to resist the ill effects of the unseasonable weather? This concern comes out especially in one section where Celsus notes which seasons are better or worse for indulgence in coitus. Sex in winter is not *too* harmful, he admits. It is safest in spring, since that is the mildest season. Sex should be avoided in autumn, because that season's changeable weather is hard on the body. But by all means, one should completely abstain in the heat of summer "if that possibly can be done."[50] Sex, which is always strenuous and depleting, should be avoided especially during times when the body will need all the reserves it can muster.

In sexual and monetary economy, strength must be held in reserve. A man may "shoot his whole wad," but in the body—as in battle or home economics—that practice is risky. And risk is usually to be avoided. Do not expend! Save! In the ancient world, strategies of capitalism and investing are rare, if one can find them at all.[51] Preservation, rather than risky "venture capitalism," is the rule. Extra money is often put into land, according to ancient ideas the safest of bets. So a notion that sex invigorates and creates energy ("Use it or lose it") is absent in these upper-class authors. Since

50. Celsus, *De medicina* 1.3.33–38.

51. It should be noted that I am referring to expressed strategies and theories about capitalist investment. Obviously, there was no theory of capitalism in the ancient world, since the system we identify as such did not exist but is a modern phenomenon. People did indeed invest money in ventures of various risk and made profit. But the dominant cultural assumptions seem to have emphasized conservation of one's property. The notion of the upper class, for example, was that a man *might* make a large profit out of some investment in a commercial venture, but he then would be expected to buy land and retire on its income, not reinvest the profit (see Cicero, *De officiis* 1.42.151; Horace, *Satire* 2.6.10–13; de Ste. Croix, *Class Struggle*, 122–24). As Moses Finley comments, the upper class lived off income from land, but agriculture in the ancient economy was never treated as a "capitalist enterprise" (*The Ancient Economy*, 2d ed. [Berkeley: University of California Press, 1985], 58, see also 110, 116–22, 144–45). For arguments that "conservative risk management" strategies are typical of "peasant societies," see Thomas Gallant, *Risk and Survival in Ancient Greece: Reconstructing the Rural Domestic Economy* (Stanford, Calif.: Stanford University Press, 1991), esp. 94–110.

sex constitutes a risky expenditure in uncertain times, it is to be avoided or carefully limited.

I mentioned above the rule we repeatedly encounter in ancient advice: "Everything in moderation." Whether in eating, drinking, or sexual intercourse, the medical writers urge balance and moderation. Importantly, though, they never really inform us exactly how much is too much. And this ambiguity, I argue, is important for the ideological efficiency of the ancient construals of masculinity and asceticism. We might imagine ancient male readers of these texts eagerly but futilely searching for specifics to answer the questions "How much is enough? How much is too much?" Like modern married couples, anxiously reading magazine surveys on how often most couples "do it" and surreptitiously calculating their own performances—is once a week "normal"? once a month? twice a month? once a day?!—ancient men could never be certain that they had "got it right," that they fit the "golden mean."

I will argue below that it is precisely this sort of ambiguity that gives the ancient ideology of masculinity much of its power. In this case, the ambiguity comes from a lack of definition and clarity about "moderation." If only certain professionals have the power to define "the moderate," that particular implement cannot be appropriated by unauthorized persons and turned against its rightful owners. Another ambiguity, though, has to do with the cultural contradiction by which the "male" is, on the one hand, defined by insemination but also, on the other, informed that true masculinity consists in avoiding, or at least restricting, insemination. Men couldn't be sure if they were failing the test of masculinity if they *did* inseminate or if they *didn't*. Before I analyze further the function of this latter contradiction, however, I turn to another location where males are caught in something of a double bind: the ideology of menstruation.

Menstruating Men

As in most cultures, menstruation was a hugely overdetermined sign in the ancient world, which is to say it meant entirely too many things in too many different contexts. Menstrual blood and menstruating women were powerful things. Agricultural manuals warn that just the presence of a menstruating woman will immediately dry up certain shrubs. Cucumbers and gourds, as may be appropriate for these delightfully phallic vegetables, were especially threatened: an entire crop of them would be ruined if a menstruating woman came near.[52] But menstruating women, or in some versions only menstruating virgins, could have positive pesticidal effects. Caterpillars in a garden would all immediately drop dead, for example, if a menstruating woman or girl walked around the plot a prescribed number of times.[53] We find many other evidences of the power and danger of menstruation in accounts of folk beliefs. Menstruating women turn purple to other colors, make boiling linen black, dull the edge of razors, rust brass, tarnish mirrors, cause mares to miscarry. Men are warned that they will die if they have sexual intercourse during a solar or lunar eclipse with a woman who is menstruating. And menstrual blood can be quite stubborn; its stain, according to Pliny, can be washed out only by the urine of the very woman from whom the blood came.[54] But menstrual flux is also said to have curative powers: spread on the soles of patients' feet, it cures fevers or epilepsy. The ash of menstrual blood, mixed with rose oil and applied to the forehead, relieves headache. Even a cloth stained with the first menstrual blood of a young girl may be tied around the head to cure headache. And menstrual fluid is often useful for undoing magic spells: smeared on doorposts it protects against mischief from magicians or other malicious forces.[55]

Menstruation was of special importance, for one thing, because it was a site where two separate highly overdetermined signs—the female and blood—came together in one place. It seems there was practically no limit to the significations of the power and problem of menstruation. So it is no surprise that ancient writers gave it much attention. They had various answers to the important question "Why do women menstruate?" In his *Table Talk*, Plutarch gives two common explanations. The subject comes up in a debate over whether females are colder or hotter than males. In Plutarch's dialogue, one speaker argues that women must be hotter than men because they obviously have more blood than men, as evidenced by their need to get rid of some of it every month or so, and as everyone knows, blood is an especially hot bodily humor. "Women have so much

52. Columella, *On Agriculture* 11.3.50; for the same effect on rue, see 11.3.38; and Pliny, *Natural History* 28.23.78.
53. Columella, *On Agriculture* 10.358–68; 11.3.64; Pliny, *Natural History* 17.47.266; 28.23.78.
54. Pliny, *Natural History* 28.23.80–82; 28.23.77 and see also 7.15.64–65; 28.23.84.
55. Pliny, *Natural History* 28.23.77–86; 28.20.70.

of it that it would burn them up and utterly consume them except for the quick recurrence of their periods of menstruation."[56] The reasoning is that women menstruate because they have an excess of blood, which will overheat their bodies if not dispensed regularly. The other point of view here expressed (that females are in general colder in constitution than males) explains that menstrual blood is harmful to the woman because it is blood that has become "corrupt and diseased." "The fact that women are apt to be seized with chills and shivering during their menstrual periods shows that the blood which has been set in motion and is now being eliminated from the body is cold and unassimilated" (651D).[57] Here the idea seems to be that the excessively cold nature of the woman's body cools the blood down and causes it to become corrupt; it becomes cold and thus unable to be assimilated by the body. The "bad blood" must be sloughed off or the woman will become ill.

Many medical writers, including the Hippocratics and Galen, combine these notions in some way. In general, the idea is that women's bodies are colder, moister, and more porous than men's. Because of their colder, slower nature, their bodies cannot process or "use up" all the blood they create. Furthermore, due to their porosity, their bodies, like sponges, retain blood and other fluids more than is healthy. The retained fluids eventually rot in the body and so must be expelled before the woman becomes sick from the corruption. According to a dominant medical idea, it is precisely the excess of blood and moisture (including female semen) that overheats the female body, causing the woman to be feverish and lustful. The woman's delicate balance of fluidity and temperature is restored by the expulsion of blood and semen in menstruation.[58]

This entire system depends on certain principles. For one thing, the human body is a system of balance between opposites: hot-cold, dry-moist, full-empty. The different humors or fluids of the body—the particulars of which vary among the different medical and philosophical systems but which often include blood, bile, phlegm, pneuma, or sometimes water or

56. Hippocrates, *Moralia* 651B.
57. Hippocrates, *Moralia* 651D.
58. Aristotle, *Historia animalium* 582b5–12 (found in book labeled 9 [7] in the Loeb edition); Hippocrates, *On the Nature of the Child* 15.3 (Lonie, *The Hippocratic Treatises*, p. 8); "Hippocrates: Diseases of Women 1," trans. and with headnote by Ann Ellis Hanson, *Signs* 1 (1975): 567–84; Rufus (Oribasius, *Libri Incerti*) 18.19–25; Galen, *On Semen* 2.4.24–25; 2.5.69–73.

other elements—also participate in this system of balance. If a fluid gets out of place in the body (goes someplace where it shouldn't, like blood in the brain or too much water in the limbs) illness results, often because that fluid is understood to corrupt or "rot" due to its state of excess or displacement. The problematic matter must be coaxed back to its place (by massage or "cupping," for instance), or a crisis must be created to get rid of the problematic matter and allow the body to reassume its natural balance.

It is difficult to overestimate the importance of *crisis* for much ancient medicine, the Hippocratics and Galen in particular. Repeatedly in the Hippocratic *Epidemics,* we see that it is good to have a crisis—some kind of hemorrhage, evacuation, or flowing abscess. These events relieve the body of the problem, and when sick people do *not* experience something drastic like this, they often die.[59] Thus, in those cases in which nature itself does not provide the crisis, the physician must provoke one on his own. Celsus offers a list of ways physicians may induce crisis: bloodletting, cupping, purging, rubbing, rocking, exercising, enforcing abstinence, inducing vomiting or sweating. The medical manuals are full of advice about and prescriptions for enemas, suggesting that for some doctors defecation seems to have been the cure for just about anything. Unprovoked bleeding is often interpreted as a good sign, and doctors are urged not to attempt to staunch such "favorable hemorrhage."[60] Doctors note the benefits of hemorrhoids and bleeding from the anus; people with hemorrhoids are said to be safeguarded from other diseases; dropsy may be caused by *suppressed* hemorrhoids (the suppression of the hemorrhoids leads to an unhealthy accumulation of fluids elsewhere in the body); even habitual bleeding from hemorrhoids is said to be not a disease, but a "purgation."[61]

Since blood was a particularly meaningful—and dangerous—substance, its displacement or excess could be particularly harmful. Women who have too much blood in their breasts, for instance, go mad. On the other hand, hemorrhoids cure insanity.[62] Nature, though, had other means by which

59. Hippocrates, *Epidemics* 1.15–19.
60. Hippocrates, *Epidemics* 1; 2.92; 3.6.
61. See the comments and list in Galen, *On Examinations by which the Best Physicians are Recognized,* ed. and trans. Albert Z. Iskander (Berlin: Akademie-Verlag, 1988), p. 173; Hippocrates, *Humors* 20; Celsus, *De medicina* 6.18.9; Galen, *On Prognosis (De praecognitione),* ed., trans., and comm. Vivian Nutton (Berlin: Akademie-Verlag, 1979), 3.15; see also commentary (on p. 86, line 22) at p. 173; *On the Natural Faculties (De naturalibus facultatibus)* 2.8.
62. Blood causing madness: Hippocrates, *Aphorisms* 5.40; Celsus, *De medicina* 2.7.27. Hem-

to dispense with excess blood besides menstruation and bleeding hemorrhoids—through the nose and mouth especially. Here it is important to remember that the ancients consistently assumed a direct physiological connection between the genitals/anus and the head. Diseases or cures in one region necessarily affected the other. Deafness due to fever may be relieved either by a flow of blood from the nose or by a bowel disorder.[63] Prolonged diarrhea may be cured by spontaneous and involuntary vomiting.[64] And vomiting of blood is often cured automatically by the onset of menstruation.[65] All these various theories operate by the common assumption that excess, surfeit, or imbalance in the body is a bad thing and normally requires some kind of crisis, spontaneous or provoked, whereby the body's balance will be reestablished. Menstruation is one of nature's ways of creating a crisis by means of which the body's balance is restored. It must be remembered, of course, that bleeding is good only if there is already a *problem* with the body. In the best of all possible bodies, menstruation would not be necessary. Unfortunately for them, women by definition seem not to be able to have such an efficient body. Thus when we come across ancient statements about the health-restoring value of menstruation, we must remember that it is only in the absence of perfect health that menstruation could receive this (qualified) approbation.

In any case, whenever one explained why women did menstruate, one was also explaining, whether intentionally or unwittingly, why men did not. Usually, the understanding was that men possessed whatever women lacked. If women were taken to be too cold, men (or at least "normal" men) were just right. The male body was hot enough (not too hot) to burn up all the fuel (blood) supplied by its intake of food. The male body was dense and compact enough that it did not inadvertently soak up and store excess fluid, which would end up rotting. The male body was dry enough that it did not produce or store excess moisture. According to Galen's system, the male body simply does not suffer from "residue" because "by its

---

orrhoids curing insanity: Hippocrates, *Aphorisms* 6.21; Celsus, *De medicina* 2.8.15; see also Caelius Aurelianus, *On Chronic Diseases* 1.5.147.

63. Hippocrates, *Aphorisms* 4.60.

64. See the confusing passage in Celsus, *De medicina* 2.7.8–10: it is unclear exactly how the nose-bleeding relates to the severe postpartum pain and abdominal congestion, whether it is a sign of the pain or that which brings its relief; but the connection of the genitals with the nose is obvious.

65. Hippocrates, *Aphorisms* 5.32; Celsus, *De medicina* 4.11.2, 2.8.16.

heat and dryness it expels all the moisture." [66] Whether the trope is heat, dryness, density, or whatever, the common factor is the efficiency of masculinity. Just as Nature in ancient systems (here especially the Aristotelian and Galenic systems) never does anything "in vain" or without a proper purpose, so the superior pole of the gender spectrum, the masculine, is teleologically sufficient and procedurally efficient. Efficiency is masculine; masculinity is efficient. So men don't menstruate.

But they do. Since all sorts of bleeding—through the mouth, nose, or anus—were construed by the ancient medical writers as fulfilling the same corporeal function as menstruation, it was painfully obvious that some men's bodies *were* capable of suffering from the same kind of excess as women's bodies. Sometimes this was recognized as a possibility for men in general, so Celsus notes that men who are "full-blooded" or very hot are in danger of hemorrhage.[67] More often, however, it is males who are closer to the "feminine" who are prone to such problems. A Hippocratic writer, for instance, notes what sort of people are most susceptible to gout: women whose menstruation has been suppressed and young men who have only recently begun having sexual intercourse. Women who menstruate regularly, young boys before the age of puberty, and eunuchs are all said not to be susceptible.[68] A common factor unites these cases: gout is caused by an excess of fluid; women do not suffer from gout if they get rid of their excess fluid (blood and semen); boys and eunuchs do not suffer from it because they do not produce semen. The bodies that *do* become gouty tend to be those on the borderline but not fully masculine: nonmenstruating women who should be menstruating and adolescent males. They are not capable of using up their fluids efficiently, but they nonetheless produce semen and associated fluids.

The same sensibility recurs in other medical issues. Young men, for example, are especially likely to spit up blood around the time of puberty.[69] Nosebleeds become important here. Nonmenstruating women are known sometimes to expel their excess and trapped blood through the nose; and young men, especially around the time of puberty, also often experience

66. Galen, *On Semen* 2.4.25.
67. Celsus, *De medicina* 2.7.2.
68. Hippocrates, *Aphorisms* 6.28–30.
69. Hippocrates, *Aphorisms* 3.29; see also Celsus, *De medicina* 2.1.21.

nosebleeds.[70] Galen relates a case in which he advised against bleeding a young man, predicting that "nature" would take care of the problem on its own by means of a nosebleed. Of course, he was proven right.[71] Since nosebleeds are understood to fulfill the same salutary function as menstruation, certain persons (those closer to the "female") are endangered when they do *not* experience them. Celsus tells us that children who have suddenly ceased experiencing nosebleeds will suffer headaches, joint ulcerations, or other diseases in the same way that women who cannot menstruate may suffer similar diseases.[72] These notions were not limited to physicians: Pliny the Elder, in his collection of what must be considered more folk knowledge than professional medicine, remarks that of all the animals, only in humans do we have cases of males regularly experiencing blood fluxes at fixed periods, through the nostrils, the mouth, or the "lower organs." Pliny knows of two cases himself; one man, he says, lived to over ninety years of age, experiencing his blood flow once a year.[73] All of these are cases of what came to be called—in early modernity and into the nineteenth and early twentieth centuries—"vicarious menstruation."[74] The idea is that although males by definition do not menstruate, some men do.

70. Women and nosebleeds: Hippocrates, *Aphorisms* 5.33; see also *Epidemics* 1.16, 19 for the healthy substitution of epitaxis for menstruation; Celsus, *De medicina* 4.27.10. Young men: Hippocrates, *Aphorisms* 3.27. Hippocrates, *Prognostic* 7, 21, 24 also points to epitaxis as a remedy, and makes the point that it is more likely to happen to people under thirty-five years of age, probably because that is a time when their bodies are taken to be producing more semen; see also Celsus, *De medicina* 2.1.19; 2.7.30.

71. Galen, *On Recognizing the Best Physicians* 4.1; for Galen's explicit connection of male nosebleeds to female menstruation, see 4.5. See also Galen, *On the Medical Sects: For Beginners,* chap. 9; *On Treatment by Venesection (De curandi ratione per venae sectionem)* 11 and passim. Eng.: Peter Brain, *Galen on Bloodletting: A Study of the Origins, Development and Validity of His Opinions, with a Translation of the Three Works* (Cambridge: Cambridge University Press, 1986).

72. Celsus, *De medicina* 2.7.7.

73. Pliny, *Natural History* 11.90.223.

74. E. Heinrich Kisch, *The Sexual Life of Woman in Its Physiological, Pathological and Hygienic Aspects* (trans. from German by M. Eden Paul; New York: Allied Book Company, 1926; original English copyright 1910), 164–66; V. Desogus, "Kehlkopf, Nase, Ohr in ihren Beziehungen zu den sexuellen Phasen," *Zeitschrift für Sexualwissenschaft* 9 (1923): 50–53; "Fliesssche Genitalstellen der Nase," *Bilder-Lexikon: Sexualwissenschaft,* vol. 5 of the 1961 reprint (1930; Vienna: Institut für Sexualforschung, Verlag für Kulturforschung), 264. These concepts were one expression of the belief, held also in both ancient and modern times,

But this observation raises several questions. Doctors doubtless encountered all sorts of men—some who might have been recognized as "feminine," but some not—who suffered from hemorrhoids, anal bleeding or nosebleeds, or who occasionally coughed up blood. Their texts mention many such cases. Pliny alone gives at least fourteen remedies for nosebleeds and at least fifty-five remedies for "spitting up blood." Were these men thereby stigmatized as effeminate? Was bleeding construed as a means of restoring a man's masculinity? or as a sign that a man was essentially not masculine enough? Did men who experienced some sort of flow of blood or semen feel ashamed? Did they take the experience as a threat to their masculinity?

Unfortunately, we have no explicit information from the ancient world that could answer these questions. I know of no case in which bleeding men are explicitly labeled as feminized and overtly shamed by the flow. Then again, we might imagine that such public labeling and discussion would have raised the contradictions of masculinity to such a level of explicitness that the result would have been uncomfortable or even intolerable for the men constructing the examinations and writing our texts. We might imagine, in other words, that the danger of bleeding was so unpredictable and uncontrollable that men did not willingly face the gendering consequences openly. After all, these ancient writers were dealing mostly with men of their own station and class. The creeping effeminacy present in the bleeding body of a neighbor may have been sensed as too threatening to be discussed openly.

I suggest, in any case, that although we have no way to ascertain what ancient men *felt* about such events, men's flows were nonetheless susceptible to many embarrassing interpretations. Although men were those who by definition did not menstruate, particular men did experience flows that were culturally and physiologically construed as equivalents to menstruation. Thus men who experienced nosebleeds, hemorrhoids, anal bleeding, or expectoration of blood were thereby susceptible to at least implicit, if not explicit, suspicion of femininity. Although the cultural construction of

---

that there were important internal connections between the genitals and the nose; see, e.g., R. Kafemann, "Zwei Fälle von sexueller Insuffienz infolge von Nasenoperationen," *Zeitschrift für Sexualwissenschaft* 11 (1924): 238–39; S. Weissenberg, "Spermageruch des Nasenschleims," *Zeitschrift für Sexualwissenschaft* 12 (1925): 258; William Buchan, *Domestic Medicine*, 13th ed. (London: Strahan, Cadell, Balfour, Creech, 1792), 328–42.

"the male" was on the surface sturdy and monolithic, particular men could never be sure their bodies would live up to that construction. *The male* was secure; but *men* were not. Particular men were caught in a contradiction within the system of ancient masculinity. By definition they could not menstruate; their bodies had to be completely sufficient and efficient. But they knew that their bodies could at any moment betray them by a feminine excess that their wills were powerless to contain.

Conclusion

Initially, perhaps, these contradictions in the ancient system of masculinity are surprising. It seems odd that the same culture (and here I speak for the moment of the conglomerate "Greco-Roman" culture) that so valued reproduction, that rewarded procreation even through legal means, that insisted so strenuously that it was particularly male to inseminate, that even reserved for men the primary role of generation, simultaneously insinuated that it was especially masculine to avoid sexual intercourse and the expenditure of semen. To inseminate was masculine; to avoid insemination was masculine. And the same culture that defined the female body by the lack of efficiency manifested in the male body, an inefficiency that signified itself in menstruation, also insinuated that men, in particular situations, might themselves menstruate. Although men by definition do not menstruate, some men do. We are surely justified in being confused and bemused by these contradictions.

On further thought, though, the presence of the contradictions makes perfect sense. In the first place, it has long been recognized that ideological systems contain contradictions, and it is by focusing on sites of contradiction that the ideological biases of those systems are exposed and deconstructed.[75] So on one level, these contradictions of masculinity simply

75. Fredric Jameson, *The Political Unconscious: Narrative as a Socially Symbolic Act* (Ithaca, N.Y.: Cornell University Press, 1981), 77–85, 253–57. I should point out that my use of "contradiction" is somewhat different from Jameson's in that he tends to use the term to refer to *social* contradictions that ideology attempts to sublimate in a mystifying system of closure. I am here using "contradiction" to point to oppositional elements within the ideological system itself. See also Ranajit Guha, "The Prose of Counter-insurgency," in *Subaltern Studies,* ed. Guha, vol. 2 (New Delhi: Oxford University Press, 1983), 1–40, see esp. 39–40; Homi K. Bhabha, *The Location of Culture* (New York: Routledge, 1994), 25, 174, 187; the Bible and Culture Collective, *The Postmodern Bible* (New Haven, Conn.: Yale University Press, 1995),

reveal the fact that the ancient construction of masculinity was indeed ideological (as opposed to some neutral observation of "nature")—that is, it was a system of meaning that served particular political interests and supported a particular, contingent structure of the exercise of power.

But we need not leave the discussion at that level of generality. Although we are here involved more in speculation than historical demonstration, we can offer some suggestion about the function of contradictions in the ancient system of masculinity. I would argue that these contradictions, rather than revealing weaknesses in the structure of the ancient ideology of the masculine, actually worked to ensure its strength. Just as earthquake-resistant buildings must contain within themselves a certain amount of flexibility, a "give-and-take," so ideologies must be malleable and flexible. Just as some bridges gain their strength by possessing within themselves opposing pressures, so the contradictions within certain ideologies render them actually less assailable, brittle, or fractious. We can imagine, therefore, that the contradictions of masculinity outlined in this essay actually rendered the ancient ideology of masculinity more serviceable, at least for the upper-class men who were the authors of practically all our surviving literature from the Greco-Roman world.

In a society for which masculinity was such a valuable commodity it could not be allowed to become the property of just anyone who happened to have been born with the prescribed genitalia. By medicalizing the assignation of masculinity, the medical writers introduced the element of class into the question of who would get to be truly male. The medical writers generally served not the entire population, but the upper class. Although one does sometimes encounter references to lower-class persons in the medical writings (more in the Hippocratic texts than those that came later, it should be noted), the overwhelming impression is that the doctors for the most part served people who could afford their (not inexpensive) services. The passing references in Galen's writings that indicate the social location of his and his colleagues' practices are almost all to situations among the

---

104; Mark Simpson, *Male Impersonators: Men Performing Masculinity* (New York: Routledge, 1994), xi; Cohen, *Law, Violence, and Community*, 68, 75, 126. For another of my attempts to focus on contradiction as a means of exposing ideological mystification, this time that of the heterosexism of modern biblical scholars, see my "Heterosexism and the Interpretation of Romans 1:18–32," *Biblical Interpretation* 3 (1995): 332–55, esp. 352–54.

propertied class.[76] And in his *On Hygiene* he quite openly admits that only someone of the leisured class would be able adequately to follow his prescriptions for good health.[77] So by making masculinity something that required the regular care of a physician, the medical writers, products of the higher class and servants of its interests, assume for themselves the power of assigning, maintaining, certifying, and restoring masculinity—at least by the standards of the upper class. And this was important. Otherwise, ignorant manual laborers, boys, and even slaves would be able to appropriate for themselves the precious commodity of masculinity. By making masculinity something that often required the care of a physician and the regimen of science, upper-class ideology could more easily retain control of the currency of masculinity and keep it out of the hands of those who did not deserve it.

76. Hippocratic texts sometimes indicate that physicians ministered to lower-class persons, such as lodgers in other people's households. And see the reference in the Hippocratic *Praecepts*, chap. 6, to refusing pay from poor patients. There are also cases involving householders themselves, their families, and their slaves. See *Epidemics* 2 and 3. Throughout chap. 9 of Galen's *On Examinations by Which the Best Physicians Are Recognized* [Berlin: Akademie-Verlag, 1988]) physicians appear as the clients and attendants of the wealthy. In fact, much of Galen's goal in writing the treatise is to free medicine from the patron-client household system, to free doctors, for example, from the necessity of the *salutatio* and other trappings of attendance on the rich (see, e.g., 9.17–19). In his *On the Passions of the Soul* (9[63]), Galen remarks that there are about 30 people in the city (probably Pergamum; see the reference to Asia Minor at paragraph 64) wealthier than his patient (the purported recipient of the treatise). That number, he notes, is out of about 40,000 citizens, which is itself out of 120,000 inhabitants in all (i.e., including noncitizens, women, slaves, etc.). See also H. F. J. Horstmanshoff, "Galen and His Patients," in *Ancient Medicine in Its Socio-cultural Context*, ed. Ph. J. van der Eijk, et al. (Amsterdam: Rodopi, 1995), 1.83–99. For the audience of Soranus's *Gynecology*, see the introduction by Temkin, xxxviii. For some comments on status issues and payment of physicians, see Fridolf Kudlein, "Medicine as a 'Liberal Art' and the Question of the Physician's Income," *Journal of the History of Medicine and Allied Sciences* 31 (1976), 448–59. Unfortunately for my purposes here, Kudlein gives scant attention to class issues and ideology or to important chronological, geographical, and cultural differences between Greece and Rome.

77. For class indicators of Galen's expected readership, see his *On Hygiene* 3.10; 6.14. Galen says that a lower-class person might be able to follow a *modified* regimen, but not the regimen he considers really sufficient for health (6.5, 7). Celsus also recognizes that the leisure available only to the upper class is necessary to maintain the kinds of moderation and regimen required by his system: *De medicina* 1.1.1.

Even more important than this particular class appropriation of the construction of masculinity, however, is the way the contradictions of masculinity rendered masculinity itself an even more precious commodity due precisely to its precarious nature. What better way to make maleness even more valuable than to make its possession never certain? Who values what he can never lose? And of course by making maleness more precious, the ideology made male power more secure, though this had to be done at the cost of making each individual man less secure in his own particular masculinity.

In spite of the apparent rigor and consistency of ancient notions of the male, therefore, ancient patriarchal ideology contained within itself significant contradictions and tensions about the definition of masculinity. But these contradictions did not render the ideology weak or insecure. In fact, the tensions and contradictions ensured that patriarchalism, and the upper-class control of it in particular, would maintain its grip on power and that the ideology of masculinity would remain secure. The ancient system of masculinity could in the end be weakened neither by the double bind that demanded both insemination and asceticism nor by the presence in its midst of menstruating men.

Menstruating Men: Similarity and Difference of the Sexes in Early Modern Medicine

GIANNA POMATA

The writer who knows exactly how exceptional,
and how unexceptional, his events should be,
possesses the key to the art.
— Thomas Hardy

I

"Men also, with great benefit to their health, are subject to menstrual flows. The servant of a big merchant from Copenhagen has a discharge of blood from his privy parts regularly every month."[1] Thus wrote Thomas Bartholin, one of the most eminent anatomists of the seventeenth century, in his collection of anatomical *historiae.* A more obscure doctor, Johann Baptist De Wenckh, sent this report to the German Academia Naturae Curiosorum in 1706:

> Among the various and indeed almost numberless phenomena of the microcosm, one should be considered as most significant: the fact that nature assigned to some men that which is common only to the female sex — viz., a regular, monthly discharge of blood from the genital parts. . . . I met myself one of these men, a peasant from Eggenberg, one hundred and five years old, the prolific parent of many children. This fellow, who is still living, from the time of puberty to the age

Abbreviations used in the following notes: AE: Acta eruditorum; AMH: Acta medica et philosophica Hafniensia; MNC: Miscellanea curiosa academiae naturae curiosorum, sive ephemerides medico-physicae Germanicae; PT: Philosophical Transactions of the Royal Society.
1. Thomas Bartholin, *Historiarum anatomicarum rariorum centuriae* (Copenhagen, 1654), cent. 5, hist. 33: "Menstruus fluxus in juvene," p. 55. Translations here and throughout mine unless otherwise noted.

of sixty-six has regularly paid this monthly toll, meanwhile enjoying very good health and generating many children. To this day he is still hale and hearty, hardly troubled by the common ailments of old age.

I met another of these men, a citizen of Leoben, when he was about the age of forty. He likewise from puberty on had been subject to the menstrual flow, and during the period in which the flow occurred he begot many children. Once the flow stopped, his fertility also ceased and he was struck by disease; beset by an obstinate fever, consumption, ravings, and frenzies, he soon ended his life.[2]

Cases of periodic bleeding in men, interpreted as "vicarious menstruation," are frequently reported in the medical literature and the learned periodicals of early modern Europe. What shall we make of these menstruating men we encounter, not in accounts from a Pacific island but while browsing over the pages of the German *Ephemerides medico-physicae*, the *Journal des savants*, the *Philosophical Transactions* of the Royal Society? Male menstruation is a phenomenon we associate — if we ever consider it at all — with cultures very distant from our own.[3] Thanks to a series of anthropological classics on New Guinea, from the works of Margaret Mead and Gregory Bateson in the mid-thirties to Gilbert Herdt's *Rituals of Manhood* in the

---

2. Johann Baptist De Wenckh, "De duobus viris styriacis fluxum menstrualem sanguinis per penem patientibus," MNC, dec. 3, ann. 9–10, 1706, obs. 136, pp. 258–61 (quotation at pp. 258–59). Biographical information on De Wenck in A. Hirsch, ed., *Biographisches Lexicon der hervorragenden Ärzte aller Zeiten und Volken,* 3rd ed. (Munich: 1963) 5:897. The Academia Naturae Curiosorum was founded in Schweinfurt in 1652. Its periodical publication, *Miscellanea curiosa sive ephemerides medico-physicae germanicae* (MNC) first came out in 1670. The *Ephemerides* were devoted to medicine and allied sciences, as it is stated in the prefatory address to the European scholars in the first volume: see Saul Jarcho, "Seventeenth-Century Medical Journalism," *Journal of the American Medical Association* 220, no. 1 (1972): 64–68; J. Walther, *Die kaiserliche deutsche Akademie der Naturforscher zu Halle* (Leipzig: 1925); Leo Stern, *Zur Geschichte und wissenschaftlichen Leistung der Deutsche Akademie der Naturforscher* (Halle: Saale, 1952).

3. In Western culture, interest for the problem of "male menstruation" has been evinced almost exclusively by psychoanalysis. See, besides Bruno Bettelheim's classic, *Symbolic Wounds* (Glencoe, Ill.: Free Press, 1954) also R. W. Lidz and T. Lidz, "Male Menstruation: A Ritual Alternative to the Oedipal Transition," *International Journal of Psychoanalysis* 58 (1977): 17–31; K. A. Menninger, "Psychogenic Influences on the Appearance of Menstrual Period," *International Journal of Psychoanalysis* 22 (1942): 60–64 (a case of profuse nose-bleeding defined as "vicarious menstruation").

eighties,[4] we have learnt that rites involving artificial bleedings — explicitly meant as vicarious menstruation — may play a crucial role in the social construction of male identity. In some Melanesian cultures male flesh is cut open to emulate the menstruating female body.

In the European case we are going to examine, in contrast, the stories of menstruating men do not seem related, at first sight, to the ritual manipulation of the body, but rather to the scholarly observation of natural phenomena. Among the men who viewed a loss of blood from the male genitals as a form of menstruation we find the most prominent anatomists of the sixteenth and seventeenth centuries: men whose names are landmarks in the history of European medical learning — men such as Thomas Bartholin, one of the "discoverers" of the lymphatics, and the prince of Renaissance anatomists himself, Andreas Vesalius.

In *De humani corporis fabrica* Vesalius reports that he once dissected "a man who suffered from the complaint called hemorrhoids . . . ; at regular intervals this man used to have a flow of blood from the anal veins, in the very same way in which women have their menstrual flux."[5] The analogy between this hemorrhoidal flow and female menstruation is so self-evident, in Vesalius's eyes, that he applies the observations gathered from the dissection of this male corpse to throw light on a problem concerning the anatomy of menstruation. (He discusses this dissection in the chapter of *De humani corporis fabrica* devoted to the uterus and the other female reproductive organs.) Vesalius was trying to solve the following anatomical question: where does the menstrual blood come from? Does it gradually collect in the cavity of the uterus or does it come from the veins of the cervix and the vagina, which discharge it monthly through their orifices? Vesalius leaned to this second hypothesis primarily on the ground of what he observed in dissecting the man who suffered from hemorrhoids.

4. Margaret Mead, *Sex and Temperament in Three Primitive Societies* (New York: W. Morrow, 1935); Gregory Bateson, *Naven* (Stanford, Calif.: Stanford University Press, 1936); Ian Hogbin, *The Island of Menstruating Men* (Scranton, Pa.: Chandler, 1970); Gilbert Herdt, *Guardians of the Flutes: Idioms of Masculinity* (New York: McGraw-Hill, 1981); J. F. P. Poole, "The Ritual Forging of Identity: Aspects of Person and Self in Bimin-Kuskusmin Initiation", in *Rituals of Manhood: Male Initiation in Papua New Guinea,* ed. Gilbert Herdt (Berkeley, Calif.: University of California Press, 1982); Gilbert Herdt, "Sambia Nose-bleeding Rites and Male Proximity to Women," *Ethos* 10, no. 3 (fall 1982).
5. Andreas Vesalius, *De humani corporis fabrica* (Basel, 1555), bk. 5, chap. 15, pp. 662–63.

Opening this cadaver — he relates — he found that "the branch of the portal vein under the final tract of the colon as well as the portion of the same vein running along the mesentery all the way to the rectum was swollen with blood." "I infer from this," concludes Vesalius, "that something similar happens in women, although I have never been able to actually observe it in the dissection of a female body." [6] Vesalius's reasoning is based on the implicit premise of a functional equivalence between hemorrhoids and menstruation. This premise allows him to extend his observations by way of analogy from the male to the female body. To his mind, somehow, both appear to be menstruating bodies.

Our notion of menstruation as a specifically female trait stands in stark contrast with these descriptions of menstruating men. These stories clearly imply perceptions of what is male and female that differ from ours in one of its most basic tenets. Furthermore, these stories seem to gainsay what has been argued insistently in recent studies of medical discourse on gender in European intellectual history. Historians have stressed that from antiquity to the late eighteenth century European medical learning was dominated by a model of sexual difference centered on the male paradigm. The model emphasized the similarity of the sexes, but the male was the dominant term of the analogy; in other words, the male body was the *Gestalt,* the paradigm that guided the perception of the female body. As it has been argued most radically by Laqueur: up to the end of the eighteenth century, there had been one basic structure for the human body, the type of the male.[7]

But was it really so? The stories of menstruating men we are dealing with in this essay seem to contradict this statement. In these stories we see early modern doctors understand male bodily phenomena through the model provided by the female menstruating body. True, also these stories empha-

6. Vesalius, *De humani corporis fabrica* 5.15.662–63. The book's subject index refers to this passage under the heading "Haemorrhoidum fluxus par ratio cum menstruo sanguine."

7. Thomas Laqueur, *Making Sex: Body and Gender from the Greeks to Freud* (Cambridge, Mass.: Harvard University Press, 1990). For a similar thesis see also Giulia Sissa, "The Sexual Philosophies of Plato and Aristotle," in *A History of Women in the West,* vol. 1, *From Ancient Goddesses to Christian Saints,* ed. Pauline Schmitt Pantel (Cambridge, Mass.: Harvard University Press, 1992), 46–82 and Danielle Gourevitch, *Le Mal d'être femme* (Paris: Les Belles Lettres 1984) for classical antiquity; Danielle Jacquart and Claude Thomasset, *Sexuality and Medicine in the Middle Ages* (Princeton, N.J.: Princeton University Press, 1988) for the Middle Ages; Londa Schiebinger, *The Mind Has No Sex? Women in the Origins of Modern Science* (Cambridge, Mass.: Harvard University Press, 1991), 189–211 for the early modern age.

size the similarity of the sexes. Just as the ovaries were perceived as "female testicles," so could a hemorrhoidal bleeding be perceived as a menstrual flow. Also in this case observation was guided by analogical inference. But with a crucial difference: the primary term of the analogy in this case was the female. Let us pay these stories closer attention.

II

I should mention, first of all, that the stories of menstruating men reported in the medical sources were based on direct empirical observation. Even when the belief in male menstruation is brought up in second-hand compilations of *loci communes,* as for instance in the comment on Aristotle and Averroes by Antonio Zimara, the author adds, after registering the opinion of another commentator according to which "men also are subject to menstrual flows": "I myself have personally known a man, now in his eighties, who every month used to have an hemorrhoidal flux."[8]

The Spanish physician Andrés a Laguna wrote in 1551: "I have seen with my own eyes several men, especially in Lotharingia and Germany, who were regularly subject to the female purgations and had milk in their breasts — men, to be sure, given to idleness and dissipation, and effeminate on account of diet and lack of exercise." According to Laguna, there is nothing strange in this phenomenon: "In just the same way in which the menstrual flow, as we know, is discharged each month in women, it stands to reason that also in men, from time to time, the superfluous excrements of the blood, which could not be dispersed through urination, sweating, or insensible perspiration, run to the testes by way of the seminal vessels and reach the neck of the bladder, to be finally evacuated through the urinary channel."[9]

In noticing these cases, early modern doctors firmly believed to be ob-

---

8. Antonio Zimara, *Tabulae dilucidationum in dictis Aristotelis, et Averrois* (Venice, 1576), fol. 239v.

9. Andrés Laguna, *Methodus cognoscendi, extirpandique excrescentes in vesicae collo carunculas* (Rome, 1551), 6–7. On Andrés a Laguna (1499–1563) see Hirsch, *Biographisches Lexicon* 3:587. Cf. Girolamo Fabrizzi (Fabricius ab Aquapendente) (1533–1619), *Opera anatomica et physiologica* (1687), pt. 2, bk. 3, chap. 13, p. 1022: "As the menses occur each month in women, thus also in some men the superfluity of blood, which could not be discharged through urination, sweating or insensible perspiration, runs to the testicles and is evacuated through the urinary channel."

serving something that "stands to reason," to use Andrés a Laguna's words; a phenomenon—we could say—that confirmed their expectations and theories about the ordinary course of nature. We need, of course, to understand these doctors' theories. But before we do that, that is, before we reconstruct the intellectual context of these stories, let us first consider the medical genre in which they appeared. This genre is usually either the *curatio*, a short narrative of the unfolding of a case from the onset of disease to its conclusion, either with recovery or death; or the *observatio*, which was devoted to the reporting of natural events in general. Both *observationes* and *curationes* have a basic narrative structure: they are always formulated as stories (*historiae*).[10]

Collections of curationes and observationes were the primary medium for the circulation of medical information in the early modern period. As a rule, both recorded firsthand observations but also frequently included— often quoted word by word—accounts of similar cases culled from earlier scholars. A seventeenth-century reader would have conveniently at hand anthologies of these stories neatly arranged by subject, such as the *Observationes medicae, rarae et novae* by Johann Schenck, published in Basel between 1584 and 1597—a massive collection, and a basic reference text for medical readers up to the eighteenth century.[11] The authors of curationes and observationes drew on a shared tradition of medical texts, regularly and precisely quoted. This tradition guided the medical observers, pointing out which phenomena were worthy of observation. Observation was meant as a cumulative contribution to a common body of knowledge, based on a Europe-wide network of scholarly exchange. The periodicals published by the learned academies in the second half of the seventeenth century[12]

---

10. The rules for writing in these medical genres were described by Hieronymus Perlinus, *Binae historiae, seu instructiones medicae. . . . Methodus compendiarie scribendi huiusmodi historias seu instructiones* (Hanover, 1613). The narrative structure of the curationes is obviously rooted in the Hippocratic tradition, particularly in the model of the case histories narrated in *Epidemics*.

11. An abridged edition, in two volumes, ed. J. Rhodius, was published in Frankfurt in 1600: see Leslie Thomas Morton, *A Medical Bibliography* (Aldershot, England: Scholar Press, 1989), p. 294.

12. The *Philosophical Transactions* (PT) of the Royal Society were first published in 1665, as was the *Journal des savants,* issued simultaneously in Paris and Amsterdam. The *Ephemerides* of the Academia Naturae Curiosorum were launched in 1670 (until 1706 they came out under the title of *Miscellanea curiosa, sive Ephemerides medico-physicae;* since 1712 under

continued and developed this tradition. Journals such as the *Ephemerides medico-physicae Academiae naturae curiosorum*, the *Acta medica et philosophica Hafniensia*, the *Journal des savants*, the *Philosophical Transactions*, adopted the narrative form of the observatio — and turned it into one of the standard forms of scientific communication of the times.

Such are the sources in which we find the stories of menstruating men. It should thus be noted that the observations of periodical bleedings in males were not the result of independent observations but of a shared intellectual tradition that singled out the phenomenon as noteworthy. This tradition dated back to classical antiquity. In Pliny's *Natural History,* for instance, in the context of a comparison between blood in animals and in the human species, we find this curious statement: "In the human race alone a flux of blood occurs in the males, in some cases at one of the nostrils, in others at both, with some people through the lower organs, with many through the mouth; it may occur at a fixed period, as recently with a man of praetorian rank named Macrinus Viscus, and every year with the City Prefect Volusius Saturninus, who actually lived to be over 90." [13] In the eighteenth century this Plinian passage was still quoted as evidence that a chronic periodical bleeding was conducive to longevity.[14] It is important to stress, however, that the early modern stories of menstruating men were not merely the rehashing of a curiosity from the repertory of the ancients. It is quite clear that medical attention to this phenomenon was prompted by a lively interest of the learned community of the time. This is shown by the fact that the observations of menstruating men, sporadic in sixteenth-century medical literature, become much more frequent in the second half of the seventeenth century. An original nucleus of stories, taken from famous Renaissance medical authors such as Antonio Benivieni, Vesalius, and Amatus Lusitanus,[15] is repeatedly quoted in the seventeenth and early eighteenth

that of *Ephemerides, sive Observationes medico-physicae*); the *Acta eruditorum* were published in Leipzig from 1682 to 1731 (see "Das medizinische Zeitschriftenwesen in Deutschland bis zur Mitte des 18. Jahrunderts," in *Sudhoffs Archiv für Geschichte der Medizin* 21 [1929]: 276). The *Acta medica et philosophica Hafniensia,* ed. Thomas Bartholin, were issued in Copenhagen from 1671 to 1679. On the history of medical journalism see W. F. Bynum, Stephen Lock, and Roy Porter, eds., *Medical Journals and Medical Knowledge: Historical Essays* (London: Routledge, 1992) (basically limited to British and U.S. journals).

13. Pliny, *Naturalis historia* 11.90 (vol. 3, p. 573 in the Loeb Classical Library ed., 1983).

14. See for instance Martin Schurig, *Haematologia historico-medica* (Dresden, 1744), p. 237.

15. The cases from Vesalius and Amatus Lusitanus are quoted here in nn. 5 and 40. For the

century. But descriptions of cases of menstruating men are found much more frequently in seventeenth-century observationes, and especially in the learned periodicals that start to be published in the second half of that century.[16] Beyond a doubt, the early modern medical community seems to have provided a particularly favorable context for the observation and discussion of these cases.

Reading the *Ephemerides*, for instance, one realizes immediately that these stories excited quite a lively interest in the medical readers. Consider, for example, how a German physician, Dr. Simon Schultz, prefaced an observatio sent to the Academia in 1673:

> Going over the second year of the German *Ephemerides* I read the observatio n. 192, entitled "Hemorrhoids flowing monthly in a man," contributed by the esteemed doctor Ehrenfried Hagendorn, practician in Görlitz. This reminded me of a similar case, in the person of the illustrious Haymon Rigius from Hamburg, bachelor of philosophy and later doctor of medicine, now practicing in Rostock, who used to be my intimate friend and confidante when we both lived in Leiden. This fellow from the age of eighteen used to have a hemorrhoidal flow for a few days each month, with great benefit to his health. And

---

case from Antonio Benivieni see his *De abditis nonnullis ac mirandis morborum et sanationum causis*, ed. Charles Singer (1507; Springfield, Ill.: Thomas, 1954), 4:26–28.

16. The largest survey of cases of menstruating men is in Martin Schurig, *Parthenologia historico-medica, hoc est virginitatis consideratio qua ad eam pertinentes pubertas & menstruatio, cum ipsarum maturitate, item varia de insolitis mensium viis . . .* (Dresden, 1729), pp. 118–25; see also of the same author, *Haematologia*, especially pp. 302–4. Schurig's review clearly shows that most of the observations were from seventeenth-century medical literature. J. D. Reuss, *Repertorium commentationum a societatibus litterariis editarum* (Göttingen, 1801–2) (a listing by subject of articles published in European scientific periodicals, compiled at the end of the eighteenth century) includes under the terms *menstrua marium* (male menstruation) and *haemorrhoides* mostly the articles published in the *Ephemerides* of the Academia Naturae Curiosorum (14:151; 13:433–34). See also W. G. Ploucquet, *Literatura medica digesta, sive Repertorium medicinae practicae, chirurgicae, atque rei obstetrice* (Tübingen, 1809), s.vv. *menstrua marium* (3:10); *haemorrhagia ex pene* (2:255). Male menstruation was also the topic of doctoral dissertations discussed at the Medical Faculty of Paris: see Jacob Nicolas and Paul Quineffault, *Ergo par feminis omnibus mensium necessitas* (Paris, 1577); Jean-Antoine Elie de la Poterie and François Thierry de Bussy, *An viris lex eadem qua mulieribus, periodicas evacuationes pati?* (Paris, 1764).

truly, if this flow did not appear at the appointed time, or was scarcer than usual, he would complain of not feeling well.[17]

As is the case here, these are often stories that the doctors learnt from having intimately known the menstruating men as personal friends rather than patients. Some of these stories appear to be based on confidential disclosures from man to man about a peculiar experience that cut across social distinctions (the cases reported concern men of every social class — beggars and peasants as well as patricians and intellectuals). Intimate male gossip, we might call it, clad in the dignified garb of medical observation. Take as one more example this story from the *Ephemerides* of 1684:

> The nobleman Felix Rauschart, counselor to the duke of Saxony and a most honored friend of mine, a man of sanguine and melancholic complexion, when he was a student in Ratisbona, at the age of twenty, was affected for the first time with a hemorrhoidal flow. Nature has ever since regularly repeated this flux every month up to the present day (although now, at the age of sixty, he enjoys somewhat less frequently this blessing of nature — as it was so appropriately called by Hippocrates in his *Aphorisms* (IV:24 and VI:11 and 21). It should be noted that every time the hemorrhoidal discharge is irregular either in time or quantity, his natural faculties appear to be disturbed and weakened in consequence: namely, he is afflicted by constipation, difficulty in breathing, inflammation of the hypochondrium accompanied by general exhaustion of body and soul. As soon as the flow comes back, all these symptoms disappear.[18]

---

17. Simon Schultz, "De haemorrhoidum menstruo & ordinario fluxu in viro," MNC, dec. 1, ann. 4–5 (1673–74), obs. 44, p. 37. Another doctor, after reading the observatio by Schultz, sent another report on the same subject (J. L. Hanneman, "De haemorrhoidum menstruo et ordinario fluxu in viro," MNC, dec. 2, ann. 1 [1682], obs. 70, p. 175).

18. J. G. Sommer, "Haemorrhoides in viro jam per quadraginta annos periodo menstrua redeuntes," in MNC, dec. 2, ann. 3 (1684), obs. 107, pp. 217–18. As one can see, the protagonists of these stories seem to have given themselves a menstrual interpretation of their symptoms, irrespective of medical opinion. Thus for example in another observatio a doctor reports: "I knew a mason, now dead, who from the age of twenty to that of sixty had a hemorrhoidal flow every month, at regular intervals like menstruation in women. He used to say that he was troubled by the same symptoms that affect menstruating women, whenever their flux is blocked or too abundant; and that the same remedies used for the menses were helpful

In these two stories the association of hemorrhoids and menstruation is quite clear.[19] In the case of other forms of periodical bleedings in males, the menstrual interpretation is not always categorically stated, but almost always openly suggested. The Roman physician Domenico Panaroli, for instance, wrote: "A certain mason, at regular intervals, presents a recurring flow of blood from a leg: an external varicose vein ruptures spontaneously and the blood flows thereof. The same vein closes up again on its own, without application of remedy of any sort. If this happened in a woman, I certainly, like any other physician, would declare confidently that her menstruation is coming out that way."[20] Many authors who relate such cases of male bleeding call it downright *fluxus menstruus* or *menstrualis*. We even find expressions such as *vir menstruatus* or *vir nenstruus* (menstruating man), and, in French, *homme réglé*.[21]

And yet these stories seem to be told without any embarrassment, often identifying the menstruating men by name and social rank. These men were openly named although still living and although (given the fact that the *Ephemerides* had European circulation)[22] the news of their menstruating condition was presumably going to be spread all over Europe. The possibility that identifying a man as menstruating might stigmatize him as effeminate, does not seem to have been a matter of concern. The fact is that,

---

also in his case" (E. Hagendorn, "Haemorrhoides in viro singulis stillantes mensibus," MNC, dec. 1, ann. 2 [1671], obs. 192, p. 294).

19. The menstrual interpretation of some cases of hemorrhoids was commonplace in the medical literature. See for instance Johann Schenck, *Observationes medicae rariores* (Frankfurt am Main, 1665), bk. 3, "De haemorrhoidibus," p. 358; in Reuss's bibliography the heading *menstrua marium* (male menstruation) is cross-listed with the heading *haemorrhoides* (*Repertorium commentationum* 14:151).

20. Domenico Panaroli, *Iatrologismorum, seu medicinalium observationum pentecostae quinque* (Rome, 1652), p. 65.

21. For example: J. M. Fehr, *De absinthio* (Leipzig, 1667), p. 138 (*nobilis menstruatus*); Georg Franck, "Vir menstruus," in MNC, dec. 2, ann. 6 (1687), p. 174; Carrère, "Observation sur un homme réglé par un doigt de la main," in *Histoires et mémoires de la Société Royale de Médecine* (1780–81), p. 287.

22. The *Ephemerides* had among its contributors, beside German authors, also English, Danish, Swiss, and Italian scholars, and seems to have addressed a correspondingly wide European public; see J. Stendel, "Die internationale Tendenz der Ephemeriden der Academia Naturae Curiosorum," *Acts of the 14th International Congress on History of Medicine* (Rome, 1954), pp. 457–59.

in contrast with what we might expect, the stories of menstruating men do not mostly concern cases of hermaphrodites. Andrés a Laguna's hint about the effeminacy of the menstruating men from Lotharingia and Germany, quoted above, is quite exceptional among these stories.[23] Much more often what is stressed is the link between vicarious menstruation (hemorrhoidal or otherwise) and positive traits such as longevity and fertility. Thus doctor Simon Schultz, whose circle of acquaintances seems to have included quite a number of menstruating men, reported to the *Ephemerides:*

> In one of my farms out of town lives an old man over eighty, but still very vigorous and lecherous [*salacissimus*] who earns his bread by making wicker baskets. This man since his early youth until now has been subject to the hemorrhoidal flow and this flow recurs every month, regularly and copiously, accompanied by pains in the lower back and abdominal colic. He lives with his father-in-law, a man over ninety, who goes around begging alms. To this other man also since his youth Nature has allotted the menstrual flow. . . . I am persuaded that this flow has been a factor of these men's longevity, because Nature rids herself of superfluous and impure blood with great advantage to health.[24]

There is no connection here between male bleeding and effeminacy. Moreover, it is clear that the description of menstruation in these men does not involve any negative association or stigma. And yet a sinister rumor about menstruating men was circulating around Europe in those same years.

---

23. It is true, however, that we find another example in a curatio by Zacutus Lusitanus: "I knew a man, without a beard or hair in all his body, like a woman or an eunuch, to whom from the twentieth to the forty-fifty year of age the menstrual purgations flowed abundantly from the genital parts, every month at the same time, for four or five days; and if occasionally they were irregular, he felt a pain with abdominal cramps, which was relieved by letting blood from the heel. He never married and died of a pleurisy, originated by the retention of the menses" (*Praxis medica admiranda* (Lyons, 1637), lib. 2, obs. 11, p. 69). Cases of hermaphrodites, to whom "the menstrual blood poured out through the channel of the penis" are reported by Martin Schurig, *Spermatologia historico-medica* (Frankfurt am Main, 1720), pp. 592ff. (but seem to be classified as different from the cases of menstruating men). 24. Simon Schultz, "De haemorrhoidum fluxu a prima juventute ad decrepitam usque aetatem durante," in MNC, dec 1, ann. 4-5, p. 54.

III

Concluding the historia I quoted in opening this essay (the case of the men-struating manservant from Copenhagen), Thomas Bartholin noted: "If we are to believe what Michael Scotus says in the tenth chapter of his *Physiognomia,* the Jews by nature have a flow of some drops of blood from the penis in connection with the moon, just as it happens to women."[25] This medieval belief was ominously associated, in the Middle Ages and still in the early modern period, with the accusations of ritual infanticide leveled at some Jewish groups.[26] As R. Po-Chia Hsia has shown, in several commu-nities of central Europe in the early modern period the Jews are accused of kidnapping and killing Christian male children, allegedly in order to use their blood for therapeutic purposes, and in particular to stop the men-strual flow which afflict their men.[27] The accusation is documented in the same period in several anti-Semitic works written in Spanish and Portu-guese circles.[28]

Isaac Cardoso, a Jewish physician of Iberic origin, the author of one of the most important texts of Jewish apologetics, *Las excelencias de los he-breos* (1679), made a direct rejoinder to this accusation.[29] Cardoso's rebuttal was aimed specifically at a tract written in 1632 by a Spanish literatus, Don Juan de Quiñones, whom Cardoso had personally known in Madrid in the years he was living in Spain as *marrano.* The occasion of Quiñones's tract had been an *auto-da-fé* conducted in Madrid in 1632. Among the persons condemned as "Judaizers" there had been one Francisco de Andrada "of whom it was said that he suffered every month the flux of blood which

25. Bartholin, *Historiarum anatomicarum,* p. 55.

26. Thomas of Cantimpré (ca. 1200–ca. 1270), *Miraculorum et exemplorum memorabilium sui temporis libri duo* (Douay, 1605), pp. 305–6 (mentions the accusation of ritual murder); Michael Scotus, *Liber physiognomiae* (Venice, 1477), chap. 10.

27. R. Po-Chia Hsia, *The Myth of Ritual Murder* (New Haven, Conn.: Yale University Press, 1988).

28. See for instance Vicente da Costa Mattos, *Breve discurso contra a heretica perfidia do Iudaismo* (Lisbon, 1623), fol. 131rv; Francisco de Torrejoncillo, *Centinela contra judios* (Pamplona, 1691), p. 174. See also Léon Poliakov, *The History of Anti-Semitism* (New York: Vanguard Press, 1965), 1:143; Joshua Trachtenberg, *The Devil and Jews* (New Haven: Yale University Press, 1943), pp. 51, 148.

29. Yosef H. Yerushalmi, *From Spanish Court to Italian Ghetto: Isaac Cardoso, A Study in Seventeenth-Century Marranism and Jewish Apologetics* (New York: Columbia University Press, 1971), pp. 122–33, 435–37. My thanks to Michele Luzzati for referring me to this book.

nature has given to women, and which is called menstruation." [30] As some people entertained doubts about this fact, Quiñones decided to write an essay aimed at proving that "among other maledictions both corporal and spiritual, within and upon its [the Jewish] body, . . . there is one which is: that every month many of them show a flux of blood in the posterior parts as a perpetual sign of ignominy and opprobrium." [31] Quiñones admitted the possibility of an alternative and natural explanation of this phenomenon: in consequence of their diet, the Jews could be disproportionately afflicted by the disease called hemorrhoids. He also conceded that some cases of male menstruation had been reported among non-Jews. But all the same he was firmly persuaded that the male menstrual flow was a bodily stigma that revealed a secret Jewish identity even in converted Jews, and he urged the Inquisition officers to carefully examine any suspect of Judaism for this sign.

Cardoso's rebuttal of Quiñones in *Las excelencias* is worth being quoted in full:

We must not omit a charming episode which occurred in Madrid about thirty years ago, more or less. There was an *alcalde* of the Court named Don Juan de Quiñones, a curiously learned man of variable erudition and a huge library, who wrote several treatises and specialized books. . . . And, among others, he compiled one . . . proving that Jews have a tail, and that like women they are subject to menstrual periods, and blood, as punishment for the grave sin which they committed. Within a very short time he developed hemorrhoids in certain parts, so great and huge, and accompanied by blood and pain, that they actually seemed tail-like. In the company of a surgeon, I then said to him: "Your honor must also be liable in the sin of that death [i.e., of Christ], for we see in you the same affliction, and just as you have written that the Jews have a tail and blood, you too have the same." And so, the conversation continuing in jest, he began to laugh and said that he did not agree with this, for he had been well proved to be an *hidalgo* of La Mancha, and the discussion moved on. But he remained with the defect which he imputed to the Jews.[32]

30. Quoted by Yerushalmi, *Spanish Court,* p. 127.
31. Yerushalmi, *Spanish Court,* p. 128.
32. Yerushalmi, *Spanish Court,* p. 23.

Undoubtedly, as Yerushalmi has argued in his excellent biography of Cardoso, the Jewish scholar's biting reply to the Christian literatus was rooted in Cardoso's passionate return to the Jewish faith and culture after his experience as marrano. But I would like to point out that Cardoso was countering the anti-Jewish legend not just as a Jew but also as a physician. For a physician, in fact, discrediting Quiñones's argument was an easy job. A doctor of Galenist training, such as Cardoso,[33] would be well aware of numerous observations of periodical bleedings in males, adequately explained by perfectly natural causes. All the stories of menstruating men that show up in the reports of the learned academies in the very same years in which Cardoso was writing *Las excelencias* did evidently contradict the anti-Jewish legend by proving that periodical bleeding occurred in men of various ethnic groups. In a communication sent to the Academia Naturae Curiosorum in 1687, the physician Georg Franck openly criticized the anti-Jewish libel: "I am utterly skeptical about this rumor, because it is clearly against both reason and experience, and because those Jews who have converted to Christianity have persuaded me of its falsity."[34] It is true instead, Franck argued, that several medical authorities such as Andrés a Laguna, Fabrizzi d'Acquapendente, Zacutus Lusitanus, and Thomas Bartholin have

33. On Cardoso's Galenist training at the University of Valladolid see Yerushalmi, *Spanish Court*, p. 77. In a later *summa* of his philosophical and medical ideas, *Philosophia libera*, Cardoso described the menses in conventional Galenist terms, admitting the possibility of "vicarious menstruation" in women and men (he quoted the case of menstrual hemorrhoidal flow reported by Vesalius). Interestingly, he also strove to reconcile the Jewish rules about menstrual impurity with the Galenic positive notion of menstruation as cleansing, by arguing that the biblical notion of "impurity" did not mean that the menstrual blood was actually physically contaminating ("aliud est esse immundum aliud esse noxium": *Philosophia libera* [Venice, 1673], 6:418–23, esp. 422–23). The problem of the interplay of ideas about menstruation in Jewish religious tradition and in ancient medical lore is complex: some Midrash sources, apparently, implied that menstruation was originally also a male lot (see Riccardo Di Segni, "Colei che non ha mai visto il sangue": Alla ricerca delle radici ebraiche dell'idea della concezione verginale di Maria," *Quaderni Storici* 25, no. 3 [1990]: 788 n. 25).

34. Georg Franck, "De viro menstruo," in MNC, dec. 2, ann. 6 (1707), p. 174. Franck repeated this argument in his *Satyrae medicae* (Leipzig, 1722), p. 93. For biographical data on him see Hirsch, *Biographisches Lexicon* 2:595. Franck does not quote Cardoso, who is mentioned instead, as a conclusive rebuttal of the legend of male menstruation among the Jews by the Abbé Grégoire's *Essai sur la régénération physique, morale et politique des Juifs* (Metz, 1789), p. 46.

affirmed that some men are prone to menstrual flows to the great benefit of their health. Only the ignorant—Franck implied—view such menstruating men with abhorrence, as evidenced by the case of "a butcher from
Sedun who every month discharged menstrual blood from the urethra.
When this news spread among the populace, the man became an object of
execration and nobody would buy meat from his shop any longer." [35]

Most likely, the physicians who reported cases of menstruating men in
the early modern period were aware of the implications of these cases as a
rebuttal of the anti-Jewish legend as well as a confutation of the idea that
menstruation (in males or females) is a punishment or stigma of God's
sending. And in the case of Dr. Franck, at least, they seemed to consider
these notions as vulgar superstition. In this respect, the reports of menstruating men implied an attitude that I would unhesitatingly define en-
lightened—an attitude thoroughly skeptical as to explanations of bodily
phenomena based on other than natural causes. It is relevant to notice, in
this respect, that the medical theory of cyclical hemorrhages was used by
these same physicians to refute the supernatural interpretation of bleeding
corpses as miracles proving the sanctity of the deceased. The same physicians who reported cases of menstruating men also argued that the bleedings from holy bodies should be understood as due to purely mechanical
or chemical causes.[36]

What was the impact of the anti-Jewish legend on the observation of
cases of menstruating men? Was the wish to refute the Jewish menstrual
stigma the main reason why the scholars reported such cases? This question is undoubtedly relevant, especially if one considers that some of the
doctors quoted so far, such as Andrés a Laguna, Amatus, and Zacutus Lusitanus, were actually of Jewish origin [37] and had therefore a direct stake in
the issue. On the other hand, it is a fact that several non-Jewish physicians,
such as Vesalius or Fabrizzi d'Acquapendente, or the many correspondents
of the Academia Naturae Curiosorum, were just as active in reporting periodic male bleedings. A careful reading of the sources admits no doubt that
these cases appeared as noteworthy to the doctors for reasons that were

35. Franck, "De viro menstruo," p. 174.

36. Schurig, *Haematologia*, pp. 310–13.

37. See Harry Friedenwald, *The Jews and Medicine* (Baltimore, Md.: Johns Hopkins University Press, 1944), 2:332–45 (on Amatus Lusitanus); pp. 307–17 (on Zacutus Lusitanus), and
p. 428 (on Andrés a Laguna, but in his case the evidence of Jewish origin is uncertain).

foremost medical. The fact is that attention to periodic bleedings was routine, so to speak, in early modern medical culture. Furthermore, a negative notion of menstruation (or any other periodic bleeding) as divine punishment did not make any sense from a medical point of view, because current doctrine held a strongly positive view of menstruation as beneficial to health. We shall see this in more detail by examining the medical theories on hemorrhoids.

IV

As we have seen, many of the stories of menstruating men concern in fact cases of hemorrhoids. Here are a few more examples, selected at random among the many that could be quoted: "A clergyman in the Duchy of Bremen was prone to hemorrhoids, and if they did not flow at the appointed time he used to be afflicted by the same symptoms that trouble women when their menses are suppressed." Domenico Panaroli described the case of an old man who in his youth, whenever ailing, would recover after a discharge of blood from the hemorrhoidal veins. In the *Ephemerides* of 1722 we read the report of a singular case of menstrual-hemorrhoidal synchronization in a couple: the case of a husband who for eight days every four weeks was subject to a hemorrhoidal flow in exact coincidence with the menstrual period of his wife.[38]

The parallel between menstruation and hemorrhoids was commonplace in the Galenist tradition. Here is how it was formulated, for instance, in an early medieval commentary on Galen's *De sectis*: "The flow of blood occurs not only through these [hemorrhoids] but also through the nose, and also by what is called menstruation or menstrual flow in women, from the fact that each month an evacuation of their bodies occurs. When the ignorants see this [the hemorrhoidal flow] they are frightened and they will say that a disease is supervening upon a disease and they strive to check the flow of blood; the learned will ask if it happens on a critical day, [and if it does] they will say that it is a great help and an indication of health and rather to be welcomed."[39]

38. L. Hannemann, in AMH, 3, obs. 18, p. 30; Panaroli, *Iatrologismorum*, p. 56; J. M. Müller, in MNC, cent. 9–10 (1722), obs. 68, p. 377.

39. Agnellus of Ravenna, *Lectures on Galen's De Sectis,* text and trans. Seminar Classics 609

The grounds for the analogy were the following: both flows (hemor-rhoidal in males and menstrual in females) are cyclical; both are due to plethora, a periodic surplus of blood in the body; both are conducive to health. Indeed, because of their analogy to menstruation, hemorrhoids were seen as a *morbus salutaris,* a symptom to which the well-informed physician would give a benign meaning. Such positive view of chronic hem-orrhoids seems to have been commonplace not only with physicians but also with the lay public. Several curationes relate cases of patients who got accustomed to hemorrhoids as a "normal" part of their life, but reacted with alarm to other forms of bleeding. Thus, for instance, in a much quoted curatio by Amatus Lusitanus:

> John Baptist Propola, a man over forty-five, once affected by the French pox, for a long time had been regularly subject, every month, to a copious evacuation of blood from the hemorrhoidal veins, in the same way in which women menstruate. But in one occasion this discharge ceased to flow in the usual way for a few days, while he started to lose blood from the mouth without any other symptoms. . . . Deeply alarmed at this, he sought medical advice. . . . I, after diligently considering every symptom, as in duty bound, enjoin the man to be of good cheer and prescribe that four leeches be immediately applied to his hemorrhoidal veins. . . . After this treatment little by little the blood once again took to its normal route. When the (hemorrhoidal) flow was resumed, the man regained his usual good health.[40]

The notion of hemorrhoids as morbus salutaris dictated what was for many centuries the canonical treatment for this condition in European medicine: therapy was supposed to avoid a total suppression of the flow, because this suppression (like the arrest of menstruation in women) would lead to more serious diseases. This therapeutic rule dated back to antiquity: it is already present in the Hippocratic corpus and was amplified, with

(Buffalo, N.Y.: State University of New York, 1981), pp. 72–73 (I have slightly revised the trans.). Cf. Galen, *Opera omnia,* ed. C. G. Kühn (Leipzig, 1821–33), 5:696; 11:165–66.

40. Amatus Lusitanus, *Curationum medicinalium centuria V* (Venice, 1653), vol. 5, cur. 3, pp. 17–21. Thomas Bartholin quotes the case of a sixty-year-old Danish nobleman, who had been subject for thirty years to a periodic vomit of blood, and who had become so accus-tomed to this "salutary evacuation" that, if it stopped occasionally, "he feared for his own life" (*Historiarum anatomicarum,* cent. 3, hist. 36, p. 76).

plenty of clinical details, in the treatise *On Acute and Chronic Diseases* by Aretaeus of Cappadocia (A.D. 81–?138)—a text that even in the eighteenth century, physicians often quote as an authority on this topic.[41] According to Aretaeus, the functional analogy between menstruation and hemorrhoids implied that a similar treatment (venesection or other forms of bloodletting) should be prescribed for both the retention of the menses or the interruption of a chronic hemorrhoidal flow, in order to avoid the more serious diseases that could derive from these conditions. Like Aretaeus, also Galen described cases of *emoptoe* (vomit of blood) caused by "ill-advised suppression of the hemorrhoidal flow" as well as instances of *hydrops* and *tabes* also occasioned by the interruption of the same. Furthermore, he argued that those who are affected by hemorrhoids are immune from more serious diseases (in particular, from melancholia).[42] This Galenic notion is emphatically reasserted in Avicenna's *Canon*: "Be advised that the blood flowing from hemorrhoids or from the anus provides immunity [*securitas*] from herpes, folly, melancholia, melancholic epilepsy, erysipelas . . . cancer, scabies, baldness, leprosy. . . . And when the blood that used to flow from these parts is retained (inside the body), one of these diseases is to be feared."[43] Repeating advice already offered in a Hippocratic aphorism, Avicenna recommended that when incising or cauterizing hemorrhoids, the practitioner leave one open so that "the corrupted blood, that Nature is accustomed to pour out in this way, can still find an outlet."[44]

Many centuries after Avicenna, the belief in the salutary character of the hemorrhoidal flow was still widespread. Here, for example, is what the famous English actor David Garrick wrote to a male friend in 1771: "Thank ye Stars for ye Piles—if you had not them, you would have gout,

41. Aretaeus, *De causis et signis acutorum et diuturnorum morborum*, ed. H. Boerhaave (Leiden 1730), p. 47c, pp. 53–54, pp. 118C and 125A.

42. Galen, *Opera* 11:170 and 166; 18A:21 (on *hydrops* and *tabes* as a consequence of the suppression of hemorrhoids); 16:453; 17A:327 and 17B:107 and 344 (hemorrhoids prevent various diseases); 16:454 and 459; 17B:108 and 286; 18A:33 (they prevent or cure melancholia).

43. Avicenna, *Liber canonis* (Venice, 1490), bk. 3, fen 17, tract. 5, chap. 2.

44. Avicenna, *Liber canonis*, bk. 3, fen. 17, tract. 5, chap. 4. Furthermore, Avicenna recommended that the so-called blind or deaf hemorrhoids (i.e., those that do not bleed) be also cut open to resume the bleeding (chap. 3). The Hippocratic aphorism recalled by Avicenna is the following: "If a patient is cured of chronic hemorrhoids, unless one is left standing, he is in danger of dropsy or phtisis" (6, 12; Loeb ed., vol. 4, pp. 182–83). Cf. Galen, *Opera* 18A:22.

or Stone or both and ye Devil and all—While I had ye Piles, I had Nothing Else, now I am quit of them, I have Every other disorder." [45] Nor was this, at this point, as we might be inclined to think, a mere "popular belief," discarded by learned medicine. In Thomas Bartholin's *Anatomia reformata* (1651) the hemorrhoidal veins are so described: "They are those veins that run to the anus and to the rectum, visible also from the outside; in some men, at regular times, they open spontaneously to let out an evacuation of thicker blood—a discharge very useful to health." [46] In the eighteenth century, the ancient medical tradition does still heavily influence the theory and treatment of hemorrhoids. Thus several curationes emphasize the adverse consequences of any attempt to stop a chronic hemorrhoidal flow. Consider for instance this case history, that describes, by the way, a very interesting interaction between doctor and patient:

A youth about thirty years old, fairly vigorous but highly hypochondriac, had had for a very long time a monthly and very abundant hemorrhoidal flow. Tired of this symptom, he sought the help of a surgeon, who prescribed astringent remedies, whereupon the hemorrhoidal flow stopped, almost by divine intervention. But after a few months he had a very plentiful bleeding from the nostrils, which kept recurring every month, making him extremely weak. . . . He tried to stop also this bleeding with refrigerants, both internally and externally applied, astringent remedies and other similar medications, prescribed by the same surgeon. With the following result: the blood, that had tried to find a vent out of the body first through the anus and then through the nostrils, now started to come out of the penis—mixed with urine . . . again at regular monthly intervals. In consequence of all this, the patient, in great anxiety, sought my advice. First of all, I proved to him that this clearly menstrual evacuation, which Nature—

45. *Letters of David Garrick,* ed. David Little and George Kahrl, 3 vols. (Cambridge: Harvard University Press, 1963), 2:743, quoted in Dorothy Porter and Roy Porter, *Patient's Progress: Doctors and Doctoring in Eighteenth-Century England* (Stanford, Calif.: Stanford University Press, 1989), p. 42.
46. Thomas Bartholin, *Anatomia reformata de circulatione sanguinis* (Leiden, 1651), p. 425. As an example of the persistence of this view of hemorrhoids in early modern clinical literature see for instance J. C. Frommann, *Tractatus singularis de haemorrhoidibus* (Nüremberg, 1677), esp. pp. 115–20 (on periodicity); 136–41 (on the analogy with menstruation); Michael Alberti, *Tractatus de Haemorrhoidibus* (Halle, 1722).

or rather the blood's orgasm—had tried to effect by various routes, ought to be accepted without fear of worse consequences; that, of all the routes taken by the blood, the initial one through the hemorrhoids was the most convenient and preferable, as being Nature's own first endeavor. I advised him that every month, right before the menstrual orgasm, whose onset he was able to anticipate and predict from general lassitude and other symptoms, he should forward the egress of the blood with a light massage . . . as well as with fomentation and hot baths. With the favor of God, this was the story's ending: . . . the hemorrhoidal flow returned and has kept returning every month to this very day, for over twenty years, with the man enjoying excellent health.[47]

Here is a poor fellow who cannot accept his condition of menstruating man and is finally reconciled to it—at least according to the doctor's version of the story—only by the failure of his repeated attempts to entrap blood that every month seeks obstinately a way out of the body. For the doctors, bleedings were an ambiguous sign: some were symptom of a fatal disease, but others—those that recurred periodically in absence of other morbid conditions—indicated instead a positive turn toward recovery. Otherwise said, they were, in early modern medical language, "critical" hemorrhages, the benign symptoms of a "crisis"—a positive step toward natural, spontaneous healing. This was considered to be the case not only for hemorrhoids but also for other forms of periodic bleeding.[48]

---

47. Schurig, *Parthenologia*, p. 124. A similar case history is narrated by the Irish physician Arnold Boate (Bootius), *Observationes medicae de affectibus omissis,* in H. Moinichen, *Observationes medico-chirurgicae* (Ferrara, 1688), chap. 7, p. 25: the Irish archbishop James Usher was subject to a periodic flow of blood from the mouth: "For a long time every remedy was tried in order to eliminate this symptom, but once it became clear that his system was accustomed to this evacuation, he stopped trying to suppress it. For I had warned him that such suppression would inevitably be injurious to him, as Nature by then had turned this flux to advantage, by eliminating in this way a superfluous burden, whenever the blood or the humors mixed with it were in excess." For another example of the futility of the attempt to stop a periodic hemorrhage, as the blood "thus stopped seeks for another outlet," see Rembert Dodoens (Dodoneus), *Medicinalium observationum exempla rara* (Amsterdam, 1571), chap. 14, p. 36.

48. On Galen's conception of "critical" hemorrhages see *Opera* 11:577 and 15:344. Various cases positively resolved by a "critical" hemorrhage are recounted by Zacutus Lusitanus, *Praxis medica admiranda* (Lyons, 1637), bk. 1, obs. 54, p. 13 (a spontaneous flow of blood from

In consequence of this the doctors viewed any effort to alter a condition of menstruating man as sheer folly: not only was it a useless effort, because nature is stronger than any remedy, but more importantly, it was a dangerous effort, which might lead to death. Thus several curationes report cases of men who tried, usually with the help of remedies prescribed by empirics and quacks, to stop a menstrual flow of blood from various parts of the body and in consequence died, or fell into more serious conditions.[49] I will quote one of these cases—one more variation in the meandering of the menses on their way out of the body—described by Dr. William Musgrave in 1701 for the readers of the *Philosophical Transactions* of the Royal Society:

Mr H. formerly a Servant to *Queen Dowager,* of late to Mrs Jennings, of Burton in Somersetshire; had (from his Infancy, as he has been inform'd, but to his certain knowledge) from as far back as he can remember, up to the twenty fourth year of his age, a Periodical Haemorrhage in one of his Thumbs. The *Time* of the Eruption was about the full of the Moon, seldom more than a day before or after it. The *Orifice* . . . on the Right side of the Nail of the Left Thumb. . . . The *Manner* of the Flux was also remarkable; for, without any Pain of Head, Straightness of Breath, or any signs of Fulness, . . . the Blood used to spin out, with a considerable force, on a sudden, in several little streams, and continue so to do, until the greater part of the quantity was discharged. Under this discharge, however copious, he was

---

the eyes heals a case of vertigo); obs. 86, p. 88 ("sanguinis ex gingivis profluvium criticum"); bk. 2, obs. 70, p. 242 ("mictus sanguinis criticus"); bk. 3, obs. 72, p. 481 ("sudor sanguineus criticus"). Many such cases are reported in the *Ephemerides* of the Academia Naturae Curiosorum: for instance, Samuel Ledel, "De fluxu haemorrhoidum per aures," MNC, dec. 3, ann. 5 and 6, obs. 365, pp. 616–17 (a bleeding from the ears cures a headache due to the stopping of a chronic hemorrhoidal flow).

49. P. Salmuth, *Observationes medicae* (Brunswig, 1648), cent. 3, obs. 47, p. 134: a clergyman afflicted by a periodical ("quasi-menstrual") passing of blood with the urine, and wishing to get rid of this symptom, sought the advice of a woman healer. She administered him a potion that stopped the flux, but a few days later the man was stricken with "great closeness of the lungs and difficulty of breathing" and died shortly thereafter. For similar cases: C. Roesler, "De haemorrhoidum fluxu (suppresso, mortem inferente)," MNC, dec. I, ann. 3 (1672), p. 543; J. Bötticher, "Apoplexia levis et pedis dextri paresis, a fluxu haemorrhoidali suppresso oborta, tandemque in apoplexiam funestam terminata," in *Acta Academiae Naturae Curiosorum* 6:162.

strong and vigorous to the age of twenty four. . . . At that age (of 24) finding this Evacuation troublesome, and being uneasie under it, he sear'd with a hot Iron the part, which used to open, and give vent to the flux of Blood. . . . This stoppage was in its effects very dangerous, and of ill consequence; for within one quarter of a year after it he fell into a *Sputum Sanguinis;* bringing up from his lungs vast quantities of Blood. This new Complaint, together with a Cough attending it, reduced him very low. . . . In short he has, ever since the stoppage of that first Haemorrhage, been weak, sickly, of a sallow, faint look; much impair'd as to health, in comparison to what he enjoy'd during the time of its Periodical Returns.[50]

As the reader may notice, the therapeutic moral of the stories of menstruating men is remarkably constant: the flow should not be inhibited but encouraged. Beyond a doubt, in these stories, the various forms of bleedings from the male body are perceived not as pathological but as salutary. Nor are they presented as a disturbing phenomenon—an anomaly that violates the order of nature. Rather, as William Musgrave points out in the text I have just quoted, they are seen as evidence that "when Nature has chosen, and for some lengths of time exercised new and extraordinary methods of Oeconomy, she seems to be as fond of their Continuance, as at other times, and in her most regular state, she is of that which is her most usual and ordinary course." One should never interfere with Nature, not even when she takes an extraordinary course.

The cases of menstruating men were clearly, for early modern physicians, something that they found "good to think," something that seemed to support a theory that they found persuasive and whose truth they wanted to advocate. We must now turn to a closer examination of these theories.

50. "A letter from Dr William Musgrave F.R.S. to the publisher concerning a very extraordinary Periodical Haemorrhage," *P T* no. 272 (1701): 864–66 (also published as "Observatio de rara haemorrhagia periodica," in *AE* [1702]: 95–96). For other cases of male menstruation under lunar influence see Richard Mead, *De imperio solis et lunae,* in William Musgrave, *De arthritide anomala* (Amsterdam, 1710), pp. 368–69; Michael Ettmüller, *Opera* (Frankfurt am Main, 1695), 2:1010.

V

The cases of menstruating men were part, for early modern physicians, of a wider issue, the problem of menstruation's "unusual pathways." It was believed that the menstrual blood, when impeded in its normal passage, would search for another way out of the body through various channels and orifices. Thus in female bodies, first of all, bleedings from the nostrils, the nipples, the mouth, and other body parts, when coincident with the absence or interruption of the menses, were commonly interpreted as "vicarious menstruation."

Also this notion derives from ancient medicine, as shown by several passages from the Hippocratic corpus.[51] Galen noted that when the menses are blocked inside, the blood can find a way out through other passageways, for example through the nose or the urethra.[52] In the Renaissance medical literature the observations of "unusual pathways" of the menstrual flow are very numerous. Antonio Benivieni, the noted Florentine physician, described many cases of devious menstrual flow, mostly discharged through vomit; the Dutch doctor Dodoens related the case of a "plethoric" virgin whose menses would flow out of her eyes, in the form of bloody tears; Johan Rode reported the case of a Bolognese nun, whose menses used to come out of the alveolus of a tooth.[53] Many, and much quoted, the cases mentioned by Amatus Lusitanus, cited by Locke, for instance, in his medical notes: "Amatus Lusitanus writes that he saw two women whose courses were stopped, and who passed blood at intervals through their breasts."[54]

51. The Hippocratic treatise *De morbis mulierum* discusses at length the theme of the menses trapped inside the body because of the obstruction of their normal outlet. But *Aphorisms* and *Epidemics* also refer several times to nosebleeds or hemorrhoids as alternative outlets of the menses: see Ann Hanson, "Diseases of Women in the Epidemics," in *Die hippokratischen Epidemien — Theorie, Praxis, Tradition: Verhandlungen des Ve Colloque international hippokratique*, ed. G. Gaader and R. Winau, Sudhoffs Archiv (1989), 7:44–45.
52. Galen, *Opera*, 17B:822 (nose-bleeding); 5:138 (blood passed with urine). See also Areateus, *De Causis et signis*, p. 13D.
53. Benivieni, *De abditis* 41:92; 60:124. R. Dodoens, *Medicinalium observationum exempla rara* (Amsterdam, 1571), chap. 15 ("De lachrymis sanguineis"); J. Rhodius (Johan Rode), *Observationes medicae*, cent. 3, obs. 51, p. 146. See also, for instance: C. Stampart van der Wiel, *Observationes rariores* (Leiden, 1687), cent. post., p. 196 ("menstrua vomitu egesta").
54. Quoted in Kenneth Dewhurst, *John Locke, 1632–1704: Physician and Philosopher* (London: Wellcome Historical Medical Library, 1963), p. 106. Cf. Amatus Lusitanus, *Curationum medicinalium centuriae septem* (Venice, 1653–54), cent. 2, curatio 21, pp. 80–81.

In the seventeenth and eighteenth centuries a vast body of medical literature — much more extensive than that dealing with menstruating men — is devoted to the problem of menstruation's "unusual pathways." [55] "It would be a massive enterprise to review all the observations that describe in how many ways and through which channels this devious evacuation finds a way out of the body," we are told in a doctoral dissertation entitled *De mensium insolitis viis,* submitted to the medical faculty of Halle in 1707, under the supervision of Georg Ernst Stahl.[56] In Lipenius's *Bibliotheca realis medica* (1679) — the most important subject guide to medical literature of the seventeenth century — we find, next to headings like *mensium suppressio* (suppression of menstruation) or *menstruorum immodicum profluvium* (excessive menstrual flow), the heading *menstruorum per os ejectio* (emission of menstruation from the mouth).[57] In a repertory by subject of the articles published on European medical journals of the seventeenth and eighteenth centuries, the topic *insolitae viae* (unusual pathways) by itself amounts to about one fourth of all the articles dealing with menstruation.[58] Beyond doubt, the issue of menstruation's unusual pathways was central to the discussion of the menstrual phenomenon within the medical community of the early modern period.

The same authors who reported cases of menstruating men were also very keen on describing instances of "unusual pathways" of menstruation in female bodies. Thus for instance the already quoted Dr. Schultz added to the vast literature documenting the issue of menses *per aliena loca fluentes* the following case: "An eighteen-year-old virgin, who from her early youth carried on her left knee, on both sides, an abscess generated by nature, started to be affected in her nineteenth year by a suppression of her menstrual flow. But soon, at the exact time when the menses were bound to flow, an opening in the abscess discharged blood in sufficient quantity, and this hemorrhage was supplemented by a vomiting of blood. The bleeding from the abscess has been coming back regularly every month for a year now."[59]

55. For an extensive review of this literature see Schurig, *Parthenologia,* pp. 84–117.

56. G. Jaeschke, *De mensium insolitis viis* (Magdeburg, 1707).

57. Martin Lipen, *Bibliotheca realis medica* (Frankfurt am Main, 1679), p. 273; we find the heading *Menstruorum per os excretio* also in the earlier medical subject index by Iohannes Antonides van der Linden, *De scriptis medicis,* 3rd ed. (1637; Amsterdam, 1662), p. 737.

58. Reuss, *Repertorium commentationum* 14:141–59.

59. Simon Schultz, "De menstruis per aliena loca fluentibus", MNC, dec. 1, ann. 4–5 (1673–

The observations of menstruating men and those of the menses unusual pathways were related to one and the same theory, which was also the theory that provided an explanation for menstruation. This was the Galenic theory of "plethora," namely a pathogenic excess of blood. For Galen, plethora was a fundamental cause of disease because excess blood fueled fevers and inflammation; whence the usefulness of natural hemorrhages such as, prototypically, menstruation.[60] Rehearsing the traditional Galenist doctrine on this argument, John Freind wrote in his *Emmenologia* (1721):

> So entirely does the menstruous Flux depend upon a plethora, that if the uterine vessels are too strong or obstructed, the Blood opens itself another passage; therefore some other evacuation frequently supplies the place of the uterine flux. There are many instances in Authors of women who, upon a suppression of the Menses, have had at a stated time, salutary discharges of Blood by the Haemorrhoids . . . ; at the nostrils . . . ; by the Pores of the Skin . . . ; by Urine . . . ; and vomit . . . , which Hippocrates in Aphorisms (V, 32, 33) rightly lays down as a token of a crisis. . . . It will not be impertinent in this place to mention that periodick Flux of Blood which is also found sometimes in Men. . . . This takes its rise from a plethora as in Women, and conduces very much to health; if it is suppressed, a distemper ensues. . . . Upon the suppression of this periodick evacuation in Men, the Health is not only destroyed, but exactly the same symptoms arise as do usually in Women destitute of a monthly Relief; so that if the suppression be of any long continuance, they become plainly Histerick. . . . This periodick Flux (for it is salutary) let it flow from what Channels soever, is excited by a Plethora and ought to be termed Menstrua.[61]

Built into the ancient theory of plethora was considerable ambiguity as to the difference of the sexes. As the reader might well wonder by now: why

---

74), obs. 74, pp. 59–60. Other examples: M. B. Valentin, "Menstrua per ulcus tibiae emissa," MNC, dec. 2, ann. 5 (1686), p. 186; J. Calder, "Two Cases of Praeternatural Menstruation (per ulcus ad malleolum)," *Memoirs of the Medical Society of London* (1776), 3:502.

60. Galen, *Opera,* 6:375; 11:164. For illuminating remarks on Galen's theory of plethora and its significance in Greek medical tradition see Shigehisa Kuriyama, *The Expressiveness of the Body and the Divergence of Greek and Chinese Medicine* (New York: Zone Books, 1999), pp. 208–27. For a Renaissance collection of texts on plethora see *Liber de plenitudine* (Paris, 1528).

61. John Freind, *Emmenologia,* trans. T. Dale (1721; London, 1729), pp. 64–67; see also pp. 40, 58.

do most women menstruate while most men do not? The answer provided by the plethora theory stressed differences both in the physical constitution and the lifestyle of males and females. Here is the traditional argument as we find it rehearsed in an eighteenth-century treatise on menstruation:

> It is well known from Hippocrates that woman is weaker than man; that her flesh is softer and more loosely knit; that she works at less arduous tasks, and in consequence dissipates less humor, and by the same account she produces and collects in her body more blood; which blood . . . finds the most convenient way out through the uterus. Whereas man, made of stronger and more tightly-knit fibers, when healthy and vigorous, more easily discharges the superfluous humors by way of insensible perspiration; and he normally has sensible evacuations more abundant than usual only once every season.[62]

These sensible evacuations, we are told, may consist "either in urine, more plentiful and thicker than usual; or in a belly discharge, or in a bleeding," this last being the case described in the stories of menstruating men.

As the reader can see, there is considerable ambiguity in this statement: on the one hand, we are told that man does not menstruate because his physical constitution is superior; but on the other hand we are told that periodic evacuations occur also in men — in other words, that something like menstruation also happens in them, somehow. In fact, and in spite of the assumption of male superiority (which implied that men do not need to menstruate), early modern medical observations betray the widespread belief that some form of periodic evacuation is absolutely necessary also for male health. Thus Santorio Santorio stated in his very influential *De statica medicina* (1614): "The bodies of men in health, and who use a moderate diet, become every month heavier than usual, by the weight of one or two pounds; and about the end of the month return to their usual weight, after a crisis has been made by urine, more than ordinary copious and turbid." [63] This "crisis made by urine" is described by Santorio as analogous to menstruation. He stresses the similarity between women's condition "at the approach of the flux" and that of men before this critical urination: "Before this monthly crisis, there is either felt a heaviness in the head, or a

62. A. Pasta, *Dissertazione sopra i mestrui delle donne* (Bergamo, 1757), pp. 41–42 and n. 13.
63. S. Sanctorius, *Ars . . . de statica medicina aphorismorum sectionibus septem comprehensa* (Duisburg, 1753), sec. 1, aph. 55.

weariness of the body, and afterward by a very plentiful evacuation of urine everything is at ease. In like manner in women, as soon as the menses have done flowing, the former vigor again returns." [64] Clearly the superiority of the male body as to capability for sweating and insensible perspiration, was not seen as sufficient to fend off the danger of plethora. Santorio's treatment of this issue, as well as the stories of menstruating men, show that a periodic critical evaluation, analogous to the female menses, was deemed indispensable also for male health.

VI

In the seventeenth and eighteenth centuries the conventional Galenic doctrine of plethora was challenged by new theories, foremost among them the iatrochemical theory, which saw the cause of menstruation in the fermentation of blood.[65] And yet the new theories did not question the "fact" of periodic bleedings in men, which seems to have been taken as an observational given. Actually, several reports of menstruating men were offered in order to disprove the theory of plethora and to support instead the newer, alternative theory. For example, Dr. de Wenck, whose observatio of two cases of menstruating men we read above, argued that the menstrual phenomenon is not caused by plethora but by a periodic fermentation of the blood manifesting itself as sexual excitement, like estrus in animals (hence his emphasis on the extraordinary fertility and "lechery" of his menstruating men).[66]

In a sense, there is nothing surprising in this: a new theory of menstruation had to cover the whole array of existing observational data, of which the stories of menstruating men were part and parcel. The increasing attention to cases of menstruating men or of the menses "unusual pathways," that is so evident in the learned journals of this period, was certainly part of

---

64. Sanctorius, Ars . . . de statica, sec. 1, aph. 55.
65. Critics of the theory of plethora who supported the fermentation theory include Regner de Graaf, De mulierum organis generationi inservientibus, in Opera (Leiden, 1677), pp. 260ff.; J. B. Verduc, De l'usage des parties (Paris, 1696), 1:236; G. Sandri, De naturali et praeternaturali sanguinis statu (Frankfurt am Main, 1712), pp. 248–49. The iatrochemical theory of menstruation is analyzed in detail by Hans Georg Müller-Hess, Die Lehre von der Menstruation vom Beginn der Neuzeit bis zur Begründung der Zellenlehre (Berlin: Ebering, 1938), pp. 35–47.
66. De Wenck, "Dissertatio physica de muliebri menstruo sanguine causisque ejusdem periodici profluvii," MNC, dec. 3, ann. 4 (1696), p. 205; see also n. 2 above.

the penchant for the preternatural, the bizarre, the marvelous, that played such a key role in seventeenth-century investigation of nature;[67] but it was also fueled, no doubt, by the lively debate on competing theories of menstruation. What is remarkable is that the new theory did not question the observational basis of the traditional theory: that is to say, the new theory raised no doubt as to the actual existence of the phenomenon classified as male menstruation. The fact is that the new theory, although advanced as an alternative to the doctrine of plethora, shared with it a deep assumption. What was this assumption?

Let us look at the stories of menstruating men or of the menses "unusual pathways" simply as *stories,* stories with an ending. They are all—either when intended to prove the theory of plethora or that of fermentation—stories with a happy ending: examples of longevity, fertility, or recovery. On condition, though, that Nature be left to work her own way. If one hinders her efforts, as we know, the outcome of the story is negative. Nature is unquestionably the protagonist of these stories. What the early modern doctors found "good to think" in these cases was the reassuring evidence of a providential notion of nature to which they were deeply attached. These stories were carefully registered and reported because they allowed to find and show, in an apparently insignificant detail such as the bleeding of a thumb, a manifestation of that wondrous force, the healing power of nature.

The importance of the *vis medicatrix naturae* in the Galenist tradition is well known. The historian Max Neuburger has devoted a detailed monograph to this subject, showing the pervasiveness of this idea in Western therapeutic theories and practices—a pervasiveness stretching well beyond the decline of Galenism.[68] From the Renaissance to the eighteenth century, the collections of *curationes* emphasize, even more than the therapeutic action of the medical practitioner, the healing endeavor of nature herself. One element is common to all the phenomena identified as signs of nature's healing effort: they are all cases of bodily discharge. The evacuation of the corrupted humor was seen as the sign and goal of a natural

67. Lorraine Daston, "Marvelous Facts and Miraculous Evidence in Early Modern Europe," *Critical Inquiry* 18 (1991): 93–124; Lorraine Daston and Katharine Park, *Wonders and the Order of Nature, 1150–1750* (New York: Zone Books, 1998), chap. 6.
68. Max Neuburger, *The Doctrine of the Healing Power of Nature throughout the Course of Time,* Eng. trans. (New York, 1932).

healing process. From Amatus Lusitanus to Thomas Bartholin to Georg Ernst Stahl, the medical texts list an impressive catalogue of remarkable cures operated by nature through various forms of evacuation: not only, as we already know, all sorts of bleeding (including menstruation, epistaxis, expectoration of blood, hemorrhoids); but also vomiting, diarrhea, sweating, skin eruptions, as well as even more unusual kinds of evacuation, astounding examples of nature's adventurous exploits in driving disease out of the body. For instance, Tulpius's *Observationes medicae* report a case of healing wrought by the passing of pus from the patient's nostrils. Valleriola describes a case of pleurisy without expectoration, in which the patient recovered thanks to a belly discharge.[69]

This notion of healing as the result of nature's effort to expel the corrupted humor is found not only in the medical literature. It was very important also in the popular perception of disease, and it guided the practice of popular healers. In ancien régime Bologna, for instance, a vernacular term employed to designate several diseases was *mal d'oppilazione* (obstruction sickness). This term covered a multitude of ailments all perceived as involving a pathogenic retention of humors inside the body.[70] The primary meaning of "oppilation" was the obstruction of a water flow: the diseased body was thus described as one whose channels were plugged. From this point of view, the main purpose of treatment was removing the obstruction, and this precisely was the goal of most of the remedies employed by popular healers. Therapy was typically seen as an artificial replica of nature's effort to push out the corrupted humor: if the body was unable to accomplish this on its own, a healer was called on to reach the same result by artificial means.

In popular culture as well as in learned medicine, the healing power of

69. Both quoted by Neuburger, *Doctrine*, p. 38. Antonio Benivieni described the case of a twelve-year-old boy whose urinary passage was obstructed: after seven days, the urine came out of the anus: "Nature, to whom all things are possible, must have opened similar channels to void the urine and save the boy. How marvelous are Her works" (*De abditis*, p. 32; see also p. 122). For Domenico Panaroli, the observation of a case of menstruation discharged from the nipples prompts a fervid eulogy of nature's healing power: "Vidimus Naturam in angustiis positam vias incognitas invenire; audivimus monstrosa, et fere incredibilia; legibus observationes quae miraculo proximae existunt. Omnia haec tamen ab immensa ipsius bonitate proveniunt" (*Iatrologismorum*, pp. 235–36).
70. See Gianna Pomata, *Contracting a Cure: Patients, Healers, and the Law in Early Modern Bologna* (Baltimore, Md.: Johns Hopkins University Press, 1998), chap. 5, esp. pp. 129–35.

nature was thus identified with the *facultas expultrix*, the "expelling faculty" of the body. This notion was basic in the Hippocratic-Galenic concept of "crisis." The crisis (a positive turning point in the course of disease) was usually identified with some form of bodily discharge. Thus "critical" evacuations, such as the cases of vicarious menstruation we have examined above, were seen as positive signs of nature's healing endeavor. In the seventeenth century, far from becoming obsolete, this idea is expressed most forcibly in Sydenham's view of disease as a process striving at the excretion of "peccant matter."[71] All this is well known. Less noticed so far have been the implications of the idea of the "healing power of nature" for the relation between male and female body. In this conception of the healing process, the abstract entity "nature" was identified with something very specific indeed: the lowest and humblest among bodily processes, the body's excretory function. The body—but which body? It was the female body that was the primary model of nature's healing. In the Galenic tradition, menstruation was the paradigm of critical evacuations, the clearest instance of nature's healing endeavor. Thus, notwithstanding the asserted superiority of the male, it was in fact the female that was exemplary from a therapeutic point of view. The arrow of the analogy between the sexes moved in this case from the female standard.

The prototypical role of menstruation within the Galenic theory of healing is most clearly indicated by the key role of bloodletting among Galenic therapies. Bloodletting, the arch-remedy against plethora, was but an artificial replica of what nature performs by means of menstruation, as Galen himself tells us in *De venae sectione adversus Erasistratum*. In the female body, nature displays the paramount example of her healing power, an example that has prescriptive value: it shows the physician what he ought to do. In defending the therapeutic usefulness of bloodletting, Galen's strongest argument is the benefit that women enjoy thanks to their natural flow:

> "Does she (nature) not evacuate all women every month, by pouring forth the superfluity of blood? . . . If you had the intelligence to understand further what great benefits accrue to the female sex as a result of this evacuation, and what harm they suffer if they are not cleansed, I don't know how you would be able to go on wasting time and not eliminate superfluous blood by every means at your dis-

71. Neuburger, *Doctrine*, pp. 38–41.

posal. . . . Has a woman ever been known to be stricken with phrenitis, or lethargy, or spasm, or tremor, or tetany, while her menstrual periods were coming? Or did you ever hear of a woman who suffered from melancholy or madness or haemoptysis or haematemesis, or headache, or suffocation from synanche, or from any of the major and severe diseases, if her menstrual secretions were well established? . . . But enough of women for the present; come now to consider the men, and learn how those who eliminate the excess through a hemorrhoid all pass their lives unaffected by diseases, while those in whom the evacuations have been restrained have fallen into the gravest illnesses. Will you not let blood from these men?[72]

I cannot deal adequately here with the issue of the connection between menstruation and bloodletting implied by this Galenic text. It is, however, a very clear connection: the reader will have noticed that bloodletting is invariably the remedy prescribed in the curationes to treat every form of retention of blood (either menstrual or hemorrhoidal), as well as to draw a devious flow of blood back to its "usual pathway." Here I would simply like to point out that for many centuries in European history bloodletting was a bleeding ritual that men willingly submitted themselves to. True, venesection was also practiced on women; but as observed in a phlebotomy textbook of 1601, "if a woman has her periods naturally and regularly, phlebotomy is not necessary."[73] These medical notions that may seem so flimsy to us today had important practical consequences. The link between bloodletting and menstruation would seem to suggest that also in the European case, as in that of the Melanesian men described by the anthropologists, the male body was cut open to emulate the menstruating female

72. Galen, *Opera*, 11:165–66 (Engl. trans. in Peter Brain, *Galen on Bloodletting: A Study of the Origins, Development and Validity of His Opinions, with a Translation of the Three Works* [Cambridge: Cambridge University Press, 1986], pp. 25–26; see also pp. 46–47, 83). The analogy between menstruation and bloodletting is obvious in ancient medicine, where the uterus is often compared to the "cupping-jar" used for letting blood: the image is present in the Hippocratic treatise *Ancient Medicine;* in Soranus's *Gynecology* (see Ann Hanson, "Continuity and Change: Three Case-Studies in Hippocratic Gynecological Therapy and Theory," in *Women's History and Ancient History,* ed. Sarah B. Pomeroy (Chapel Hill: University of North Carolina Press, 1991), pp. 89 and 107 n. 87; and also in Rufus of Ephesus (98–117 A.D.) *Oeuvres de Rufus d'Ephèse,* ed. C. Daremberg (Paris, 1879), p. 183.
73. Simon Harward, *Phlebotomy; or A Treatise of the Letting of Blood* (London, 1601), p. 79.

body. And perhaps when European anthropologists in the thirties interpreted the male bleeding rituals in Oceania as "vicarious menstruation," the idea was suggested by practices in their own culture. This can be legitimately surmised at least in one case. When Ashley-Montagu in 1937 explained the rite of penis subincision in Australia by arguing that with it "men were trying to produce an artificial menstruation in their bodies," he noted also that "bloodletting has among most people been practised for the same reason, and is still so practised to this day among the peasantry of Europe."[74]

My readers will forgive me if I ask them at this point to read one more story of menstruating man. What is special about this story is that it is a "self-observation": here a man tells us in the first person how he perceived his own (menstruating) body. Dr. Schultz, some of whose contributions to the Academia Naturae Curiosorum we have already read, sent one more, entitled *De haemorrhagia menstrua critica*. By *haemorrhagia*, he explained, he meant "that critical flow by which means Nature, at regular intervals, ejects . . . through the nostrils that (blood) which is noxious or harmful to her."

> Such hemorrhage I have long experienced myself since the age of eighteen: almost every month the blood used to flow plentifully and easily [*cum euphoria*] from my right nostril. I am still occasionally subject to this flux, although no longer each month but much more rarely, and it is still beneficial to my health. The flow, in fact, is always preceded by heaviness or headache and inflammation of the face, symptoms that disappear immediately once the flow starts. And to tell the truth, if the blood does not run spontaneously, I have the habit of irritating the tiny veins in my right nostril with a goose quill, whereupon the blood flows, bringing me the accustomed relief.[75]

---

74. M. F. Ashley-Montagu, "The Origin of Sub-Incision in Australia," *Oceania* 8 (1937–38): 205. Interestingly, also Hogbin (*Island of Menstruating Men*, p. 207 n. 34) noted a European analogue to Melanesian notions observing that "the Galenic conception of menstruation is very similar to the Wogeo notion of menstruation." The parallel between Australian bleeding rites and European bloodletting has been discussed recently by another anthropologist, James L. Brain: "Male Menstruation in History and Anthropology," *Journal of Psychohistory* 15, no. 3 (1987): 311–23.

75. Simon Schultz, "De haemorrhagia menstrua critica," MNC, dec. I, ann. 4 and 5 (1673–74), obs. 45, pp. 37–38.

What we see here is a man whose perception of his own body is deeply influenced by the model of female physiology. The periodic flux of blood that gives him relief is something that he perceives as part of his normal condition: "a regular and ordinary aspect of nature," as he calls it—of his own nature, not just of that of women. A female conception of nature, as we see, may have very important consequences, theoretical as well as practical.

VII

The stories of menstruating men are thus related to a complex set of ideas, deeply rooted in European medical learning, according to which menstruation was viewed as of great prophylactic and therapeutic value. The sources of such a view are legion. Beside Galen (who expounds it very clearly in the passage quoted above) we can easily trace it already in the Hippocratic texts, where menstruation, together with nosebleeds, diarrhea, copious urination, and the like are listed as "crises" that bring about recovery.[76] Avicenna calls menstruation "the cause of women's health and of the body's cleansing."[77] In the Middle Ages, Albertus Magnus attributed women's superior longevity, among other things, to the effect of menstruation.[78] Sixteenth- and seventeenth-century commentators on the Hippocratic and Galenic texts rehash, as common opinion, the notion that "this evacuation preserves women from many diseases." In the seventeenth century, the therapeutic value of menstruation is stressed by Sydenham, among others. Freind calls it unambiguously "a salutary crisis, not a disease: a remedy given by nature."[79] Even the Hippocratic notion that some ailments can

76. See Hanson, "Diseases of Women in the Epidemics," pp. 44–45; Leslie Dean-Jones, "The Cultural Construct of the Female Body in Classical Greek Science," in Pomeroy, *Women's History*, p. 119.

77. *Liber canonis*, bk. 2, fen 21, tract. 3, chap. 1, 291v: "causa sanitatis mulierum et mundificationis corporis."

78. Albertus Magnus, *Quaestiones super De animalibus*, 15, qu. 8, in *Opera omnia* 12 (Muenster: Verlag der Aschendorffscher Velagsbuchhandlung, 1955), p. 263. Cf. Vern Bullough and C. Campbell, "Female Longevity and Diet in the Middle Ages," *Speculum* 55, no. 2 (1980): 107; and C. T. Wood, "The Doctor's Dilemma: Sin, Salvation and the Menstrual Cycle in Medieval Thought," *Speculum* 56, no. 4 (1981): 724.

79. Thomas Sydenham, *Morborum acutorum historiae*, quoted by Freind, *Emmenologia*, p. 69; Freind, *Emmenologia*, p. 16 for the definition of menstruation as "a salutary crisis, not a disease."

be healed by the onset of menstruation (menarche) is retained by early modern commentators.[80] And as we might expect, the *Philosophical Transactions* of the Royal Society and the *Ephemerides* of the Academia Naturae Curiosorum print stories of recoveries brought about by the onset of menstruation.[81] As a matter of fact, the early modern term used to indicate the menses in several European vernaculars—purgation—clearly shows that the therapeutic meaning of the menstrual phenomenon was foremost even in everyday language.[82]

And yet the history of medicine has asserted that European medical discourse ever since antiquity has viewed menstruation negatively as a stigma, a brand of women's physical inferiority. Even scholars of deep knowledge of ancient medicine, such as Esther Fischer-Homberger and Paola Manuli, have uncritically repeated this stereotype. Fischer-Homberger, for instance, wrote in her book *Krankheit Frau*: "From the viewpoint of humoral pathology, a woman was constitutionally sick."[83] She did not perceive the contradiction between this statement and the fact that, as she

80. See for instance Valesius (Francisco de Vales, 1524–1592), *Commentaria in septem libros Hippocr. De morbis popularibus* (Orleans, 1655), sec. 7.

81. See for instance J. C. Westphal, "Menstrua dysenteriam solventes," in MNC, dec. 2, ann. 8 (1689), p. 537; G. Heintke, "Menstruatio dysenteriae remedium," in MNC, dec. 2, ann. 5 (1686), p. 108; J. G. Gulerand, "Epilepsia tum gravidae tum lactantis infanti innoxia, et paralysis eruptis catameniis soluta," in AMH 1:84.

82. *Purghe* was a common term to indicate menstruation in Italian (see, e.g., Scipione Mercurio, *La commare o riccoglitrice* [Venice, 1621], p. 72); for the English "purgations," see Patricia Crawford, "Attitudes to Menstruation in Seventeenth-Century England," in *Past and Present*, no. 91 (1981): 50. Schurig, *Parthenologia*, pp. 27–29, offers an extensive review of the vernacular terms for menstruation in several European languages.

83. Esther Fischer-Homberger, *Krankheit Frau* (Bern, 1979), p. 49; Paola Manuli, "Donne mascoline, femmine sterili, vergini perpetue: La ginecologia greca fra Ippocrate e Sorano," in *Madre materia: sociologia e biologia della donna greca*, ed. Silvia Campese, Paola Manuli, and Giulia Sissa (Turin: Boringhieri, 1983), p. 159. In his pioneering work on ancient gynecology (*Die Frauenheilkunde der Alten Welt: Handbuch der Gynaekologie* 12, pt. 1 [Munich, 1937]) Paul Diepgen has also fallen into this contradiction. He does recognize that the gynecological treatises of the Hippocratic corpus as well as the Galenic texts attributed a therapeutic function to menstruation. He also observes that "the Hippocratic authors never said that a woman is impure or poisonous during her menstrual period." And yet he concludes that the ancient authors "viewed menstruation as an excrement, like feces or urine. Through this notion, the popular belief in the impure and polluting character of the menstrual blood found support in scientific medicine" (pp. 128–29).

herself pointed out, menstruation was seen as "a form of natural blood-letting." Indeed one of the most widely held prejudices about our past is the idea that menstruation has always been seen as an abomination and pollution. Definitely, as shown by the legend of the menstruating Jews, a negative view of menstruation as divine punishment did have currency in Europe among the learned as well as the common people. There is clear evidence of the survival of this idea also in some early modern medical texts.[84] Even the notion that the menstrual blood is poisonous, passed on from Pliny to the Renaissance, can still occasionally be found in the six-teenth and seventeenth century.[85] But more widespread by far among the medical authors of this period, starting with Vesalius (who scornfully dismissed Pliny's opinion on this issue) is the notion that the menstrual blood is neither noxious nor impure.[86] On the ground of the evidence presented in this essay, I would argue that the notion of a negative view of menstruation in the Hippocratic-Galenic tradition should definitely be reconsidered. The concept of menstruation that early modern doctors inherited from Greek medicine was a far cry from the notion of menstruation as a chronic infirmity, the cause of the weakness and sickliness of the female body. On the contrary, as we have seen, menstruation was seen as the paramount "critical evacuation," the very model of the healing power of nature.

Perhaps, as is often the case, our perception of these ancient ideas has been dimmed by the distorting medium of more recent notions. In fact, the therapeutic value of menstruation was rooted in a conception of nature that came under severe attack in the second half of the seventeenth century.

---

84. See Mueller-Hess, *Die Lehre von der Menstruation,* pp. 35–36.

85. Pliny, *Naturalis historia,* bk. 7, ch. 15 (Loeb ed., pp. 546–48); P. A. Matthioli, *Commentarii in lib. VI Pedacii Dioscuridis* (Venice, 1554), bk. 6, chap. 25, p. 672. Schurig, *Parthenologia,* pp. 226–29 cites several sixteenth- and seventeenth-century authors (such as Fernel, van Helmont, and Musitano) who held this belief.

86. Vesalius, *De humani corporis fabrica,* p. 662; Giulio Cesare Claudini, *Responsiones & Consultationes* (Frankfurt am Main, 1607), responsio 23, p. 158 ff. and responsio 24, p. 165; Mercurio (*La commare, o riccoglitrice,* pp. 72–73) stresses that the menstrual blood is not "vitioso e velenoso" but "of the same nature as the rest of the blood in the veins." This is the prevailing thesis in seventeenth-century medical texts: see Schurig, *Parthenologia,* pp. 228–32. Similarly, most authors argue that intercourse with a menstruating woman is normally not dangerous (Schurig, *Parthenologia,* p. 232). On the belief in the dangers of intercourse with a menstruating woman see Ottavia Niccoli, "Menstruum quasi monstruum: Parti mostruosi e tabu' mestruale nel '500," *Quaderni storici* 44 (1980): 402–28.

We all know that in this period the ancient providential notion of nature—so well expressed by the image of her healing power—was rejected and replaced with a notion of nature as a set of mechanical laws. In medical discourse, the advent of mechanical philosophy implied abandoning the idea of nature's healing power. And significantly, it was especially the theory of critical evacuations that was discarded. This is not surprising, as the critical evacuations had been the cornerstone of the argument for the healing power of nature. Thus when Robert Boyle attacked the concept of nature as a purposeful agent in *An Inquiry into the Vulgar Notion of Nature* (1682), one of his main targets was the belief in the healing function of the critical evacuations, which he saw as the "strongest" evidence that could be brought in support of the received notion of nature. In truth, Boyle argued, not all critical evacuations lead to a positive outcome; some, on the contrary, bring about a worsening of the patient's condition: "[A]s some crises are salutary, so others prove mortal. And among those, that do not directly kill the patient, there are several which leave him in a worse condition than he was before."[87] Furthermore, he maintained that the bleedings interpreted as "unusual ways" of menstruation were not due to the healing effort of nature, but to congenital or acquired anatomical anomalies.[88] Friedric Hoffmann, a German physician who adopted some of Boyle's ideas, argued that the healing effects of the various forms of bleeding, vomiting, and so on were merely accidental. He called the critical evacuations "purposeless reactions," the product of merely mechanical causes.[89] In medical circles influenced by mechanical philosophy, bleeding and other forms of discharge came to be viewed as we would view them today, that is as pathological symptoms, or "errors of nature," which it would be meaningless to encourage or reinforce by medical means.

Between the seventeenth and the eighteenth century the conception of healing in European medicine underwent a sea change. The role of that entity—Nature—that had been the undisputed protagonist of the curationes of the Renaissance was questioned and drastically curtailed. Together with it, the very notion of critical evacuations was also put into question. Additional evidence of this change can be found in the debates on natu-

87. Robert Boyle, *A Free Inquiry into the Vulgar Notion of Nature*, in *The Philosophical Works of the Honourable Robert Boyle*, ed. Peter Shaw (London, 1725), 2:129–32 (quotation at p. 130).
88. Boyle, *Free Inquiry*, p. 132.
89. Friedric Hoffmann, *Medicina rationalis systematica*, quoted in Neuburger, *Doctrine*, p. 60.

ral and supernatural healing. At the beginning of the seventeenth century, when Paolo Zacchia, papal archiater and author of the celebrated *Quaestiones medico-legales,* set about drawing the distinction between natural and miraculous healing, he unhesitatingly identified the "critical evacuations" as the clearest sign of a recovery wrought by nature.[90] A century later, when Cardinal Lambertini, the future Pope Benedict XIV, dealt with the same issue in his fundamental work on canonization proceedings, he no longer saw the "critical evacuations" as the clearest sign of natural healing. Aware of the plurality of medical opinions on this issue, he distinguished between "critical" (that is, positive and therapeutic) evacuations, on one side, and "symptomatic" evacuations, on the other side, these last seen as pathological symptoms.[91]

The notion of the healing power of nature, however, survived the attack of mechanical philosophy. At the beginning of the eighteenth century Georg Ernst Stahl was one of its champions and still considered bleeding, vomiting, sweating, diarrhea, and the like as examples of the healing action of nature.[92] The notion of *morbi salutares* (diseases which it is recommended to leave untreated) had currency yet later in the century. In Raymond's *Traité des maladies qu'il est dangereux de guerir,* a chapter is devoted to vomiting, diarrhea, fluor albus, as well as, of course, spontaneous bleedings, as manifestations of the healing power of nature.[93] But although the notion of nature's healing power lingered on, it lost its close association with the *facultas expultrix* (and therefore with menstruation). By the end of the eighteenth century, the "critical evacuations" have become a marginal aspect of the discussion on the healing power of nature, which is centered instead on fevers or on anatomically observable phenomena (such as, for instance, the formation of cysts, the spontaneous healing of aneurysms, etc.).[94]

90. Paolo Zacchia, *Quaestiones medico-legales* (1612–30; Lyons, 1662), bk. 4, tit. 1, quaestio 8, p. 13: "Crises, praesertim quae per insignes evacuationes fiunt, maxime ostendunt, sanationem Naturae vi successam."

91. Prospero Lambertini, *De servorum dei beatificatione et beatorum canonizatione,* 2nd ed. (Padua, 1743), tit. 4, pt. 1, chap. 16.

92. Georg Ernst Stahl, *Dissertatio de medicina sine medico* (Halle, 1707); *Theoria medica vera* (Halle, 1708), t. 2, pt. 2, sec. 1.

93. D. Raymond, *Traité des maladies qu'il est dangereux de guerir* (Avignon, 1757), t. 1, pp. 261–382. For other eighteenth-century medical authors who believe in *morbi salutares* see Neuburger, *Doctrine,* p. 98.

94. Neuburger, *Doctrine,* pp. 69–78, 102–3.

But the crucial factor in the demise of the ancient view of menstruation as salutary crisis was probably the establishment of a link between menstruation and ovulation. In the first half of the nineteenth century the discovery of the mammalian ovum led to a better understanding of the role of ovaries in reproduction—a role that had been a subject of anatomical speculation, for lack of conclusive experimental evidence, since the second half of the seventeenth century.[95] At this point, menstruation started to be seen as closely related to the ovaries and was in fact explained by means of the so-called ovular theory.[96] With the ovular theory, much more than in the past, menstruation was directly related to reproduction, while its cleansing function, so central in ancient and early modern medicine, lost significance. Furthermore, in the ovular theory we can notice a tendency toward the pathologization of menstruation. According to the ovular theory, the process of cell growth in the ovaries determined a constant stimulation of their nerves. This stimulation, periodically reaching a threshold, led to an arterial congestion of the genitals by means of a nervous reflex. This periodical congestion was seen as the cause of the release of the ovum (ovulation) as well as of the simultaneous hemorrhage of the uterine membranes (menstruation). (According to this theory, menstruation was concomitant with ovulation.) The ovular theory drew an explicit parallel between the nervous etiology of menstruation and that of the epileptic crisis, stressing the particular weakness and irritability of the female nervous system.[97] In this way, menstruation moved from the

95. On the discovery of the mammalian ovum by Karl von Baer in 1827, see Carlo Castellani, *Storia della generazione* (Milan: Longanesi, 1965), pp. 346ff.; on anatomical research and speculation on the role of ovaries in the seventeenth and eighteenth century, see Jacques Roger, *Les Sciences de la vie dans la pensée française du XVIIIe siècle: La génération des animaux de Descartes à l'Encyclopédie* (1963; Paris: A. Colin, 1993), pp. 256–93; Clara Pinto-Correia, *The Ovary of Eve: Egg, Sperm and Preformation* (Chicago: University of Chicago Press, 1997).
96. On the theories of menstruation in the nineteenth century, from the "ovular theory" to the beginnings of endocrinology, see H. Fels, *Beiträge zur Lehre von der Menstruation vom Beginn der Zellenlehre bis zum Beginn der Lehre von der inneren Sekretion*, Ph.D. diss., Faculty of Medicine, Berlin, 1961. For a detailed historical analysis of the ovular theory see H. H. Simmer, "Pflüger's Nerve Reflex Theory of Menstruation: The Product of Analogy, Teleology and Neurophysiology," *Clio Medica* 12 (1977): 57–90.
97. Simmer, "Pflüger's Nerve Reflex Theory," pp. 74–75; Fisher-Homberger, *Krankheit Frau*, pp. 72–74 (more generally, on the association between menstruation and periodical mental crises in the medicine of this period, see pp. 74–78). On the pathologization of menstruation

realm of physiology to pathology. To quote from an influential medical encyclopedia of the late nineteenth century: "Even when running a perfectly normal course, menstruation has a disturbing influence upon the general condition. . . . Disturbances of the circulatory apparatus and of the digestive organs, and particularly of the nervous system, are quite commonly developed . . . [which often] lead to the most serious disturbances in bodily and mental condition."[98] Similarly, the "unusual pathways" of menstruation were reconceptualized in the nineteenth century as pathologies caused by a nervous condition. They were redefined as "neuropathic hemorrhages," for instance, in a French study of 1859, which argued that a disorder of the nervous system was the source of almost all the cases of so-called vicarious menstruation.[99]

By the end of the nineteenth century, however, the scientific discussion on vicarious menstruation was not over yet. In 1885, the *Lancet* published an article on this topic. The author, the obstetrician Alfred Wiltshire, advanced once again a version of the ancient plethora theory, arguing that menstruation is accompanied by increased vascular tension, which the body tries to release by discharging the superfluous blood out of the "places of least resistance," such as ulcers or wounds. Wiltshire thought that forms of "vicarious menstruation" can occur also in men as a consequence of the "primal law of periodicity," which he believed to regulate both male and female physiology.[100] Four physicians wrote letters to the journal in response to Wiltshire's article; three of them declared to be utterly skeptical about vicarious menstruation. In one of these letters, the belief in vicarious menstruation was likened to the belief in witchcraft and was attributed to

---

in the nineteenth century see also Emily Martin, *The Woman in the Body: A Cultural Analysis of Reproduction* (Boston: Beacon Press, 1987), pp. 34–35.

98. *Cyclopaedia of the Practice of Medicine,* ed. H. von Ziemssen (New York, 1875), 10:326–27.

99. J. Parrot, *Etude sur la sueur du sang et les hémorrhagies névropathiques* (Paris, 1859). This new view of "vicarious menstruation" is adopted in the *Dictionnaire encyclopédique des sciences médicales,* 2nd ser. (Paris, 1873), vol. 6, s.v. *menstruation* ("déviation des règles": pp. 732–33).

100. Alfred Wiltshire, "Clinical Lecture on Vicarious or Ectopic Menstruation, or Menses Devii," *Lancet* (Sept. 19, 1885): 513–17. On the theory of "vital periodicity," developed by the English neurophysiologist Thomas Laycock in the 1840s, see Ornella Moscucci, *The Science of Woman: Gynecology and Gender in England, 1800–1929* (Cambridge: Cambridge University Press, 1990), pp. 19–20.

ignorant students: "It is not unusual when under examination, and asked for the causes of haemoptysis or haematemesis, for them to give vicarious menstruation as the first cause."[101]

Two years later the *British Gynecological Journal*, the periodical of the newly formed British Gynecological Society, devoted an issue to a long discussion on vicarious menstruation. In a meeting of the society, one of its founders, Dr. Robert Barnes, read a paper in defense of the theory of vicarious menstruation, now relabeled "ectopic menstruation." Like those of Wiltshire, Barnes's arguments were basically a rehash of the theory of plethora: "The state of hyperaemia preceding menstruation, expressed by the term *molimen haemorrhagicum*, must be relieved. If the normal route fails, the excess of blood which is manifest in every part of the system seeks a vent elsewhere, and will escape at the *locus minoris resistentiae*."[102] The hemorrhages we observe in cases of "ectopic menstruation," Barnes argued, are basically safety valves of the system which "relieve systemic and local hyperaemia," thereby "lessening or averting evil."[103] He listed several cases of vicarious menstruation that he had either personally observed or read in the medical literature. It is the old list of "unusual pathways": bleedings from wounds, nipples, eyes, hemorrhoids, and so on. He indicated the appropriate cure, this also no novelty — drawing blood from the foot.

And yet there was something new: the discussion that followed Barnes's paper shows very clearly that most of the physicians in the meeting were strongly skeptical not just as to the theory but also — and this is the novelty — as to the actual existence of the phenomenon called "vicarious menstruation." These doctors argued that the periodicity of the bleedings existed only in the minds of the patients, and did not pass the test of rigorous clinical observation. For several participants in the debate, "vicarious menstruation" was just a misnomer for what was simply a diagnostic error. One physician, for instance, reported the case of a woman who, twelve months after her menopause, started to spit blood, which she herself interpreted as a return of her period; in truth, her lungs were affected by tuberculosis — a better explanation for the blood-spitting.[104] It is clear that hemorrhages,

---

101. *Lancet* (Sept. 26, 1885): 575.

102. R. Barnes, "On Vicarious Menstruation," *British Gynecological Journal* 2 (1886–87): 151–83 (quotation at p. 158).

103. Barnes, "Vicarious Menstruation," pp. 157 and 177.

104. Barnes, "Vicarious Menstruation," pp. 188–207, esp. pp. 178, 183, 198. On the ground

far from being associated with the healing endeavor of nature, were now conceptualized, already prima facie, as a pathological symptom, which, even if accompanied by amenorrhea, did not have anything to do with it. Furthermore, amenorrhea itself was now classified as a symptom, not a disease. Late-nineteenth-century doctors had moved very far away from the notion that the absence of menstruation is the fundamental pathology of the female body — the notion that had been the cornerstone of ancient gynecology.

A medical encyclopedia of the late nineteenth century argues that one must be very cautious of interpreting as vicarious menstruation those bleedings that are concomitant with amenorrhea, because "periodical hemorrhages from ulcers, etc. occur also in men." [105] Here the question is put in entirely new terms: if periodic bleedings occur in men — in whose case the possibility of menstruation is excluded — then when these phenomena are observed in women, their link with menstruation cannot be taken for granted. As we can see, an implicit premise of this reasoning is that menstruation is exclusively female. We are now in a mental framework in which menstruation, from being conceptualized as an element of similarity between the sexes, has come to stand as a marker of their difference.

Thus it is not surprising that, when we find observations of menstruating men at the turn of the nineteenth century — and they are still to be found — these cases are usually classified as examples of pseudo-hermaphroditism in which, notwithstanding the external aspect of the genitals, the inner anatomical structure is feminine. It is so, for instance, in a case reported in the *Wiener klinische Rundschau* of 1906: a seventeen-year-old gymnasium student "menstruated" regularly from the penis. A medical examination found that, notwithstanding the masculine appearance of the external genitals, he had a uterus and one ovary, which were later surgically removed because the boy wished "to keep his penis and to get rid of his menstruation." [106]

———

of this evidence, I would dissent from Ornella Moscucci's opinion (*Science of Woman*, p. 18) that the theory of "vicarious menstruation" went unchallenged in late-Victorian medicine. Both the correspondence to the *Lancet* and the debate in the *British Gynecological Journal* show instead that the theory was viewed with considerable skepticism by many members of the medical profession.

105. *Cyclopaedia of the Practice of Medicine* 10:328–29.

106. A. Heymann, "Heterotypischer Hermaphroditismus femininus externus," in *Wiener Klinische Rundschau* (1906), no. 26. The case is cited also by Magnus Hirschfeld in his *Sexualpathologie: Sexuelle Zwischenstufen* (Bonn, 1922), pt. 2, p. 24.

The occurrence of vicarious menstruation in individuals seemingly of the male gender was decidedly classified, by now, under the category of anatomical aberrations that hid, under male appearances, an identity that was biologically female.[107]

And yet relics of the ancient folklore on male menstruation survived through the radical change of the medical theory. Also in the nineteenth century we can find, though much more rarely than in the past, medical reports of cases of menstruating men based less on clinical observation than on intimate disclosures from man to man. For instance, the American physician V. O. King published in 1867 an article on a "Case of Menstruation in the Male." The menstruating man was a friend of his, a fellow student at the University of Louisiana Medical School. King claimed to have personally observed the phenomenon in several occasions, but he gave very few clinical details.[108] The British obstetrician Alfred Wiltshire, in the *Lancet* article quoted above, declared to have personally known "a distinguished London surgeon," who told him that from the time of puberty he had had a crop of herpes on the left side of his penis every three weeks, accompanied by increased urination and sacral pain. For Wiltshire, this was clearly a case of vicarious menstruation.

Some men, then, were still fascinated by the apparent periodicity of their bleedings, and kept interpreting them through the female model. Moreover, the popularity of the so-called law of vital periodicity in Victorian medical circles suggests that the ancient paradigmatic character of the female body kept some currency even in scientific medicine. The law of periodicity was going to have some interesting developments in the medi-

---

107. F. von Neugebauer, "58 Beobachtungen von periodischen, genitalen Blutungen menstruellen Anscheins, pseudomenstruellen Blutungen, Menstrualia vicaria, Molimina menstrualia usw. bei Scheinzwittern," *Jahrbuch für sexuelle Zwischenstufen* 6 (1905): 277; and Hirschfeld, *Sexualpathologie*, pp. 24, 81, and 84. In a case described in a letter to a U.S. periodical in 1885 (W. D. Halliburton, "A Peculiar Case," *Weekly Medical Review and Journal of Obstetrics* [St. Louis, 1885], p. 392), vicarious menstruation is attributed, rather than to a latent female anatomical structure, to an effeminate mental disposition. It is the case of a "druggist, who has menstruated regularly since he was nineteen years of age." Notwithstanding the fact that "the penis and testes are well developed," this man, married and with one child, "has rather a feminine disposition, wears a corset, can do any kind of sewing or housework."

108. V. O. King, "Case of Menstruation in the Male," *Canada Medical Journal* 2 (1867): 472. I have not been able to consult F. A. Forel, "Cas de menstruation chez un homme," *Bulletin de la société médicale de la Suisse romande* (1869): 53–61.

cine of the turn of the century. Wilhelm Fliess, the Viennese physician who was Freud's friend and close collaborator, reelaborated this theory, arguing that both male and female physiology were regulated by biological cycles. This periodicity, according to Fliess, was the cause of the bleedings occasionally observable in males. On this ground Fliess posited the theory of the essential bisexuality of all human beings—a theory which was going to exert a deep influence on psychoanalysis.[109]

In a letter to Fliess of July 20, 1897, Freud wrote: "My special dates that had been on the decline have appeared again (July 17: menstruation in its most developed form, with occasional bloody nasal secretions before and afterwards)." A few months later, again writing to Fliess, he complained that his self-analysis suddenly ceased for three days during which "I had the feeling of being tied up inside . . . and I was really disconsolate until I found that the same three days (28 days ago) were the bearers of identical somatic phenomena. . . . From this one should draw the conclusion that the female period is not conducive to work."[110] Like Dr. Schultz two centuries earlier, another European doctor observes his body through the lens of the female model. But in these two centuries much has changed: in particular, we can notice that whereas for Schultz the periodic nose-bleeding was associated with a restorative and relaxing effect, for Freud the paramenstrual symptoms are accompanied instead by an unpleasant sensation of constraint, unfavorable to concentration and work. The stereotypes of menstruation in the two cases could hardly be more different.

And what shall I say finally, after trying so hard to understand all these doctors in their effort to grasp the elusive nature of menstruation? I am sorely

109. In Wilhelm Fliess, *Die Beziehungen zwischen Nase und weiblichen Geschlechtsorgan, in ihrer biologischen Bedeutung dargestellt* (Leipzig, 1897), p. 198. Fliess interpreted the occasional passing of blood with the urine in some boys as a sign of "vicarious menstruation." On the influence of the "law of periodicity" on psychoanalysis, see Moscucci, *Science of Woman*, pp. 20ff.

110. Sigmund Freud, *The Complete Letters of Sigmund Freud to Wilhelm Fliess, 1887–1904*, ed. Jeffrey Moussaieff Masson (Cambridge, Mass.: Belknap Press of Harvard University Press, 1985), pp. 256 and 270. Sander L. Gilman ("The Struggle of Psychiatry with Psychoanalysis: Who Won?" *Critical Inquiry* 13 [winter 1987]: 34–35) argues (to my mind, not persuasively) that Fliess's and Freud's belief in male paramenstrual phenomena was connected with the anti-Jewish legend. According to Gilman, by theorizing the essentially bisexual nature of all human beings, Freud and Fliess (both Jews) tried to make the traditional sign of Jewish separateness (male menstruation, and therefore bisexuality) into a universal human trait.

tempted to adopt the skeptical conclusion reached by Mlle de l'Espinasse in the *Dream of D'Alembert* and to say with her that "there is no difference between a physician who's awake and a philosopher who's dreaming." [111]

But seriously—no, the skeptical attitude won't do for me. The observations of cases of menstruating men do not prove the futility of all observation. There is in these stories an effort to register phenomena that contradict the a priori belief in the male standard—a dogma that has certainly exerted a narrowing influence on the scientific study of the body. We find in these stories deep curiosity and respect for the female body as a marvelous product of nature's virtuosity. Present-day historians are wrong when they say that in early modern European medicine the male was invariably held as the standard of bodily processes. In empirical observation, in therapeutic practice, things looked to many doctors more complex than that. The stories of menstruating men were an attempt to record this multifaceted perception. Empirical observation that keeps us alert to complexity is always precious, even when it leads into error.

111. Denis Diderot, *Rêve de D'Alembert,* in *Oeuvres* (Paris: Gallimard 1951), p. 890.

The Psychomorphology of the Clitoris, or, The Reemergence of the *Tribade* in English Culture

VALERIE TRAUB

We have long realized that in women the development of
sexuality is complicated by the task of renouncing that genital zone
which was originally the principal one, namely, the clitoris, in favour
of a new zone—the vagina.—Sigmund Freud

Freud considered the clitoris a problem. From Anne Koedt's early feminist critique, "The Myth of the Vaginal Orgasm," to Thomas Laqueur's "Amor Veneris, Vel Dulcedo Appeletur," many critics have elucidated the strategies whereby Freud attempted to reconcile women's physiology with a heterosexual imperative.[1] His theory—that in the Oedipal phase the female child must renounce clitoral stimulation in favor of vaginal penetration—is widely acknowledged to be an attempt to secure phallic privilege by imposing a cultural solution on what he deemed a biological problem. Such psychosexual adaptation is enabled by Freud's equation between the clitoris and the penis, an equivalence that simultaneously is physiological (the clitoris and penis are analogous in structure and function), psychological (both organs indicate an active masculine aim), and metaphorical (during the infantile "phallic" stage, "the little girl is a little man").[2]

This essay is a revised version of "The Psychomorphology of the Clitoris," which appeared in *GLQ: A Journal of Lesbian and Gay Studies* 2, no. 2 (April 1995), 81–113. A more extended version will appear in my book, *The Renaissance of Lesbianism in Early Modern England.*

The epigraph is from Sigmund Freud, "Female Sexuality" (1931), in *Sexuality and the Psychology of Love,* ed. Philip Reiff (New York: Macmillan, 1963), pp. 194–211, esp. p. 194.

1. Anne Koedt, "The Myth of the Vaginal Orgasm," in *Radical Feminism,* ed. Anne Koedt, Ellen Levine, and Anita Rapone (New York: Quadrangle, 1973), pp. 198–207; and Thomas Laqueur, "Amor Veneris, Vel Dulcedo Appeletur," in *Fragments for a History of the Human Body,* ed. Michael Feher (New York: Zone, 1989), 1:90–131.
2. Freud, "Femininity" (1932), in *New Introductory Lectures on Psychoanalysis,* ed. and trans. James Strachey (New York: Norton, 1965), pp. 99–119, esp. p. 104.

For Freud, the clitoris also is linked inextricably to lesbianism. Female resistance to forgoing pleasure in the clitoris is associated with an inability to replace the first object of desire, the mother, with the more proper object, the father. Just as vaginal satisfaction is the developmental sign of mature heterosexuality, clitoral attachment is the symptom of a recalcitrant, immature homoerotic desire. Retrospectively, every woman moves through a psychosexual stage in which her clitoris threatens fixation on homoerotic objects; lesbians fail to follow the dictates of culture, narcissistically remaining attached to "anatomy" and "mother," and projecting their envy of the male organ onto their own "phallic" genitality. A Freudian system of equivalencies, whereby the penis = the clitoris = lesbianism = penis envy, sets up a smooth continuity among terms, the effect of which is a transposition of bodily organs by psychic states. The circularity of this equation despecifies female erotic experience by referring woman's body and desire back to the phallus—in modernity, the privileged term that links sexuality to identity. The formalization of two incommensurate object choices (homo and hetero) based on two separate genital "zones" (clitoral and vaginal) moderates the more radical implications of Freud's theory of bisexuality and polymorphous perversity, and resecures the direction of female desire toward men, toward reproduction, and, if all goes well and there is no slippage of identification within heterosexuality, toward the reproduction of patriarchal culture.

Since the advent of psychoanalysis, then, the clitoris and the lesbian have been mutually implicated as sisters in shame: each is the disturbing sign (and sign of disturbance) that implies the existence of the other. Underlying the perversion of lesbian desire is not only the polymorphous perversity of the infantile body and the inherent bisexuality of all drives but also an anatomical organ that is shared by the vast majority of females, regardless of age, gender identification, or sexual orientation. Joined through the imperative of repression, the clitoris and the lesbian together signify woman's erotic potential for a pleasure outside of masculine control. At the same time, Freud's binary (and teleological) model of incommensurate pleasures (clitoral or vaginal, not clitoral and vaginal) produces a bodily schema of lesbian eroticism that obscures the range of erotic activities, including vaginal penetration, historically performed by women with women.

Freud's views have been credited with exerting enormous influence on modern understandings of "homosexuality." Indeed, even when they emphasize the agency of gay people, most historians of sexuality attribute to psychoanalysis, sexology, and related epistemologies such as criminology and anthropology an originary, constitutive force in the construction of the "homosexual subject." However, neither Freud's association of clitoral pleasure with lesbian desire nor his equation of the clitoris and the penis were original to him or his culture. Sixteenth- and seventeenth-century European anatomists, physicians, and midwives regularly employed a penis-clitoris analogy as part of a system of representation that asserted the homologous yet hierarchical relation between male and female bodies. Likewise, the association between the clitoris and tribadism (an early modern antecedent to lesbianism) has an equally long cultural history. The system of equivalencies between the penis, the clitoris, and same-gender female desire predate Freud by several centuries; such analogies are less an *effect* of the modern construction of female "homosexuality" than the cultural material out of which such a category was created.

My essay details the conjunction between the clitoris and the tribade during the period in which both were given their first sustained early modern articulation as objects of Western anatomical inquiry. A circular, self-referential relation, whereby the clitoris and the tribade imply, necessitate, and support one another, structures the terms of intelligibility that governed an influential representation of female homoerotic desire in the early modern period. Indeed, the structural association between the clitoris and the tribade has operated historically as one primary condition of intelligibility for such desire. Freud's recapitulation of this paradigm both reformulates and occludes this link; in his hands, what was previously conceptualized as a spatial, metonymic connection between body and body part becomes the symptomatic sign of a psychosexual phase.

This shift from a spatial (metonymic) logic to a temporal (developmental) one is less of an advance than might at first appear. Under the guise of explorer of the psyche, Freud converted earlier paradigms of scientific discovery, imposing a teleological narrative of psychosexual development onto a preexisting map of the female body. The map Freud appropriated was born of protocolonialist and patriarchal imperatives which instigated and invigorated the quests of early modern science. Freud's own exploration did not elicit a new mapping, for his narratives of space and time depend on a form of analogical thinking prevalent in the early modern period that forcibly fuses body part to erotic behavior. Rather, Freud solicited the authorizing power of discourse that, in its replay of the "discovery" of the clitoris through the invention of clinical psychoanalysis (and the invention of the vaginal orgasm), materially affected the pleasures and possibilities of the modern female body. At the same time, the prior conceptual paradigms to which Freud was indebted were obscured by the institutional power of psychoanalysis. Peter Hulme's assertion regarding colonialist discourses that "the gesture of 'discovery' is at the same time a ruse of concealment" is true not only of Freud's reconstitution of earlier spatial metonymies but also of the concealments imposed by those earlier maps upon alternative conceptualizations of the female body.[3]

The terms of embodiment that have governed the construction of the clitoris as the metonymic, material sign of same-gender female desire were engendered by a complex cultural interplay of psychic and material forces. Analysis of these forces demonstrates that the meanings of clitoral structure, size, and function are not merely a matter of empirical knowledge; rather, they are constituted by, and include traces of, anxieties about the illicit use to which the clitoris might be put. The morphology of the clitoris is thus a *psychomorphology*. "Rediscovered" in the mid-sixteenth century and immediately subjected to cultural expectations, fantasies, fears, and warnings about its proper structure, size, function, and use, the clitoris and its attendant psychomorphology highlight the historicity of the terms by which Freud contributed to the modern consolidation of lesbian identity—that is, as an essential, and essentially pathological, subjectivity.

The point is not simply to historicize Freud or to refute his narrative of lesbian pathology. Rather, my aim is to demonstrate the extent to which feminist figurations of lesbian desire and subjectivity are implicated within the same psychomorphology that gave rise to Freud's mapping of the lesbian body. In the critique of Freud that pervades contemporary lesbian scholarship, a logic of reversal structures analytic resistance to the psychoanalytic narrative; rather than pathologize, as Freud does, the equation between the lesbian and the clitoris, many theorists and critics celebrate (and unwittingly reify) this analogy as the enabling truth of lesbian existence. In rejecting the self-evident nature of the clitoris-lesbian connection, I want to suggest that metonymies that presume the commensurability of body parts to erotic desires and practices, whether presented in spatial or tempo-

3. Peter Hulme, *Colonial Encounters: Europe and the Native Caribbean, 1492–1797* (London: Methuen, 1986), p. 1.

ral terms, continue rather than challenge the history from which modern terms of female embodiment evolved.

The most historically detailed and analytically elaborated account of the cultural representation of the clitoris is the work of Thomas Laqueur. In *Making Sex: Body and Gender from the Greeks to Freud* and the essay "Amor Veneris, vel Dulcedo Appeletur," Laqueur reconstructs a history of the female body that shows how anatomical knowledge is constructed through the coordinates of gender ideology.[4] Laqueur argues that the anatomical "rediscovery" of the clitoris in the sixteenth century drew from and reinforced the view of the two sexes as isomorphic: whereas the vagina visually resembled the penis, the clitoris *functioned* like the male organ, becoming erect when aroused and emitting seed during orgasm. According to Laqueur, the apparent conceptual contradiction involved in women having two penises (vagina and clitoris) while men possessed only one did not trouble medical conceptualizations, confined as they were within a Galenic one-sex model in which difference was inconceivable: "Thus, the elaboration in medical literature . . . of a 'new' female penis and specifically clitoral eroticism, was a re-presentation of the older homology of the vagina and penis, not its antithesis."[5]

In constructing a ruptural model derived from the archaeology of Michel Foucault, Laqueur upsets the body's presumed naturalism, demonstrating the degree to which eroticism and the body partake of, and are only knowable through, discursive formations. However, even as Laqueur brilliantly insists upon the force of social construction to impact "biology," and even as he resists teleological narratives of causality, his work remains caught within an epistemic paradigm that results in a unifying rubric of explanation. According to *Making Sex,* all medical literature up to the eighteenth century speaks cohesively and insistently of gender isomorphism; intent on demonstrating an epistemic shift from a one-sex to a two-sex body, Laqueur's macroscopic view tends to obscure differences and discontinuities among temporally proximate discourses. In particular, Laqueur discards conventional periodizations (the Renaissance, the Enlightenment, modernity), replacing them with a binary epistemic model organized along

4. Thomas Laqueur, *Making Sex: Body and Gender from the Greeks to Freud* (Cambridge, Mass.: Harvard University Press, 1990).
5. Laqueur, "Amor Veneris," p. 119.

the temporalities of the *before* and *after*—before the one-sex model gave way to the two-sex model, after the two-sex model initiated the regime of oppositional difference. Social conflict and contestation among and between different discourses are subordinated to a master rubric that is statically organized along the temporal axes of the pre- and the post-. To put this another way, Laqueur constructs a diachronic narrative of historical change that nonetheless carries with it vestiges of a structural model of how change happens. The result is that, within each axis, contest is translated into uniformity, struggle into consensus. The multiplicity of discourses, their dialogic character, is transformed into a monologic homogeneity, which gains its existence from one overarching mode of intelligibility: the difference between the one- and two-sex body. What is lost is the specificity by which human actors experience their relationship to multiple and often conflicting discourses, as well as a more precise diachronic charting of the advent and processes of change.

Laqueur has been critiqued, by Katharine Park among others, for his silencing of those medical voices in the sixteenth and seventeenth century that do not concur with the paradigm of the one-sex body.[6] Though he records some of these alternative voices in *Making Sex,* he does so only to assert their ineffectiveness in challenging the dominance of the Galenic model. In particular, Laqueur's contention that the "rediscovery" of the clitoris had no impact on the one-sex model is refuted by Park, who argues that knowledge of the clitoris pressured the paradigm of homology, and helped to initiate, much earlier than Laqueur suggests, the shift to a model of two diametrically opposed genders.

---

6. See Katharine Park and Robert Nye, "Destiny Is Anatomy," review of *Making Sex: Body and Gender from the Greeks to Freud* by Thomas Laqueur, *New Republic* (18 Feb. 1991): 53–57; Lorraine Daston and Katharine Park, "The Hermaphrodite and the Orders of Nature: Sexual Ambiguity in Early Modern France," in *Premodern Sexualities,* ed. Louise Fradenburg and Carla Freccero (New York: Routledge, 1996), pp. 117–36; and Katharine Park, "The Rediscovery of the Clitoris," in *The Body in Parts: Fantasies of Corporeality in Early Modern Europe,* ed. David Hillman and Carla Mazzio (London: Routledge, 1997), pp. 171–94; Joan Cadden, *Meanings of Sex Difference in the Middle Ages: Medicine, Science, and Culture* (Cambridge: Cambridge University Press, 1993); and Heather Dubrow, "Navel Battles: Interpreting Renaissance Gynecological Manuals," *American Notes and Queries: A Quarterly Journal of Short Articles, Notes, and Reviews* 5, nos. 2 and 3 (1992): 67–71. Laqueur's gender bias is analyzed in general terms by Gail Kern Paster in *The Body Embarrassed: Drama and the Disciplines of Shame in Early Modern England* (Ithaca, N.Y.: Cornell University Press, 1993).

My essay attempts to unpack Renaissance discourses about the clitoris, analyzing them, as Laqueur does not, from the angle of female specificity. The "rediscovered clitoris" is not entirely subsumed under the reproductive discourses that are Laqueur's primary concern; although early modern anatomy treats clitoral orgasm as vital to reproductive success, it also emphasizes the clitoris's capacity to provide autonomous female pleasure. But pleasure per se is not Laqueur's concern; nor, given his concern to demonstrate the stranglehold of Galenism, is the specificity of the female body. For in analytically visibilizing the female body *only in relation to* the male — either as homologous or as oppositional — Laqueur reiterates the conceptual bias he purports to analyze.

Indeed, several problems endemic to the archaeological project converge in Laqueur's account. If his focus on dominant discourses elides cultural contestation, his reliance on an epistemic model of change endorses Foucault's contention that the appearance of the "homosexual" as a category of identity became available only after the rise of a modern disciplinary apparatus. Laqueur's uncritical adoption of this view leads to the analytical assertion that "Lesbianism and homosexuality as categories were not possible before the creation of men and women as opposites," that is, before the two-sex model.[7] References to tribades in Laqueur's account thus become merely gestural, as the focus is more on the social construction of an anatomical part (the clitoris) than the varied uses to which that part could be put. Resistance to examining the specificity of same-gender female eroticism prior to the inauguration of "homosexuality" then allows Laqueur to describe and reaffirm a male-oriented paradigm in which the only erotic possibility is homoeroticism between men: "When among themselves, [these Renaissance authors] seem to be saying, women rub *their* penises together. . . . Indeed, all sex becomes homoerotic."[8]

Each of us makes interpretative choices. Laqueur has read the clitoris-as-penis analogy in terms of a putative masculine norm; by extension, he presents tribades as imitators of men and all sexual activity as male homoeroticism — thus reinscribing the hierarchy that his account ostensibly seeks to address. Neglecting to insert a wedge between his interpretative voice and that of early modern writers, Laqueur employs without demurral descriptions of the tribade such as "taking the man's role in love-

7. Laqueur, "Amor Veneris," p. 119.
8. Laqueur, "Amor Veneris," p. 118.

making" and "playing the man's part during intercourse."[9] I ask rather what is at stake in the cultural effort to disavow the gender specificity of the clitoris and of erotic acts among women, even as those acts are interpreted via a phallic model. The following discussion attempts to reassert such gender specificity, not in the interest of locating a pre-Enlightenment lesbian identity, but to demonstrate the conditions of emergence *for* modern identity categories. Lesbians did not arrive on the modern scene as fully formed social objects; nor did the ascendancy of a two-sex anatomical model ensure their arrival. The category of the lesbian was fashioned only after available rubrics for understanding and assimilating erotic variation failed to account adequately for activities women had been pursuing—under widely divergent conceptual systems—at least since Sappho.

Just as the "birth" of the lesbian is not a discrete social occurrence, the emergence of anatomy as a field of knowledge production is not a singular scientific phenomenon. Rather, the consolidation of anatomy as a separate epistemology occurred in concert with the development of other domains of knowledge, and it was enabled by the ability of anatomists and popularizers of medical texts to appropriate and reformulate the knowledges of other genres, including natural histories, herbals, Latin commentary on Greek and Roman literature, and travel narratives. Early modern travel accounts, in particular, contribute significantly to the construction of the contours and meanings of the early modern body. Generated at the same historical moment and governed by similar tropes of exploration and discovery, anatomies and travel narratives share a common imperative to chart, catalogue, and colonize the body.[10] Both genres synthesize received authority, observation, and invention as they commit highly interpretative acts under the guise of disinterested description. Their narrative strategies and cultural functions are allied closely: both are dedicated to rendering intelligible and distinct that which appears chaotic, primitive, or previously

9. Laqueur, *Making Sex*, p. 136; see also pp. 137 and 279.
10. I explore the relations between anatomy and cartography in constructing a normative body in the early modern period in "Gendering Mortality in Early Modern Anatomies," in *Feminist Readings of Early Modern Culture: Emerging Subjects*, ed. Valerie Traub, M. Lindsay Kaplan, and Dympna Callaghan (Cambridge: Cambridge University Press, 1996), pp. 44–92, and "Mapping the Global Body," in *Early Modern Visual Culture: Representation, Race, Empire in Renaissance England*, ed. Clarke Hulse and Peter Erickson (Philadelphia: University of Pennsylvania Press, 2000).

unknown by employing strategies of description, nomination, and classification. Metaphorically, anatomical texts act as a discourse of travel, visually traversing the body in order to "touch" and reveal a cosmically ordained corporeal whole, while travel narratives observe and dissect peoples and countries, interrogating and reaffirming their place in the cosmic order. Together, their exploratory gazes create the possibility of looking "inward" and "outward," as they formulate the contours of bodily, social, and geographical boundaries. Their processes fashion two sides of the same coin: whereas the dissection of the corpse and its textual reconstitution create a normative, abstracted body whose singularity encompasses and signifies all others, travel accounts compose an exoticized body which often, though not inevitably, reveals the very antithesis of (Western) normativity. Locating bodies within prevailing epistemic hierarchies by charting corporeal cartographies, anatomies and travel narratives not only function as colonialist discourses but urge colonialism into being.

Whether primarily concerned with commerce or conquest, Western European travelers to foreign lands chart a cultural anthropology that functions similarly to a physical geography. Describing the New World, Africa, and the East, narrators obsessively remark upon those cultural practices that distinguish native inhabitants from Europeans, often employing rhetorics of gender and sexuality as explanatory tropes.[11] Marriage rituals, dowries, divorce, and polygamy excite Western curiosity and provide travelers to Africa and Arabia, in particular, a means of deploying the sexual status of indigenous women as a primary marker of cultural definition and civility.[12] A spatial geography of erotic behavior constructs women (and by implication, the nation) as beautiful and chaste (for instance, Persians) or hideous and loose (black Africans). The assumption of female lasciviousness gains self-evident power through the structure of a cross-cultural

11. As Louis Montrose has noted, the identification of territory with the female virginal body provided explorers of the New World powerful justifications for their right to conquer and subject native inhabitants, while simultaneously providing an image of one's own nation as inviolable; see Montrose's "The Work of Gender in the Discourse of Discovery," *Representations* 33 (1991): 1–41. Likewise, Jonathan Goldberg shows how the discourse of sodomy could be manipulated to rationalize European ascriptions of bestiality onto South American tribes, while occluding the very desires that constitute the colonial imaginary in *Sodometries: Renaissance Texts, Modern Sexualities* (Stanford, Calif.: Stanford University Press, 1992).
12. Kim Hall, *Things of Darkness: Economies of Race and Gender in Early Modern England* (Ithaca, N.Y.: Cornell University Press, 1995).

polarity: whereas the partial nudity of women in various African nations authorizes readings of female incontinence, the practice of Muslim purdah constructs the woman whose body is hidden as a highly desirable (and also desiring) object. Although same-gender female eroticism is mentioned only rarely in these accounts (and nowhere as often as charges of male sodomy), its presence routinely is associated with certain locales. Travelers to Turkey, in particular, curious about Muslim attitudes toward cleanliness and intrigued by the Ottoman segregation of women, typically relay rumors about women pleasuring one another—or themselves—within all-female spaces.

Ogier Ghiselin de Busbecq, a Flemish ambassador to the Sultan who penned four lengthy letters, explains to a fellow ambassador why women are segregated from men:

> The Turks are the most careful people in the world of the modesty of their wives, and therefore keep them shut up at home and hide them away, so that they scarce see the light of day. But if they have to go into the streets, they are sent out so covered and wrapt up in veils that they seem to those who meet them mere gliding ghosts. They have the means of seeing men through their linen or silken veils, while no part of their own body is exposed to men's view. For it is a received opinion among them, that no woman who is distinguished in the very smallest degree by her figure or youth, can be seen by a man without his desiring her, and therefore without her receiving some contamination; and so it is the universal practice to confine the women to the harem.[13]

Yet, a narrative by Robert Withers, published in 1587, which describes the architectural arrangements regulating the women in the sultan's seraglio, suggests that the practice of confining women entails certain problems:

> Now, in the Womens lodgings, they live just as the Nunnes doe in their great Monasteries; for, these Virgins have very large Roomes to live in, and their Bed-chambers will hold almost a hundred of them a

13. Ogier Ghiselin de Busbecq, *The Life and Letters of Ogier Ghiselin de Busbecq*, ed. Charles Foster and F. H. Daniell (London: Kegan Paul, 1881), pp. 228–29. I am grateful to Doug Bruster for alerting me to the existence of this passage. The first of de Busbecq's "Turkish Letters" was published in Latin in 1581. The first edition of all four letters was printed in 1589. The first "Englished" edition was printed in 1694.

piece: they sleepe upon Sofaes, which are built long wise on both sides of the Roome, so that there is a large space in the midst for to walke in. Their Beds are very course and hard, and by every ten Virgins there lie an old woman: and all the night long there are many lights burning, so that one may see very plainely throughout the whole Roome; which doth both keepe the young Wenches from wantonnesses, and serve upon any occasion which may happen in the night.[14]

Keeping "young Wenches from wantonnesses" involves taking precautions with their provisions: "Now it is not lawfull for any one to bring ought in unto them, with which they may commit the deeds of beastly uncleannesse; so that if they have a will to eate Cucumbers, Gourds, or such like meates, they are sent in unto them sliced, to deprive them of the meanes of playing the wantons; for, they being all young, lustie, and lascivious Wenches, and wanting the societie of Men (which would better instruct them) are doubtlesse of themselves inclined to that which is naught, and will be possest with unchast thoughts."[15] The idea that cucumbers would be used by women on themselves or with one another is reiterated in many subsequent narratives.

As Withers's account demonstrates, the sultan's harem generated comparisons to convents which, in anti-Catholic polemic, were reputed to be a haven for "unclean" behaviors. But whereas associations with the nunnery led to a focus on sleeping (and eating) arrangements, the communal nudity of the *hannam*, or Turkish bath, occasioned even more explicit comment about women's bodily behaviors. Nicholas de Nicholay's *Navigations into Turkie*, published in 1585, depicts typical procedures involved in visiting the public baths, and concludes his description of female bathers in this way: "[They] do familiarly wash one another, whereby it commeth to passe that amongst the women of Levan, ther is very great amity proceding only through the frequentation & resort to the bathes: yea & sometimes become so fervently in love the one of the other as if it were with men, in such sort that perceiving some maiden or woman of excellent beauty they wil not ceasse until they have found means to bath with them, & to handle & grope them every where at their pleasures so ful they are of luxurious-

---

14. Robert Withers, *The Grand Signiors Serraglio* in *Purchase His Pilgrimes,* ed. Samuel Purchase, 2 vols. (London, 1625), 2:1586–87.

15. Withers, *Grand Signiors,* p. 1590.

nes & feminine wantonnes: Even as in times past were the Tribades, of the number whereof was Sapho the Lesbian."[16] Other travelers reproduce such rumors. De Busbecq, for instance, writes in his third ambassadorial letter:

> The great mass of women use the public baths for females, and assemble there in large numbers. Among them are found many girls of exquisite beauty, who have been brought together from different quarters of the globe by various chances of fortune; so cases occur of women falling in love with one another at these baths, in much the same fashion as young men fall in love with maidens in our country. Thus you see a Turk's precautions are sometimes of no avail, and when he has succeeded in keeping his wives from a male lover, he is still in danger from a female rival! The women become deeply attached to each other, and the baths supply them with opportunities of meeting. Some [men] therefore keep their women away from them as much as possible, but they cannot do so altogether, as the law allows them to go there. This evil affects only the common people; the richer classes bathe at home.[17]

De Busbecq augments this description of a class-specific eroticism with an anecdote about an elderly woman who, having fallen in love with a young woman, crossdresses as a man, obtains permission to marry, and is foiled only upon being recognized by her beloved as someone she encountered at the baths. Thomas Glover, secretary to the English ambassador, concludes his description of Turkish baths with this terse condemnation: "Much unnaturall and filthie lust is said to bee committed daily in the remote closets of the darkesome Bannias: yea, women with women; a thing uncredible, if former times had not given thereunto both detection and punishment."[18]

---

16. Nicholas de Nicholay, *The Navigations, Peregrinations, and Voyages, Made into Turky . . .*, trans. T. Washington (original French, 1567; English translation 1585), in *A Collection of Voyages and Travels*, ed. Thomas Osborne (London, 1745), p. 60. De Nicholay's work was first brought to my attention by Mario DiGangi.

17. De Busbecq, *Life and Letters*, p. 231.

18. Thomas Glover, *The Muftie, Cadileschiers, Divans: Manners and attire of the Turkes. The Sultan described, and his Customes and Court;* and George Sandys, *A Relation of His Journey Begun Anno 1610,* both in Samuel Purchase, *Purchase His Pilgrims 1293–1306,* 2:1299. As far as I know, Glover's text was not published prior to its inclusion in Purchase, although it was also

The seraglio and the hannam are not the only locales that engender anxiety about same-gender female activity. In *The History and Description of Africa,* translated into English in 1600, Leo Africanus describes the erotic practices of fortune-tellers in Fez:

> But the wiser and honester sort of people call these women *Sahacat,* which in Latin signifieth *Fricatrices,* because they have a damnable custome to commit unlawfull Venerie among themselves, which I cannot expresse in any modester termes. If faire women come unto them at any time, these abominable witches will burne in lust towardes them no otherwise then lustie yoonkers [young men] doe towardes yoong maides, and will in the divels behalfe demaunde for a rewarde, that they may lie with them: and so by this meanes it often falleth out, that thinking thereby to fulfill the divels command they lie with the witches. Yea some there are, which being allured with the delight of this abominable vice, will desire the companie of these witches, and faining themselves to be sicke, will either call one of the witches home to them, or will send their husbands for the same purpose: and so the witches perceiving how the matter stands, will say that the woman is possessed with a divell, and that she can no way be cured, unlesse she be admitted into their societie. With these words her silly husband being persuaded, doth not onely permit her so to doe, but makes also a sumptuous banket [banquet] unto the damned crew of witches: which being done, they use to daunce very strangely at the noice of drums: and so the poore man commits his false wife to their filthie disposition.[19]

These exoticizing tales, most of them written during the period when the Ottoman Empire posed a viable military and religious threat to Western

published in other Purchase editions under the following title: *The Journey of Edward Barton Esquire, her Maiesties Ambassadour with the Grand Signior, otherwise called the Great Turke, in Constantinople, Sultan Mahumet Chan. Written by Sir Thomas Glover then Secretarie to the Ambassadour, and since employed in that Honourable Function by his Maiestie, to Sultan Achmet.*
19. Leo Africanus, *The History and Description of Africa and of the Things Herein Contained,* trans. John Pory (London, 1600), ed. Robert Brown, 2 vols. (London: Haklyut Society, 1896), 2:458–59. I am grateful to Kim Hall for alerting me to the existence of this passage and to her analysis of it in *Things of Darkness.*

Europe, enable a number of observations about the rhetorics and figures of female-female eroticism in the early modern period. First, even though these texts attempt to create an illusion of eye-witness veracity, they are extremely intertextual; they draw freely from one another, often quote each other verbatim, and blithely neglect to cite original sources. Second, these texts treat eroticism among women as a real and present danger that is made intelligible largely through signifiers of an ancient past. A specific vocabulary—the Greek *tribas,* Latin *fricatrice,* and Arabic *sahacat*—provide the historical lexicon and the authorizing lens through which to condemn the witches of Fez and bathers of Turkey. The repetition of these terms conveys a consistent manner of nominating women erotically engaged with other women, who, even if they are unaware of it, are allegedly following the classical example of "Sapho the Lesbian."

Third, no consensus regarding the cause of female-female eroticism emerges from these accounts. All of the writers attest to the inherent "feminine wantonnes" of women, and all of them judge women's desire as boundless; but they variously attribute the catalyst for the commission of "unnatural acts" to the segregation of women from men, to witchcraft, and to emulation of male sodomites. Fourth, an architectural logic structures these accounts, as certain physical spaces enable "unnatural" female contact. As spaces originally built to block male access and protect female chastity, the harem and the bath are described as enabling the circulation of desire enclosed within. And as one of the few places that women could congregate in public, the bazaar brings into contact modest wives with "abominable witches," who then invade the patriarchal household.

Fifth, such narratives assume not only that women willingly deceive their husbands or masters, but that homoerotic pleasures, once experienced, prove to be irresistible. The "burning lust" that de Nicholay and others figure as flowing indiscriminately through the waters of the Turkish bath is represented by all the narrators as undermining the patriarchal authority of the harem or household. Sixth, despite their ostensibly descriptive purpose, and despite their convenient use of ready-to-hand labels, these travelers employ what seems to modern ears to be a vague, euphemistic rhetoric: "commit unlawful Venerie," "burn in lust," "inclined to that which is naught," and "handle and grope them everywhere." Leaving the precise nature of erotic acts unspecified, these narratives both assume and occlude the reader's knowledge of "deeds of beastly uncleannesse."

Finally, and most importantly, in the absence of similar narratives about

166   *Valerie Traub*

Englishwomen, tales such as these imply that African and Muslim women are uniquely (if amorphously) amoral in their erotic desires and practices.

The "exotic," of course, is produced through a cultural exchange—psychic, material, rhetorical—between self and other. It is thus perhaps unnecessary to aver that, despite their assertion of eye-witness authority, these travel accounts are hardly empirical, truthful reports of the activities of Middle Eastern and African women. It is true that throughout the Islamic world, the seraglio and hannam may have spatially enabled female homoeroticism. According to Kathryn Babayan, early modern Iranian women during the Safavi empire often exchanged vows of sisterhood and, in the enclosure of the harem, developed intimate friendships, some of which formed the basis for political unions, some of which were erotic.[20] My project, however, is not to write a social history of female affectivity within the Muslim world, which in any case would need to distinguish between the various empires and states of North Africa and the Middle East. And whereas the figural intertwining of the erotic and the exotic within an evolving racialized discourse of European colonialism is also worthy of its own analysis, such a project would best be pursued by situating erotic tropes within the complex political relations among the various state and mercantile powers, east and west, north and south.

Instead, I want to focus here on the way the protocolonialist imperatives of travel narratives ultimately contribute to the erotic representation of Englishwomen. For, in 1671 Jane Sharp, the first Englishwoman to write her own midwifery, alludes to the dissemination of travel accounts as she describes in *The Midwives Book* women whose clitorises grow "so long that it hangs forth at the slit like a yard, and will swell and stand stiff if it be provoked, and some lewd women have endeavoured to use it as men do theirs." "In the Indies, and Egypt," she says, such incidents "are frequent"; but she goes on to assert that illicit contact among women occurs primarily beyond England's borders: "I have never heard but of one in this Country." She then concludes with the ambiguous statement, "[I]f there be any they will do what they can for shame to keep it close," an admonition that, in conflating the enlarged clitoris with the use to which it could be put, could

20. Kathryn Babayan, "The *Aqâ'id al-Nisâ'*: A Glimpse at Safavid Women in Local Isfahani Culture," in *Women in the Medieval Islamic World: Power, Patronage, Piety*, ed. Gavin R. G. Hambly (New York: St. Martin's Press, 1998), pp. 349–81.

refer either to keeping enlarged genitals hidden or illicit erotic practices secret. In a later passage, she writes: "I told you the Clitoris is so long in some women that it is seen to hang forth at their Privities and not only the Clitoris that lyeth behind the wings [labia] but the Wings also. . . . In some Countries they grow so long that the Chirurgion cuts them off to avoid trouble and shame, chiefly in Egypt; they will bleed much when they are cut, and the blood is hardly stopt; wherefore maids have them cut off betimes, and before they marry, for it is a flux of humours to them, and much motion that makes them grow so long. Some Sea-mem [sic] say that they have seen Negro Women go stark naked, and these wings hanging out." [21] Although Sharp does not marginally gloss these passages describing clitoral hypertrophy and clitoridectomy with textual authorities, she does cite Leo Africanus elsewhere in her book. I want to suggest that her minimizing of the frequency of Englishwomen's same-gender contacts, and her displacement of "unnatural" erotic practices onto women of Egypt and the Indies, is not simply a conventional English effort to refer the origin of unwelcome behaviors and disease to other countries. Nor is it merely an instance of the colonial imaginary that, as Jonathan Goldberg has shown, "is particularly prone to a desire to other its own desires." [22] Rather, Sharp's gesture is actually *invited* by the racialized travel literature that underlies and authorizes her account, which structures the difference between west and east, north and south, as partly a difference of erotic morality. At the same time, her strategy of displacement inadvertently acknowledges (and likewise attempts to dispel) the anxiety that erotic contact among Englishwomen was in fact occurring—a fear that may have had as much to do with the rising circulation of representations of female-female eroticism as with any upsurge of homoerotic practices.

Increasingly esteemed as a heroine of seventeenth-century English midwifery, Sharp is viewed as performing a crucial service in contesting the growing dominance of male-midwives and challenging male-dominated medical knowledge through the publication of her own midwifery. Sharp attempted to counter male disgust about the female genitals and, as part of her effort to undermine misogyny, even poked fun at male sexual dysfunc-

21. Jane Sharp, *The Midwives Book, or the Whole Art of Midwifry Discovered* (London, 1671), pp. 45–47.
22. Jonathan Goldberg, ed., "Introduction," *Queering the Renaissance* (Durham, N.C.: Duke University Press, 1994), pp. 1–14, esp. p. 13.

tion.[23] However, as Eve Keller notes, Sharp's text "contains much that is normative, much that enforces the prevailing gender assumptions."[24] Sharp's discussion and condemnation of tribadism, like every other seventeenth-century anatomy and midwifery, immediately follows the description of the clitoris and its possible enlargement. Thus, if it is the case, as Keller argues, that Sharp's rhetorical strategies, which propose the female body as the norm as frequently as the male, undercut the male dominance of the Galenic model, then it is all the more significant that Sharp rehearses conventional wisdom in regard to "some lewd women [who] have endeavoured to use [the clitoris] as men do theirs." In her effort to reorient the traditional masculine hierarchy of perfection and to assert the unique structure and function of the female body, Sharp figures the tribade as foreign, shameful, and expendable.

The rediscovery of the clitoris in the mid-sixteenth century gave female erotic pleasure a new, albeit ambivalent, articulation. With that articulation, I want to suggest, came a representational crisis. This crisis stemmed less from the rancorous disputation among anatomists regarding the clitoris's existence than the fact that anatomical representation of the clitoris became a focal point for the expression of anxieties about the cultural meanings of the female body. As anatomical plates and texts from Italy, France, Spain, and Germany made their way into England, as English physicians and midwives contributed their own methods of textually communicating the "new science" of anatomy, strategies of accommodation — of, quite literally, in-corporation — were developed. The trajectory of these strategies suggests that this clitoral "age of discovery" was a pivotal moment in the cultural history of English women, embodiment, and eroticism. Over the next century, as information about this "new" anatomical organ was incorporated into, and helped to refigure, an old corporeal framework, a discourse evolved that increasingly fixated on the clitoris as the disturbing emblem of female erotic transgression.

We need only turn to Helkiah Crooke's conclusion of his description of the clitoris in his popular vernacular anatomy, *Microcosmographia,* to recog-

23. Jane Sharp, *The Midwives Book,* p. 53.
24. Eve Keller, "Mrs. Jane Sharp: Midwifery and the Critique of Medical Knowledge in Seventeenth-Century England," in *Natural Eloquence: Women Reinscribe Science,* ed. Ann Shteir and Barbara Gates (Madison: University of Wisconsin Press, 1997). I am grateful to Eve Keller for sharing her work prior to publication.

nize the contours of this crisis: "[Y]et sometimes it [the clitoris] groweth to such a length that it hangeth without the cleft like a mans member, especially when it is fretted with the touch of the cloaths, and so strutteth and groweth to a rigiditie as doth the yarde of a man. And this part it is which those wicked women doe abuse called *Tribades* (often mentioned by many authors, and in some states worthily punished) to their mutuall and unnaturall lusts." [25] Crooke also cites Leo Africanus and Caelius Aurelianus (a fifth-century Latin translator of Soranus) in his marginal gloss under the heading "Tribades odiosae feminae."

Drawing from previous authorities to bolster his claim of knowledge, Crooke makes specific use of the racialized, "anthropological" images first put into play by travel narratives only a few decades earlier. And yet something crucial has changed in this intertextual transfer from one discursive domain to another: none of the travel writers mention the "abuse" of a particular body part. Though the words *tribade, fricatrice,* and *sahacat* are used, and cucumbers and public baths loom large, no enlarged clitoris haunts travel accounts; rather, there is simply a boundless, deceitful desire of which all foreign, non-Christian women presumably are suspected. With the publication of anatomical descriptions of the clitoris, however, imprecision gives way to pseudoscientific accuracy, as the site of transgressive female eroticism shifts away from the social excesses of Mediterranean climes to the excessive endowment of female bodies.

By the early seventeenth century, under the auspices of anatomical research, a paradigm of women's boundless desire present in travel literature is transmuted into a paradigm of discrete and empirically verifiable bodily structure. In the emerging terms of early modern medicine, it is not the tribade's inconstant mind or sinful soul, but her uniquely female yet masculinized morphology that either propels her to engage in, or is itself the effect of, her illicit behavior. Clitoral hypertrophy is posited as one cause of early modern tribadism, but perhaps more importantly, early modern tribadism increasingly is inconceivable without clitoral hypertrophy. Anatomy provides a map of this connection.

The mapping of the tribade's body produces and is produced by an anatomical essentialism — the riveting of body part to behavior — that continues to underpin modern discourses of sexuality. Such essentialism is the result

25. Helkiah Crooke, *Microcosmographia, or the Body of Man* (London, 1615) p. 238.

not of natural, empirical facts, but of a strategy to organize and make intelligible the plurality of corporeal structures and behaviors within the conceptual confines of Renaissance cosmological and earthly hierarchies. The early seventeenth-century production of anatomical essentialism is related to other intertextual shifts: as the discourse of anatomy early in the century appropriated the tropes of travel narratives, the racialized "anthropology" born of a protocolonialist imperative was first used to authorize anatomy and then was displaced momentarily in favor of an articulation and consolidation of normative bodily form. This is not to suggest that cross-cultural, anthropological comparisons were no longer relevant; after all, colonialism was gathering, not losing, steam. Rather, the aims of anatomy and travel discourse, linked as they were to different institutional and material practices, began to diverge: as anatomy defined its project as the construction of a normative bodily schema, the myriad forces of colonial expansion expended their material, financial, and ideological energies in an unprecedented exploration of otherness. The temporary displacement of anthropological concerns by anatomy is evident in *Microcosmographia:* figuring tribadism as a "mutual lust" that is "often mentioned by many authors" and "worthily punished" in other nations, citing Leo Africanus but failing to locate illicit practices in any particular nation or locale, Crooke's medical text is uninterested in making explicit cultural comparisons. One effect of this lack of concern is that Crooke ignores the possibility of tribadism in England.

And yet, the unspoken assumption of tribadism's foreign otherness that gives Crooke's account such an air of unflappability begins to break down by mid-century. Thomas Bartholin's 1653 English translation and expansion of his father's Latin anatomy draws on Crooke for his entry "Of the Clitoris," and then proceeds to recontextualize "tribadic" practices. After terming such women *Confricatrices* or Rubsters, Bartholin introduces a reference to the "lascivious Practice" of Philaenis and Sappho. Then, after citing Romans 1:26 ("for this cause God gave them up unto vile affections: for even their women did change the natural use unto that which is against nature"), he asserts that such lascivious practices cause the clitoris to be called *Contemptus virorum* or "the Contempt of Mankind" (an ambiguous construction that fails to specify whose contempt is thereby invoked).[26] Bartholin continues in this vein as he discusses clitoral size:

26. Thomas Bartholin, *The Anatomical History of Thomas Bartholin* (London, 1653), p. 76.

Its Size is commonly small; it lies hid for the most part under the Nymphs in its beginning, and afterward it sticks out a little. For in Lasses that begin to be amorous, the Clitoris does first discover it self. It is in several persons greater or lesser: in some it hangs out like a mans Yard, namely when young Wenches do frequently and continually handle and rub the same, as Examples testifie. But that it should grow as big as a Gooses neck, as Platerus relates of one, is altogether praeternatural and monstrous. Tulpius hath a like Story of one that had it as long as half a mans finger, and as thick as a Boys Prick, which made her willing to have to do with Women in a Carnal way. But the more this part encreases, the more does it hinder a man in his business. For in the time of Copulation, it swells like a mans Yard, and being erected, provokes to Lust.[27]

By morphologizing the tribade, anatomy paradoxically moves her closer to home: the erotic excess that was attributed to foreign women now can be found on the Christian bodies of "Lasses" and "young Wenches" who handle themselves as well as each other. This Englishing of anatomical rhetoric implies that it is not merely the clitoris's enlargement that might "hinder a man in his business," but women's erotic interest in their own and other women's bodies.

Bartholin's "Englished" anatomy includes the first anatomical illustration of the clitoris in an English book, where it is shown to be the "commonly small" outgrowth of a normative body. But despite this visual schematization of an anatomical norm, and despite Bartholin's ambiguous rejection of Platerus's story as "praeternatural" (does Bartholin mean impossible or simply monstrous?), the discursive exaggeration of the clitoris continued unabated. Nicholas Culpeper's *Complete Midwife's Practice Enlarged* states that the clitoris "hath been observed to grow out of the body, the breadth of four fingers."[28] And in France, Jean Riolan repeated Platerus's story of the goose's neck and offered two accounts of the clitoris "as long and thick as my little finger."[29] This reiterated link between what must have been proportionately insignificant physical aberrations to what was in all likelihood a small number of erotic transgressions indicates an

27. Bartholin, *Anatomical History*, p. 77.
28. Nicholas Culpeper, *Complete Midwife's Practice Enlarged*, 4th ed. (London, 1680), p. 57.
29. Jean Riolan, *Anthropographia* (1618); cited by Park, "Rediscovery of the Clitoris," pp. 178–79.

anxiety less about the body unnatural than the unnatural use to which *any* female body might be put. As the potential measure of *all* female bodies, clitoral hypertrophy metonymizes women's supposedly inordinate capacity for pleasure. As anatomies like Bartholin's begin to invoke cautionary references and biblical citation (assuming more and more frequently the function of conduct books), and as the anatomist's repudiation of women's pleasure grows more insistent, the specter of the enlarged clitoris looms larger: if not as big as a "Gooses neck," yet as big as a "Boys Prick."

Market exigencies within the print industry no doubt played a part in this amplification as well. In the genre of marital advice books that developed out of the intersection of anatomy and conduct literature, anatomical hyperbole promoted excellent sales. Nicholas Venette's immensely popular *Conjugal Love, or The Pleasures of the Marriage Bed,* for instance, first describes the size of a typical clitoris as "longer more or less than half a finger," then terms the clitoris "the fury and rage of love," and finally asserts: "This part lascivious women often abuse. The lesbian *Sappho* would never have acquired such indifferent reputation, if this part of her's had been less. I have seen a girl eight years of age, that had already the *clitoris* as long as one's little finger; and if this part grows with age, as it is probable it may, I am persuaded it is now as long as that of the woman mentioned by Platerus, who had one as big and long as the neck of a goose." [30] With the clitoris of most women measured at the length of "half a finger," it is perhaps less fantastical that within a Renaissance economy that correlates quantity of lust with physical size, the clitorises "abused" by "lascivious women" could be asserted to attain the length of a goose's neck. It is, I believe, the discursive amplification of the threat posed by this ever-growing female "prick" that motivates Jane Sharp to resurrect the colonialist imperative, rise to a sisterly defense of Englishwomen, and exile the tribade from England.

As the observations of travel writers are appropriated by anatomical discourse, the clitoris and the tribade are positioned paratactically as mutually constitutive forms of female matter. Not only does the tribade function as the abject other against which a normative female body is defined, but the clitoris comes into representation as the metonymic sign of the unnatural,

---

30. Nicholas Venette, *Conjugal Love, or The Pleasures of the Marriage Bed* (New York: Garland, 1984), pp. 18–19. Also known as *The Art of Conjugal Love,* Venette's book went through eight printings before his death in 1698; the 1750 English edition I quote is designated as the twentieth edition.

transgressive tribade. Despite the sense of an inevitable progression struc-
turing these accounts, however, the actual meaning of tribadism and the
precise nature of the acts this term was supposed to denote were less than
clear. Katharine Park follows Lillian Faderman in reserving the use of the
term "tribadism" for the activity of rubbing, claiming that "French writers
made a clear distinction between female homoerotic behavior that involved
rubbing the genitals . . . and any activity that involved the penetration of
one woman by another." [31] Certainly it is true that penetration (with any
object) was widely construed as the most readily recognized transgression
and also the crime most harshly punished. But the medical, theological,
moral, and legal texts on which Park and Faderman base their assertions
are not exhaustive measures of the range of meanings circulating in early
modern culture. Thus, rather than interpret writers' "exceedingly clear distinctions" as a sign of clarity, I propose that we read the effort involved in
making such discriminations as a sign of cultural anxiety; whatever success they may have achieved was by virtue of an ideological backformation,
imposed after a considerable amount of confusion and contestation.

The seriousness with which anatomists took the tribade's "imitation"
of men is evinced in the rhetorical linkages forged in their work between
anatomy, eroticism, and surgery. If the narrative trajectory of these texts
monotonously moves from a description of normative genitalia to a discussion of clitoral hypertrophy, and from there to excoriation of the tribade, it perhaps comes as no surprise that the narrative often ends with
a recommendation of genital amputation. The French surgeon Ambroise
Paré, who in his early discussion of tribadism confuses the clitoris with the
labia, recommends labial amputation;[32] and Bartholin approvingly cites the
practice of female circumcision of ancient and Eastern nations. Culpeper
goes one step further in his *Fourth Book of Practical Physick,* providing precise if erroneous instructions for how to excise both the enlarged clitoris
and the labia.[33] *The Chyrurgeons Store-house* (1674) — an English translation

31. Park, "Rediscovery of the Clitoris," p. 185; Lillian Faderman, *Surpassing the Love of Men:
Romantic Friendship and Love between Women from the Renaissance to the Present* (New York:
Morrow, 1981).
32. T. Johnson, *The Workes of That Famous Chiurgion: Ambrose Parey, Translated out of Latine
and Compared with the French* (London, 1634).
33. Nicholas Culpeper, *A Directory for Midwives and The Fourth Book of Practical Physick: Of
Women's Diseases* (London, 1684).

of *Wundarztneyishes Zeughaufs* (1665), a surgical textbook by Johannes Scultetus—includes a pictorial depiction of an adult clitoridectomy as a treatment for "the unprofitable increasing of a Clitoris."[34] Whereas none of these writers explicitly recommends eradicating the social phenomena of tribadism through clitoridectomy, the narrative logic of their entries makes clear that, if clitoral hypertrophy causes problems, surgical intervention is available. Within this hypertropic discourse, whether the clitoris or the labia are cut off, what is excised *ideologically* is a pleasure that grows beyond its own abjection.

The discursive appropriation by anatomy of travelers' descriptions and preoccupations demonstrates the emergence of a social *conflict* about the terms by which female desire, pleasure, and embodiment were to be represented. Such a conflict is the result of a *psychomorphology*—the fantasies that structure and the structures that fantasize—of the clitoris in the sixteenth and seventeenth centuries. I am not suggesting that such a conflict did not previously exist, nor do I mean to occlude the prehistory of the tribade in the ancient and medieval periods. The association of the clitoris with immoderate desire, and of clitoral hypertrophy with the putative tribadism of African women, crops up in the medical works of classical and medieval Arabic authors, and is one source of early modern accounts.[35] References to tribades can be found as well in Latin literature from the second century B.C.E. through the second century C.E.,[36] as well as in occasional religious commentary.[37] By focusing on the interaction between sixteenth- and seventeenth-century discourses, I mean to underscore that this prior history situates the tribade primarily in the Mediterranean, and that discussion of her in Western Europe was hindered by religious conflict, political divisions, and linguistic differences.

Nor, in concentrating on medical and travel accounts, do I mean to imply

34. Johannes Scultetus, *Wundarztneyishes Zeughaufs* (Frankfurt, 1655 and 1666); trans. as *The Chyrurgeons Store-house* (London, 1674) p. 194.
35. See Park, "Rediscovery of the Clitoris"; Bernadette Brooten, *Love between Women: Early Christian Responses to Female Homoeroticism* (Chicago: University of Chicago Press, 1996); and Cadden, *Meanings of Sex Difference*.
36. Judith P. Hallett, "Female Homoeroticism and the Denial of Roman Reality in Latin Literature," *Yale Journal of Criticism* 3, no. 1 (fall 1989): 209–27.
37. See Brooten, *Love between Women*.

that they are the only genres relevant to the formation of early modern erotic categories. The work of Judith Hallett and Harriette Andreadis demonstrates the extent to which intimations of female-female eroticism remained alive within the Latin literary tradition, particularly as continental commentary on Ovid's *Heröides* was supplemented by English translations of Ovid and Martial.[38] As the references to Sappho by the physician Bartholin and the traveler de Nicholay evince, this literary heritage was appropriated to bolster the judgmental commentary of their texts. However, it took the early modern interaction between travel literature and anatomy, with their shared cartographical impulse to map the bodies of both self and other, to reposition the tribade in England. The convergence of these discourses in seventeenth-century England is a function not merely of the routes whereby knowledge is transmitted, but of specific social processes that granted a renewed relevance to concerns about female erotic transgression.

That is, under the auspices of emerging epistemologies and under pressure from new cultural exigencies, an ancient linguistic and social category was revivified and transfigured, giving rise in England to new and, I want to argue, specifically early modern significations. As the ancient logic of sexual activity and passivity that gave rise to the Greek *tribas* survived in early modern Galenic medicine,[39] it interacted with new conceptual schemes for figuring gender, erotic, racial, and cultural difference. The early modern category of the tribade is a product of the negotiation not only between modern and ancient modes of knowledge but also between various epistemological domains that sought to map the early modern body. In this sense, the early modern tribade is not a creature of exotic origins imported to Europe by travel writers, but rather is the discursive effect of (1) travel writers' transposition of ancient and medieval categories of intelligibility onto foreign "matter," and (2) anatomy's appropriation and refashioning of these "travel maps."[40]

38. See Harriette Andreadis, "Sappho in Early Modern England: A Study in Sexual Reputation" in *Re-Reading Sappho: Reception and Transmission*, ed. Ellen Greene (Berkeley, Calif.: University of California Press, 1996), pp. 105–21.

39. My characterization of the ancient logic of activity and passivity is drawn from the work of Brooten and David Halperin (*One Hundred Years of Homosexuality and Other Essays on Greek Love* [New York: Routledge, 1990]), who stress the importance of this binary system for organizing the meanings of sexual activity.

40. I thank David Halperin for helping me to see that the tribade is not so much invented

It is through women's common clitoral inheritance — an inheritance that is as much historical and psychological as biological — that the oppositional dyads of modernity (homo/hetero) develop. If the clitoris comes into representation accompanied by the tribade, if the tribade only takes up residence in England when endowed with an enlarged clitoris, and if the clitoris must be threatened with removal whenever the tribade rears her head, then these associations provide the raw material out of which the identity categories of lesbian and heterosexual would begin to be constructed. The inauguration of "the heterosexual" as the original, normative, essential mode of erotic behavior is haunted, from its first recognizably modern articulation, by an embodiment and practice that call the conceptual priority of heterosexuality into question. In historical terms, then, lesbianism is not, as Freud's developmental narrative would have it, the preoedipal embryo of an adult heterosexuality, but rather that troubling potential which always accompanies and threatens to disrupt heterosexuality. In the psychomorphology that our clitoral inheritance instantiates, lesbianism is less an alternative to female heterosexuality than its transgressive twin, "born" into modern discourse at the same ambivalent cultural moment.

To make this assertion is to challenge the adequacy of several analytical models currently circulating in lesbian studies. On the one hand, my effort to produce a nuanced account of erotic discourses prior to 1700 challenges the presentist bias of much recent work, particularly that which implies that little can be said of same-gender female eroticism before the inauguration of modern discourses of identity. One example of such presentism, as well as a lesson in what can result from a wholesale adoption of Laqueur's thesis, is found in an essay on clitoridectomy in Victorian Britain by Ornella Moscucci:

Throughout the sixteenth and seventeenth centuries, it was accepted that the clitoris was the seat of woman's sexual pleasure; medical writers were not worried about the potential of the clitoris for lesbianism or masturbation, nor about its size, which was seen positively, as a healthy mark of female lustfulness. By the end of the eighteenth century, however, the clitoris had become much more problematic.

or discovered in this period as refashioned according to new cultural exigencies. See his entry, "Homosexuality," in the *Oxford Classical Dictionary*, 3rd ed. (Oxford: Oxford University Press, 1996).

As the emerging notion of two opposite sexes made heterosexual coupling "natural," the capacity of the clitoris for homo- and autoeroticism was increasingly perceived as a threat to the social order.[41]

Moscucci follows Laqueur's lead in homogenizing a range of early modern discourses, constructing them as both univocal and unambivalent about female erotic power; more egregiously, she fails to follow his example of attention to historical specificity, instead condensing his treatment of the early modern period to a series of sound bites. If Moscucci's aim is to anatomize the gender and racial dynamics informing the practice of clitoridectomy in the mid-nineteenth century, she would do well to extend her historical gaze beyond the "enlarged clitoris and labia of the Hottentot," which became such "an important criterion of racial classification" by the late eighteenth century.[42] The eighteenth-century imperialist construction of a "torrid zone," a geography of both the equatorial regions of the globe and the female body that, as Felicity Nussbaum argues, "was formative in imagining that a sexualized woman of empire was distinct from domestic English womanhood," owes much to the earlier discourses of the clitoris and the tribade I have been tracing.[43] So too, the early sexologists' understanding of inversion as a deviation in gender produced under special circumstances and marked by geographical otherness has a long and involved colonial prehistory, which can be traced from the ambassadorial letters of de Busbecq to Richard Burton's *A Thousand and One Nights*.[44] Indeed, these traditions emerge in one of the most notorious accusations of tribadism in the early nineteenth century, the libel trial of Marianne Woods and Jane Pirie, during which one of the justices used classical sources to argue, much like Jane Sharp, that the "imputed vice has been hitherto unknown in Britain."[45]

41. Ornella Moscucci, "Clitoridectomy, Circumcision, and the Politics of Sexual Pleasure in Mid-Victorian Britain," in *Sexualities in Victorian Britain*, ed. Andrew Miller and James Eli Adams (Bloomington: Indiana University Press, 1996), pp. 60–78, esp. 69.
42. Moscucci, "Clitoridectomy," p. 70.
43. Felicity Nussbaum, *Torrid Zones: Maternity, Sexuality, and Empire in Eighteenth-Century English Narratives* (Baltimore, Md.: Johns Hopkins University Press, 1995), p. 7.
44. Both the stories themselves and the "Terminal Essay" appended to *The Book of The Thousand Nights and a Night* (1885–88) (trans. Richard Burton [New York: Heritage Press, 1934]) were an influential source of information about tribadism in the Middle East.
45. See the trial transcripts of 1810, *Miss Marianne Woods and Miss Jane Pirie against Dame Helen Cumming Gordon* (New York: Arno, 1975), "Speeches of the Judges," p. 8. See also Lillian

Although late-nineteenth-century psychoanalysis, sexology, anthropology, and criminology solidified erotic identities, the critical tendency to subsume early modern eroticism under modern categories obscures the indebtedness of these categories to prior discourses and conflicts. This presentist tendency thwarts inquiry both into the construction of the homo/hetero divide and the regulatory function of identity. The early modern reinvention of the tribade demonstrates that both the anatomical essentialism and colonial imaginary that underpin modern formations of lesbianism are not original to the Enlightenment regime of "the subject"; rather, they predate and help to constitute such modern formations. That is, under the auspices of protocolonialist discourses a new nexus of modern knowledge about female bodies was produced. Within the logics of this emerging epistemology were some of the primary terms by which certain female bodies subsequently would be pleasured as reproductive capital, while others would be condemned for their usurpation of masculine prerogatives and their pursuit of autonomous pleasures. If the regimes of Enlightenment knowledge inaugurated the category of "the subject" out of which a lesbian identity would be generated (by Freud among others), such epistemologies inherited from early modern travel narratives and anatomies the bodily contours of that subject.

Inherited, but not without significant change. For tribades were not lesbians; and if the early modern mapping of the tribade's body provides a means of understanding the historical antecedents to modern identities, it does not reinscribe such identities as historically invariable or self-evidently knowable. My study thus contravenes the (re)essentializing account making a resurgence in lesbian studies, perhaps most influentially in *The Apparitional Lesbian* by Terry Castle. In arguing that the lesbian "is not a recent invention,"[46] Castle bypasses the more difficult issue of just when, and under what auspices, the lesbian was constructed. Her attempt to bring the "apparitional lesbian" into visibility prior to 1900 assumes rather than explores the cohesion of lesbianism with the Enlightenment; as a result,

Faderman's condensation of the trial in *Scotch Verdict: Miss Pirie and Miss Woods v. Dame Cumming Gordon* (New York: William Morrow, 1983), as well as Lisa Moore's critique of Faderman's book in *Dangerous Intimacies: Toward a Sapphic History of the British Novel* (Durham, N.C.: Duke University Press, 1997), pp. 78–83.

46. Terry Castle, *The Apparitional Lesbian: Female Homosexuality and Modern Culture* (New York: Columbia University Press, 1993), p. 8.

the "dark ages" from which she attempts to rescue and revivify the lesbian are simply pushed farther back in time. If one of the pleasures of reading *The Apparitional Lesbian* is that it demonstrates the centrality of lesbianism to modern Western culture (much as Eve Sedgwick does for male homoeroticism), one of the disappointments is that Castle does so without formulating the historical *terms* of the lesbian's ghostly centrality. Lack of interest in these historical terms allows Castle to make the misguided proclamation that "[b]y its very nature . . . lesbianism poses an ineluctable challenge to the political, economic, and sexual authority of men over women [and] implies a whole new social order." [47] I hope to have called into question the idea that lesbianism has any such transhistorical "nature." Furthermore, Castle's empiricist, "commonsense" assumption that one knows, in an "ordinary," "vernacular" sense, what a lesbian "is," that this meaning is to be found in dictionaries,[48] and that on the basis of such tautologies one can forge stable connections across time and culture, obscures the recognition that such knowledge is less a position from which one can make autonomous claims than the result of normalizing discourses, the history of which I have been tracing.

The modern psychoanalytic discourse of lesbianism both recuperates and refigures the seventeenth-century psychomorphology of the clitoris, accepting the analogy between penis and clitoris, yet reading that analogy through the developmental narrative of castration. The indebtedness of modern discourses to preexisting corporeal maps, then, impels us not only to question the provenance of definitional tautologies ("lesbianism as we know it"), but to query the adequacy of the trope of metonymy to organize our understanding of the relation between bodies, identities, and desires. If the psychomorphology of the clitoris demonstrates the extent to which the clitoris and the lesbian are mutually constituted by a colonialist and patriarchal dynamic (which represses as much as it reveals same-gender female desire), then perhaps we can recognize the impact of this history on our attempts to think beyond the pathologies inscribed by Freud. In particular, we can trace the lineages of this occluded history in feminist strategies to displace the phallus by a female corporeal imaginary; for, as important as this displacement of the phallus by the labia has been in refiguring female sexuality as something other than lack, the theoretical recourse to female

47. Castle, *Apparitional Lesbian*, p. 62.
48. Castle, *Apparitional Lesbian*, pp. 9 and 15.

genitals tends to reiterate the logic of metonymy through which same-gender female desire has been anatomized and colonized.

The problem extends beyond the inability to conceive of the pleasures of vaginal penetration (by fingers, penis, tongue, or dildo) or the possibility of a nonphallocentric heterosexuality—although these are crucial issues as well.[49] Paula Bennett, for instance, recognizes that female sexuality is not limited to clitoral stimulation; and yet she concludes her essay on clitoral imagery in nineteenth-century poetry by asserting that "[w]ithout the clitoris, theorists have no physical site in which to locate an autonomous sense of female sexual agency. . . . With the clitoris, theorists can construct female sexuality in such a way that women become sexual subjects in their own right. . . . No longer married . . . to the penis or the law, they can become . . . by themselves healthy and whole."[50] Locating the possibilities of psychic health, wholeness, and agency in the clitoris seems a lot to ask of any one organ, particularly if women's embodied experience of desire, pleasure, and orgasm is, according to many testimonies, more fragmented and diffuse than unitary. But more is at issue here than the humanist basis of such claims: for the elevation of the clitoris (or labia) as the sine qua non of lesbian sexuality overvalues not only the genitals as a source of pleasure, but the power of bodily metonymy to represent that pleasure.

By far the most sophisticated (if slippery) expression of a metonymical mode of interpretation is that performed by Luce Irigaray. By situating a mechanics of fluids against the specular economy of the phallus, Irigaray challenges the humanist tradition of phallomorphic logic, with its emphasis on singularity, unity, and visibility, mobilizing instead a ternary, labial logic characterized by multiplicity, movement, fluidity, and tactility. Irigaray's invocation of vaginal and facial "lips" that "speak together" disperses the singularity of the signifier into a plurality of pleasures, zones, and sites of articulation: "[W]oman's pleasure does not have to choose between clitoral activity and vaginal passivity. . . . The pleasure of the vaginal

49. The need to reassert the pleasures of the vagina and penetration is advocated by Jane Gallop in *Thinking through the Body* (New York: Columbia University Press, 1988). For analyses of the lesbian use of dildoes, see Colleen Lamos's "The Postmodern Lesbian Position: On Our Backs," and Cathy Griggers's "Lesbian Bodies in the Age of (Post)Mechanical Reproduction," both in *The Lesbian Postmodern*, ed. Laura Doan (New York: Columbia University Press, 1994), pp. 85–103 and 118–33.

50. Paula Bennett, "Critical Clitoridectomy: Female Sexual Imagery and Feminist Psychoanalytic Theory," *Signs* 18 (1993): 235–59, esp. p. 257.

caress does not have to be substituted for that of the clitoral caress. They each contribute, irreplaceably, to woman's pleasure. . . . Among other caresses . . . [f]ondling the breasts, touching the vulva, spreading the lips, stroking the posterior wall of the vagina, brushing against the mouth of the uterus, and so on. . . . woman has sex organs more or less everywhere." [51] Supplementing the clitoris with the labia and the vagina, Irigaray charts a new "geography of feminine pleasure" that would seem to bypass and subvert the history of analogies between penis and clitoris that I have been tracing. [52]

Or does it? Does Irigaray's vulvomorphic "geography" actually sustain the deconstructive project she announces in *This Sex Which Is Not One?* Or does Irigaray's labial morphology reenact the anatomical essentialism that links body part(s) to erotic desire, and then enforces this link through the identification (and abjection or celebration) of a social type? I want to suggest that the metonymic association of female bodily organs (no matter how plural) with an erotic identity (no matter how "deviant") doesn't so much refigure female desire, as reproduce the contours of the colonialist geographies and anatomies out of which lesbian identity emerged.

To respond to Irigaray in this way is not simply to rehash the problems of essentialism and referentiality that have so dominated the reception of this theorist's work in the North American academy. [53] As Diana Fuss and Jane Gallop have argued persuasively, Irigaray's bodily aesthetic can be read as a strategic *composition*, a *poiesis*, rather than a referential *reflection* of the female body. [54] Nonetheless, this strategy of reading Irigaray rhetorically and performatively fails to take into account the extent to which the terms

51. Luce Irigaray, *This Sex Which Is Not One*, trans. Catherine Porter and Carolyn Burke (Ithaca, N.Y.: Cornell University Press, 1985), p. 28.

52. Irigaray, *This Sex*, p. 90.

53. See Ann Rosalind Jones, "Writing the Body: Toward an Understanding of l'Écriture féminine," in *The New Feminist Criticism: Essays on Women, Literature, and Theory*, ed. Elaine Showalter (New York: Pantheon, 1985), pp. 361–77; and Toril Moi, *Sexual/Textual Politics: Feminist Literary Theory* (London: Methuen, 1985).

54. Diana Fuss, *Essentially Speaking: Feminism, Nature, and Difference* (London: Routledge, 1989); Jane Gallop, "Lip Service," in *Thinking through the Body*, pp. 92–100. For defenses of Irigaray, see Margaret Whitford, *Luce Irigaray: Philosophy in the Feminine* (New York: Routledge, 1991); and *Engaging with Irigaray: Feminist Philosophy and Modern European Thought*, ed. Carolyn Burke, Naomi Schor, and Margaret Whitford (New York: Columbia University Press, 1994).

of that (re)composition carry with them a particular history. This igno-rance of historical terms is evinced by Gallop: "Volvomorphic logic, by *newly* metaphorizing the body, sets it free, if only momentarily." Although Gallop, a feminist Lacanian, recognizes that "as soon as the metaphor be-comes a proper noun, we no longer have creation, we have paternity," she nonetheless asserts: "Metaphor heals." [55]

I propose to read Irigaray's bodily poetics, not from the perspective of philosophy, but from the angle of genealogy. Lineages of a colonialist his-tory of embodiment become evident if one recognizes *This Sex Which Is Not One* as an effort to articulate not only a specifically "feminine" voice and desire, but also a lesbian subject; this subject is brought into being by a tex-tual progression of chapters within *This Sex Which Is Not One* which asserts the commensurability of body part(s) to erotic identity under the guid-ing auspices of metonymy. To read Irigaray genealogically, in other words, means to move from the problem of ontology (the task of defining what a woman "is") and mimesis (the adequacy of the signifier to denote the real) to the problem of metonymy (the adequacy of the part to stand for the whole). It is metonymy that enables Irigaray's valorization of a tactile over a visual economy, that allows her to envision the possibility of a touch un-mediated by culture and bodily difference. And it is metonymy that enables, over the course of her text, the supplanting of the category "woman" by the category "lesbian." In chapter 2, "This Sex Which Is Not One," the two lips that cannot be parted (except through phallic violence) represent the inher-ent autoeroticism of the female body; in chapter 11, "When Our Lips Speak Together," they become the lips of (at least two) women erotically plea-suring one another. What began as an assertion of bodily self-sufficiency ("she touches herself in and of herself without any need of mediation") [56] ends in a poetics of female merger: "You? I? That's still saying too much. Dividing too sharply between us: all." [57] In a move reminiscent of Adrienne Rich's lesbian continuum but devoid of Rich's acknowledgment of differ-ences along that spectrum, Irigaray slides from celebrating a unique female positivity to lauding the special effects of homoerotic desire. Negating the difference between one and two (bodies, subjects, erotic practices), Irigaray collapses the labia, the female voice, and lesbian(s) into a unified expres-

55. Gallop, "Lip Service," p. 96, emphasis mine.
56. Irigaray, *This Sex*, p. 24.
57. Irigaray, *This Sex*, p. 218.

sion of feminine *jouissance*. If Irigaray's strategic "concentrism" is a reversal and displacement of phallocentrism, it is nonetheless the case that her construction of lesbianism is indebted to a conflation of pre-Oedipal desire for the mother, autoeroticism, and narcissism. In a utopian gesture that elides the material conditions of lesbians, lesbianism is defined as that Imaginary plenitude which is both prior to and beyond the Symbolic.[58]

Where this correlation positions women who are not lesbian,[59] just where the exteriority of lesbianism is located, how lesbians may relate psychoanalytically to their mothers, and the extent to which lesbians may not enact a transgressive politics, are all questions left unanswered by Irigaray's bodily composition. But, more importantly for my argument, Irigaray's conflation of body part(s) and erotic identity maintains the psychomorphology of the clitoris by positing body part(s) as a sufficient sign of desire, and desire as adequately expressed through the rubric of (constructed) identity.[60] Although the specific terms of embodiment have changed, the logic of metonymic equivalence still holds: if not penis = clitoris = lesbian, then labia = lesbian desire = lesbian identity. Despite the erasure of phallomorphism from the equation, the underlying structure of commensurability secured by the phallus remains: body part = embodied desire = erotic identity. The phallus remains secure because this metonymic logic enacts and reinforces the power and propriety of naming. Indeed, one reason the relational structure I've described is so resistant to alteration is that it functions as a metanarrative of legitimation.[61] Although

58. This is the basis of an important critique by Annamarie Jagose, "Irigaray and the Lesbian Body: Remedy and Poison," *Genders* 13 (spring 1992): 30–42, who argues that Irigaray problematically relies "on a concept of exteriority . . . *as the very condition of female homosexuality*" (p. 33). According to Jagose, Irigaray's construction of femininity is even more insidious than this, for its ultimate goal is not the elaboration of a lesbian politics, but a "renegotiation of an emancipated heterosexuality across the repressed and unrepresentable body of the female homosexual" (p. 38).

59. See Joan Elizabeth Cocks, "Power, Desire, and the Meaning of the Body," in *The Oppositional Imagination: Feminism, Critique, and Political Theory* (London: Routledge, 1989).

60. Irigaray's reliance on metonymy authorizes her notoriously problematic conflation of male homosexuality and male patriarchal homosociality as "an economy of the same" in her coinage "hom(m)osexuality." See Fuss, *Essentially Speaking*, p. 111; Jagose, "Irigaray," pp. 36–37; and Craig Owens, "Outlaws: Gay Men in Feminism," in *Men in Feminism*, ed. Alice Jardine and Paul Smith (London: Routledge, 1987), pp. 219–32.

61. My thinking about legitimation as a metanarrative has been enhanced by Judith Roof's

the clitoris is no longer posited as an equivalent to the penis, female genitals are still invested with the power conventionally attributed to the phallus: they serve as the authorizing signature, the "proper name" of erotic desires, practices, and identities.

The problem with these bodily metonymies, then, is the synecdochical presumption that a part *can* stand for a whole, and that there is in fact a whole to be represented. I do not mean to imply that bodily metonymy invariably is colonialist. As a local, strategic, performative strategy, metonymy may be as good a trope as any: one continually is in the process of narrativizing one's own body, and the more rhetorical figures at one's disposal the better. However, the particular metonymies at issue here have functioned hegemonically as a master narrative that occludes not only its own historical construction, but the (anatomical) emergence of the body it purports to represent.

As long as this metonymic logic of legitimation holds steady, same-gender female desire is caught within the coordinates of a colonialist and patriarchal history. At the same time, this history is positioned as irrelevant to most lesbian scholarship, which seems unaware of or indifferent to any past prior to the eighteenth century. What finally is most troubling about the strategy to refigure the lesbian as a body composed of multiple lips is the extent to which it allows us to forget the centuries-long material processes that have identified and pathologized those psyches and bodies that desire other women. Indeed, it would seem that the feminist return to metonymy registers a longing to escape not only the logic of phallomorphism but also an awareness of the embodied history through which such a logic is lived. And yet lesbianism (the category of identity whose antecedents I have been tracing) is *constituted* by phallocentrism—or rather by the history that grants both phallocentrism and lesbianism their embodied meanings as ontology and identity. The very intelligibility of lesbianism, in other words, has devolved from the recitation of a past that exerts its power precisely because it is so rarely self-consciously cited.

Our task now is not to revise or reject Freud's narrative of lesbian pathology; several critics already have done so brilliantly.[62] Rather, in order

---

"Lesbians and Lyotard: Legitimation and the Politics of the Name," in *The Lesbian Postmodern*, pp. 47–66.

62. Freud's reading of the lesbian body is deconstructed by Irigaray, Roof, and Judith Butler, *Bodies That Matter: On the Discursive Limits of "Sex"* (New York: Routledge, 1993).

to resist the overdeterminations of history, we need to acknowledge the force of the psychomorphology that contributed not only to the psycho-analytic narrative of lesbian pathology but also to the feminist counter-narrative of lesbian identity, health, and wholeness. As two sides of the same identity coin, both narratives offer the lesbian body as the diacritical marker of female subjectivity, even as they value that body differently. As someone who is called, interpellated, identified by that name, I protest. But rather than simply repudiate or disavow these versions of lesbianism (a strategy that remains caught within an oscillating prison of identification/disidentification), I suggest that we pry apart the terms — the equation of body part and embodied desire, of embodied desire and erotic identity — through which the metonymic logic of anatomical essentialism continues to delineate, define, and discipline erotic possibility. Only by disarticulating these links can we extend the meanings of same-gender erotic desires be-yond the geographies and anatomies that would circumscribe them; only by articulating the incommensurability of desires, bodies, and identities can we move beyond the history from whence, inscribed, abjected, and unintelligible to ourselves, "we" came.

III

FEMALE GENEALOGIES

Genealogies in Crisis:
María de Zayas in Seventeenth-Century Spain
MARINA SCORDILIS BROWNLEE

> When life seems full and absolute, and men, out of
> all-consuming faith, are resigned to their destinies, novels
> perform no service at all. Religious cultures produce poetry and
> theater, not novels. Fiction is an art of societies in which faith
> is undergoing some sort of crisis, in which it's necessary to
> believe in something, in which the unitarian, trusting
> and absolute vision has been supplanted by a
> shattered one and an uncertainty about
> the world and the afterworld.
> —Mario Vargas Llosa

If we consider the case of Golden Age of Spain—a period rich in the production of fiction, poetry, and theater, Vargas Llosa's observation should be recast to indicate that the theater and poetry produced at the time tended to valorize official discourses, while the novelistic production often interrogated them. At times María de Zayas ostensibly supports the institutional rhetoric—going so far as to express at the end of her second novella collection, *The Disenchantments of Love,* nostalgia for the imperially great era of the Catholic monarchs, Ferdinand and Isabella, and the "golden age of gender relations" she imputes to it.[1] Yet she pays only intermittent lip ser-

---

The epigraph is from Mario Vargas Llosa, "Is Fiction the Art of Lying?" *New York Times Book Review,* October 7, 1984, I, 40.
1. In the epilogue to *The Disenchantments of Love* Lisis, the frame protagonist of the second half of Zayas's two-part collection of tales, laments the contemporary state of gender relations by making a pointed contrast between their seventeenth-century situation and the heroic age of the Catholic Kings, Ferdinand and Isabella: "I swear if you did love and cherish women as was the way in former times, you'd volunteer not just to go to war and fight, but to die, exposing your throat to the knife to keep from falling into the hands of the enemy. This is

vice to the establishment. Her novelistic prose offers to an equal—indeed greater degree—an exposé of the corrupted genealogies of gender, class, and racial purity that pervade the Spain of her day.

Even before the reader encounters the genealogical particularities of María de Zayas's texts, matters of literary lineage emerge provocatively in evaluations made by her peers. In keeping with the literary fashions of the seventeenth-century Spanish book trade, Zayas's novella collection is preceded by a series of laudatory endorsements that take the form of sonnets penned in her honor by other prominent writers. Yet, while it may be argued that promotional material of this sort was the order of the day, the repeated evocations of Zayas as a "tenth muse" and "sibyl" gesture toward a particular kind of appreciation of her by her contemporaries—namely, of her extraliterary effect.

Each of these mythical ascriptions provides a revealing perspective not only of Zayas's literary project but also of the wide-ranging possibilities that these female paradigms themselves entail. The sibyl has traditionally been depicted as a laconic female prophet with an ability to see beyond the civic chaos of a given period and a desire to offer guidance leading to the restoration of social order. Thought to live in oracular caves, the sibyls were ten in number, their most illustrious representative being Deiphobe, the Cumean sibyl, credited with such genealogical feats as guiding the Trojan Aeneas through the underworld so that he could visit with his father, Anchises. Since she had asked of Apollo that she live for as many years as there were grains of sand in her hand, she had clearly acquired the wisdom of age. According to another legend, she offered the last king of Rome, Lucius

---

the way it was in earlier days, particularly under King Ferdinand the Catholic. Then it wasn't necessary to conscript men, forcing them into service almost with their hands tied, the way it is today (causing our Catholic king unhappiness and great misfortune). Men used to offer up their possessions and their lives, the father to defend his daughter, the brother to defend his sister, the husband to defend his wife, the suitor to defend his lady. They did so to keep their women from being captured, taken prisoner or, worst of all, being dishonored. I feel sure this is what will come to pass if you men don't gather the courage to defend women." María de Zayas, *Parte segunda del sarao y entretenimiento honesto* [*Desengaños amorosos*] (Barcelona: Sebastian de Cormellas, 1647); Eng. trans. by H. Patsy Boyer, *The Disenchantments of Love* (Albany: State University of New York Press, 1997), p. 400. Zayas's first novella collection, *Novelas amorosas y eiemplares* (Saragoça: Pedro Esquer, 1637) was published in English by Boyer as *The Enchantments of Love: Amorous and Exemplary Novels* (Berkeley: University of California Press, 1990). All subsequent quotations in English from Zayas's *Enchantments* and *Disenchantments* refer to Boyer's translations.

Tarquinius Superbus, nine prophetic books—a compendium of sibylline wisdom—at a high price. When the monarch refused to buy them, she destroyed three of the volumes, destroying an additional three when he again refused. Tarquin finally bought the remaining three tomes at the price initially demanded for all nine. These books were preserved in the temple of Jupiter in Rome and were regularly consulted in times of great strife. The original Sibylline Books were destroyed in a fire in 83 B.C., and a new collection was subsequently compiled, though this also perished, in 405 A.D.

Zayas is referred to repeatedly as a sibyl because of her short stories, which figure the decay of the Spanish Empire through the male-female relations of her day. Her fiction goes far in illustrating the extent to which "the recesses of domestic space become sites for history's most intricate invasions," which Homi Bhabha insightfully identifies as a cultural constant.[2] While her prose has been explored for its indictment of patriarchal abuses, two further aspects of her writing require explanation. First, the level of violence done to women—primarily uxoricide—far exceeds any historical archival evidence, and second, her domestic narratives—often lurid in their detail—point, beyond gender relations, to the most hotly contested features of Spain's imperial enterprise, namely, the nature and function of class, race, and nationhood. No doubt it is as a result of this wide-ranging cultural commentary that Zayas is regarded by her contemporaries as a sibyl. María Caro de Mallén and Alonso Castillo y Solórzano, among other notable authors of the time, praise her as a latter-day, modern sibyl, the "Sibyl of Madrid," while Caro and Lope de Vega provide an additional association with Sappho: "nueva Safo," the "new Sappho" of Spain.[3]

This identification with Sappho is intriguing for several reasons. First, Zayas, like Sappho (650–590 B.C.), wrote literature, teaching her art to women and eschewing the company of men. Late writers of antiquity, because of Sappho's preference for the company of women, accused her of "Sapphism," that is, lesbianism. Zayas, too, has been likened to Sappho in this way. For while she was the toast of literary salons, a literary figure of major stature, lauded and applauded by other literary stars, a best-seller as

2. Homi Bhabha, *The Location of Culture* (London: Routledge, 1994), p. 9.

3. E.g., María Caro de Mallén, "Crezca la gloria española,/ insigne Doña María,/ por ti sola, pues podría/ gloriarse España en ti sola;/ nueva Safo, nueva Pola" in Zayas, *Novelas amorosas y ejemplares,* ed. Agustín de Amezúa (Madrid: Aldus, 1948), p. 10. Subsequent quotations from the first part of the Spanish text refer to the Amezúa edition. In his *Laurel de Apolo,* Lope de Vega offers a similar analogy.

well, virtually nothing has been recorded of her biography except that she was very close to and lived, for several years, with a woman by the name of Ana Caro—perhaps a kindred spirit in sexual preference as well as literary taste.[4] The fact that the women of her extended fictional soirée figured in the novelas, retreat, at the book's conclusion, to the convent to reject the company of men has contributed further to the Sapphic association. Yet the mythological association with Sappho is not entirely analogous.

Zayas masterfully weaves plots that address the abuses of the period, but in such a way that, far from being silenced, she attains tremendous success in print. She is more than a staunch critic of the abusive male-female relations of her day. If she were exclusively concerned with subverting the patriarchy, how do we account for seeming inconsistencies is her discourse, where she appears to uphold the "system"? If she is as programmatically subversive of the patriarchy as recent critics allege, how do we account for Zayas's status in her day as a best-selling author (surpassed in sales only by Cervantes, Quevedo, and Alemán)?—especially given the low female literacy rates in the Spain of her time. Likewise, how do we explain the fact that her work remained uncensored by the literary expurgators of the Inquisition? What do we make of her contradictory self-presentation as author in her *Novelas amorosas y ejemplares* (*The Enchantments of Love*)—on the one hand reviling the abuses perpetrated by men, advocating escape to the convent in the voice of her principal female character; declaring, on the other hand, the recuperability of men (if they read her twenty-novella collection properly), calling for a return to the "golden age" of gender relations she situates in the era of the Catholic Kings? Within the tales themselves, what do we make of the at times shockingly cruel exploitation of women (and men) by other women? Finally, why do a number of her tales verge on the pornographic if her only ambition is to illustrate the blamelessness of her sex? She is an accomplished marketing strategist who manages to captivate readers with notably divergent alliances—conservative and radical, sentimental and sadistic—eluding censorship while cashing in on the "tabloid" craze that gripped Spain in the seventeenth century.[5]

4. See Margarita Nelken, "*Las novelas amorosas y ejemplares* de doña María de Zayas y Sotomayor, y la escuela cínica," in *Las escritoras españolas* (Barcelona: Labor, 1930), pp. 151–55. Castillo Solórzano, in his *Garduña de Sevilla,* alludes to the fact that Ana Caro was Zayas's companion and that Caro lived with Zayas in Madrid. See *La garduña de Sevilla,* ed. Federico Ruiz Morcuende (Madrid: Espasa-Calpe, 1957), pp. 66–67.
5. In this connection, see Henry Ettinghausen, "The Illustrated Spanish News: Text and

Let the reader beware of additional pitfalls engineered by Zayas in her seemingly transparent, didactic prose. The words "amorous" and "exemplary" in the title of her collection of stories (two volumes published at a twenty-year interval, the first in 1637, the second in 1647) are notoriously overdetermined during the period in which she wrote them. Michel Foucault and others have observed that in the seventeenth and eighteenth centuries the "solidity of language was dissolved." [6] Hence, the notion that a text could exert an "exemplary" pedagogical function is questionable on principle. Because humanist as well as posthumanist exempla call for judgment rather than unquestioning acceptance, such texts are problematizing rather than illustrative. Yet, as Victoria Kahn notes, they "also give rise to the temptation to theorize this (in)coherence." [7] It is a largely futile exercise, however, in which many critics of Cervantes' *Novelas exemplares* are still engaged. It is, I maintain, just as fruitless in the case of Zayas.

The other term—"amorous"—is likewise problematic, on at least two counts. First, when a woman writes about male-female relations, her work should not be construed as sociological tract, as mimetic evidence of "real life," any more than a man's writing should. Much Zayas criticism has erred in this direction, which is a temptation, especially since she insists that her narratives detail empirically real events. Second, seduction narratives are intricate in terms of gender and genre. As Ros Ballaster indicates, "The telling of a story of seduction is also a mode of seduction. The struggle for control over the identification and interpretation of amatory signs between male and female protagonists which is enacted on the level of content can be taken as a metaphorical substitution for the struggle for epistemological authority between male and female readers on the level of form." [8]

In the case of Zayas, this struggle is made explicit by a group of inscribed mixed-gender narrators and auditors who by turns tell, listen to, and in-

---

Image in the Seventeenth-Century Press," in *Art and Literature in Spain: 1600–1800, Studies in Honor of Nigel Glendinning,* ed. Charles Davis and Paul Julian Smith (London: Tamesis, 1993), pp. 117–33, and his "Sexo y violencia: Noticias sensacionalistas en la prensa española del siglo XVII," *Edad de Oro* 12 (1993): 95–107.

6. Michel Foucault, *The Order of Things* (New York: Vintage Books, 1973), p. 43.

7. Victoria Kahn, "Humanism and the Resistance to Theory," in *Literary Theory/Renaissance Texts,* ed. Patricia Parker and David Quint (Baltimore, Md.: Johns Hopkins University Press, 1986), p. 380.

8. Ros Ballaster, *Seductive Forms: Women's Amatory Fiction from 1684 to 1740* (Oxford: Clarendon Press, 1992), p. 24.

terpret the narratives, as well as by the implicit struggle in which we—her extratextual readers—engage. What becomes clear in the process of reading her work is that she does not construct her characters or her readers' responses along predictable gender lines, even when she at first appears to do so.

If we return to the Zayas's association with Sapphic genealogy, we may recall that Sappho is traditionally referred to as the tenth muse—a distinction ascribed to her two centuries after her death by Plato in recognition of her poetic prowess. And this is, significantly, the other identification made with respect to Zayas by her contemporaries. What is particularly interesting in this regard is the appearance of the "tenth muse" paradigm in the early modern period and its contextualization within the framework of imperial discourse. It is a genealogical trope evoked during this period by its promoters for purposes of imperial self-justification, as Stephanie Jed has recently argued.[9]

More broadly, women writers of the early modern period seem to be obsessively categorized by their male counterparts in genealogical as well as biological terms—deemed to be either legitimate or illegitimate, type-cast at one extreme or the other, either, like Aphra Behn, as "whores" who dare to leave the privacy of the domestic sphere and its patriarchal authority to "go public" with their writing, hence becoming "public women," as Catherine Gallagher has documented, or as the unthreatening, unsexed ("neuter") mythological muse figures that Stephanie Jed has studied.

The laudatory attribution of tenth muse status to Zayas conforms strikingly to Jed's typology of this modern muse: as being neither male nor female.[10] Such an attribution of a woman writer's status as "neuter" reflects a whole system of assumptions about authorship—that men wrote and women inspired them to do so as muses and that real women did not write. The epithet "tenth muse" eliminates these problems; given that they are capable of writing, they must not be women in the normal sense. Thus, the tenth muse trope is a way of justifying—or of making less threatening—the perceived problem of being both a woman and an accomplished writer.

9. Stephanie Jed, "The Tenth Muse: Gender, Rationality, and the Marketing of Knowledge," in Women, "Race," and Writing in the Early Modern Period, ed. Margo Hendricks and Patricia Parker (London: Routledge, 1994), pp. 195–208.
10. Alonso Bernardo de Quirós, "Del olvido y de la muerte/ hoy redimes tu renombre, / ni eres mujer ni eres hombre;/ nada es humana, tú fuerte." Zayas, Novelas amorosas, p. 16.

The provocative study of this phenomenon offered by Jed focuses on Sor Juana Inés de la Cruz and on Anne Bradstreet — two writers who had a significant impact on the colonial literature market. Both authors speak of themselves as neuter, and both construct themselves by means of genealogical references that defy gender norms. Bradstreet's title is very revealing: *The Tenth Muse, Lately Sprung Up in America,* which, as Jed observes, "evoked an image of parthenogenesis: this muse was not born from any inseminated figure of Mother America, but she sprang up rather from the soil of New England, seemingly without the help of English seed" (197). This parthenogenic potential has, paradoxically, an ability to link the Old World with the New to, in Bradstreet's case, represent "the power of English (and European) culture to dominate the world, a new category [able to] assimilate new manifestations of this power in places far from London" (198).

Sor Juana performs a similar function vis-à-vis the Spanish Empire, speaking of her own body as "neuter" ("neutro"), with the title page of the first edition of her works describing her as the "Musa dézima . . . que en varios metros, idiomas, y estilos fertiliza varios assumptos" ["Tenth muse . . . who in various meters, languages, and styles fertilizes various issues." [11] She, like her Puritan counterpart Bradstreet, is invoked as a museum piece of sorts: referred to by a fellow nun as the "glorioso honor del mexicano museo" ("glorious honor of the Mexican museum"). It is no accident that Zayas is just as worthy of inclusion within the museum, "el Museo te alabe en voz canora." [12] The reason for associating the tenth muse figure with the Museum has to do, in the case of Sor Juana and Anne Bradstreet, with their potential as New World propaganda in the service of the Old World. Their compelling literature, their very existence in remote lands, could be used as a tool to engage Old World investors in the New, and to underscore the powerful influence of the empire in places far removed from it.

If the tenth muse is a constructed genealogy designed to lure European investors and consumers and to valorize colonial discourse itself, then this is where Zayas parts company from her sisters. She too is a muse of empire, but one who cannot be appropriated as imperial propaganda, given the problematic depiction she offers in her repeated representations of this

11. Quoted in Jed, "The Tenth Muse," p. 195.
12. In his laudatory sonnet, Victorián Josef de Esmir y Casanate writes: "Ocupa el mucho desplendor luciente,/ el Museo te alabe en voz canora,/ el rubio Apolo que los obres dora/ honre con claros círculos tu frente." Zayas, *Novelas amorosas,* p. 19.

enterprise. What differentiates Zayas from her illustrious literary sisters, the other tenth muses, is her persistent interrogation of state policies pertaining to gender, race, and class. For while at times voicing approval of Spain's imperial discourse and its status quo, her project is to stage the instability and injustices of Spanish society—from its most intimate individual domestic case studies to their universal implications for the officially sanctioned discourses and the values that subtend them. In this way she breaks dramatically with the genealogical relationship that links the tenth muse to empire. To a large degree, Zayas brings about her extended indictment by rejecting the genealogical imperative on an individual scale— offering human relationships that do not conform to the enshrined heterosexual paradigms of courtship, marriage, and procreation. And in so doing, she offers dramatic substantiation of Elizabeth Grosz's observation that "bodies have all the explanatory power of minds."[13]

Slavery is a case in point, a topic that Zayas addresses provocatively in her text. Amid the existence of white and black slaves owned by various masters, we find depicted in *El prevenido engañado* (*Forewarned but Not Forearmed*), for example, a widow who fends off a suitor, invoking as the reason for her behavior the obligatory year of celibacy to which she must adhere in memory of her dead husband. Yet what we learn from her suitor's surveillance is that she is sexually obsessed with her slave—a black man. Far from being the bereaved widow in search of consolation, she is the cause of the slave's death, which occurs as a result of her monstrously insatiable sex drive. This scene is striking in its implications in terms of both gender and class. Namely, it figures woman as being implicitly as libidinous as men are, including their potential for rape. Yet, given the relentless nature of her repeated excess, the widow seems even more sinister. The fact that her partner is sick adds to the repugnance of this impression. The fact that the tables are turned—that it is a woman sexually abusing a man, rather than the normatively male predator, offers a comment on the much more widespread abuse of women, as well as a meditation on class differences; usually it is the male head of household who takes advantage of his female servant.

The shock value of the black-white liaison clearly reflects the fascination and fear of the other, the obsession with blood purity which had, since the

13. Elizabeth Grosz, *Volatile Bodies: Toward a Corporeal Feminism* (Bloomington: Indiana University Press, 1994), p. vii.

mid-1400s in Spain, been an official policy. This terror of "impurity" and fascination with the forbidden other was very real in seventeenth-century Spain, documented even in the well-known sensationalist account of a lady from Seville and her husband who—much to their dismay—produced a black child because a black maid's baby lay in their bed at the time of procreation.[14] A different instance of racial anxiety exists in Zayas's tale entitled "Tarde llega el desengaño" ("Too Late Undeceived"), a narrative that is a lurid remake of Marguerite de Navarre's thirty-second *Heptameron* tale.[15] Beginning with a white woman who treats her white lover as a prostitute (receiving him only blindfolded, concealing her identity for the duration of their month-long liaison, and paying him each time for his services), the text thereafter depicts a black female slave who victimizes an exemplary (white) wife, convincing the lady's husband that the wife has defiled his honor. In order to punish the unjustly maligned wife, the husband substitutes the black slave for her in every way—giving her the jewels, clothes, even, it appears, the sexual prerogatives of the lady—who must witness the substitution in public and on a daily basis, while she herself is tortured both physically and psychologically. The effect of this mixed couple on the inscribed audience, like the effect on the extradiegetic reader of the story, is one of fascination, but even more, of fear and loathing—given the predatory nature of the black woman who destroys the life of her exemplary mis-

14. Quoted in Agustín Redondo, "Les 'Relaciones de sucesos' dans l'Espagne du siècle d'Or: Un moyen privilégié de transmission culturelle," *Cahiers de l'UFR d'Etudes Ibériques et Latino-Américaines* 7 (1989): 63. See also the essay by Valeria Finucci.

15. Zayas actually conflates key aspects of two of Marguerite de Navarre's *Heptameron* tales, numbers 32 and 43 (Marguerite de Navarre, *The Heptameron,* ed. and trans. Paul Anthony Chilton, New York: Penguin, 1984). In the first model, an adulterous wife is punished by her husband, who confines her to her (albeit "beautiful") bedroom, shaves her head, and makes her use the skull of her executed lover as a drinking cup. No one speaks to the lady, moreover. This macabre punishment is revoked, however, when a traveler convinces the dishonored husband that her remorse warrants forgiveness. They are reconciled and have several lovely children. Zayas recounts the definitive punishment of a totally blameless wife, only part of whose torment is figured by the mendacious slave who replaces her. The other model text, *Heptameron* 43, also reflects Zayas's more grisly rendition. In the French original, a woman named Jambique, who does not wish her lover to know her identity, tells him that if he attempts to learn who she is, their love will be destroyed. When he ascertains her identity, she refuses to see him ever again. Here too, Zayas "turns up the heat" by making her female protagonist much more vindictive, by having her attempt to kill the lover after treating him as nothing more than an anonymous sex object.

tress. A stern indictment of the husband is also registered, given his—like other husbands'—haste in condemning his wife before attempting to determine her guilt or innocence. An overwhelming number of chaste wives in Zayas are similarly condemned, a pattern she uses to indict the misnamed "honor code" that can lead to such injustice.[16]

While the first case offers a seductive portrait of the black slave, and the second a repulsive one, a third example of slavery evoked by Zayas centers, in "La esclava de su amante," around a white woman named Isabel who turns the slave-of-passion metaphor into a literal reality, offering another case study designed to expose the injustices of gender relations in her homeland. In this case it is the Christian Isabel Fajardo who disguises herself as the Moorish slave Zelima in order to pursue her rapist, Manuel, who had sworn eternal fidelity before abandoning her. This story is unique to Zayas's collection because it is presented autobiographically—Isabel tells her own story to the assembled soirée members. As Amy Katz Kaminsky explains, Zelima/Isabel "makes material the metaphor of the lover's abiding presence within her and determines to advertise his base and unchristian behavior by wearing outwardly the marks of estrangement from Christian society (Muslim dress) and enslavement (the brand on her face) which his actions have occasioned."[17]

In so doing, the behavioral "femininity as masquerade" identified long ago by Joan Rivière (the role-playing that a woman undertakes in order to comply with the cultural constructions of femininity) is replaced by a literal masquerade that inverts those constructions. Her rape leads her (after she tries to kill Manuel and then herself) to seek revenge for the crime in a more calculated manner, a goal on which she spends six full years of intense pursuit. Manuel interprets her challenge to boundaries of gender, class, ethnicity, and religion as repulsive and to be avoided at all cost. Meanwhile another man, Felipe, who has always loved Isabel but belongs to a more modest economic milieu, avenges her by murdering Manuel. This act leads

16. See in this regard Melveena McKendrick, *Woman and Society in the Spanish Drama of the Golden Age* (Cambridge: Cambridge University Press, 1974), and Matthew Stroud, *Fatal Union* (Lewisbery, Pa.: Bucknell University Press, 1990).

17. Amy Katz Kaminsky, "Dress and Redress: Clothing in the *Desengaños amorosos* of María de Zayas," *Romanic Review* 79 (1988): 380. For a fine series of essays on sexuality, narrative, and other aspects of Zayas, see Amy R. Williamson and Judith A. Whitenack, eds., *María de Zayas: The Dynamics of Discourse* (Madison, N.J.: Farleigh-Dickinson University Press, 1995).

Isabel to consider briefly—but ultimately reject—marriage to Felipe, who has defended her honor in spite of her impurity as a nonvirgin. Instead, she chooses to "enslave" herself to God, the lover who will never mistreat her, ending her narrative by announcing that she plans to enter a convent.[18] As such, she rejects the heterosexual paradigm entirely, exposing the ideologically corrupt, unchristian norm of male-female relations through her "impure" disguise as a Moor.

Genealogies of "honor," male-female relations, the validity of blood purity—indeed all the institutionalized categories used by church and state to officially define "Spanishness" are interrogated in Zayas's stories. Beyond the predatory representation inherent in prostitution, to which she resorts on several occasions, she signals the disfunctional nature of Spain's most influential classes by other means as well. The institution of marriage is relentlessly attacked as predatory, whereby chaste wives are victimized by unjustifiably cruel husbands, brothers, and other male relations. The dictum to "be fruitful and multiply" is similarly problematized in these texts. If one counts the number of offspring produced by the couples represented in the *Enchantments* and *Disenchantments,* we find a virtual absence of procreative activity. Indeed, there are virtually no children produced by the couples figured in these tales, and when there are, they are either abandoned or killed by their parents, or the parents express the unnatural desire to have them die.

We are left to survey a bleak human landscape, devoid of biological productivity. At the same time, the integrity of the human body—virtually always the female body—is shattered as we encounter severed heads and hands, women who are blinded, poisoned, crushed, burned, and bled to death by vengeful males. While Zayas's grisly accounts of male brutality have been the object of considerable attention lately, it should be noted that, on a number of occasions, women retaliate. The broken and dismembered bodies of both genders in Zayas's seventeenth-century Spain signal an analogous societal alienation that Francis Barker describes in the case of Jacobean and Elizabethan England and the move toward the emerging modern subject: "If the once-full body is so often presented as a shattered

18. Zayas, "Because of a thankless and ungrateful lover I've suffered great misfortunes always wearing the brand and the name of being a slave. How much better it is to be God's slave, offering myself to Him with the very same name: 'slave to her own lover'" (*Disenchantments,* p. 81).

wreckage of disarticulated fragments, it is because the disintegration of this world and its signification is already upon it. As modern subjectivity begins to emerge, it turns destructively on that older body from which it struggles to free itself."[19] Society's alienation from a corrupt ideology expresses its violent verbal response by means of violent physical response.

This is why not only integral human bodies but gender relations, Christian matrimony, the family structure, race, and also the official guarantors of the system—such as mayors, priests, even the king—are portrayed as ineffectual in providing a just system of civic order.[20] For the same purpose she figures various alternative lifestyles into her texts with a remarkable degree of complexity. The presence of such traditionally marginal and un- or underrepresented categories as homoerotic and lesbian desire, as well as the complex treatment Zayas offers of witchcraft, all serve to illustrate the insufficiency of traditional categories of literary and societal representation and the need to rethink the inauthentic nature of their values.

Witchcraft is an issue that Zayas addresses repeatedly, posing a significant threat to patriarchal authority with an at times very unorthodox matri-

19. Francis Barker, *The Tremulous Private Body* (Ann Arbor: University of Michigan Press, 1995), p. 37.
20. Zayas even figures woman as valiant and triumphant soldier in her tale "El juez de su causa" ("Judge Thyself"). Indeed, Estela (cross-dressed and circulating as a man by the name "Fernando") is so adept and fearless that for the valor she demonstrates in saving the life of Charles V, the Holy Roman Emperor bestows upon her the title of duke, thereafter being honored by him as he designates her a member of the prestigious Order of Santiago and, ultimately, appointing her to the position of viceroy. Zayas is indebted to Lope de Vega for the gender-bending involved in this tale; and it is indicative of a whole tradition of "manly females," *mujeres varoniles,* that frequently surface in the literature of the period. In the case of Zayas's tale, order is definitively restored not by Estela/Fernando's heroic feats, but by the revelation of her female sexual identity which results, among other things, in the transfer of her titles as viceroy and Knight of the Order of Santiago to her fiancé, don Carlos, while she is given the more appropriate title of princess of Buñol. Although this tale is amusingly far-fetched, and calculatedly so, it points to a category of female depiction as amazon that exists in seventeenth-century Spain and beyond. Speaking of the English eighteenth-century tradition of the female warrior and its misogynistic implications, Laura Brown has written insightfully that "under the sign of difference, the Amazon illuminates a whole constellation of ideological categories and functions. As a proxy or scapegoat, the representation of difference serves discursively to deflect the responsibilities and anxieties of empire" ("Amazons and Africans: Gender, Race, and Empire in Daniel Defoe," in Hendricks and Parker, *Women, "Race," and Writing,* p. 135).

archal model.[21] Lesbian attraction is suggested, albeit momentarily, in "La burlada Aminta y venganza del honor" ("Aminta Deceived and Honor's Revenge"). As Flora offers to help Jacinto seduce and abandon the innocent Aminta, she tells her accomplice to allow her to approach the lady alone and unaccompanied, saying that "you know my tastes are more those of a gallant than of a lady, and whenever I see a lady, particularly one as beautiful as this lady, I can't take my eyes from her beauty, and my heart grows tender." [22] As Valerie Traub observes of such allusions on the English stage, they are allowable so long as they do not pose a threat to patriarchal prerogatives.[23] While Flora and the old crone who helps her in the seduction are depicted as watching with pleasure as Aminta loses her virginity, Zayas almost immediately returns the narrative to its heterosexual point of reference. Nonetheless, this move back to the more traditional model of love between men and women does not cancel out the suggestion.

Zayas uses the representation of gender boldly — as a way to figure cultural anxieties about the validity of the patriarchal structure itself — along with its implications for the Christian notion of matrimony. Her concerns for this troubled social system are nowhere more apparent than in "Mal presagio casar lejos" ("Marriage Abroad: Portent of Doom"), a tale that plays out fears pertaining to the issue of nationalism as well.

This is a story of grotesque cruelty in which five children — one son and four daughters — lose their parents and all suffer great personal tragedies. In spite of their innocence, beauty, intellect, and nobility, each of the women is brutally maimed or murdered. The first, named Mayor, accompanied by her youngest sister, Maria, goes to Portugal when she takes a Portuguese husband. In a totally feigned and unwarranted testing of his new wife, this man writes her a love letter, pretending to be not her husband but a suitor. As she reads the letter, the husband rushes in, killing both her and the unsuspecting page who delivered it. Seeing this monstrous behavior, the young sister jumps out the window in an attempt to escape it, in the process breaking both legs, which leaves her an invalid for life. We are

21. For the implications of witchcraft see Peter Stallybrass and Allon White, *The Politics and Poetics of Transgression* (London: Methuen, 1986), especially the introduction.
22. Zayas, *Enchantments*, p. 55.
23. Valerie Traub, "Lesbian Desire in Early Modern England," in *Erotic Politics*, ed. Susan Zimmerman (London: Routledge, 1992), p. 164.

given an explanation based on nationalism and the powerful hatred it can engender, that the Portuguese do not welcome Castilians, that this is why Mayor lost her life in an unprovoked attack. We also learn that Maria was rescued by some Castilians who returned her, in her permanently crippled state, to Spain.

In this way the topic of nationalism—especially the abuse of Spanish women abroad—is firmly established from the opening moments of the unfolding narrative. And it is reinforced with each new casualty. The second sister of this unfortunate genealogy, Leonor, marries an Italian by whom she has a son. When one day and without any ulterior motive she praises a Spanish captain in her husband's hearing, he strangles her as she is in the process of shampooing her hair, murdering their now four-year-old son as well. The third sister, Blanca, meanwhile marries a prince from Flanders who seems to her brother to be a suitable match. We are told by the narrator that if she had known the tragic fates of her three sisters, however, she would surely have chosen the convent instead of agreeing to any marriage.

Unaware as yet of her sisters' deaths, she agrees to this marriage of convenience on condition that the prince who has proposed to her come to Spain and court her for one year, thereby hoping to become sufficiently acquainted with him to know whether his love for her is genuine. They marry at the year's conclusion, and almost immediately thereafter Blanca learns of the violent deaths of her sisters. But now it is too late, since she has officially become her husband's property. Virtually as soon as they leave Spain, Blanca's husband begins to mistreat her, we are told, because Spanish women always suffer at the hands of foreign husbands.[24] Yet the misogyny extends beyond national boundaries, for even Marieta, the prince's sister, is hated by her husband although they share the same nationality. No simple overlapping of categories obtains.

We learn in addition that the prince's mistreatment of Blanca is nothing by comparison with her relentlessly cruel father-in-law. The day that the newlyweds arrive in Flanders, the prince's father, impatient at the one-year delay in the marriage, meets his daughter-in-law for the first time with words of abuse: "¿Cuándo había de ser esta venida? Basta que las españolas sois locas. No sé qué extranjero os apetece, si no es que esté desespe-

---

24. Zayas, "I don't understand the misfortune Spanish women have with foreign husbands, who never esteem them but instead tire of them in two days and treat them with contempt. I say this because I've seen it happen many times" (Disenchantments, p. 254).

rado" (273–74). This remark is indicative of his attitude toward her, treating her with nothing but rage and ridicule. Why, we may ask, does the prince marry Blanca in the first place, given the prejudice against Spaniards that he and especially his father feel? It would appear from the violent deaths that Blanca's sisters have experienced and from the equally terrible fate that she herself will soon undergo that Zayas constructs an exemplum of the perils involved for the woman who marries a foreigner. Yet other causes are suggested as well. Marieta, her sister-in-law, who is not married to a foreigner, dies garroted by her husband—either because she defended Blanca in an altercation she had with her husband, or because the husband was jealous of her servant: "un gentilhombre de la señora Marieta, que daba la mano cuando salía fuera, mozo de mucha gala y nobleza" (281). It is never made clear whether the jealousy was justified or not. Yet, though this ambiguity is never resolved, there exists no doubt as to the misogynistic environment pervading the household of the prince and his father. In any case, the narrator's categorical statement concerning the issue of nationalism—that it brings the demise of blameless women—is called into question.

What becomes increasingly evident in this tale is that the prince's brutal attitude toward women results less from nationalistic prejudice than from a homoerotic complication. Blanca herself walks in on the prince as he is having sex with his favorite page, Arnesto. Whereas Blanca had assumed that the prince's radical change in behavior toward her once he returned to Flanders was the result of a liaison with another woman, she is shocked to find him in bed with another man.[25] At last we find articulated a motive for all the seemingly unmotivated and excessive barbarity against women that fills the pages of this narrative. Apparently, the prince, his father, and Arnesto form a fiercely loyal homosexual community. That Zayas would represent this possibility in an extended fashion in seventeenth-century Spain seems daring indeed. It is a topic that even today is often viewed as transgressive and controversial. This departure from the canon of appropriate themes corresponds in part to the new reading practices that Roger Chartier identifies with the privatization of reading during the early modern period.[26] Silent reading encouraged an atmosphere of intimacy

25. Zayas, "In the bed she saw her husband and Arnesto engaged in such gross and abominable pleasures that it's obscene to think it, let alone say it" (*Disenchantments*, p. 265).
26. See Roger Chartier, "The Practical Impact of Writing," in *A History of Private Life*, vol. 3, *Passions of the Renaissance*, ed. Roger Chartier, trans., Arthur Goldhammer (Cambridge,

that shut out the outside world, permitting the reader to indulge in all types of fantasies, including the voyeurism that Blanca — and later her sister Marieta — experience. And, while it is a profoundly negative experience for Blanca the character, the transgressive nature of its representation is titillating for the reader, representing as it does a highly transgressive activity in the context of early modern mainstream society. Although it is not described in great detail, its very suggestion borders on the pornographic, which private reading made possible in respectable circles for the first time in history.[27] In effect, in the privacy of his or her own room, the reader is now offered the exciting prospect of becoming a voyeur.[28]

Beyond the treatment of a transgressive theme, Zayas offers a remarkable, admirably complex vision of homosexuality. For if we trace carefully the speech and actions of the prince, we see that he, like her females, reveals inconsistent and contradictory subject positions to a dramatic degree. Paul Julian Smith has written insightfully of the male-female relations in this text, speaking of the "negative female exchange" as opposed to the "productive economy of men" embodied by the homosocial community of the prince, his father, and Arnesto. In so doing, Smith affirms that "(according to Zayas and Irigaray) 'hom(m)osexualité' (sexual commerce between men) is the logical result of a system which persists in excluding women. In this 'circulation of the same' women can figure only as objects of exchange and can never transcend a state of permanent exile."[29]

It is true that these women are forever silenced as a result of unwarranted male brutality, but the "productivity" of the male group is debatable. Moreover, such a coherent presentation of the male community is not the case,

Mass.: Harvard University Press, 1989), pp. 111–60; and Fernando Bouza Alvarez, Del escribano a la biblioteca: La civilización escrita europea en la edad moderna (siglos XV–XVII) (Madrid: Síntesis, 1992).

27. On the rise of pornography and its connection with print culture, see Lynn Hunt, ed., The Invention of Pornography (New York: Zone Books, 1993), esp. pp. 9–45.

28. To be sure, voyeuristic moments have been represented in earlier literature, e.g., Decameron 2.9, or in the various accounts of Mélusine, who becomes victimized by her husband's forbidden gaze. But unlike the type of public reading entailed by the Boccaccian text or the medieval romance, Zayas's stories are intended for individual, private reading. The effect of the voyeuristic environment becomes much more transgressive as one individual (the reader) spies on another.

29. Paul Julian Smith, "Writing Women in Golden Age Spain: Saint Teresa and María de Zayas," Modern Language Notes 102 (1987): 238.

given that at several important junctures in the text the prince reveals himself to be conflicted about his sexuality and affective affiliations. Why did he seek a wife at all if he formed part of a productive and stable male community? It is important to note that the text does not explicitly articulate any motivation for this behavior, for example, pressure regarding social appearances. Contradictions in his behavior surface from the start of the one-year courtship stipulated by Blanca. When Blanca's trial period is criticized by many of her friends and acquaintances, among them María, her maid since childhood, she responds quite logically by indicating that since all commodities (dresses, jewels, etc.) are seriously contemplated before the choice is made to purchase them or not, serious scrutiny is even more essential in committing oneself to a husband—who cannot be resold. She adds, marriages should not be agreed upon for the sake of someone else.[30]

We learn that the prince's father is furious at this obligatory year of courtship, although his son seems not to be, since he wanted to "see Spain," as the narrator indicates. Thus the extent of his affective commitment to Blanca is uncertain from his response to the delay in marrying her. We also learn from Blanca's faith in pure reason that she is unaware of the complexities of human subjectivity, that her testing of her future husband may very well not disclose his true nature. Zayas underscores Blanca's blind faith in reason as a way of pointing to the unpredictable, labyrinthine nature of multiple subject positions. At the same time, she is rejecting the time-worn dualism that depicts the female psyche as spontaneous sentiment and the male as reason.

Further ambiguous signals concerning the prince's sexual and affective identity are given by the narrator and by Blanca's response to the prince. We learn from the narrator that the prince "was so enamored of Doña Blanca, or so he feigned to be, for a man's heart is fundamentally cunning" (278). Blanca is similarly conflicted: "Porque confesar que le agradaba el príncipe, no negar que le amaba, haberle parecido bien y no desear la posesión, antes pesarle de que para llegar a tenerla era corto plazo el de un año, y que quisiera fuera más dilatado, cosas son que admiran" (266).

30. Zayas, " 'Is it better for a woman to marry a man she's never seen, never spoken to, who might be ugly, stupid, harsh, deformed, so that too late she may find herself despairing because of her misjudgment in not ascertaining what kind of a man her husband was? Before you buy merchandise like a dress or a jewel, you always examine it first to determine in the examination whether it pleases your taste" (Disenchantments, p. 246).

Blanca's desperation stems from her contradictory impulses at the thought that she must reluctantly marry (thus forfeiting her freedom) and her simultaneous love for the prince. This ambivalent reaction, the "tan diferentes efectos de amor y desamor" (271), is hotly debated by the frame characters who listen attentively to the grisly details of this account. Some say that Blanca was wise in making the prince pay full price for her beauty, while others claim that it was sheer madness, since she already belonged to him. For his part, the prince is said to be so desperate as a result of the yearlong delay that he would have returned to Flanders had it not been for Blanca's brother, and that his father, the elderly prince, had in fact ordered him to return home. The father seems to construe this one-year testing period as an insult, which would account in part at least for his negative reception of Blanca.

What is left unsaid but becomes progressively clear is that, given his detestation of all women (evident from his murderous acts), the old prince does not want his son to marry at all. Did he permit the marriage to keep up appearances, or was he perhaps yielding reluctantly to a desire on the part of his son to assert himself as bi- or heterosexual against his father's will? The motive is not clarified explicitly; Zayas leaves it to her readers to determine the cause for themselves.

Even more telling and unanticipated is the fact that the prince sides with the unfortunate women of the group, especially his sister, Marieta, and wife, Blanca, at two key moments in the text. The first occurs when he discovers his sister dead as a consequence of the garroting administered jointly by her husband (his cousin) and his father. We are told that had he known their intentions he would surely have prevented his sister's death and that he was grief-stricken by the servant's death as well.[31] Seeing his sister's corpse on one side and Blanca's unconscious body on the other, the prince reviles his father. The father simply calls him a coward, after which the prince helps revive Blanca from her faint, all the while grieving for his viciously murdered sister.

The other crucial moment at which the prince tries to defend a woman, it is Blanca herself, at the moment when his father and Arnesto reveal their

31. "The prince hadn't been a party to the dreadful scene and indeed knew nothing of it, or you can be sure he would never have allowed it. He would have saved his sister because he loved her dearly" (Disenchantments, p. 262).

intention to bleed her to death slowly. Blanca's sister Maria helplessly witnesses this repulsive spectacle through a keyhole, while the prince begs his father not to go through with his sadistic plan. His father's only response is to call his son "womanish coward, traitor" (542). Following this exchange we are told in no uncertain terms that it was the prince's father and Arnesto who had created the animosity that he developed toward Blanca. By means of the displays of grief and compassion and also from the narrator's commentary, it becomes clear that much of the time the prince feels conflicted about the consequences of his male bonding.

The story does not create an unproblematic, coherent male community as Smith suggests. Nor is its female community as passive as he suggests either. Smith states of Blanca, for example, that "her one positive act is to burn the bed in which her husband and his page have made love, a symbolic rejection of desire in all its forms" (237). Yet the urge of a faithful wife to burn her marital bed once it has been defiled by another coupling does not constitute a rejection of "desire in all its forms." It is a sign of rage at the fact that she has been displaced, and by a type of union that writes her out of the economy of desire in absolute terms. Zayas emphasizes this point by a programmatic use of beds in this tale. The first refers to Blanca's sister María, who is crippled for life, hence bedridden, as she tries to elude the wrath of her brother-in-law. The second depicts Blanca in bed while she is convalescing from the beating given her by the prince, the third is the scene revealing the prince in bed with Arnesto. As a result, beds for Blanca are hateful reminders of physical pain inflicted by men on women or of the wife's personal marital humiliation as a result of her husband's preference for male bonding.

An additional, highly significant "positive act" is Blanca's disbursement of her jewels to her servants when she understands that her days are numbered once she has discovered the liaison that exists between the prince and Arnesto. This type of bequest by one woman to another was a way by which the boundaries of the self could be affirmed by a woman in early modern Europe. As Natalie Zemon Davis explains, paradoxically: "A strategy for at least a thread of female autonomy may have been built precisely around [the] sense of being given away, that women sometimes turned the cultural formulation around, and gave themselves away. . . . The women's wills carefully describe the gifts — 'my fur-lined gray cape,' 'my third-best petticoat' — and the items are distributed according to the status and closeness of the recipients."[32] Moreover, this ritual of the bequest held true for poor women as well as affluent ones. It was a way of demonstrating the bond of female community. In this way, during her last moments of life Blanca finally attains a margin of autonomy that had been denied to her within the bonds of the marriage she initially believed would respect her individuality.

With its nuanced and conflicting presentation of both the prince and Blanca, "Marriage Abroad: Portent of Doom" offers a vivid testimony to Zayas's ability to understand and represent conflicting subject positions, as well as the importance and unpredictability of agency. The notable absence of consistent subjects makes possible the articulation of nonhegemonic voices.[33] This tale, like the other novelas, is illustrative of the way in which Zayas uses gendered discourses as she uses other discourses — political, racial, even supernatural, as a means of staging the complexity of the emerging modern subject. It is also as a means for the self-staging of her own daring literary enterprise. Perhaps it is for this reason that she figures herself in the introduction to her twenty tales not as an official muse or sybil but with the identification of herself as a sort of witch figure — offering the reader her "crucible of letters."[34]

32. Natalie Zemon Davis, "Boundaries and the Sense of Self in Sixteenth-Century France," in *Reconstructing Autonomy, Individuality and the Self in Western Thought,* ed. Thomas C. Heller, Morton Sosna, and David Wellbery (Stanford, Calif.: Stanford University Press, 1986), p. 61.

33. For an interesting treatment of this perspective see, Valerie Traub, M. Lindsay Kaplan, and Dympna Callaghan, *Feminist Readings of Early Modern Culture* (Cambridge: Cambridge University Press, 1996).

34. "Quien duda, lector mío, que te causará admiración que una mujer tenga despejo, no sólo para escribir un libro, sino para darle a la estampa, que es el crisol donde se averigua la pureza de los ingenios; porque hasta que los escritos se rozan en las letras de plomo, no tienen valor cierto, por ser tan fáciles de engañar los sentidos, que la fragilidad de la vista suele pasar por oro macizo lo que a la luz del fuego es solamente un pedazo de bronce afeitado" (Zayas, *Novelas amorosas,* 21) [Who doubts, my reader, that you will be amazed that a woman has the audacity not only to write a book, but to publish it; given that publication is the crucible which determines the worth of authors since only once texts are set in leaden type do they have any certain value. This is the case because the senses are so easily deceived; the sense of sight is so readily fooled that a piece of barely disguised bronze can be mistaken for pure gold. (my trans.)].

Incest and Agency:
The Case of Elizabeth I

MAUREEN QUILLIGAN

At age eleven, the princess Elizabeth Tudor translated a poem by Marguerite de Navarre, *Le Miroir de l'âme pécheresse* (*Mirror of the Sinful Soul*), from French into English. Why the eleven-year-old Elizabeth should have translated this particular poem, to give to her stepmother, Katherine Parr, will doubtless have to remain a matter for speculation. But it does not need to be Elizabeth's own poem in order for the choice to be significant in demonstrating not only how even so august a personage as a royal princess might need to be empowered by constructing a connection to two royal females who wrote (Katherine Parr had written a similar confession) but also how fantasized incestuous genealogies could provide profoundly enabling terms for female authority in the Renaissance.

Although Marguerite's *Miroir* is a pivotal text in its own right, and important not only for her authority but for the crucial part that its publication (if not its strangely overlooked theology) played in the early politics of the wars of religion in France, it is the history of the publication of Elizabeth's translation that most interestingly extends the life of this text for another sixty years, reiterating the conjuncture of royal female authority in two languages and the trope of incest through a long and pivotal period of Renaissance culture.[1] Published first in 1548, next in 1569–1570, then in two different editions in 1582, and finally in 1590, the editions span virtu-

---

1. D. F. McKenzie, *Bibliography and the Sociology of Texts* (London: British Library, 1986) argues that bibliography "has an unrivaled power to resurrect authors in their own time, and their readers at any time." My emphasis will be on the "social motives" one may decipher in the repeated recyclings of two royal female authors' texts about incest. For a discussion of the odd scholarly silence about the subject of her poem, see Marc Shell's useful edition with facsimile of the manuscript, *Elizabeth's Glass* (Lincoln: University of Nebraska Press, 1991), pp. 6–7.

ally Elizabeth's entire reign and in their different presentations decade by decade, have much to tell us how Elizabeth's discourse of incest could be put to very different uses. Along with the autograph manuscript presently at the Bodleian, the physical objects reveal a great deal about changing attitudes toward female agency.

But first, a bit of anthropology may help to make the idea of incest as an enabling condition for female agency somewhat less drastic. Annette Weiner has theorized that "sibling intimacy" can help to articulate an understanding of female agency in traditional societies. Women circulate among themselves gifts that are not "alienable" but like family heirlooms, which pass down through the generations of a family, accruing status to it. Such circulation among women is radically different from the "exchange" practiced by men; Weiner names it the "paradox" of "keeping while giving." [2] According to Weiner, sisters of brothers within a high-status family remain tied by a "sibling intimacy," which increases the status of the woman and of her family. Such a theory helps to explain the usefulness of the fantasy that Marguerite, and Elizabeth as her translator, entertain: that the female soul is both mother and daughter as well as sister to Christ. Inhabiting all three familial positions simultaneously, the soul is imagined to remain within a natal family, not traded out or exchanged, as is usually the case with female family members. Kinship is complicated and genealogical relations doubled in a process that disrupts the normal "traffic in women." While Marguerite, of course, is only casting her own voice in the voice of the Virgin Mary (who was traditionally the mother and daughter of Christ, as well as "sister" in the general Christian siblinghood), her penitential stance in this familial position as a sinful soul gives the rhetorical position great personalized force.

That incest is the central trope of the poem becomes clear immediately; it is the first major metaphor in the meditation by the soul on the affective intimacy that binds "her" to God. The introduction of the trope presents the multiply incestuous relations of the soul to God as a solution to the problem, specifically, of bad bread and doctrine and of the soul's panicked recognition that no intermediary is potent enough to work the soul's desire for salvation. The familial metaphor is thus, from the outset, immediately

2. Annette Weiner, *Inalienable Possessions: The Paradox of Keeping While Giving* (Berkeley: University of California Press, 1992).

connected to a Protestant desire for an unmediated relationship to God that bypasses church-authorized intercessors.

> Car trop estoit mas paoure ame repue
> De mauluais pain, et damnable doctrine:
> En deprisant secours et medecine.
> Et quant aussi l'eusse voulu querir
> Nul ne cognois, qu'eusse peu requerir:
> Car il n'y a homme, ny sainct, ny ange,
> Pour qui le cueure iamais d'ung pecheur change.
> Las bon IESUS, voyant ma cecité
> Et que secours en ma necessité
> Ne pu-ys avoir d'auleune creature,
> De mon salut auéz faict l'ouerture
> Quelle bonté, mais quelle grand'doulceur:
> Est il pere à fille, ou frere à soeur,
> Qui ung tel tour iamais eust voulu faire.
> .   .   .
> Bien suffiroit saillant de tel danger,
> De me traicter ainsi qu'ung estranger.
> Mais mon ame traictéz (si dire j'ouse)
> Comme mere, fille, soeur, et espouse.
> (Lines 132–72)[3]

Oftentimes have I broken with Thy covenant, for my poor soul was too much fed with ill bread and damnable doctrine, I despising succor and physic such as would have helped me. And if I had been willing to look for it, I know no man who I had required, for there is neither man, saint nor angel for whom the heart of a sinner will change.

Alas, good Jesus! Thou seeing my blindness and that at my need I could have no succor of men, then didst Thou open the way of my

---

3. Marguerite de Navarre, *Le Miroir de l'âme pécheresse,* ed. Renja Salminen (Helsinki: Tiede-akatemia, 1979), pp. 171–72; all citations are to this edition.

salvation. O what goodness and sweetness! Is
there any father to the daughter, or else brother
to the sister, which would ever do as He
hath done?

      .   .   .

For it should suffice me (I coming out of such
a danger) to be ordered like a stranger; but
Thou dost handle my soul (if so I durst say) as a
mother, daughter, sister, and wife.[4]

Doing away with any priestly intermediary, the familiar intimacy of the
metaphor insists upon the soul's multiple but consistently gendered relationship to God. In substituting incestuous intimacy for bad "bread" and
"doctrine," the poem's argument implicitly makes the metaphor answer a
problem posed by the ideology of communion, specifically referring to the
nature (good or bad) of bread. It is not only Marguerite's metaphor that
speaks to the powerful hold that incest rules had in maintaining church authority. Elizabeth's father, Henry VIII, had broken from the church strictly
over an issue of incest. He maintained that the pope did not have the authority to override the taboo against incest when he allowed Henry to
marry his elder brother Arthur's widow, Catherine of Aragon. Their lack of
a male heir was proof to Henry that he had sinned in marrying Catherine.
When the pope refused to grant him a divorce on the ground of consanguinity, holding that the earlier dispensation made the marriage perfectly
legal, Henry, in order to ensure a chance for his dynasty's survival with
the birth of a male heir, dissolved England's relationship with Rome and
assumed control over the English church. Religious reformation operated
by personal fiat in England.

The problem was that Henry then compounded his incest problems by
marrying a woman (Ann Boleyn) with whose older sister he had previously
had an affair, thus making their relationship, by the rules of the day, also
incestuous.[5] This prior relationship was part of the grounds on which Cran-
mer later granted Henry a divorce from Ann. It is not so much that Henry
revealed his hypocrisy (or confusion) in contracting this marriage, but that

4. Shell, *Elizabeth's Glass*, p. 117.
5. Shell, *Elizabeth's Glass*, p. 14.

he knew his relationship with Ann Boleyn fell within the interdicted degrees.[6]

Elizabeth was the daughter of this tainted union between Henry and Ann. Never made legitimate, she was always haunted by an unspoken specter of incest. Elizabeth would never have ruled as the famous Virgin Queen if her father had taken his patriarchal duties toward her seriously and, rather than bastardizing her at the age of three, had formed up marriage alliances for her. In the dynastic traffic in women that lasted from when first her father, then her brother, and then her sister ruled, Elizabeth was never as useful as an untainted daughter would have been; she was still unmarried at the advanced age (for a royal female) of twenty-five. Wallace MacCaffrey points out that at age five, Elizabeth had been "ticketed" for one of the Hapsburg princes and later for a Valois son. "None of the overtures came to anything," MacCaffrey admits, "but they made it clear that [Elizabeth's and Mary's] technical illegitimacy was not to disqualify the royal girls for the traditional role of princesses in the diplomacy of Europe."[7]

However, at least in some part, Elizabeth's position as an unmarried and potentially autonomous virgin princess at age twenty-five was due to the complications of her situation, of which illegitimacy and incest were fundamental elements. Although these deficits did not prevent her from entering the matrimonial game, they might well have played a part in the lack of success with which various matrimonial possibilities were pursued. Indeed, with uncanny specificity, Elizabeth's situation demonstrates how incest can enable active females. Although the incest at issue here belongs to her parents, Elizabeth, as a product of that union, becomes freer to exercise her own desire actively. Where the traffic in women stops, the female is not traded by another male but is allowed to turn inward, to a nonexogamous arena over which she may imagine she exerts control and where she may lay claim to an active and erotically charged agency for herself. That Elizabeth chose repeatedly not to marry meant that, as her own patriarch, she maintained the open discursive space for herself as an endogamously withheld woman. In this sense then, her conflicts with Parliament over marriage in the early years of her reign can be seen as being as much about the need for

6. Jasper Ridley, *Henry VIII: The Politics of Tyranny* (New York: Viking Press, 1985), p. 214.
7. Wallace MacCaffrey, *Elizabeth I* (London: E. Arnold, 1993), p. 50.

FIGURE I

male control over her female agency as it was about the need to secure the succession to the throne. What is at issue is not so much incest seen only as sexual congress between close family members (consanguine partners or "affines," as in the case of Henry and Ann), but incest as an action that brings about a most spectacularly scandalous halt in the traffic in women.

Elizabeth covered the manuscript volume that she presented as a gift to her stepmother with fabric from an embroidered sleeve or chemise, for which she, apparently, had done the needlework (figure I).[8] Embroidered in bright turquoise blue and decorated with an interlaced design picked out in still shiny silver thread, the volume makes an elaborate gift, with Katherine Parr's initials, "K.P." raised in cotton-batting-stuffed relief in the center of

8. Margaret H. Swain, "A New Year's Gift from the Princess Elizabeth," *The Connoisseur* 36 (1973): 258–66. I am indebted to Martin Kauffman, Department of Western Manuscripts, Bodleian Library, for this reference and for aid in handling the volume.

both back and front covers. Raised-work embroidered silver flowers are at each of the four corners. The same batting is used to raise cord-marks on the book's spine, as if the embroidered cover were part of the manuscript's actual binding. The fact that she dedicated the volume to her stepmother may be no more than an attempt to please one queen of pronounced Protestant sympathies by translating the work of another, but it is uncanny that the text of this translated poem, sent from one female family member to another, covered in a personally worked textile, results in a gesture that looks oddly like the trade in woven heirloom items that Annette Weiner finds generic to female communities in the present-day South Pacific. Indeed, using Weiner's theory of inalienable possessions as central to her understanding of the function of some gift-giving in Elizabethan society, Lisa M. Klein has argued that the cover, with its embroidered pansies, provides a witty pun on "pensées," meaning "thoughts": 1544 was the year Elizabeth had been established in the succession by an act of Parliament, although she was still illegitimate.[9] Klein never discusses the actual contents of Elizabeth's translation (her concern is for the embroidery), but the central trope of incest insists upon the endogamous noncirculation of the female speaker. As a gift to a female member of her father's family—in which Elizabeth now had a slightly more secure place—the woven nature of the object calls attention to its inalienable status.

It is clear from the dedicatory letter to her stepmother that the eleven-year-old expected Katherine Parr to keep the volume private, at least until its faults had been corrected: "But I hope that after having been in Your Grace's hands there shall be nothing in it worthy of reprehension and that in the meanwhile no other (but your highness only) shall read it or see it, lest my faults be known of many" (112). In essence, in asking for collaborative correction, Elizabeth suggests that she expects that many will read the volume and, while not exactly assuming "publication" thereby, she reveals her concern for the performance as one by which she will be judged. Elizabeth's brief letter to Katherine Parr is notable also for the emphasis it puts upon the familial fluidity of the speaker's position. The only thing she has to say about the actual content of Marguerite's poem insists upon the centrality of the trope of the incestuous woman:

9. Lisa M. Klein, "Your Humble Handmaid: Elizabethan Gifts of Needlework," *Renaissance Quarterly* (1997): 459–93.

The which book is entitled, or named, *The Mirror or Glass of the Sinful Soul*, wherein is contained how she (beholding and contemplating what she is) doth perceive how of herself and of her own strength she can do nothing that good is, or prevaileth for her salvation, unless it be through the grace of God, whose mother, daughter, sister, and wife by the scriptures she proveth her self to be. (111)

The slipperiness of the familial positions, here understood to be the central point of the poem, is predicted on a metaphorical elision that sacrifices no sense of concrete affect to the metaphorical nature of the position. Marc Shell has very powerfully argued that, in claiming herself to be both mother and spouse of the nation of England, the "mature Elizabeth . . . institutionalized that collapse on a national plane at once secular and chaste" which she had first essayed in her translation (66). And it is indeed very probable that Elizabeth learned the effectiveness of such multiple positions—so useful for preserving her autonomy—from her experience with such discourse in translating Marguerite's poem.

Susan Snyder has argued that Marguerite, in her use of the biblical story of Miriam, Moses's sister, lets that older female sibling vent frustration at having been preempted in rule by her younger brother.[10] Marguerite's sister-soul Miriam plays Aaron-like rebel rather than loyal aide to the brother, a vicious act for which she gains the inexplicable grace of forgiveness. Snyder points out that Elizabeth too, at the time she translated Marguerite's text, was in the same situation vis-à-vis her younger brother, Edward, and so she would have been able by this means to articulate, as an experience shared with her royal "sister," any sense of disentitlement she might have felt. The biblical story about sisterly betrayal speaks more directly to the actual historical facts, Snyder argues, than the trope of incest, and she is doubtless right. Yet the section is less than a hundred lines out of Marguerite's original fourteen hundred and, therefore, the major weight of the poem necessarily falls on the trope as the sacredly scandalous means to heal the soul's sinfulness.

10. Susan Snyder, "Guilty Sisters: Marguerite de Navarre, Elizabeth of England, and the *Miroir de l'âme pécheresse,*" *Renaissance Quarterly* (1997): 443–58.

A Godly Medytaty
on of the christen sowle, concer=
ninge a loue towardes God and
hys Christe, compyled in frenche by lady
Margarete quene of Nauerre, and apte=
ly translated into Englysh by the
ryght vertuouse lady Elyzabeth
Doughter to our late soueraync
Kynge Henri the.viij.

Inclita filia, sereniƒƒimi olim Anglorum
Regis Henrici octaui Elizabeta, tam Græ
cæ quam latine fœliciter in Christo
erudita.

FIGURE 2

Bale's 1548 Imprint

When John Bale took Elizabeth's familial manuscript in hand to publish
it three years after she wrote it, he printed her text in a black-letter type-
face that lends it a traditional weightiness that underscores the devotional
nature of the work. Although he kept Marguerite's preface, humbly excus-
ing itself as the "homely speech" of a "woman" (B ii), Bale did not reprint
Elizabeth's private letter to Katherine Parr, providing instead a long dedicatory epistle and an elaborate woodcut (at the beginning and end of the
volume) that shows a kneeling, book-holding princess Elizabeth before a
nimbus-crowned Christ, who is pointing upward (figure 2). The Roman-
looking pillars and walls show cracks and stress marks as if the triumphal,
banner-hung pillar had sustained some damage and therefore was in need

of some reform by means, perhaps, of the immediacy of the relationship presented in front of it. Bale's opening argument, correspondingly, is an attack on the illegitimacy of the "Romaish clergy" who have made themselves, falsely, into a "nobility digged out of the dunghill." In contrast to this nobility is the nobility of blood, represented by Elizabeth and her brother Edward IV—but even more singularly, the nobility of kindred attested to in scripture, that is, the "heavenly kindred" of John, by which means a man "becometh . . . the dear brother, sister, and mother of Christ" (Avii v). Bale underscores the power of the familial metaphor to attack the fundamental structure of the Roman Church. He mocks the clergy for their foolish assumption that they could remake Christ in the Eucharist, using familial terms that he empties out as if to make them available to the language of holy incest: "Such power hath a priest (say they) as hath neither angel, nor yet man, be he of never so great authority, science, or virtue; for a priest by word may make Him and bear Him, whereas his mother Mary begat Him (bore Him they would say) but once. . . . O blasphemous belly-beasts and most idle-witted sorcerers!" (A iiii v).

Bale's conclusion is given over to a roll-call of illustrious queens and women warriors—Boadicea, Martia, Helena Salvia, the mother of Constantine—only a few of which Bale points out ruled alone; they include "Cordilla the doughter of Kynge Leyer, and least of all her systers, as her father was deposed, & exiled out of hys lande, she recyued, conforted, and restored hym agayne to hys princely honoure, and reigned alone after hyse dethe, for the space of v. yeares" (F ii). Marc Shell argues that Bale's imperial Protestant vision anticipates Elizabeth's rule—but it is also striking that Bale cannot imagine her ruling alone, as most of the examples of history assume women's marriages. Bale published his text when Elizabeth was fifteen. She would not inherit the throne for another ten years, and in the meantime, she very nearly suffered the fate of Ann Askew, one of the women in Bale's roll-call of honor. Bale's sense of Elizabeth's virginity is of one proper to an eleven-year-old girl, which does not rule out the possibility of later marriage. At the end of his preface he prays that she will be a "nourishing mother" to God's "congregation."

Cancellar's Versions

The text of what Bale had titled the "Godly Meditation" was not published again until 1569–1570 by John Cancellar, chaplain to Mary Tudor. In 1553

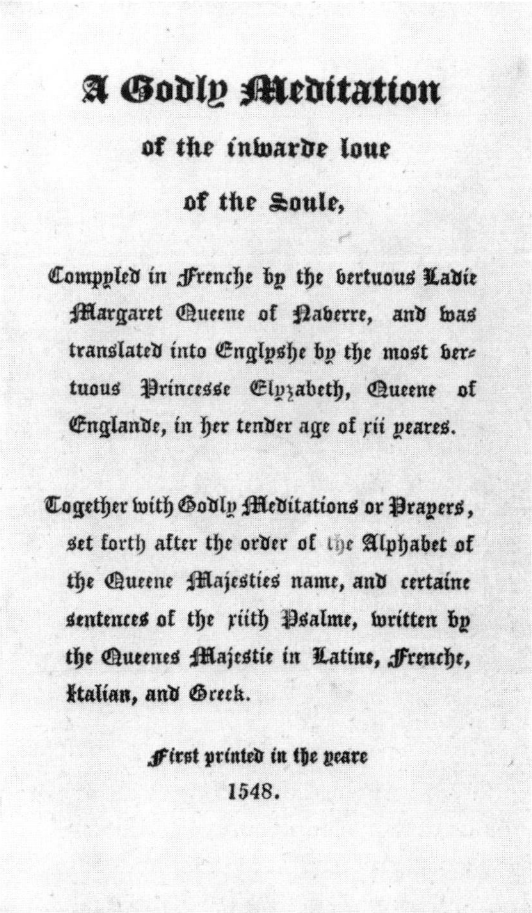

A Godly Meditation

of the inwarde loue

of the Soule,

Compyled in Frenche by the bertuous Ladie
Margaret Queene of Naberre, and was
translated into Englyshe by the most bertuous Princesse Elyzabeth, Queene of
Englande, in her tender age of xii yeares.

Together with Godly Meditations or Prayers,
set forth after the order of the Alphabet of
the Queene Majesties name, and certaine
sentences of the xiith Psalme, written by
the Queenes Majestie in Latine, Frenche,
Italian, and Greek.

First printed in the yeare
1548.

FIGURE 3

Cancellar had dedicated to Mary a volume entitled *The Path of Obedience,*
in which he instructs his readers in the prayers that good subjects should
use in relationship to their prince, who is not merely head of a secular
government. Bale's Protestant poetic gives way to a volume in which Elizabeth's book on holy incest is made to serve the purposes of a resurgent
Catholic Church. Cancellar printed the text twice in two different versions,
once in 1568–1569 (the *Short Title Catalogue* guesses), and again in 1580, both
by the same printer, Henry Denham. The differences between these two
versions are profoundly instructive of the slipperiness of the metaphor of
the soul's erotic address to God and of the difference a decade makes.

FIGURE 4

The first reprint offers the text of the meditation, newly emphasized to be the "inward loue of the Soule" (figure 3). Cancellar drops Marguerite's preface, which Bale had provided, as Marguerite's humility in offering the work of a "mere" woman may not have suited Elizabeth who is now queen. The title pager makes clear, however, that the translation was done in "her tender age of xii yeares" and announces that it comes to the reader "[t]ogether with the Godly Meditations or Prayers, set forth after the order of the Alphabet of the Queene Majesties name." Separated from the text of the meditation by an elaborate frontispiece (figure 4), Cancellar's "Alphabet" is very similar to one he had made for Robert Dudley in a volume printed a few years before, in 1564 (figure 5). These elaborate frontispieces provide Dudley's and Elizabeth's arms respectively, circled by the belt of the "garter" with parallel mottoes and boxed "alphabets" of each of their names; although they were printed four to five years apart, the two formats call attention to a noticeable effort to pair them.

Dudley's shows the bear and ragged staff with a motto (in black letter): "It is good for every estate, these fewe lynes to imitate." There follows the

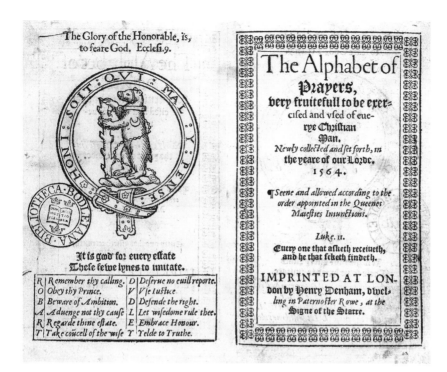

FIGURE 5

acrostic on Dudley's name, the first sentences reading: "Remember thy Calling." "Obey thy Prince." "Beware of Ambition." This last, of course, speaks directly to Dudley's infamous designs on Elizabeth and the throne. The book is specifically announced on its title page to have been "Seene and allowed according to the order appointed in the Queenes Maiesties Iniunctions." In 1564 Dudley had been three years a widower and was making a concerted effort to become Elizabeth's consort (they were cousins—but first-cousin marriage was legal in England). In a volume sent to Elizabeth by Catherine de Medici in 1564, a dedicatory epistle to Leicester by Ronsard makes it clear that the French court assumes they might well marry and beget children.[11] In Cancellar's text similarly, the dedicatory epistle to Dudley as the Earl of Leicester (a title he had been given only that year), promises that—like the biblical David—the earl might "after that hee had long trauailed and had passed thorowe the gate of vertue, [enter] the faire

---

11. Pierre Ronsard, *Oeuvres Complètes* (Paris: Paul Laumonier, 1948), vol. 2.

and pleasaunt garden of humilitie." In this garden, King David had been promised by God, "I will set vp thy seede after thee, which shall proceede out of thy body. Which sentence most worthy Earle (although not spoke of your Noble parentage) in your honor may be approved, which I doubt not your honor considereth" (A ii r).

Included in the Dudley alphabet is a "prayer for the Queene," plus a remarkable group of polemic prayers "against the Enimies of the Catholike Church":

> Cruellye haue they (on euery syde) shead like water the bloud of thy faithfull; and have despisd to bury them.
> Deceitfullye haue they crept into thine habitation: and wyth scorne and derision, haue they (O Lorde) spoken against thee. (C iiii v)

Apparently, in an effort to gain a larger base of power, Dudley had made deals with Catholics, and especially de Quadra (the Spanish Ambassador), that if they were to help him to marry Elizabeth, he would work to restore the church.[12] Such a program makes Cancellar's participation understandable.

The program for the restoration of the church is less obvious in the alphabet addressed to Elizabeth five years later, but the agenda of David's son being set upon the throne is repeated. Between 1564 and 1569 Elizabeth had entertained marriage proposals from the Archduke Charles of Austria, but he had been definitively rejected by 1569. In the prayer attached to the letter "T" of Elizabeth's name, Cancellar writes:

> Thou did promise unto Abraham, a Sonne when he was aged: thou fulfilledest thy promise in olde and barren Sara, bicause thou louest truth.
> Thou madest promise unto David thy seruant, saying, of the fruite of thy body, will I set upon thy regall throne: and it came to passe, bicause thou louest truth. (F iiii v)

Cancellar also makes clear that Elizabeth herself is not the spouse of Christ: the Church, separate from Elizabeth, is that spouse and is an authority to which the queen herself must listen:

12. George Smith et al., *Dictionary of National Biography* (1921; Oxford University Press, 1967).

Giue me also (O holy Father) a perfite hearing, and not a corrupt hearing, but that I may throughe the teaching of the holye ghost heare thee, out of the Prophets, out of the Apostles, out of the penne of the Evangelist, and out of the mouth of thy Spouse the Catholike Church: to whom thou saydest, I will send you as comforter, euen my spirite, which shall leade you into all truth. (C i r)

The boxed acrostic on the frontispiece of the alphabet makes the secular eroticism of the queen's position reasonably clear. She is addressed in Latin as the daughter of her father, Henry VIII, and she is told in the motto to "Embrace Vertue," a neutral enough exhortation. For the "L" of her name she is commanded to "Loue perfectlye."

It is as if Cancellar were mining the terms of Elizabeth's text about the soul's erotic address of divinity for those elements that could speak to Dudley's program (active statement of sexual desire), and specifically writing against others. Elizabeth is thus exhorted to "Love perfectlye," but she is not the spouse of Christ, as she claims in the text of her translation; rather, the Catholic Church is. Whom then, should she love perfectly? She is not the daughter of Christ; she is the offspring of Henry VIII. Perfect love here would seem to aim at an earthly spouse and an earthly child—a not impossible request of a woman who was, in 1569, thirty-six years old.

When, in contrast, Cancellar reprints the text again in 1580, Elizabeth has been excommunicated by the pope for over ten years, and it has been treasonous to suggest reconciliation with Rome since that time. Correspondingly, Cancellar provides a massive amount of different front matter, a dedicatory epistle, and a preface, for which he mines Bale's "Conclusion," and thereby gives his text a properly Protestant tone.

In his dedication, Cancellar praises Elizabeth's adolescent virginity, which he makes congruent with her education—both of which continue to empower her as a divinely protected ruler:

O how greatlye maye wee all glorie in such a peerelesse floure of Virginitie, as is your grace, who in the middest of Courtly delices, and amiddes the intisement of worldlye vanities, haue by your owne choyse and election, so vertuousley and fruitfullye translated this vertuous worke in your childhood and tender youth. O royall exercised in deed of a virginly education: O right precios fruite of Maydenlye studies, worthie immortality of fame and renowne. (A iiii r)

Cancellar calls attention to the failings of the earlier version (not pointing out that it was his, even taking to task its many corruptions):

> This precious Pearle of your trauayle (most gracious and Soueraigne Lady) long hath lyen hidden from the sight of your louing subiets: and now come to the hands of your faithfull obedient seruaunt, and day-lye Orator, and the corruption & faultes of the olde print corrected and amended is now by him (for the worthinesse thereof) dedicated to your Maiestie, as to the verie Patronesse and Author of the same. Whervnto most gracious Ladye, your humble Orator hath added cer-tayne vertuous and godly Meditations, collected and gathered out of the holy Scriptures orderly set forth after the Alphabet of your Ma-iesties name. Minding also most gracious Ladie, vnder your gracious favour, further to enlarge the same with godly Psalmes and prayers, to be the comfort of the godly Reader of the same: craving your gracious pardon, that so boldlye (being so vnworthy of myselfe) would take in hande to present to your Maiestie (so simple as I am) so precious a Iewell. (A iiii r)

Quoting what appears to be the queen's own desire to have the text re-published so that, as he says, she "would say . . . folks" would be made "familiar" with her treatise, he echoes language familiar from Elizabeth's speeches, when "folk" is turned into her "family." It is, however, in the rep-resentation of the queen's relationship to Christ that Cancellar makes the greatest change of tune, reflecting the growing "cult" of Elizabeth.[13] His final prayer is Bale's, in which the speaker requests that Elizabeth be given a special place in heaven after her death:

> Wherefore, I beseeche Almightie G O D that it may (in the hartes of the readers therof) take no less place and effect, of godly knowl-edge, and innocent liuing, that by your Grace was ment in the trans-lating of the same: whose act, most noble and gracious Princesse, hath

---

13. Helen Hackett, *Virgin Mother, Maiden Queen: Elizabeth I and the Cult of the Virgin Mary* (New York: St. Martin's Press, 1995), argues that the full-blown cult of Elizabeth's virginity only became paramount after the threat of the Anjou marriage had passed in 1579, and that representations of the queen still were open to the possibility even after that date. Philippa Berry, *Of Chastity and Power* (Cambridge: Cambridge University Press, 1997) also argues for a nuanced, decade-by-decade chronology for an evolving discourse of chastity throughout Elizabeth's reign.

deserued in this worlde, condign fame and renowne, with perpetu-
all meoire, & after this life a crown of imortall glorie and blesse in
Heaven, eternally there to raigne with Christ our Lord, and sauior.
Amen. Our Maiesties humble, seruaunt and dayly Orator, Iames Cancellar. (A v v and A v r)

After the request that Elizabeth rule with Christ, Bale had printed a short
sentence "So be it." Cancellar cuts the phrase, but even with this trunca-
tion, the queen manages to take a place as Christ's royal spouse, just as the
main metaphor of the poem and Elizabeth's autonomous power force even
so staunch a recusant as Cancellar to acknowledge the fact.

The 1582 Monument of Matrons

Henry Denham was Cancellar's printer for both versions of the text; in 1582
he brought out yet a third edition of the queen's translation, this time as
the "Second Lampe of Virginitie," that is, the second of a five-part, multi-
volumed, elaborately printed book entitled *The Monument of Matrons* and
put together by Thomas Bentley. Bentley's dedicatory epistle places Elizabeth's work within the context of literally voluminous female authority:
where Bale had merely listed famous women, Bentley collects and pub-
lishes a massive number of female authors, as if he were attempting to
provide a thousand testimonies to match the thousand wise virgins of his
biblical text. This placement amid a welter of female voices poses a very
interesting question about the cultural authority possessed, at this point, by
Elizabeth's translation: does its context limit the potential power of Elizabeth's voice by submerging it among other women's prayers, or does it, as
I think, empower those female voices in the aggregate?

  After printing numerous prayers specifically by women recorded in the
Bible in the "First Lamp" (figure 6), Bentley prints Elizabeth's translation
in the "Second Lamp" (pp. 1–36), followed by Katherine Parr's "Lamenta-
tions of a Sinner" (complete with the preface by William Cecil, pp. 37–79),
as well as short prayers by Elizabeth on her imprisonment and her coro-
nation, and by Lady Jane Grey Dudley at the time of her imprisonment
and death, plus various prayers by Elizabeth Tyrwhit (pp. 103–38), Lady
Frances Aburgavennie's prayers at death committed to her daughter May
Fane (pp. 139–213), Mistress Dorcas Martin's prayers (pp. 221–46), including a catechism for children, and sundry prayers made by an anonymous

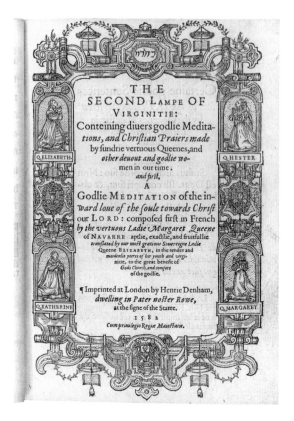

FIGURE 6

"Gentlewoman." The first four lamps run to 479 pages in the first volume; two more "lamps" were printed in subsequent years.

Elizabeth's uniqueness among women is here submerged in a massive demonstration of articulate female piety and learning, across classes and from the standpoint of the many different social roles women play, as mothers, daughters, queens, housewives, and so on. In the dedication to Elizabeth, Bentley explains his sense of his task, to "bring profit to the mysticall bodie, whereof I trust I am a member,"

> out of the admirable monuments of your own Honourable works and some other noble Queenes, famous laides and vertuous Gentle-women . . . to address and make readie these seven Lampes of your perpetuall virginitie, to remain unto women as one entire goodlie monument of praier, precepts, and examples meet for meditation, in-

struction and imitation to all posteritie. [I offer them to] your maiestie the most natural mother and noble nurse thereof; the cause of a virgin to a Virgine, the works of Queenes to a Queene, your owne praiers to yourself.

In turning Elizabeth herself into the church, which is the "sweet spouse" of Jesus Christ and Bentley's own "deer mother" and a "virgin," Bentley appropriates the metaphor for Elizabeth's own text. Thus he prays that God will "as your spiritual spouse . . . set your Maiesty (a most worthie and mightie gouernor of the same) ever as a seal upon his hart, to tie you as a bracelet upon his arm . . . to set his eie over you continuallie for your health, wealth, and prosperitie, to bend his desires alwaies towards you." Louis Montrose has argued that Elizabeth was unique in being allowed to inhabit the three different roles of an Elizabethan woman simultaneously —"Maiden, Matron, and Mother."[14] But in Bentley's collection we see Elizabeth's language in the poem on holy incest—itself authorizing if not instigating this simultaneous inhabitation of roles—leading off a truly impressive amount of eloquence raised in praise and supplication for the often daily round of women's activities—eating, speaking, working, teaching, at church and at home. In 1582 other women (and men) participate in the familial activities authorized by the queen's familiar relationship to God.

The "Third Lampe" prints a number of Elizabeth's Accession Day prayers, including one specifically for the twenty-fourth year of her reign, that is, 1582. She asks God to help her in

reigning blessedlie ruling prudentlie, and like a louing mother, and tender murse, giuing my fostermilke the good of thy word and Gospell aboundantlie to all, in all places of my dominion, and endeuouring my self faithfullie to discharge the great truth commited unto me: why thy sonne, to whome not onlie the sea and windes, but all creatures are subiect, shall come as King of kings to require an accompt of the counter charge committed unto me, I may be found faithfull, and not faile finallie in heauen, but in the pureness of my virginitie,

14. Louis A. Montrose, "The Fantasies of Elizabethan Culture," in *Rewriting the Renaissance,* ed. Margaret Ferguson, Maureen Quilligan, and Nancy Vickers (Chicago: University of Chicago Press, 1986), pp. 80–81: "Because she was always uniquely herself, Elizabeth's rule was not intended to undermine the male hegemony of her culture. Indeed, the emphasis upon her *difference* from all other women may have helped to reinforce it."

and holinesse of mine innocencie, be presented to the lambe my sov-
erign Lord and onlie God, my heauenlie Bridegroom and spirituall
Spouse, my euerlasting king deer Christ and onlie sweetsaviour Jesus,
ther to see the Saints, and to be a Saint, and with all the holie Patri-
arches, Judges, Kings and Queenes, . . . to reigne with him over spirituall powers and pincipalities for euer, and sing the sugred songs of
my wedding daie to my perpetual ioie. (272)

Here Bentley also prints the alphabet Cancellar had used in 1569–1570 and
in 1580, repeating for the "T" of her name the same prayer that promises David a son. But this time, sonship and all family metaphors are also
juxtaposed to a very peculiar text entitled the "King's hest" or "God's familiar speech" to the queen as "expounded by Theodore Beza out of David's
psalms." In the compilation from Beza, presumably done by Bentley himself, we find the language of holy incest writ large again, if also a trifle more
regularized than in the language of Elizabeth's translation of Marguerite's
poem. God the Father directly addresses Elizabeth as the "perfect virgin"
chosen from the rest of the people:

And now then, deere daughter, consider diligentlie with thy selfe
awhile, what maner of husband thou art coupled and conioined unto:
learne of him alone (thy spouse Christ mine onlie Son I mean) to
whom as this daie I married thee, what he requireth of thee: name-
lie that thou shouldest forget thine owne Nation, thy fathers house,
and all other worldlie things, how that thou art come under his au-
toritie and into the fanmily and spirituall societie of thy heauenlie
Bridegroom. (309)

God's voice counsels Elizabeth to use an erotic address to his son:

O kiss this my sonne christ thy spouse betimes, least he be angrie, and
then thou suddlenly perish, when his wrath shall flame forth. Worship
the lord I saie with due worship, and trust in him alone, as she that
wholie dependeth upon his mercie, favour, and protection: so shalt
thou be blessed, and thy throne shall neuer be shaken.

The text continues with a response in Elizabeth's fevered voice:

Rabboni, my heart so boileth within me that I must needs burst forth
that which it hath conceived; even a magnifical vow of a Queene consecrated to the king of heaven himself, and that with such zeale and

fervencie, that no penne may seem to be able to attain unto the voice of the speaker. (321)

E. C. Wilson, Peter McClure, Robin Headlam Wells, and Helen Hackett all see Bentley's text as the further appropriation of Mariology for the growing cult of Elizabeth.[15] But it is entirely possible that Bentley was led by Elizabeth's own language in compiling from Beza's translation his scriptural dialogue between a loving father and an erotically responsive daughter. The connection between Mary and Elizabeth may have become typological as Elizabeth's reign and virginity wore on, but the very first articulation of Elizabeth's incestuous spousalship of God was her own very erotically charged one — and anyone who read her text along with the prayers of the other women surrounding it in Bentley's volume would have found the Beza-based prayer to be simply an enactment of the relationship she there had begun to describe. If Elizabeth learned this erotic language from Marguerite, Bentley and the culture he represents learned it from Elizabeth, and circulated it as such.

Ward's 1590 Edition of Bale's Text

The final edition of the text is Ward's 1590 reprint of Bale's text, presenting merely his preface (in Roman type) and conclusion, lacking the woodcut of the 1548 printing, which would have been inappropriate for a reigning queen just shy of sixty years of age (fig. 7). To reprint Bale's text is somehow commemorative of what would have been merely promissory in Bale's polemic, which would again, just after the Armada and still under the threat of Catholic Spain, be a useful articulation of an again important anti-Catholic attack. Ward thus reprints Bale's excuse for the repetitiousness of the text: "If the humble speech here do too much offend, consider it to be the work of a woman, as she in the beginning thereof hast most meekely desired" (E viii). He repeats Bale's translation of Elizabeth's term "homely" as "humble," thereby erasing what might have been offensive in the "familiar" metaphor of home. As to the tediousness of the repetition, Saint John the Evangelist does the same, and Ward prints Bale's reminder to the reader that "a thing twise or thrise spoken entereth much more dayly into the remembrance then that is uttered but once" (E viii). Ward does

15. Cited in Hackett, *Virgin Mother,* pp. 124–25.

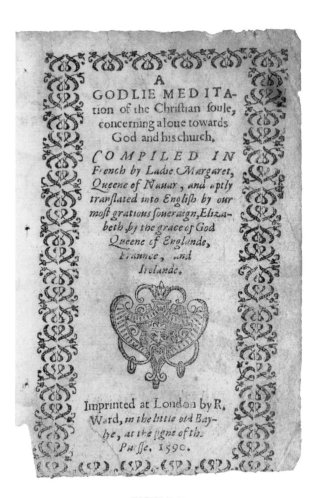

A
GODLIE MEDITA-
tion of the Chriftian foule,
concerning aloue towards
God and his church,

COMPILED IN
French by Ladie Margaret,
Queene of Nauar, and aptly
tranflated into Englifh by our
moft gratious foueraign, Eliza-
beth, by the grace of God
Queene of Englande,
Fraunce, and
Irelande,

Imprinted at London by R.
Ward, in the little old Bay-
lye, at the figne of th:
Purfe, 1590.

FIGURE 7

not update the text in any way—thus Elizabeth is still the "king's sister" and not queen in her own right. Only on the title page is Elizabeth "our most gracious Soveraign."

Elizabeth's familiar metaphor, borrowed from a sister queen, Marguerite, herself sister to a king, reprinted at regular intervals throughout her career, entered deeply into the memory of the culture that surrounded her. Capable of serving not only the erotics of a very earthly Robert Dudley but also the chastity that made Elizabeth into the church—who could thereby be both married to and a mother of her people—the discourse she first learned in her translation of the French poem had a long and complicated life. It was also capable of authorizing a vast array of prayerful eloquence by numbers of high- and low-born women in the *Monument of Matrons,* and of exemplifying female learning through four decades of the sixteenth century — indeed, five decades, if we include Marguerite's French texts. In short, this "meditation," with its bizarre metaphor of an incestuous genealogy offered a remarkably supple and long-lived discourse for articulating female agency in the sixteenth century.

IV

THE POLITICS OF
INHERITANCE

In Search of the Origins of Medicine:
Egyptian Wisdom and Some Renaissance Physicians

NANCY G. SIRAISI

In Renaissance medicine, as in Renaissance philosophy, concepts of reform—and actual innovations—often went hand in hand with a search
for the most ancient and authentic wisdom. In either field, critics of traditional academic doctrine or method seldom proclaimed their own origi-
nality. Rather, they were apt to claim to have discovered and restored an
earlier, purer genealogy of their discipline. In most instances, such claims
pointed to Greek thinkers who preceded the standard school authorities,
Aristotle and Galen. Thus for orthodox (as distinct from Paracelsian) physicians, as for natural philosophers, Greek antiquity was almost always, in
one form or another, an essential point of reference. The enduring influence of the classicizing impulse of humanism, the importance of some of
the philosophical and scientific texts that humanists brought to light, and,
in medicine, the continuing dominance of Galenic physiology ensured that
this situation remained unchanged throughout the sixteenth century.

But Greek tradition itself also authorized an alternative ancient genealogy of wisdom. Among ancient Greek authors writing in a variety of contexts, the wisdom and the wonders of Egypt were a recurring topos. Until
the late sixteenth century, the writings attributed to "Egyptian Hermes"
(Hermes Trismegistus) were widely accepted a source of the most ancient
philosophical wisdom.[1] In the case of medicine, as we shall see, some an-

---

1. For a brief account of the philosophical *Hermetica* and their fortuna in Renaissance and
early modern Europe, see the translator's introduction to *Hermetica*, trans. Brian P. Copenhaver (Cambridge: Cambridge University Press, 1992); Garth Fowden, *The Egyptian Hermes*
(Cambridge: Cambridge University Press, 1986) stresses the presence of some Egyptian elements in these Hellenistic Greek writings; on some late sixteenth-century critics of the authenticity of the *Hermetica*, see *Das Ende des Hermetismus*, ed. Martin Mulsow, forthcoming.

cient origin stories—told by Greek authors—located the beginnings of medicine in Egypt. Moreover, the widespread Renaissance fascination with Egypt rested not only on the assertions of ancient authors but also on material remains transported to Europe in antiquity—for example the obelisks of Rome and the hieroglyphics with which they were inscribed. In the sixteenth century, furthermore, reports of travelers and political and economic contacts spread awareness that contemporary Egypt, a Muslim country under Ottoman rule, was indeed an enduring repository of some of the wonders—pyramids, obelisks, hieroglyphs, for example—testified to by ancient authors.[2]

In the cultural environment just described, some physicians seem to have hoped to find in Egyptian medicine an alternative disciplinary genealogy and a source of medical knowledge that was both new and authentically ancient. Any such hope was ultimately doomed to disappointment: by the second half of the seventeenth century, as will become apparent, the myth of Egyptian origin survived only among some Paracelsian physicians. Nevertheless, the subject of Egyptian medicine engendered sixteenth-century discussions that include highly revealing examples of Renaissance scientific endeavor, characterized by the confrontation of ancient opinion with personal experience, of Christian observation of a contemporary Muslim society, and even of the impact on medicine of the rival economic interests of eastern and western Mediterranean powers. Accordingly, this essay will sketch the lines of some of these medical debates about Egypt and the origins of medicine. The extensive interests of Venice in the eastern Mediterranean ensured that some of the earliest western medical travelers to Egypt were associated with the University of Padua (which lay in Venetian territory), and it is with their circle that I shall begin. Their discussions were, of course, not informed by the data, issues, or attitudes involved in modern controversies about the possible antecedents of Greek science. Rather, the issue revolved around the confrontation of an-

---

In the latter work a fuller version of the present essay, including discussion of connections with philosophical circles will appear.

2. On Renaissance enthusiasm for Egypt in general, see Karl H. Dannenfeldt, "Egypt and Egyptian Antiquities in the Renaissance," *Studies in the Renaissance* 6 (1959): 7–27. On the obelisks, see, for example, Brian Curran and Anthony Grafton, "A Fifteenth-Century Site Report on the Vatican Obelisk," *Journal of the Warburg and Courtauld Institutes* 58 (1995): 234–48.

cient Greek or Hellenistic opinion with knowledge of contemporary Egypt obtained in the context of the interaction of Venetian and Ottoman power in the eastern Mediterranean.

One such physician who knew Egypt at first hand was Prospero Alpino. In a work entitled *De medicina Aegyptiorum* he reported his investigations into medicine, health, and disease in contemporary Egypt during a three-year stay in that country from 1581 to 1584.[3] Alpino, who graduated from the University of Padua in 1578, was the favorite student of Melchior Guilandinus, prefect of the university's botanic garden from 1561.[4] He cast *De medicina Aegyptiorum* in the form of a dialogue with Guilandinus, who earlier in his career had also visited Egypt.[5] For Guilandinus and Alpino, Egypt (ancient and modern) and the origin and sources of medical knowledge were connected themes. But interest in medicine's origins, especially in the sense of the foundations of medical literature and medical theory, was also shared by other members of the medical faculty at Padua at about the same time. One of the most important was the professor of *practica* and Hip-

3. The first edition is Prospero Alpino, *De medicina Aegyptiorum libri quatuor* (Venice, 1591). In what follows, I cite from the second edition (Paris, 1646). Several subsequent editions were published in the eighteenth and early nineteenth century. There is also an Italian translation by Angelo Capparoni, *La medicina degli egiziani* (Rome: Istituto di Storia della Medicina dell' Università di Roma, 1961), with brief biographical introduction. On Alpino (1553–1616), see further Giuseppe Ongaro, "Contributo alla biografia di Prospero Alpini," *Acta medicae historiae patavina* 8–9 (1961–62): 79–168, with appendix of documents at pp. 143–68 (the whole of this issue of the journal is devoted to the proceedings of a conference on Alpino); G. Lusina, "Alpino (Alpini), Prospero," *Dizionario biografico degli italiani* (Rome: Instituto della Encyclopedico Italiana, 1960), 2:529–31; Jerry Stannard, "Alpini, Prospero," *Dictionary of Scientific Biography* (New York: Scribners, 1970), 1:124–25; Giuliano Lucchetta, "Viaggiatori, geografi e racconti di viaggio dell'età barocca," in *Storia della cultura veneta*, ed. Girolamo Arnaldi and Manlio Pastore Stocchi (Vicenza: Neri Pozza editore, 1980), part 4, vol. 2, pp. 215–23. In this article, I follow the *Dizionario biografico degli italiani* in using the form of the name Alpino (rather than Alpini).

4. On Guilandinus (ca. 1520–1589), see Loris Premuda, "Wieland (or Guilandinus), Melchior," *Dictionary of Scientific Biography* (New York: Scribners, 1976), 14:335–36; G. C. Pisanski, *Nachricht von dem gelehrten Königsberger M. Guilandin* (Königsberg, 1785).

5. As recorded in Melchior Guilandinus, *Papyrus, hoc est commentarius in tria C. Plinii maioris de papyro capita. Accessit Hieronymi Mercurialis Repugnantia, qua pro Galeno strenue pugnatur. Item Melchioris Guilandini Assertio sententiae in Galenum a se pronunciatae* (Venice, 1572). I am grateful to Anthony Grafton for the loan of a microfilm of the copy in Cambridge University Library (Adu. C. 19. 1), with critical annotations of J. J. Scaliger. I have also consulted the copy in the New York Public Library.

pocratic scholar Girolamo Mercuriale, who engaged Guilandini in debate and was also among Alpino's teachers.[6]

The opening exchange of Alpino's dialogue with Guilandinus will serve to provide a starting point:[7]

6. On Mercuriale (1530–1606), see Italo Paoletti, *Girolamo Mercuriale e il suo tempo* (Lanciano: Cooperativa editoriale tipografia, 1963). He first met Guilandinus at Padua in 1554, when he (Mercuriale) was still a medical student: "Agitur iam decimus et tertius annus doctissime Guilandine, ex quo ego Patavii philosophiae, ac medicinae studiis operam navans, Falloppiique praeceptoris consuetudine familiariter utens, cognovi. . . ." (Mercuriale, *Repugnantia* [as in note 5, p. 235]). The work is dated 1567 (p. 240).

7. Alpino, *De medicina Aegyptiorum* 1. 1., fols. 1r–2v (my translation):

"Alpinus: Sed quid obsecro me de medicis Aegyptiis dicturum arbitraris? an quia multis persuasum est ibi medicinam primas habuisse radices, plurimosque illustres viros tum in medicina, tum in aliis scientiis olim in Aegypto floruisse, iisdem etiam hac tempestate ornari regionem illam ac florere?

"Guilandinus: Quidni omnes istud ipsum sentiant? Quando usque adeo etiam ibi bruta multa animalia reperiantur, quibus ars insita curandi morbos aliquos existimetur? quemadmodum de Hippopotamo equo marino in Nilo flumine degente apud quosdam legitur. Hunc enim equum in quadam medendi parte etiam magistrum esse aliqui affirmant. Assidua namque ipse, ut aiunt, ingluvie et satietate obesus, exit in littus, recentes indagaturus arundinum caesuras, atque ubi acutissimum earum stipitem cernit, id in corpus adigens, venam quandam sibi in cure vulnerat, atque ita profluvio sanguinis excitato morbidum alias corpus exonerat, mox plagam rursus limo obducit. . . . Si itaque bestias ipsas in ea orbis parte natura medicinam docuisse creditur, quid de hominibus erit ratione ac discursu praeditis existimandum? Atque eo magis cum priscis saeculis Agyptus plurimis doctissimis medicis semper floruerit?

"Alpinus: Hippopotamum et alia bruta animalia, de quibus ea medendi miracula praedicantur, ibi reperiri certum est, at quod ego de hominibus medicinam profitentibus hisce annis observarim, in medium nunc tibi proferam, paucisque narrabo, quae ex his scitu digna mihi fuere visa, ac primum dico, Cayri aliisque in locis Aegypti plurimos tum viros, tum mulieres reperiri, qui publice per urbem medicinam faciunt, non tamen ullos existere, qui hanc artem aliqua ratione atque Hippocratice faciant. . . .

"Guilandinus: Cum medici illi ita negligantur, neque multum lucri faciant, quae occasio erit, qua ad medicinam valenter perdiscendam illi moveantur. Non est igitur mirum inter illos paucos perfectos medicos reperiri. Quod cum explicatum a te sit, nunc reliquum est praeterea nihil, nisi ut susceptum de medicina Aegyptiorum sermonem claudas, ac de aliis rebus loquaris.

"Alpinus: Quamobrem?

"Guilandinus: Quoniam ex indoctis medicis, quid boni, ac scitu digni ex te observatum audire possum?

"Alpinus: Intelligo unde tu in eam deveneris sententiam. Sed hoc fortasse non est ita existimandum, quando scientia atque doctrina ignaros homines Empirice tamen multa in arte

Alpinus: But what do you think I am going to say about Egyptian medical practitioners? Can it really be that, because many people believe that medicine had its first roots there and many illustrious men in both medicine and in other sciences flourished in Egypt, that region is also ornamented and flourishing with them at the present time?

Guilandinus: Why should everyone not think that very thing? When right up to the present many animals are found there by which some people think the art of curing diseases was [originally] discovered? Just as we read in some authors about the hippopotamus, a marine horse living in the Nile. . . . If therefore the very animals in that part of the world are taught medicine by nature, what should we think about the human inhabitants, who are endowed with reason and speech? And the more so because in the earliest centuries, Egypt always flourished with very learned physicians?

Alpinus: The hippopotamus and other animals of which those miracles of healing are related are certainly found there, but I am now about to offer you what I recently observed about the human beings practising medicine . . . and first I say that in Cairo and many other places in Egypt there are many people, both men and women, who practice medicine publicly through the city but none who exercise this art rationally or Hippocratically. . . .

Guilandinus: Now that you have explained that, the only thing to do is to stop discussing the medicine of the Egyptians and talk about something else.

Alpinus: Why?

Guilandinus: Since what can I expect you to have observed that was good or worth knowing from unlearned medical practitioners?

Alpinus: I understand how you came to hold that opinion, but perhaps one should not think so, since who will deny that men ignorant of science and doctrine can nevertheless empirically know many secrets of the art [of medicine]? Such are many most noble secrets of healing of the highest utility once invented among the earliest Egyptian physicians [apud Aegyptios priscos medicos]; these, rather than any theo-

---

secreta posse dignoscere, quis negabit? qualia sunt multa medendi secreta auxilia summam ob utilitatem nobilissima, apud Aegyptios priscos medicos olim inventa, haereditarie potius ab aliis praeclassimis medicis his relicta, quam aliqua doctrina ab his acquisita."

retical doctrine acquired by them, were left as an inheritance by other outstanding physicians.

As this little exchange illustrates, claims about the superiority and or antiquity of Egyptian wisdom relating to medicine were made on several grounds and appealed to different physicians for different reasons. Alpino's opening neatly — and, to judge by Guilandinus's other writings, quite realistically — positioned himself and Guilandinus with regard to Egypt and medicine. Guilandinus's Egypt was the Egypt of doxographical tradition. During his own travels in Egypt he "used to inquire with the greatest care into all the plants of the region," but he used his observations primarily to make points about ancient Egyptian history and classical philology.[8] One of the plants he saw growing in Egypt was papyrus. Subsequently, in 1572, he published a lengthy commentary on the chapters on papyrus in Pliny's *Natural History,* in which he supported Pliny's contention, against Varro, that the invention of papyrus paper for writing long predated the Hellenistic period. Joseph Scaliger poured justified scorn on Guilandinus's classical scholarship in this work, though not on his main contention or his botanical knowledge.[9]

The comments attributed to Guilandinus in the exchange at the beginning of *De medicina Aegyptiorum* suggest that he associated Egyptian medicine primarily with accounts — first appearing in late antiquity and many times repeated in the Renaissance — of the invention of medicine in Egypt and of the wisdom of Egyptian physicians in remotest antiquity. His remark about animals alluded to one set of origin myths that attributed the discovery of standard therapeutic techniques — bloodletting and the clyster — to observation of the behavior of distinctively Egyptian animals, the hippopotamus and the ibis. (According to these stories, the hippopotamus, when satiated with overeating, restored itself to health by slashing a vein in its thigh with a sharp reed; the ibis used its beak as a syringe for a self-administered enema of Nile water.) Another variety of origin story attributed the discovery of medicine to named individuals, human or semidivine. Throughout the sixteenth century a convenient

8. "Cum enim in Agypto perigrinarer, et magna cura in omnes eius regionis stirpes inquirerem . . . ." Guilandinus, *Papyrus,* p. 107.

9. See note 3. For analysis of this work of Guilandinus and of Scaliger's critique, see Anthony Grafton, "Rhetoric, Philology and Egyptomania in the 1570s: J. J. Scaliger's Invective against M. Guilandinus's *Papyrus,*" *Journal of the Warburg and Courtauld Institutes* 42 (1979): 167–94.

collection of such accounts, assembled from ancient authors, was readily available in Polydore Vergil's widely disseminated *De inventoribus rerum*. In most of them, the originators of medicine were Greek; candidates ranging among Apollo, Chiron the centaur, and Homeric warrior-surgeons were presented as constituting a kind of prehistory to Asclepius and Hippocrates. But Polydore also noted that Diodorus Siculus said that Mercury first invented medicine among the Egyptians although according to the ancients "Apis, king of the Egyptians" discovered it, while Clement of Alexandria ascribed it completely to the Egyptians.[10] Clement of Alexandria's *Stromateis* was in fact one of the principal sources that could be cited in support of a specifically Hermetic, not just Egyptian, ancient medicine, since it alleged the existence of six medical books of Hermes — not corresponding to any of the surviving philosophical Hermetic literature — covering, respectively, anatomy, diseases, instruments, medicines, opthalmology, and gynecology.[11]

One of the philosophical Hermetic treatises actually known in the Renaissance provided yet another apparent witness to an Egyptian origin of medicine. The Latin *Asclepius* identifies the eponymous interlocutor's grandfather, also named Asclepius, as an Egyptian god (or deified human) who invented medicine.[12] Egypt was also the site of the first beginnings of medicine in a less flattering account purportedly by medicine's own leading authority. The pseudo-Galenic *Introductio seu medicus* gives roles to both Egypt and Greece. The author credited the perfection of medicine to the Greek Asclepius and his successors, especially Hippocrates, but ascribed previous practical rudiments to Egypt. The latter included observation of

<hr/>

10. Polydore Vergil, *Adagiorum liber. Eiusdem de inventoribus rerum libri octo* (Basel, 1524), *De inventoribus* 1.20, "Quis primus medicinam invenerit," fols. 11v–12r (second series of foliation). "Hanc [medicinam] enim (teste Diodoro) volunt Mercurium apud Aegyptios primum invenisse: secundum vero veteres, Apis Aegyptiorum res reperit. . . . Clemens autem Aegyptiis omnino ascribit" (11r). On this work, which first appeared in 1499 and went through numerous sixteenth-century editions, see Brian P. Copenhaver, "The Historiography of Discovery in the Renaissance: Polydore Vergil's *De inventoribus rerum*, I–III," *Journal of the Warburg and Courtauld Institutes* 41 (1978): 192–214. Regarding earlier accounts of the origins of medicine, see Wesley D. Smith, "Notes on Ancient Medical Historiography," *Bulletin of the History of Medicine* 63 (1989): 73–109, and Chiara Crisciani, "History, Novelty, and Progress in Scholastic Medicine," *Osiris* 6 (1990): 118–39.

11. Clement of Alexandria, *Stromateis* 6.4.

12. *Asclepius* 37, now most readily consulted in *Hermetica*, trans. Copenhaver, p. 90.

the ibis, surgical skills developed as a result of Egyptian burial practices, and knowledge of medicinal properties of plants native to Egypt (as testified by Homer).[13]

In the mid-sixteenth century, interest in ancient Egypt as a source of medical wisdom may have been stimulated by the appearance of the collected "medical epistles" of the Heidelberg practitioner Johann Lange; they certainly provide striking evidence of the author's fascination with the subject. Lange's collection was first published in 1554; a second edition enlarged with a second book appeared in 1560 and a third (including a third book) in 1589.[14] A letter apparently written during student days in Italy—Lange graduated M.D. from Pisa in 1522 or 1523—describes a trip to Venice, where he had a conversation with his former Greek teacher, Petrus de Aegina, about the origins of medicine. As reported by Lange, Petrus declared—amid much else—that the Greeks were only apes of the much more ancient Egyptian *scientia* in all disciplines. The Egyptians had shone forth in the study of medicine from the origin of the world, effecting wonderful cures by means of natural magic. Democritus, Pythagoras, and Plato had gone to Egypt to learn the secrets of magic to which medicine was annexed. When Democritus returned home, he taught Hippocrates what he had learned. Although the speech Lange attributed to Petrus concludes with admonitions to the effect that medicine is a gift of God bestowed on all nations, the overall thrust is that of an encomium to a most ancient Egyptian medi-

13. *Introductio seu medicus,* in Galen, *Opera,* ed. C. G. Kühn (Leipzig, 1821–33) 14:674–76. For Egypt in Galen's authentic writings, see Vivian Nutton, "Galen and Egypt," in *Galen und das hellenistische Erbe,* ed. Jutta Kollesch and Diethard Nickel (Stuttgart: F. Steiner Verlag, 1993), pp. 11–31. Most references concern Galen's disdain for contemporary Hellenistic medicine in Alexandria, where he spent several years. Nutton points out that his information about indigenous Egyptian remedies as well as prejudices concerning Egypt and the Egyptians came from Greek written sources. A concise account of modern historical and archaeological knowledge of early Egyptian medicine is provided in J. Worth Estes, *The Medical Skills of Ancient Egypt* (Canton, Mass.: Science History Publications, 1989); for the Egyptian origin of some plant remedies and possibly also some concepts and techniques used in Greek medicine, see Estes, *Medical Skills,* pp. 122–23.

14. On Lange (1485–1565) and his epistles, see Vivian Nutton, "John Caius und Johannes Lange: medizinischer Humanismus zur Zeit Vesals," *NTM* 21 (1984): 81–87, and Nutton, "Humanist Surgery," in *The Medical Renaissance of the Sixteenth Century,* ed. A. Wear, R. K. French, and I. M. Lonie (Cambridge: Cambridge University Press, 1985), pp. 75–99, at pp. 91–96. I have consulted Johann Lange, *Epistolarum medicinalium volumen tripartitum* (Frankfurt, 1589).

cal wisdom closely allied with natural magic.[15] But darker connotations of Egyptian medicine appear in some of Lange's other epistles, in which it is associated with pagan worship, demonic magic, and nefarious forms of Jewish magic, which the Jews (whom Lange repeatedly excoriated) were said to have learned in captivity from the idolatrous Egyptians.[16]

The medical Egypt presented by Alpino in the exchange with Guilandinus quoted above and in the rest of *De medicina Aegyptiorum* was very different. Even though Alpino, as already noted, described Egyptian medical practitioners as poorly paid empirics, he greatly admired some of their therapies. He particularly advocated an Egyptian method of bloodletting

---

15. Lange, *Epistolarum . . . volumen* 2. 2, pp. 522–50: "Graeci vero, scientiae Aegyptiorum mancipia et simiae, Epidaurum incolentes, ea in Aesculapii templo tanquam donaria eidem consecrata, recondebant: quae vulgo contractare nefas erat" (526).

"At Egyptii ab origine mundi omnes medicinae studio adeo flagrarunt . . . . ipsi nempe medicinam magia naturali admirandam effecerunt, et illustrarunt adeo ut pleraque pharmaca vel hodie videantur esse *epodoi*, carmina, vel incantamenta. Haec enim ex rerum naturalium sympathiae et antipathiae peritia, conspirantibus astrorum, et non raro etiam spirituum vicibus constabat, qua admiranda in morbis prodigia peragebant. Quid multis? Fateri ingenue cogor, Graecos omnes artium ingenuarum disciplinas a barbaris accepisse. Primus omnium Cadmus, Agenoris filius ex Phoenicia, Orpheus ex Thracia literas, deorum caeremonias, simulacrorum consecrationes, hymnos attulere. Ac Persae magiam Graecos docuerunt, qui haec ab Aegyptiis primum hauserunt, ad quae discenda Democritus, Pythagoras et Plato in Aegyptum migrarunt, ut arcana magiae, cui medicina annexa fuit, ab Aegyptiorum magis et Hebraeis qui tum in servitute Aegyptiorum vitam misere traducebant, addiscerent" (528–29).

"Quum ista Democritus in Aegypto didicisset, reversusque domum, Hippocratem, quo cum familiariter vixit, haec erudisset, grassante in Graecia peste, discipulis comitatus, in Illyriam profectus, aerem ignis incendio a pestis contagione expurgavit" (530).

16. Notably in 1.72, pp. 434–44, headed "Veteres ex Aegypto philosophos divina herbarum medicamenta, magica et anili superstitione infamasse turpiter," and 2.46, pp. 772–80: "De magica Aegyptiorum medicina, ac magiae speciebus." In the latter, Lange classified Egyptian magical medicine into natural and demonic varieties: "Est quoque alia nefanda magiae species, a pharmacis deleteriis Pharmacia dicta, veneficio Circes infamis: quae ex medicamentis phyltra, amoris pocula conficere docuit. Huius inventor fertur Thoon rex Aegypti. . . . Altera vero Aegyptiorum magia, inquit apud Heliodorum Calafiris, revera est sapienta, a qua illa adulterina degeneravit, quam nos sacerdotes et antistitum genus, ab ineunte aetate excolimus, supra res naturales, naturales contemplatur, deorum convictrix, et naturae praestantioris particeps astrorum motus inquirens, futurorum scientiam in lucro ponens, ab his terrenis malis remota, omnia ad honestatem et utilitatem hominum accommodans studia. Haec enim secretioribus philosophiae rationibus innixa, ex medicina et astrologia nata fertur, quibus rerum sympathias scrutatur" (778–79).

by scarification of the legs. As explained by Alpino and illustrated by a woodcut in his book, this procedure involved making rows of small vertical incisions in the patient's legs. On his return to Italy, he had immediately introduced the technique into his own medical practice, enthusiastically scarifying old and young, male and female among his patients at Bassano. He considered the procedure particularly suitable for women (though the patient shown in his illustration is a man) and used it for complaints ranging from double tertian fever, through difficulty in breathing, to pestilence. Alpino ascribed much therapeutic success to his use of this Egyptian technique, although he admitted that almost all patients initially feared "the many and deep scarifications." Perhaps as a result, his *condotto* as town physician of Bassano was not renewed for a second term.[17]

Alpino's focus on the medical techniques actually used by contemporary medical practitioners in Egypt under Turkish rule to treat their own patients was so sharp that he completely omitted discussion of Renaissance Europe's favorite Egyptian—or supposedly Egyptian—medical import, *mumia*.[18] Instead, he devoted many pages to Egyptian methods of

17. Alpino, *De medicina Aegyptiorum* 3.3–10, fols. 80r–96v, with illustration at 92r. "Ab Egypto ego in patriam reversus, Bassanum oppidum loci amoenitate pulcherrimum, meorum studiorum gratia, me contuli, ibique medicinam publice faciendo multos scio aegrotos crurum scarificatione, sanguinis saepe evacuatione more Aegyptiorum procurata, sanitati restitutos. Scis enim postquam in Italiam ex illis locis pervenerim, me perpetuo optima Aegyptiorum vestigia in medendo sequi voluisse, praesertimeque in sanguinis vacuatione molienda, maximeque in usu crurum scarificationis. . . . Quod mihi feliciori cum successu semper evenit. . . . In principio dum ea uti coeperim, propter multas magnasque ac profundas scarificationes fere omnes hoc auxilium formidabant. Deinceps vero multi fuere, tum viri, tum mulieres, quae ab utilitate persuasi hoc genus remedii facile complexi sunt." Alpino, *De medicina Aegyptiorum* 3.4, fols. 82r–83r. For the case histories of six patients, all children, adolescents, or elderly women, see fol. 82r–v. For the nonrenewal of the *condotto*, Ongaro, "Contributo alla biografia di Prospero Alpini," pp. 97–98.

18. The term *mumia* referred to an exudate from corpses of spices used in burial or to bituminous substances supposed to have been used in burial. See K. H. Dannenfeldt, "Egyptian *Mumia*: The Sixteenth-Century Experience and Debate," *The Sixteenth Century Journal* 16 (1985): 163–80; and Michael Camille, "The Corpse in the Garden: *Mumia* in Medieval Herbal Illustrations," in *Micrologus*, vol. 7, *Il cadavere* (Turnhout: Brepols, 1999), pp. 296–318. Alpino mentioned the drug *mumia* in passing, in the course of his description of ancient Egyptian burial practices in his *Historiae Aegypti naturalis pars prima* (first published posthumously in 1735), but did not dwell on its merits and did not associate it with the medicine practiced by the Egyptians themselves; see *Histoire naturelle de l'Égypte, 1581–84 par Prosper Alpin*, ed. and trans. R. de Fenoyl, *Collection des voyageurs occidentaux en Égypte*,

bloodletting, Egypt's disease environment, and the Egyptian lifestyle, including the use of opium, cannabis, lemon sherbet, and a beverage usually identified as coffee. If so, this is one of the earliest European references to coffee, the cultivation of which is said to have spread throughout the Arabic world in about the fifteenth century.

These chapters are filled with observations either made by Alpino himself or reported to him by another Venetian physician in Egypt. An account of recreational opium use describes mood alteration, dreams, and withdrawal symptoms. The subject of coffee elicits appreciative testimony to its stimulating effect first thing in the morning. Alpino also waxed enthusiastic about the refreshing qualities of lemonade, "most enjoyable to thirsty people," and provided a recipe.[19] Of special interest was Egyptian theriac, both because the Egyptian version of this supposedly universal remedy (first described by Galen) was highly prized and probably also because the correct composition of theriac was currently a controversial issue among the Italian physicians.[20] Alpino's Egypt was thus a contemporary

---

vol. 20 (4 vols. in 2, Cairo: Institut français d' archéologie orientale de Caire, 1979), 1.7, 1: 73–75.

19. Book 1 of *De medicina Aegyptiorum* has eighteen chapters, devoted, respectively, to the medical profession in Egypt (1–4); the geography and climate of Egypt (5–8); the physique, longevity, and diet of the inhabitants (9–12); the disease environment, especially plague (13–18). Book 2 (sixteen chapters) is devoted to bloodletting and cupping; book 3 (nineteen chapters) to scarification; book 4, on medication, has fifteen chapters devoted, respectively, to (1) alterative medicines, (2) opiates used to obtain dream visions, (3) decoctions, (4) syrups, (5–7) purgatives, (8–12) theriac, (13) other compound medicines, (14) enemas, and (15) fever medications. On coffee (4.1, 118r): "Est etiam illis in usu frequentissimo semen illud bon ab ipsis appellatum, et quo illud decoctum parant, de quo posterius loquemur. Huic omnes non secus quam nostri in publicis tabernis, vinorum potationibus, operam dant. De eoque singulis diebus saepe ad modum calenti interdiu, sed maxime mane ieiundo stomacho large bibere consueverunt. Siquidem ipso ventriculum calefieri, roborique apud eos compertum sit, non minusque etiam viscerum obstructiones tolli, quotidie experiantur." On lemon sherbet or lemonade (4.3, 124r): "Pro potu vero non in aegrotis modo, verum multo magis in sanis corporibus hanc potionem frequentant, quae sitientibus est iucundissima, quam sarbet, quasi potum per excellentiam vocant: illud etenim nomen, potum, simpliciter explicat: ipsam parant, in aqua multa saccharum dissolventes, eique admiscentes tantum limonum succi recentis, quantum modice aquam acidam reddere queat. Hanc aquam in aestivis caloribus omnes libentissime potant, tum at sitim extinguendam, tum ad refrigerandum."
20. On the controversies in Italy during the 1560s and 1570s over the correct composition of theriac, for which Galen had given a recipe involving vipers and sixty-three other ingredients, see Paula Findlen, *Possessing Nature: Museums, Collecting, and Scientific Culture in*

land of empirical "secrets" and practical hands-on techniques that could yield innovations of current medical usefulness. Moreover, Alpino spoke of individual Egyptian medical practitioners with a respect born of close personal contact: there was for example Mohammed ibn Ali, who was in charge of the manufacture of the much prized Egyptian theriac and who "even though he was a Muslim" was "a man of such integrity as to be worthy of respect." Alpino learned of this integrity at first hand, when he failed to persuade the Egyptian to reveal the recipe for the theriac, which was closely guarded as a valuable commercial secret. More trusting was "another Mohammed, with whom I was very friendly, who was by far the most learned of all the Egyptians in the *res herbaria,* to whom every day new medicaments were sent by friends from Arabia, Ethiopia, India and other places." It was through this practitioner that Alpino claimed ultimately "by chance" to have come into possession of the treasured recipe.[21]

In Italy as well as Egypt, as William Eamon has shown, sixteenth-century empirics such as Leonardo Fiorovanti made powerful claims for alleged

Early Modern Italy (Berkeley: University of California Press, 1994), pp. 241–45, 272–85; an account of the manufacture of theriac in Egypt in the seventeenth century is edited and translated in Gary Leiser and Michael Dols, "Evilya Chelebi's Description of Medicine in Seventeenth-Century Egypt," *Sudhoffs Archiv* 71 (1987): 197–216.

21. "Is, autem qui eo tempore, quo Cayri ego medicinam faciebam, compositionem hanc [sc. of theriac] moliebatur, fuit Mahemet ebne Haly, vir quidem quamvis Mahemetis assecla, morum tamen integritate non spernendus, quique advenas plurimi facere prae se fert: fingit tamen ingenti spe lucri, ex multa theriaca, quam advenis continue vendit. Nunquam tamen ego, etsi multi admodum domesticus, ac familiaris esset, theriacae compositionem, quam illi servant, ex eo discere potui, nunquam voluit me ipso etiam praesente legere. Timent enim, si nos ipsorum compositionem, quam caeteris absolutiorem ac praestantiorem esse opinantur, ab ipsis didicissemus, multi lucri, quod cum advenis plurimis Italis, Germanis, Polonis, Anglis, Gallis, Flandris, aliorumque multarum nationum hominibus saepissime in Aegyptum navigantibus continue faciunt, se non parvam iacturam ac damnum passuros. Vel etiam quia illis lege interdictum est, Christianos homines eam compositionem posse docere. Hincque nemo advena potest, ullo pretio ab illis eam compositionem intelligere.

"Guilandinus: Hoc iamdiu sciveram sed tu quanam arte usus fuisti, ut eam ab illis intelligeres? . . .

"Alpinus: Nullo meo consilio id accidit, sed casu atque ab alio Mahemete mihi valde familiari, rei herbariae longe omnium Aegyptiorum doctissimo, cui quotidie ex Arabiae, atque Aethiopiae, Indiaeque locis aliqua nova medicamenta ab amicis mittebantur, theriacae, quam Aegyptii componunt, integram ac veram habui descriptionem." Alpino, *De medicina Aegyptiorum* 4.8., fol. 133v.

secrets of therapy.[22] Moreover, the actual therapies employed by empirics and by academically trained medical practitioners often resembled one another. Yet as a university-educated physician Alpino was a member of a profession that traditionally regarded empirics with contempt. Hence his care to endow the techniques he picked up in contemporary Egypt with the prestige of putative ancient Egyptian origin and the approval of recognized medical authorities. Even if the practice of letting blood from children, common in Egypt, was not praised by Galen, "other very distinguished men in the medical art, such as Rasis, Haly, Avenzoar, Avicenna, and Celsus thought differently."[23] In fact, because he believed that the glories of ancient Egyptian medicine had lasted until the Mamelukes took over the country, Alpino assimilated the medical wisdom of Egyptian antiquity with Arabic medical tradition.[24] He claimed simultaneously that the physicians of ancient Egypt had practiced dogmatic (that is rational, as distinct from empirical) medicine, which Hippocrates may have learned from them, and that their wisdom had been preserved in Egypt until the Turkish conquest (1517) in the form of an Arabic book.[25]

22. William Eamon, *Science and the Secrets of Nature: Books of Secrets in Medieval and Early Modern Culture* (Princeton, N.J.: Princeton University Press, 1994), especially chap. 5.

23. "Quam in his missionem etsi Galenus non laudaverit, aliis etiam praeclarissimis viris in arte medica, ut Rasi, Haly, Avenzoar, Avicennae, Celso, secus persuasum est." Alpino, *De medicina Aegyptiorum* 2.4, fol. 46r.

24. "Ut ex Aegyptiis historiarum peritis audivi, a barbara priscorum Aegypto imperantium tyrannide tempore enim quo Mamaluchi illiusce regionis obtinebant imperium, omnia ea loca medicis doctissimis florebant, qui dogmatice summaque cum ratione medicinam faciebant . . . ." Alpino, *De medicina Aegyptiorum* 1.2, fol. 5v.

25. "Les anciens, en effet, connurent bien la médecine dogmatique, et beaucoup d'entre eux écrivèrent à son sujet beaucoup de choses, et fort belles, qui sont toutes contenues dans un livre très utile et très distingué, appelé *Sife,* composé par un Egyptien et écrit dans cette langue. Lorsque l'empereur des Turcs soumettait l'Egypte, il trouve ce livre caché parmi les objects les plus précieux. . . . Mais je n'ai jamais pu en obtenir des Egyptiens un exemplaire. Les Egyptiens ont aussi un livre appelé *Ebnagel ducam,* dans lequel sont décrits tous les remèdes simples et composés propres à supprimer les maladies. Ce livre est très familier à tous et j'ai pu, non sans peine, en obtenir un exemplaire. Parmi les anciens ils ont tous les médecins arabes: Avicenne, Albumazare, Rasis, Averroès, Ambibetar. Les anciens Egyptiens eurent donc autrefois une médecine très perfectionnée; et cela est normal, car, non loin de l'Egypte, ils avaient Cyrène, où l'on sait que la vraie médecine dogmatique fut autrefois brillante; et certains pensent qu'Hippocrate reçut d'eux autant que des habitants de Crotone les plus importants principes de la médecine." Alpino, *Histoire naturelle*

Alpino's invocation of ancient Egypt in support of his endeavor to import manual techniques new to conventional Galenic medical practice into Italy may have been novel. But his was by no means the first claim that innovations in medicine were endorsed either by ancient wisdom that preceded the standard school authorities or by those authorities themselves if properly interpreted. Although Galenism continued to represent the medical mainstream throughout the sixteenth century, criticisms of specific aspects of Galen's teaching were from time to time accompanied by appeals to the wisdom of ancients who had preceded him. Vesalius's references to the (pre-Galenic) ancients who allegedly taught boys anatomy in their homes are of this type. So are Cardano's endeavors to show that Galen's Hippocratic commentaries misinterpreted the true Hippocratic wisdom.[26]

Doxographic and medical tradition, as well as previous endeavors to call on the most ancient authority in medicine thus helped to shape the responses of Guilandinus and Alpino to the medical wisdom of Egypt. No doubt, too, both were affected by the contemporary interest in all manner of things Egyptian, which extended beyond hieroglyphics, papyrus, and obelisks to include such medical specialities as mumia and balsam. Colorful descriptions of the last two were, for example, featured in the popularized account of Egypt in André Thevet's *Cosmographie de Levant*.[27]

---

de l'Égypte 2.9, 1:224–25. The editor suggests Arabic identifications for the books named by Alpino.

26. "Veteres qui domi pueros sedulo dissecandi rationem docebant . . . ." Andreas Vesalius, *De humani corporis fabrica libri septem* (Basel, 1543) 1.3, p. 7; similarly, 1.15, p. 67; 1.18, p. 83; 2.23, p. 264; 5.13, p. 524; 6.5, p. 579; the preface of the *Fabrica* also makes reference to "priscos dissectionum professores" (fol. *3r). See further, Vivian Nutton, " 'Prisci dissectionum professores': Greek Texts and Renaissance Anatomists," in *The Uses of Greek and Latin: Historical Essays*, ed. A. C. Dionisotti, Anthony Grafton, and Jill Kraye (London: The Warburg Institute, 1988), pp. 111–26, at p. 117; R. Toellner, " 'Renata dissectionis ars,' Vesals Stellung zu Galen in ihren wissenschaftsgeschichtlichen Voraussetzungen und Folgen," in *Die Rezeption der Antike,* ed. August Buck (Hamburg: Hauswedell, 1981), pp. 85–95; and Nancy G. Siraisi, *The Clock and the Mirror: Girolamo Cardano and Renaissance Medicine* (Princeton, N.J.: Princeton University Press, 1997), pp. 128–42.

27. See Dannenfeldt, "Egypt and Egyptian Antiquities," and Grafton, "Rhetoric, Philology, and Egyptomania."

According to Thevet: "De ces Momies usent les Apoticaires: mais aucuns d'eus errent en ce, qui'ils pensent que sesdis corps se trouvent sous les sables. Car moy estant sur le lieu avec deus Medecins Veniciens, et quatres marchans de Rhaguse, acompagnez de six

But Guilandinus's and Alpino's own travels to Egypt belonged to a particular local, subdisciplinary, and institutional context. Although sixteenth-century travelers to Egypt came from various parts of Western Europe, for both political and commercial reasons interest in the eastern Mediterranean was especially pronounced in the Venetian Republic.[28] Moreover, Venetian diplomatic representatives or trading communities in the east in some instances employed medical practitioners as well as affording protection to favored travelers. Thus, the physician Andrea Alpago of Belluno used his time in Venetian service in Syria to produce an emended version of the *Canon* of Avicenna with a glossary of Arabic terms, a work that was officially endorsed by the University of Padua in 1521.[29] In addition, the public for works on "eastern" topics was more likely in Venetian territory than elsewhere to include readers who could bring the test of personal experience to bear. For example, the publication of Alpino's book on Egyptian plants in 1592 involved him in a long correspondence with Onorio Belli, a former acquaintance from Padua, who disagreed with some of Alpino's

---

Iannissaires, fut trouuee une femme en son entier, ayant les ongles grands à merveilles, et les cheveux iusqu'à demi iambe, en sorte qu'on eust dit qu'il n'y avoit pas deus ans qu'elle estoit morte. . . . Or toutes ces choses diligemment vues, et considerees fut question de poursuiure notre voyage, à raison de quoy nous vinmes en un vilage nommé la Mataree, ou il y ha une fonteine, qui arrose le iardin ou se trouue le baume, qui ha une odeur fort plaisante aus viperes . . . ." André Thevet, *Cosmographie de Levant,* ed. Frank Lestringant (Geneva: Librairie Droz, 1985), chap. 42, pp. 157–59. Thevet also informed his readers that the Egyptians were the healthiest of all people, after the Africans, and lived a hundred years (chap. 35, p. 125), and of the health benefits of Nile water and crocodile fat (chap. 37, pp. 139, 141). Thevet was in Egypt for about four months in 1551–52, most of which he spent in Alexandria, with short side trips to other points of interest; much of his account of the country is derivative. The work was first published in 1554 (pp. xvi–xvii).

28. See Giuliano Lucchetta, "L'oriente mediterraneo nella cultura di Venezia tra il Quattro e il Cinquecento," *Storia della cultura veneta* part 3, vol. 2: 375–432.

29. See Francesca Lucchetta, *Il medico e filosofo bellunese Andrea Alpago (+ 1522) traduttore d'Avicenna, profilo biografico* (Padua: Editrice Antenore, 1964); and Giorgio Vercellin, ed., *Il Canone di Avicenna fra Europa e Oriente nel primo Cinquecento: L'interpretatio Arabicorum nominum di Andrea Alpago* (Turin: UTET, 1991). Other medical practitioners who served Venetians in the Middle East included Gian Giacomo Manni of Salo and the pharmacist and surgeon Domenico da Re, both of whom Alpino encountered in Egypt, and Tommaso Minadoi of Rovigo (d. 1615), who, after his return from Syria, published a *Historia della guerra fra Turchi e Persiani* (Rome, 1587), and became a professor of *medicina practica* at Padua. See Alpino, *Histoire naturelle de l'Égypte,* pp. 6–7, and Lucchetta, "Viaggiatori," pp. 218–19.

plant descriptions and identifications on the basis of experience gained during his (Belli's) ten years' residence in Crete.[30]

Furthermore, with the exception of Pierre Belon, most sixteenth-century travelers to Egypt from parts of Europe other than the territories of the Venetian Republic were chiefly concerned with the wonders of Egypt in general rather than specifically with natural history or medicine.[31] By contrast, Guilandinus and Alpino were committed to the methods and goals of humanist pharmacology and botany. The remarkable development in the sixteenth century of these subdisciplines—which combined botanical description with philological or historical investigation and sought to relate actual plants to descriptions in ancient sources—occurred across Europe. But at the University of Padua and in Venice a special context was provided by Venice's role as a great mart for all kinds of medicaments and medicinal ingredients, many of which were, or purported to be, imported from the eastern Mediterranean.[32] Venetian and Paduan civic and academic authorities appreciated the endeavors of Guilandinus and Alpino to describe Egyptian plants at first hand as well as to identify various remedies or ingredients that Dioscorides, Galen, or other ancient writers had characterized as "Egyptian." Guilandinus's journey to various parts of the eastern Mediterranean and Egypt had been supported by a Venetian senator who was a member of the Riformatori dello Studio, the Venetian magistracy in charge of the University of Padua. The patrons who ransomed Guilandinus from pirates who had captured him on the voyage home included another Venetian noble. It was presumably his Venetian patrons who, shortly thereafter, in 1561, secured his appointment to the university botanic garden. Alpino's works on the genuine balsam (1591) and the plants of Egypt (1592) helped to obtain his appointment as lecturer on simples at the University of Padua

---

30. Milan, Biblioteca Ambrosiana, ms. D 191 inf., fols. 137r–158v. Consulted on microfilm, Ambrosiana Microfilm Collection, University of Notre Dame. I am most grateful to Dr. Louis Jordan, librarian of the Ambrosiana Microfilm Collection, and to Professor Cornelius O'Boyle for assistance obtaining access to this material and to that cited in notes 38 and 43.

31. See *Voyage en Égypte de Pierre Belon de Mans 1547*, ed. Serge Sanneron, *Collection des voyageurs occidentaux in Égypte*, vol. 1 (Cairo: Institut français d'archéologie orientale de Caire, 1970). Belon, a physician, sought out information regarding materia medica and simples. Nevertheless, he devoted much space to natural history and general travelogue.

32. See Richard Palmer, "Pharmacy in the Republic of Venice in the Sixteenth Century," in *The Medical Renaissance of the Sixteenth Century*, pp. 100–117.

in 1594 and, ultimately, also to make him Guilandinus's second successor as prefect of the botanic garden in 1603.[33]

But the various claims made for Egypt by Guilandinus and Alpino did not convince Girolamo Mercuriale. Judging by his powerful patrons (the Farnese family) and wide network of scientific and intellectual correspondents, Mercuriale's was an exceptionally successful medical career. At Padua, where he was professor of *medicina practica* from 1569 until 1587, he earned renown both as a practitioner among an elite clientele — notwithstanding an unfortunate episode in which he failed to identify a major epidemic of plague in Venice — and as the author of works on practical medicine.[34] Before then, in 1567, he had already been engaged in an epistolary debate with Guilandinus over Galen's identification of the ingredients of "Egyptian ointment."[35] In this exchange Guilandinus criticized and Mercuriale defended Galen. Throughout his academic career, Guilandinus devoted much energy to disputes over the proper identification of plants or medicines named by ancient authors, his usual opponent being Mattioli, whose commentary on Dioscorides made him one of the most influential medical botanists of the period.[36] The letters between Guilandinus and Mercuriale, although lavish with mutual expressions of esteem, included nasty insinuations from Mercuriale about Guilandinus's incompetence in philology and rival claims to have consulted superior Greek manuscripts.[37]

33. See, in addition to the various biographical sources for Guilandinus and Alpino cited above, Lucchetta, "Viaggiatori," pp. 220–23. Guilandinus's *Papyrus* is dedicated to one of his Venetian patrons.

34. See note 6.

35. Guilandinus prefaced these letters — Mercuriale's *Repugnantia* and his own *Assertio* — with a dedicatory epistle to Giovan Vincenzo Pinelli and published them along with his *Papyrus* in 1572 (as in note 3, above). Mercuriale's *Repugnantia* is dated 1567 (p. 240).

36. On Mattioli, see *Pietro Andrea Mattioli, Siena 1501–Trento 1578, la vita le opere,* ed. Sara Ferri (Perugia: Quattroemme, 1997), and Paula Findlen, "The Formation of a Scientific Community: Natural History in Sixteenth-Century Italy," in *Natural Particulars: Nature and the Disciplines in Renaissance Europe,* ed. Anthony Grafton and Nancy G. Siraisi (Cambridge: MIT Press, 1999).

37. Mercuriale first praised Guilandinus for "ingenium tuum, ac miram in pervestigandis plantarum naturis sedulitatem," but continued: "Ego vero Guilandine, tantum abest ut credam Galenum hac in re nos fefellisse, quo potius te (nisi gravioribus rationibus aliud sentire cogar) vel pravos Athenaei et Galeni codices habuisse, vel horum auctorum verba, pro tuis multis occupationibus minus sedulo examinasse puto" (Mercuriale, *Repugnantia* pp. 235, 236).

Guilandinus and Mercuriale had another difference of opinion two years later, but neither this nor the correspondence about Egyptian ointment, nor the publication of the latter by Guilandinus (as an appendix to Guilandinus's *Papyrus* in 1572) seems to have caused lasting ill-feeling, since the two men were apparently friends in 1574.[38] Furthermore, Mercuriale, who, as already noted, had also been among Alpino's teachers, took a leading role in urging the latter to publish the results of his Egyptian voyage soon after his return in 1584.[39]

Mercuriale shared the interest in the most ancient medicine, but his interest did not take the form of enthusiasm for Egypt. He wrote a book advocating the revival of Greek gymnastic practice as a form of health care[40] and was a prominent figure in the late-sixteenth-century reassessment of Hippocrates. Despite the continued dominance of Galen, belief in the superior antiquity and purity of Hippocratic medicine led to some efforts to isolate Hippocratic teaching from Galenic interpretation, to make use of a wider range of Hippocratic texts than those traditionally studied, and to distinguish authentic works of Hippocrates. Mercuriale wrote commentaries on several Hippocratic treatises and supervised the 1588 Giunta edition of the Hippocratic corpus.[41] But his most significant contribution to Renaissance Hippocratism was a *Censura operum Hippocratis*, first pub-

---

Guilandinus termed Mercuriale a man of "singularis doctrinae et perspicacis ingenii," but retorted that he had found his information in an "antiquissimo exemplo" of Athenaeus, *Deipnosophistae* (in which Egyptian ointment was mentioned) (Guilandinus, *Assertio*, pp. 242, 244).

38. In 1569, Guilandinus wrote to Giovan Vicenzo Pinelli, commenting unfavorably on Mercuriale's interpretation of the ingredients of types of bread mentioned by ancient authors (Bibliotheca Ambrosiana, ms. S 109 sup., fols. 26r–v [Mercuriale to Pinelli] and 27r [Guilandinus to Pinelli], consulted on microfilm, Ambrosiana Microfilm Collection, University of Notre Dame). But a letter of 1574 from Sperone Speroni to Mercuriale requests "A quelli nostri signori amici, infra li quali i primi sono il sig. Pinelli e Guillandini, tenetemi caro colla vostra autorità," in *Lettere inedite di dotti italiani del secolo XVI tratte dagli autografi della Biblioteca Ambrosiana*, ed. Antonio Ceruti (Milan, 1867), p. 23.

39. Alpino, *De medicina Aegyptiorum*, prefatory letter, "eruditis lectoribus," eii verso.

40. I have consulted Girolamo Mercuriale, *De arte gymnastica libri sex* (Venice, 1601). The work was first published Venice, 1569, with the title *Artis gymnasticae apud antiquos celeberrimae, nostris temporibus ignoratae, libri sex*.

41. *Hippocratis Coi Opera quae extant graece et latine veterum codicum collatione restitua, novo ordine in quattuor classes digesta, interpretationis latinae emendatione, et scholijs illustrata, a Hieronymo Mercuriale Forliviensi* (Venice, 1588).

lished in 1584, in which he made one of the first attempts to classify the Hippocratic books according to authenticity.[42]

In Mercuriale's works, the few comments on the contribution of Egypt to the origins of medicine are dismissive. Egypt is not even mentioned in an account of the "most ancient origin, inventors, and practitioners" of medicine contained in an oration he delivered upon taking up his professorial duties, probably at Padua.[43] A chapter, "On the beginnings of medicine," that opens his *De arte gymnastica* informs the reader that because early people did not overindulge, they had no need of medicine, did not use it, and knew nothing of its principles, even though Homer says the Egyptians had many herbs. Subsequently, overindulgence in sex, gourmet food, and strong drink brought on diseases that made it necessary to discover the first, very crude, beginnings of empirical medicine. But medical knowledge was perfected much later, by the Greeks.[44] Mercuriale allowed the ancient Egyptians merely the dubious credit of having invented the *ars cosmetica*.[45] He presented Egypt's contribution to empirical medicine in a somewhat more favorable light in one of his Hippocratic commentaries, when he asserted (citing Galen) that at the time of Hippocrates the Egyptians preserved the remedies they had discovered by inscribing them on columns in the temple of Isis.[46] But if in Mercuriale's view ancient Egypt

---

42. Girolamo Mercuriale, *De morbis puerorum. Item de venenis et morbis venenosis. Quibus adiuncta est Censura Hippocratea* (Basel, 1584). The *Censura* is separately paginated at the end of the volume; Subsequent reprintings included one with the edition of Hippocrates cited in the previous note. See also I. M. Lonie, "Cos versus Cnidus and the Historians: Part 1," *History of Science* 16 (1978): 49. Mercuriale was still largely following Galen's opinion regarding the authenticity of Hippocratic treatises.

43. Milan, Biblioteca Ambrosiana, ms. S 84 sup., fols. 309r–313v; survey of history of medicine at fols. 309r–310v. Consulted on microfilm, Ambrosiana Microfilm Collection, Notre Dame University.

44. "Qua de re tunc temporis medicinae aut paucos omnino, aut nullos usus, nullaque principia extitisse certum est: etsi Homerus antiquissimus auctor scripserit Aegyptum multas herbas, multaque medicamenta habuisse. Postquam vero intemperantiae nefanda lues, coquorum exquisitae artes, delicatissima epularum condimenta, vinorumque peregrinae temperaturae inter homines irrepsere, morborum simul varia continuo genera succrescentia ad inveniendam medicinam eos coegerunt: qua semper carere profecto licuisset, nisi humana, vel potius ferina ingluvies omnium vitiorum soboles eius usum omnium maxime necessarium effecisset"—and so on. Mercuriale, *De arte gymnastica* 1.1, p. 1.

45. Mercuriale, *De arte gymnastica*, 1.2, fols. 3v–4r.

46. Girolamo Mercuriale, *Commentarii eruditissimi, in Hippocratis Coi Prognostica, Prorrhetica,*

had contributed little to the beginnings of medicine, Hellenistic Egypt had positively hindered its further progress. Hippocrates had either left few writings or few had survived. But in the centuries after his death, the Ptolemies, greedy to build up their famous library, had offered lavish rewards for copies of books by well-known authors, with the result that they had acquired numerous forgeries, especially of works attributed to Hippocrates. The later dissemination of these forgeries was, in Mercuriale's view, responsible for all subsequent confusion about the identity of the genuine works of Hippocrates — and hence, from the standpoint of the late sixteenth century, about the fundamental principles of medicine itself.[47]

Thus, physicians at Padua held very diverse views about Egypt. Guilandinus and Alpino were in their different ways both exceptionally interested in and knowledgeable about Egypt. But Alpino, whatever his rhetorical obeisance to Egyptian antiquity, made it clear that he knew that antecedents of the contemporary Egyptian medical practices he described were to be found in Arabic medicine. Mercuriale, one of the most influential members of the professoriate, took what seems on the whole to have been a rather negative view of Egyptian medical history.

Ultimately, professors of medicine in the Galenist tradition would have little use for appeals to ancient Egyptian medical wisdom. Their reservations were not due only to simple conservatism, though this may have played a part. One problem was probably the connotation of magic — and not necessarily only benign natural magic — that hung around some accounts of Egyptian medicine, as Lange's epistles showed. Another may have first become apparent at Padua in the last third of the sixteenth century as a result of the work of Guilandinus and Alpinus. The more attention was devoted to Egypt, the more it became clear that what Egypt had to offer was medical botany and remedies — whether plants and remedies

De victus ratione in morbis acutis et Epidemicas historias (Frankfurt, 1602; bound with his Medicina practica), p. 358 (in the commentary on De victus in acutis).

47. "Caeterum cum posterioribus temporibus Aegypti Reges locupletendae bibliothecae cupidissimi, quemque ad adferendos antiquorum auctorum commentarios, propositis eximiis praemiis, invitarent, factum est, ut complures a lucri studiosis, libri falso probatorum auctorum adscripto nomine offerrentur, qui deinceps, vel surrepti, quo tempore ea bibliotheca dissoluta est, vel inde transcripti falsis titulis ad posteritatem longe lateque propagati sunt, id quod Hippocratis Coi commentarios potissimum esse passos existimandum est." Mercuriale, Censura operum Hippocratis, printed before Hippocratis Coi Opera quae extant (as in note 41), p. 3. This opinion, too, is attributed to Galen.

associated with Egypt by ancient authors or noted on the spot by recent observers. Notwithstanding Alpino's assertions about rationalism in ancient Egyptian medicine, a textual or theoretical basis for a system of medicine was lacking. The Hermetic medical literature claimed by Clement of Alexandria, if it had ever existed, did not survive, and actual Egyptian medical or surgical papyri were not known in the sixteenth century. By contrast, Renaissance physicians had available to them a large body of Greek medical texts. Moreover, their discussions of theoretical topics such as the nature of the elements — a subject of fundamental importance to medicine, since it underpinned the entire elaborate physiological system of qualities, humors, and temperaments — could and did draw in addition on the whole range of ancient Greek philosophical writing.

Late in his career Alpino himself moved away from an Egyptian model for the reform of medical techniques toward a Greek model for the revision of underlying medical theory. An interest in the revival of ancient medical methodism led him to espouse atomism. He was, of course, by no means the first Renaissance physician to introduce unconventional authorities or ideas about the elements and theory of matter into his medical writings. Among well-known earlier endeavors of this kind are, for example, Paracelsus's radical revisions of element theory, Fracastoro's use of ancient atomism to explain contagion, and Cardano's exclusion of fire from the number of the elements.[48]

Perhaps Alpino was originally drawn to methodism by a desire to attribute some form of systematic medicine to contemporary Egyptians; at any rate, he remarked in De medicina Aegyptiorum that, since they rejected attention to causes they could be described as practicing methodist as well as empirical medicine.[49] By 1601, he was committed to a program of re-

48. Vivian Nutton, "The Seeds of Disease: An Explanation of Contagion and Infection from the Greeks to the Renaissance," Medical History 27 (1983):1-34; Nutton, "The Reception of Fracastoro's Theory of Contagion: The Seed That Fell among Thorns?" Osiris 6 (1990): 196-234; Alfonso Ingegno, Saggi sulla filosofia di Cardano (Florence: La nuova Italia, 1980), pp. 223ff.
49. "Ut per eos annos, quibus Cayri moram traxi, observare potui, potius methodicae simulque empiricae ipsos addictos iudicavi, quando ad indicandam morborum curationem partium laesarum, causarum, naturae, aetatis, virium, habitus coeliique observationem esse necessarium negent, quibusdamque medendo utantur communissimis propositionibus, quae methodicorum sectam referre videntur. Ipsi etenim affirmant omnia morborum genera, vel a caliditate, vel a frigiditate oririi, vel morborum omnium praecipuam causam

viving the ancient sect; ten years later he published a large volume entitled *De medicina methodica*.[50] The salient medical doctrines of the ancient medical methodists (about whom most information comes via hostile accounts by Celsus and Galen) were the repudiation of lengthy study of causes as irrelevant to therapy and the belief that all disease was the result of excessive constriction or excessive relaxation of pores that made every part of the body transpirable. To these ideas they allied an atomist physics.[51] Hence, Alpino rested his case for methodism as a medical system on the authority of pre-Socratic philosophers—Democritus, Epicurus, and Leucippus for atoms in a void and Anaximenes and Heraclitus for the importance of density and rarity.[52] Although Alpino classified disease and remedies according to their relaxing or constricting nature, his actual prescriptions in *De medicina methodica* seem mostly to have been traditional herbal compounds, with frequent allusions to and recipes from Galen and Dioscorides. His endeavor may thus deserve a minor place in the history of the revival of atomism.[53]

---

in calorem praeter naturam, vel frigiditatem referunt. Alpino, *De medicina Aegyptiorum* 1.2, fol. 3r.

50. Prospero Alpino, *De medicina methodica libri tredecim* (Padua, 1611). A century later, this work still retained the esteem of Hermann Boerhaave, who was responsible for a second edition (Leiden, 1719). Alpino announced his intention to revive methodism in a prefatory epistle in his *De praesagienda vita, et morte aegrotantium. Libri septem,* published in 1601 (a work reissued in many subsequent editions and an English translation, the latter also sponsored by Boerhaave). On Alpino and medical methodism, see Loris Premuda, "Prospero Alpini: Il rilancio delle antiche dottrine fisiche in medicina nella Padova di Galileo Galilei," *Acta medicae historiae patavina* 8–9 (1961–63): 9–28, with appendix of excerpts from *De medicina methodica* in Italian translation following at pp. 28–63.

51. Celsus, *De medicina*, 3 vols., proem 54–67, ed. W. G. Spencer (Cambridge, Mass.: Harvard University Press, 1971), 1: 28–36; Galen, *On the Sects for Beginners,* chaps. 6 and 7, now most readily consulted in Galen, *Three Treatises on the Nature of Science,* trans. Richard Walzer and Michael Frede (Indianapolis: Hackett Publishing Company, 1985), pp. 10–13.

52. Alpino, *De medicina methodica* (1611) 1.5, pp. 8–10. "Quare philosophorum vacuum ponentium, quos eruditissimos, gravissimos viros fuisse scimus, auctoritate etiam ea communitas confirmatur" (p. 9).

53. Premuda, "Prospero Alpini," places Alpino's atomism in the context of innovations in physics in the age of Galileo. However, Alpino is seldom, if ever, mentioned in standard accounts of the history of atomism, although William Newman has recently drawn attention to the corpuscular theory of matter espoused by another prominent medical author of the time, namely Daniel Sennert. See William Newman, "The Alchemical Sources of Robert Boyle's Corpuscular Philosophy," *Annals of Science* 53 (1996): 567–85, at pp. 573–76. For a

As regards medicine, Alpino's turn to methodism is also suggestive of a shift. In orthodox academic medical circles, the quasi-mythical history of medicine before Hippocrates diminished in significance as the seventeenth century wore on. What finally undermined Galenic physiology was not appeals to remotest antiquity but new competing theories based on persuasively presented observations.[54] Meanwhile, much Galenic therapy survived the new science largely unscathed. Thus in 1696, Daniel Le Clerc, author of what has been claimed as the first systematic history of medicine, devoted a hundred pages to perhaps the most exhaustive survey ever written of all the diverse ancient accounts of Egyptian and pre-Hippocratic Greek medicine.[55] But he concluded that it all amounted to very little: "Everything appears fabulous or uncertain, or at least extremely confused." The only thing that mattered, he thought, about any of this most ancient medicine was that it evidently already included "the fundamental remedies . . . bleeding and purgation."[56]

Yet belief in an Egyptian genealogy of medicine lived on in a different milieu. The supposed Egyptian deity (or deified human) Thrice-Great Hermes was claimed as a founding father of Paracelsian medicine and alchemy. Alchemical treatises of Arabic origin attributed to Hermes, of which the best known is the *Tabula smaragdina,* had been available in Europe

---

recent evaluation of atomism in this period, see also Christoph Meinel, "Early Seventeenth-Century Atomism: Theory, Epistemology, and the Insufficiency of Experiment," *Isis* 79 (1988): 68–103.

54. The bibliography of the history of seventeenth-century physiology is far too extensive to be listed here, but mention may at least be made of the most recent study of the reception of Harvey, Roger French, *William Harvey's Natural Philosophy* (Cambridge: Cambridge University Press, 1994).

55. I have consulted Daniel Le Clerc, *Histoire de la médecine* (Amsterdam, 1702), bks. 1–2, pp. 1–103. The first edition appeared in 1696.

56. "Tout y paroît presque fabuleux ou incertain, out du moins extremement confus. . . . Néanmoins, si la Médecine consiste plûtôt dans les effets, que dans les discours; et si *l'invention des remedes* est plus importante que *tous les raisonnemens qu'on peut faire sur les maladies,* comme on le verra ci-après, il se trouvera que ces premiers Médecins ont connu ce qu'il y a presque de plus essential dans la Médecine, ou de moins ce qui passe pour tel encore aujourdui dans toute l'Europe; et qu'ils ont pratiqué tous les remedes *fondamentaux,* et ceux sur lesquels on conte le plus. Tous les Médecins, à la reserve d'un bien petit nombre, regardent *la saignée* et *la purgation* commes les remedes les plus universels. Or il paroît par les preuves que l'on a rapportées, que ces deux remedes ont été mis en usage dans l'espace de temps don't il s'agit." Le Clerc, *Histoire,* 2. 9, p. 102 (italics are the author's).

since the Middle Ages (these treatises were distinct from the philosophical *Hermetica* esteemed by Marsilio Ficino and other Renaissance philosophers).[57] Paracelsian medicine, which drew on earlier alchemical tradition, thus acquired veneration for Hermes. Moreover, historical claims about the Egyptian origin of both alchemy and spagyric medicine served to provide a respectably ancient lineage for current Paracelsian ideas and practice. Emphasis on Egyptian origins seems to have gained prominence in Paracelsian literature during the second half of the sixteenth century.[58] But for the medical faculty at Padua any association with Paracelsianism would probably have been a further deterrent to interest in ancient Egyptian medical wisdom. By the 1570s or 1580s, Paracelsian ideas and remedies had some adherents in Italy, but were generally disapproved by the orthodox medical community.[59] Thus, for example, writing some time after 1586, Orazio Augenio, professor of medical theory at Padua from 1596, declared that it would be ridiculous for a Hippocratic-Galenic physician to consult with a Paracelsian, since their systems were completely different.[60]

As for the Paracelsians, they continued to attribute the invention of their medicine to Egyptian Hermes long after Isaac Casaubon's demolition, in 1614, of the authenticity and great antiquity of the philosophical *Hermetica*. The persistence of the claim in the mid-seventeenth century induced the German polymath Hermann Conring to devote a lengthy treatise to attacking it. In this work, which Conring first published in 1648 and reissued in an enlarged version over twenty years later, he not only demolished the specific claim that Egyptian Hermes had founded medicine, but provided a dis-

57. On the medieval tradition of the *Tabula*, see Chiara Crisciani, "Aspetti della trasmissione del sapere nell'alchimia latina. Un'immagine di formazione, uno stile di commento," *Micrologus* 3 (1995): 149–84, at pp. 177–84.

58. See Robert Halleux, "La Controverse sur les origines de la chimie de Paracelse à Borrichius," *Acta Conventus Neo-Latinus Turonensis, Université François-Rabelais, 6–10 septembre 1976. Troisième congrès international d'études néo-latines, Tours*, ed. Jean-Claude Margolin (Paris: J. Vrin, 1980), 2: 807–19. I am grateful to William Newman for this reference.

59. On Paracelsianism in Italy, see Palmer, "Pharmacy in the Republic of Venice," pp. 110–14 (naming individuals at Padua on p. 114), and Marco Ferrari, "Alcune vie di diffusione in Italia di idee e di testi di Paracelso," in *Scienze, credenze occulte, livelli di cultura* (Florence: L. S. Olschki, 1982), pp. 21–29.

60. Orazio Augenio, *Epistolarum et consultationum medicinalium alterius tomi libri XII* (Venice, 1602) (bound with his *Epistolarum et consultationum medicinalium. Prioris tomi libri XII* [Venice, 1592]) 4.9, fol. 60H; cited from another edition in Palmer, "Pharmacy in the Republic of Venice."

missive evaluation of ancient Egyptian medicine in general.[61] He acknowledged that ancient sources testified that a form of indigenous medicine practiced by priests flourished in ancient Egypt. But the famous medicine of Hellenistic Alexandria was Greek, not Egyptian. When the Egyptian temples were destroyed the ancient Egyptian medicine practiced by priests came to an end (1.9). The (Arabic) medicine practiced under Muslim rule ultimately derived, he noted, from Greek sources, as was abundantly evident from Alpino's book on Egyptian medicine.[62] Thus, whatever Alpino's own intentions, for Conring he served as an important witness against the significance or survival of the medicine of ancient Egypt.

Conring went on to analyze such information about the content of ancient Egyptian medicine as could be gathered from ancient sources. In the first place, it had nothing whatsoever in common with Paracelsian teaching. Unlike the Paracelsians, the ancient Egyptians did not use chemically prepared or mineral medicines. They did not make much use of metal and all the sources testified to their use of medicinal plants (1.11, pp. 99–100). In terms of element theory, they certainly never introduced the Paracelsian triad mercury, sulphur, and salt (1.10, pp. 89–90).

Secondly, Conring asserted that considered as natural knowledge, the medicine of the ancient Egyptians was at a low level. Their anatomy was crude and erroneous. Their astrology—like all astrology—was groundless. They could perhaps be credited with the concepts of man the microcosm and critical days, both of which Conring deemed futile (1.10). No prudent physician could commend their therapy, which relied on excessive

---

61. Hermann Conring, *De hermetica Aegyptiorum vetere et Paracelsicorum nova medicina liber unus. Quo simul in Hermetis Trismegisti omnia, ac universam cum Aegyptiorum tum Chemicorum doctrinam animadversitur* (Helmstadt, 1648). The revised edition is Hermann Conring, *De hermetica medicina libri duo. Quorum primus agit de medicina, pariterque de omni sapientia veterum Aegyptiorum: altero non tantum Paracelsi, ed etiam chemicorum, Paracelsi laudatorum aliorumque, potissimum quidem medicina omnis, simul vero et reliqua universa doctrina examinatur. Editio secunda infinitis locis emendatior et auctior* (Helmstadt, 1669). In this essay, references are to book, chapter, and page numbers in the 1669 edition. If no page number is given, the reference is to the general topic of the chapter as a whole.

62. "Et vero, etsi post Aegyptus in Muhamedanorum potestatem pervenerit, sola tamen Graecanica Philosophica in Medicina in pretio mansit: ipsis Arabibus artem medicam ex Graecorum, et quidem praecipue Galeni, scriptis suam in linguam versis, petentibus. Quem morem ne nunc quidem desinere cum alias notum et fide plurimorum qui terras illas cum cura lustrant, tum abunde constat ex preclaro opere Prospero Alpini de Medicina Aegyptiorum . . . ." Conring, *De hermetica medicina* (1669), 1.9, p. 88.

use of laxatives and emetics (1.11, p. 98). Even the number and effectiveness of medicinal herbs native to Egypt had been exaggerated by the ancient authors, as Alpino's works showed (1.11, p. 104).

Thirdly, and most importantly, ancient Egyptian medicine was inextricably involved with the cult of demons, superstition, magic, and incantations. To this charge Conring returned repeatedly (1.8; 1.11, pp. 105–8; 1.13). Against Johannes Lange (whom he cited by name) he insisted that Egyptian medicine was not a form of *magia naturalis* depending on hidden forces in nature, but a fully demonic magic.[63] Furthermore, Conring opined that when the Egyptians left off the cult of demons (i.e., ceased to worship the gods of Egypt) the offended spirits took care to reduce Egyptian medicine to an even lower level (1.11, p. 116). Conring thought that an especially pernicious modern propagator of magical medicine was the Danish Paracelsian Severinus, "whom many people [now] follow rather than Paracelsus. . . . So that today this new discipline really seems like a hydra with many heads."[64]

Far from slaying the hydra, Conring's book moved Severinus's countryman Olaf Borch to an indignant reply. In 1674 Borch published a 448-page opus entitled *The Wisdom of Hermes of the Egyptians and the Chemists Vindicated Against the Animadversions of Hermann Conring*.[65] He devoted its first book to insisting that Hermes had invented medicine and expatiating on the anatomical and botanical prowess and all-round wisdom of the ancient Egyptians. In the second book, he defended every aspect of Paracelsian medicine. And in 1696, Le Clerc still found it necessary to deny that chemically prepared medicines had been invented in ancient Egypt by Hermes Trismegistus.[66]

The multiplicity of sources alluding to ancient Egyptian medicine, none of which provided detailed information about it, left sixteenth-

63. "Ita enim pene usu venit ubi magica sunt in pretio venit ut quae natura suppeditat contemnantur, nec possint facile illa ab aliis distingui: usque adeo sese commiscente cum natura vi daemonum, ut perfrequenter in illius locum horum ludibria obrepant. nec vero est quod magicam illam medicinam Aegyptiorum arcanis naturae viribus attribuere cum Joanne Langio et aliis . . . ." Conring, *De hermetica medicina*, 1.11, p. 115.

64. "Jam vero plaerique Severinum potius quam Paracelsum sectantur: multi magicas artes dudum sepultas . . . profitentur. . . . Ut hodie Hermetica illa nova disciplina vere hydra quaedam sit multorum capitum." Conring, *De hermetica medicina*, 2.1, p. 179.

65. Oluf Borch (Borrichius), *Hermetis Aegyptiorum et chemicorum sapienta ab Hermanni Conringi animadversionibus vindicata* (Copenhagen, 1674).

66. Le Clerc, *Histoire de la médecine*, 2.9, pp. 102–3.

and seventeenth-century medical practitioners free to evaluate its significance according to their own preconceptions and preferences. In these circumstances, discussions of Egyptian medicine were almost always profoundly conditioned by attitudes to Galenic medical orthodoxy, to magic, to alchemy, and to ancient Egypt in general. But the late-sixteenth-century University of Padua provided a possibly unique instance in which discussion about ancient Egyptian medicine took place in a medical milieu in which there was substantial firsthand knowledge of Egypt and of contemporary Egyptian medicine. The context for this knowledge was Venetian interest, political and economic as well as cultural, in eastern Mediterranean and Middle Eastern affairs. The stimulus for Alpino's endeavors to find out about Egyptian medicine for himself and his eagerness both to learn from and to exploit current Egyptian medical practice and living Egyptian practitioners came both from the humanistic search for the most ancient (and thus purest) medical wisdom and from his immediate political and economic environment.

The Conflicted Genealogy of Cultural Authority: Italian Responses to French Cultural Dominance in *Il Tesoretto*, *Il Fiore*, and *La Commedia*

KEVIN BROWNLEE

By the mid-thirteenth century, French language and culture enjoyed a uniquely dominant position among the various Romance vernaculars of Western Europe. It is the case of Italy that concerns me in the present context,[1] in the sense that an almost caricatured genealogical/generational conflict can be seen to have been staged between the aggressively rebellious "son" of a nascent Italian literature, which seemed to feel obliged to kill its obvious vernacular cultural "father" — French — in favor of a claim to the more prestigious, more "legitimate" (and also safer, more distant, less immediately threatening) cultural father of Latin, by means of a "direct" link — that is, unmediated by French — to this same Latin, propagandistically presented as involving a privileged, deep-structure cultural genealogi-

An earlier, shorter version of this essay appeared in *Forum for Modern Language Studies* 33 (1977): 258–69.

1. See Paul Meyer, "De l'expansion de la langue française en Italie pendant le moyen-âge," in *Atti del congresso Internazionale di Scienze Storiche* (Rome: Tipografia della Reale Accademia dei Lincei, 1904–1907), 4:61–104; and esp. the exaggerated summary: "L'examen des ouvrages composés ou simplement remaniés par des écrivains italiens nous amène à fixer approximativement entre les années 1230 et 1350 l'époque où le français fut la langue littéraire pour l'Italie septentrionale," p. 93. Cf. E. Jeffrey Richards, *Dante and the "Roman de la Rose"* (Tübingen: Max Niemeyer, 1981): "Old French was a literary *koiné* in 13th- and early 14th-century Italy," p. 20. Ronald Witt is currently doing ground-breaking (and, I hope, complementary) work on the degree to which the "birth" of Italian vernacular culture as such constituted, to an important degree, an aggressive reaction against and, indeed, erasure of, the clear and facile dominance of twelfth- and thirteenth-century Francophone culture, commerce, and so on, throughout the Mediterranean basin. I am grateful to him for generously sharing with me several of his speculative, but, to my mind, fully convincing interpretations along these lines.

cal authority. In essence, this simply (but very polemically) involved the claim of a special genealogical connection between the language (and cultural prestige) of Virgil, Ovid, and Cicero to that of the self-perceived key Tuscan writers of the late Duecento and the early Trecento.

If my own language here might seem to be exaggeratedly metaphoric, one need only recall the extraordinary power of the twelfth- and thirteenth-century Western European myths of the *translatio studii et imperii:* the (still) potent notion that both cultural and political legitimacy can most effectively be figured by means of genealogically and geographically *transferable* tropes of an authority that manages always to remain intact as a specifically chronological power structure/inheritance, even as it moves, changes places.[2]

In this essay, I would like to examine how, within the powerful context of medieval genealogical myths of the "transference" of cultural authority, three particular Italian texts respond to (and rebel against) the "fact" of French cultural hegemony: (1) Brunetto Latini's *Il Tesoretto;* (2) the anonymous *Il Fiore;* and (3) Dante's *Commedia.*[3] In all three cases I will be focusing (from the "Italian" cultural point of view) both on the status accorded to the French language (including the ways in which it is represented) and on the function of a specially privileged canonical French vernacular literary text, the *Roman de la Rose,* as model. In this context, I am particularly concerned with the status of the *locus amoenus* setting and with the French-vernacularized Ovidian god of love as an authority figure. In addition, I will be concerned with the ways in which these three Italian writers utilize in

2. See, in this context, Karl D. Uitti, *Story, Myth, and Celebration in Old French Narrative Poetry, 1050–1200* (Princeton, N.J.: Princeton University Press, 1973); R. Howard Bloch, *Etymologies and Genealogies: A Literary Anthropology of the French Middle Ages* (Chicago, Ill.: University of Chicago Press, 1983); and Sarah Kay, *Chansons de Geste in the Age of Romance: Political Fictions* (Oxford: Oxford University Press, 1996).

3. Editions used: Julia Bolton Holloway, ed. and trans., *Brunetto Latini: Il Tesoretto* (New York: Garland, 1981); Gianfranco Contini, ed., *"Il Fiore" e il "Detto d'Amore" attribuibili a Dante Alighieri,* Edizione Nazionale 8 (Milano: Ricciardi, 1984); Giorgio Petrocchi, ed., as found in Charles S. Singleton, trans. and comm., *Dante Alighieri: The Divine Comedy,* 3 vols. (Princeton, N.J.: Princeton University Press, 1970–75). Translations are either selectively modified, or are mine. I would like to declare my overall intellectual debt to Margrete de Grazia's probing critical reading of Nietzsche's notion of cultural (tropes of) genealogy in her trenchant critique of his essay *On The Genealogy of Morals* in her book, *Shakespeare Verbatim: The Reproduction of Authority and the 1790 Apparatus* (Oxford: Oxford University Press, 1991), pp. 7–77.

their own works, and with regard to French culture, the construct of *trans-latio*, which was so central to how French medieval writers established their own cultural authority vis-à-vis the ultimately prestigious starting point (from their point of view) of *latinitas*. Again, the fundamental, empowering metaphor is genealogical.

For the purposes of this essay, I understand *translatio* to involve the re-writing/continuation of a classical (i.e., Latin) *auctor*, which serves both to authorize a specific vernacular literary enterprise and the vernacular as lit-erary language. At the same time, of course, the model Latin text is itself valorized. This process of reciprocal authorization between the French ver-nacular and classical language is first evident in the late-twelfth-century *romans d'antiquité*, most explicitly in Benoît de St. Maure's prologue to his *Roman de Troie*.[4]

As a final preliminary note, I wish to make clear that I do not propose the three Italian texts that are the subject of my essay as exemplars of a general historical progression with regard to Italian reception of French culture, which, indeed, was characterized by a rich variety rather than a simple unity in terms of chronological developments from the thirteenth through the fifteenth centuries.[5] I am, rather, interested in the particular practices of the three specific Italian texts on which I focus. At the same time, however, there is a striking progression to be observed with regard to responses to the authority of French culture in these texts, which are themselves interrelated in a number of important ways.

The Florentine notary and politician Brunetto Latini was deeply involved with the Guelph party. After the Florentine Guelphs were defeated by King Manfred of Sicily and the Sienese Ghibellines at the battle of Montaperti

---

4. See Ernst Robert Curtius, *European Literature and the Latin Middle Ages* (Princeton, N.J.: Princeton University Press, 1953), pp. 17–35; esp. 28–29; Uitti, *Story, Myth, and Celebration*, pp. 128–231; Richards, *Dante and the "Roman"* pp. 20, 42–70. Another important articu-lation of the *translatio studii* topos—with the progression Greece-Rome-France—occurs in the well-known prologue to Chrétien's *Cligés* (lines 25–42; ed. Alexandre Micha). See Michelle A. Freeman, *The Poetics of "Translatio Studii" and "Conjointure": Chrétien de Troye's "Cligés"* (Lexington, Ky.: French Forum, 1979).

5. See Günter Holtus, Henning Krauss, and Peter Wunderli, eds., *Testi, cotesti e contesti del franco-italiano: Atti del 10 simposio franco-italiano (Bad Homburg, 13–16 aprile 1987)* (Tübingen: Niemeyer, 1989).

in 1260, Brunetto began a six-year period of exile in France, which ended when Charles d'Anjou (whose French army included a division of exiled Tuscan Guelphs) decisively defeated Manfred at Benevento in 1266. Brunetto stages the composition both of his *Tesoretto* in Italian (and of his *Livres dou Tresor* in French) during his exile in France, between 1260 and 1266. Both because of his French exile and because of the key Angevin role in ending that exile (and in continuing to give essential support to the Florentine Guelphs) there is a significant political dimension to Brunetto's relation to France and to his attitude toward French culture. For my purposes in this essay, I would simply like to acknowledge this generally positive political orientation, while avoiding any discussion of its complex details and their sparse but suggestive documentation.[6]

In the course of the first-person journey that constitutes the plot line of the *Tesoretto*, Brunetto-protagonist arrives at a "grande piano giocondo" (1221) (great smiling plain) where he encounters a series of allegorical characters. There ensues a prologue-like passage in which Brunetto-author explicitly distinguishes between his writing in Italian and in French:

> Di tutte quattro queste
> Lo puro sanza veste
> Dirò 'n questo libretto:
> Dell' altre non prometto
> Di dire né di contare;
> Ma chi 'l vorrà trovare,
> Cerchi nel gran tesoro
> Ch'io faró per coloro
> C'anno lo cor più alto:
> Là faró il gran salto
> Per dirle più distese
> Ne la lingua françese.
> (1345–56)

(Of all four of these [allegorical characters] I will speak plainly, without adornment, in this little book: about the others I do not promise

---

6. See Francis J. Carmody, ed., *Li Livres dou Tresor de Brunetto Latini* (Berkeley: University of California Press, 1984), pp. xvii–xix. Citations to *Livres dou Tresor* in the text will be to this edition.

to speak or to recount; but whoever wants to find this should look in the great *Treasure* that I will make for those who have a higher heart: there I will make the great leap to speak of these at greater length in the French language.)

The positive way in which Brunetto here characterizes both the French language as a literary medium and the Francophone reading public as culturally superior is elaborated in the prologue to his *Livres dou Tresor,* the other book to which he refers here as containing a more comprehensive treatment of the subject of the virtues. In the well-known conclusion to the *Tresor's* prologue, the Italian author explains why he writes this book in French:

> Et se aucuns demandoit pour quoi cis livres est escris en roumanç selon le raison de France, puis ke nous somes italien, je diroie que c'est pour .ii. raisons, l'une ke nous somes en France, l'autre por çou que la parleure est plus delitable et plus commune a tous langages. (p. 18)

> (And if any one should ask why this book is written in the vernacular speech of France, since we are Italian, I would say that there are two reasons for this: the first is that we are in France; and the second, because that language is more delightful and more widespread than all others.)

Within an awareness of the multiplicity of Romance vernaculars, Brunetto again marks French for prestige and dominance. In this context it is at once a national and a supranational language, functioning outside the geographic boundaries of France in a wider area of Francophone culture, extending from the eastern Mediterranean through both southern and northern Italy to Great Britain. As such, French as language and as culture exists as a potent and useful resource to a writer like Brunetto. Yet there is also, perhaps, at least implicitly, some kind of perception that an Italian writing in French needs to justify this linguistic choice; some hint of a potentially problematic dimension to the apparently unproblematic hierarchical relationship Brunetto explicitly describes as existing between the two languages.

This extremely positive characterization of both the French language as a literary medium and of the Francophone reading public as culturally superior functions as Brunetto's "official" authorial stance in the *Tesoretto*.[7] When we consider his response to French culture in terms of Brunetto's writerly practice in the *Tesoretto*, however, a more complex, a more nuanced stance emerges, especially in the passage (2198–393) which I take to be his *rifacimento* of Guillaume de Lorris's *Roman de la Rose*, considered as a canonical (and thus "representative") French text.[8] Here Brunetto employs most strikingly two rhetorical and intertextual procedures: *abbreviatio* and corrective inversion.

His encounter with the god of love begins when Brunetto-protagonist enters a locus amoenus on the first day of May, presented in abbreviated terms (2201–5) that contrast strikingly with the prolonged presentation in Guillaume, whose elaborate and potent valorization of courtly erotic discourse in the corresponding narrative moment in the *Rose* is significantly undermined:[9]

> Io giunsi in un bel prato
> Fiorito d'ongni lato,
> Lo più riccho del mondo.

7. While Brunetto's "official" authorial attitude toward French language and culture are, as has just been shown, repeated, though perhaps more ambiguously, in the famous passage at the end of the prologue to the *Livres dou Tresor* (p. 18), unresolvable questions remain concerning the relative chronology of these two works, especially since the future "farò" of line 1352 appears as "fatt' ho" in at least five manuscripts, though the "farò" of line 1354 remains consistent (ed. Contini [1960], in *Poeti del Duecento* [Milano: Ricciardi, 1960] T. 2, p. 173). I find valuable Contini's suggestion of "uno svolgimento contemporaneo, magari per intermittenza, d'un medesimo assunto" (p. 173).
8. It has been argued by several scholars that in the *Tesoretto* Brunetto is responding not just to Guillaume de Lorris, but also to Jean de Meun, that is, to the entire *Rose* text. This view presupposes a much later date for the composition of the *Tesoretto* (as opposed to its setting), that is, during the late 1280s. See Richards, *Dante and the "Roman,"* pp. 24–29; Luigi Foscolo Benedetto, *Il "Roman de la Rose" e la letteratura italiana* (Halle-Niemeyer, 1910); Francesco Mazzoni, *Brunetto in Dante*, pp. x–liii, in *Brunetto Latini: "Il Tesoretto", "Il Favolello,"* ed. P. G. Pozzi (Alpignano: A. Tallone, 1967). Indeed, Mazzoni proposes that the *Rose*'s diffusion in Italy took place through Brunetto (see Richards, *Dante and the "Roman,"* p. 34). See also David Wallace, *Chaucer and the Early Writings of Boccaccio* (Woodbridge, Suffolk-Dover, N.H.: Brewer, 1985), pp. 10–15, 53–59. I confine myself to the key sequence in which the *Tesoretto* rewrites—indeed, deconstructs—Guillaume de Lorris's *Rose*.
9. Benedetto (*"Roman de la Rose,"* p. 94) proposes that Brunetto's locus amoenus involves a simultaneous reference to Guillaume's *Jardin* and Jean's *biau parc*.

Or mi parea ritondo,
Or avea quadratura.
(2201–5)

(I came to a beautiful meadow with flowers everywhere, the richest in the world. Sometimes it seemed round to me, sometimes four-sided.)

There are no courtly personifications or intermediaries as in Guillaume's extended narrative of Amant's encounter with Deduit and his followers, but rather a simple (though nominally courtly: "per cortesia," 2233) request for information about the place addressed to four flying Cupid figures ("fanti," 2228). The response is brief and to the point, serving to situate the author-protagonist by name in the Garden: "Sappie, mastro brunetto, / Che qui sta monsengnore / Ch'è capo e dio d'amore" (2240–42) (Know, Master Brunetto, that here rules the lord who is chief and god of love). Again there is a significant contrast with Guillaume, who never names himself. In a sense, Brunetto is here displacing his French model author, marking difference rather than continuity.

The *Tesoretto*'s initial presentation of the god of love is as a Cupid whose identity and function are explained by the authoritative voice of Brunetto-author, which thus replaces that of Guillaume's character, the authoritative god of love himself. Again, the contrasts with Guillaume's text are significant. First, this event loses the centrality that it had had in the *Rose,* where it had also preceded the god of love's ten commandments and his general treatment of the pains, joys, and techniques of lovers (*Rose,* lines 2077–580; 2595–764). Second, its importance is still further undercut by a quantitative reduction: it is recounted in a mere nine lines (2343–51). At the same time, it is recounted indirectly and summarily, and is thus strikingly de-dramatized: Guillaume's detailed representation of Amant's ambush by Amors, and the sequential account of each of the five arrow wounds, is simply suppressed. Furthermore, the entire experience is presented from the severely critical perspective of Brunetto-author for whom the falling in love of his "younger" self appears as a mistake to be condemned.

The valence of love is also changed significantly in the *Tesoretto,* where it receives a predominantly negative context. Brunetto-author presents "love from the heart" (2334) ("l'amor corale") as an untranscendent desire for "dilecto corporale" (2333) (corporeal delight). The courtly erotic linguistic and behavioral codes of Guillaume de Lorris are thus undermined and dismissed.

It is only after this general treatment of love and lovers is concluded, that the *Tesoretto*'s first-person protagonist's *innamoramento* is presented, but from the severely critical perspective of Brunetto-author, for whom the falling in love of his "younger" self appears as a mistake to be condemned. The positive context provided in Guillaume by the deployment of courtly discourse is absent here, as the protagonist appears to have attempted resistence to love and to have been unwisely overcome. In contradistinction to Brunetto-author's own recent description of the love experience there is no mention of the "persona piaciuta" (2329) the sight of whom incites desire:

> Assai mi volsi intorno,
> E la nocte e lo giorno,
> Credendomi campire
> Del fante che ferire
> Lo cor non mi potesse;
> E s'io questo tacesse,
> Farei maggior savere,
> Ch'io fui messo in podere
> E in força d'amore.
> (2343–51)

(Often I turned around, both night and day, believing that I was fleeing from the boy, who would not be able to wound me in the heart; and if I were silent about this, I would show greater wisdom, for I was caught in the power and in the force of love.)

Finally, Brunetto-protagonist's object of desire simply is not mentioned in his text: there is no lady, there is no flower. The focus is entirely upon the first-person self. Significantly, Brunetto-protagonist, unlike Guillaume-protagonist, only experiences the negative side of love.

It is at this point in the *Tesoretto*'s narrative that the key figure of Ovid appears as a character, standing in the *bel prato* of *amore*. Brunetto's Ovid is both a *magister amoris* and a detached, philosophical observer who can provide the cure for love:

> E in un ricco manto
> Vidi Ovidio maggiore,
> Chelgli atti del amore,
> Che son così diversi,

Rassempra e mette in versi.
E io mi trassi appresso,
E domandi lui stesso
Ch'elli apertamente
Mi dica il convenente,
E la bene e la male,
Del fante e dell'ale
Ch'a le saette e l'arco.
(2358–69)

(And in a rich mantle I saw great Ovid, who collected and put into verse the acts of love, which are so diverse. And I drew near, and asked the man himself that he should openly tell me the workings, both the good and the evil, of this child with wings, who has the arrows and the bow.)

In response to Brunetto-protagonist's request for advice, Ovid tells him to study in himself both the good and the evil effects of love. The result of this self-scrutiny is that the protagonist is freed from love's domination and reoriented upon the right path:

Così fui giunto, lasso,
E messo in mala parte!
Ma Ovidio per arte
Mi diede maestria,
Sì ch'io trovai la via
Ond'io mi traffugai.
(2388–93)

(And so I was hit, alas, and put in a bad predicament! But Ovid through artistry gave me the mastery [self-control], so that I found the way from which I had strayed.)

The entire episode in the "bel prato" of *amore* is thus presented as a mistake, a diversion, a dangerous detour on the journey of Brunetto-protagonist which constitutes the plot line of the *Tesoretto*. In the bel prato sequence, there is no translatio-type relation set up between Guillaume de Lorris and Brunetto Latini, who does not "continue" the French model text, or depend upon it for authorization. Brunetto rather *corrects* Guillaume by means of an authoritative intervention by the character of Ovid, who provides the true legitimation for Brunetto's authorial perspective. On the one hand, this involves a translatio-type relation between the Italian and the Latin poets, which, as it were, evokes only in order to bypass the French intermediary. On the other hand, Brunetto's use of Ovid in this way involves a confrontation with and correction of Guillaume de Lorris's use of Ovid in the *Rose*.

Guillaume de Lorris had presented his work as, among other things, a vernacularization of the Ovidian *Ars amatoria*, in which Guillaume-author claims the authority of a new vernacular Ovid figure. This French translatio of the Latin *auctor* is itself simultaneously situated within an ongoing French literary tradition as exemplified, for example, by the prologue to Chrétien's *Cligés* (lines 2–3). In Guillaume's *Rose*, Ovid's *Ars amatoria* and *Amores* are valorized as privileged model texts, while the voice of Ovid the love poet is conflated with that of the God of Love as character.

In the *Tesoretto*, by contrast, Brunetto carefully distinguishes between, even opposes, the two characters of Ovid and the god of love. Indeed, the former's critique of the latter involves a special valorization by Brunetto-author of Ovid's *Remedia amoris*, which serves as the key operative Ovidian text in the *Tesoretto*, displacing the Ovidian erotic poetry privileged by Guillaume. In addition, Brunetto's particular designation of the figure of Ovid in his text involves a clever strategy: the appellation "Ovidio maggiore" (2359) attributes to the author of the *Remedia amoris* the prestige of the author of the *Metamorphoses*, for it is that work that the Middle Ages normally referred to as "Ovidius major." [10]

The *Tesoretto* does not utilize Guillaume's *Rose* for purposes of literary self-authorization, but rather miniaturizes, corrects, and finally dismisses the French model text in favor of an ethical, moral, religious perspective. It is rather the classical *auctoritas* of the Ovid of the *Remedia amoris* that Brunetto uses both to legitimate his literary enterprise on its own terms, and in contradistinction to the French *Rose*. [11]

10. For a different interpretation, cf. Michelangelo Picone, "L'Ovidio di Dante" in Amilcare Iannucci, ed., *Dante e la Bella Scola della Poesia* (Ravenna: Longo, 1993), p. 117; and Hans Robert Jauss, *Alterità e modernità della letteratura medievale* (Torino: Bollati Boringhieri, 1989), pp. 135–74.

11. In terms of classical-model authors, Brunetto then moves on from the Ovid of the *Remedia amoris* to a politicized Cicero in the *Tesoretto*. For Brunetto's use of Cicero both here and in other texts (esp. *La Rettorica*), see Charles T. Davis, "Brunetto Latini and Dante," in *Dante's*

In Brunetto's *Tesoretto*, therefore, we can see an interesting dichotomy in terms of the response to French cultural dominance and prestige. The French language is assigned a kind of superior position among the Romance vernaculars, a response also found in Brunetto's *Tresor* (especially in the author's justification in the prologue for writing the work in French). The literary practice of the *Tesoretto* seems, however, to reveal a different kind of response to French culture in Brunetto's reduction and deconstruction of a key French model text, Guillaume de Lorris's *Roman de la Rose*, which is not utilized within the context of translatio to authorize the Italian author's own innovative literary enterprise. Indeed, the *Tesoretto* does not seem to involve this kind of response to the French canon at the level of literary practice.

The anonymous Italian work known as *Il Fiore* (a name given by its first modern editor, Ferdinand Castets [1881], on p. 5 of the preface) was composed, we now think, in the late 1280s. It is an adaptation of the *Roman de la Rose* into a sequence of 232 Italian sonnets.[12]

It is also, in a sense, an adaptation of the French language into Tuscan, because of its extremely high number of gallicisms. Gianfranco Contini, the poem's modern editor, has gone so far as to describe its language as a "literary 'creole'" of French and Tuscan.[13] Luigi Vanossi identifies hun-

---

Italy and Other Essays (Philadelphia, Pa.: Univ. of Pennsylvania Press, 1984), pp. 166–97; and Elisabetta Pellegrini Sayinor, in the chapter devoted to *La Rettorica* in her doctoral dissertation, "The Rhetoric of Didacticism: Brunetto Latini and Dante Alighieri," University of Pennsylvania, 1998.

12. I will not here be treating the question of the possible Dantean authorship of the *Fiore*, a question that has consumed an extraordinarily large percentage of scholarship on the Italian text. For an excellent set of treatments of all aspects of *Fiore* studies, see Patrick Boyde and Zygmunt Baranski, eds., *The "Fiore" in Context: Dante, France, Tuscany* (South Bend, Ind.: 1997. For readings of the *Fiore* on its own terms (including its literary relations to the *Rose*), see Zygmunt Baranski, Patrick Boyde, and Lino Pertile, eds., *Lettura del "Fiore"* (Ravenna: Longo, 1993); Peter Armour, "The *Roman de la Rose* and the *Fiore*: Aspects of a Literary Transplantation," *Journal of the Institute of Romance Studies* 2 (1993): 63–81; Robert Pogue Harrison, "The Bare Essential: The Landscape of *Il Fiore*," in *Rethinking the "Romance of the Rose": Text, Image, Reception*, ed. K. Brownlee and Sylvia Huot (Philadelphia, Pa.: Univ. of Pennsylvania Press, 1992), pp. 289–303; Richards, *Dante and "Il Fiore*," pp. 27–32; Wallace, esp. 54–56; and John Took, "Towards an Interpretation of the *Fiore*," *Speculum* 54 (1979): 500–527.

13. Contini, "*Il Fiore*," p. xcvii; as quoted by Armour, "Aspects," p. 72.

dreds of gallicisms in the Italian text,[14] and speaks of a "compenetrazione col sistema lessicale del francese" (243). Peter Armour notes that the "Fiore is littered with gallicized prefixes . . . , suffixes . . . , grammar . . . , and much else" (73). While the status and the function of the strong French presence in the language of the *Fiore* have been variously and elaborately debated,[15] the fact and the importance of this presence is indisputable. From my present point of view, it is significant that the *Fiore* does not explicitly mention the French language as such, but rather treats it "implicitly."

The same is true for the *Fiore*'s treatment of French literature in general and the *Roman de la Rose* in particular: there are no explicit mentions of the *Rose,* and a minimal French literary presence. This is, of course, particularly significant in the case of the *Rose,* which is the *Fiore*'s model text. I would like to suggest that these absences function as part of the *Fiore*'s overall strategies of rewriting the *Rose* in such a way as to suppress constructs both of *translatio* and of literary genealogy. These suppressions, I would argue, significantly problematize the Italian poem's relation to its French model precisely qua French model.

Of particular importance in this regard is the *Fiore*'s radical reduction of the *Rose*'s consistent and extensive citation of classical *auctores* who are explicitly named, often along with their books.[16] In this way, the *Fiore* programmatically writes out one of the *Rose*'s most important uses of translatio, for the extremely frequent citation of the works of the *auctores* (especially in Jean de Meun) authorizes the French work by (among other things) presenting it as a vernacular continuation of the Greek and Latin canon. Indeed, John Fleming has pointed out that the only two French authors cited by name in the *Rose* are Guillaume de Lorris and Jean de Meun, who are thereby made to share in the high status of the *auctores* whom they are presented as continuing.[17] The *Fiore* eliminates this program. At the same time, it replaces the *Rose*'s double-author figure by a single author,[18] and

14. See the chapter on "L'impronta linguistica della *Rose,*" in Luigi Vanossi, *Dante e il "Roman de la Rose": Saggio sul "Fiore"* (Florence: Olschki, 1979), pp. 223–58.

15. See, e.g., Luigi Peirone, *Tra Dante e "Il Fiore": Lingua e parola* (Genoa: Tilgher, 1982); and Richards, *Dante and the "Roman,"* pp. 5–41.

16. See Peter Armour, "Lettura dei sonetti 61–90," esp. p. 57, in Baranski, Boyde, and Pertile, *Lettura.*

17. John Fleming, "Jean de Meun and the Ancient Poets," pp. 81–100, in Brownlee and Huot, *Rethinking.*

18. See Brownlee, "Jason's Voyage and the Poetics of Rewriting: *Il Fiore* and the *Roman de la*

as a result eleminates any trace of the translatio (from Guillaume to Jean) that plays such a key role in the *Rose's* visible presentation of its own composition.

A particularly significant example of this is found in sonnet 33, which occurs structurally in *Il Fiore* at the point in the plot line that corresponds to the transition from Guillaume to Jean in the *Rose:*

> Quand' i' vidi i marosi sì 'nforzare
> Per lo vento a Provenza che ventava,
> Ch' alberi e vele e ancole fiac[c]ava,
> E nulla mi valea il ben governare,
>   Fra me medesmo comincìa' a pensare
> Ch'era follïa se più navicava,
> Se quel maltempo prima non passava
> Che dal buon porto mi facé' alu[n]giare:
>   Sì ch'i' allor m'ancolai a una piag[g]ia,
> Veg[g]endo ch'i' non potea entrar in porto:
> La terra mi parea molto salvaggia.
>   I' vi vernai co-molto disconforto.
> Non sa che mal si sia chi non assagia
> Di quel d'Amor, ond' i' fu' quasi morto.

(When I saw the waves strengthening because of the wind blowing from Provence, which was striking the masts and sails and anchors, and steering well no longer did any good, within myself I began to think that it was folly for me to continue sailing, if this bad weather did not finish first, which was pushing me farther from the good port. So I then cast my anchor onto a shore, seeing that I was not able to get to port. The land struck me as very wild. I wintered there in great discomfort. He does not know what pain is, who does not taste the pains of love, from which I was almost dead.)

Instead of the seamless textual joining effected by the (conjoined) *Rose,* which maintains in the opening of part 2 (by Jean de Meun) the same basic metaphoric structure (my lady is like a rose) in place at the end of part 1

Rose," in Baranski and Boyde, *Context*, pp. 167–84; and Armour in Baranski, Boyde, and Pertile, *Lettura*, pp. 67–68. See also Baranski, *"Sole Nuovo, Luce Nuova": Saggi sul rinnovamento culturale in Dante* (Torino: Scriptorium, 1996), esp. pp. 287–89.

(by Guillaume de Lorris), in *Fiore* 33 (continued in sonnet 34), we have the introduction of a new basic metaphor, that of the voyage by boat for the protagonist's erotic quest.

Sonnet 33 is thus crucially important to the *Fiore*'s strategic rewriting of the *Rose* in which the Italian poem is read, intertextually, *against* its French model. At least four key points should be made in this connection. First, *Fiore* 33 functions to emphasize Durante's *difference* from his model text, the *fact* of his rewriting as such. Second, it both effects and emphasizes Durante's replacement of a double-authored text (with its built-in translatio structure) by a single-authored one. This takes place by virtue of Durante's transformation of the moment (the locus) of textual transition from Guillaume to Jean, a locus normally marked as such in *Rose* manuscripts. Special attention is called to the fact that this transition is not operative in the *Fiore*. Third, sonnet 33 stresses the "rhetorical independence" of the *Fiore* vis-à-vis the *Rose* by treating the French poem's base metaphor as "replaceable," as "interchangeable." In a sense, this continues (though in a qualitatively different manner) the process begun by the initial transformation of the *rose* into a *fiore*. Fourth, from a narrative perspective, sonnet 33 involves a key relocation *outside* the garden for Durante-protagonist, and by implication, for Durante-narrator. We have, thus, a rewriting of the *Rose* from a perspective outside the *Rose,* and an incorporation of that *Rose-*external perspective at the level of the *Fiore*'s plot.

Within the context of the *Fiore*'s various programmatic transformations and abridgments of the *Rose,* one particular passage in the Italian poem stands out: sonnet 82, where the notion of translatio may be seen to be brilliantly problematized by the strikingly negative manner in which the Italian poem represents its relationship to its authoritative French model.

At the heart of the *Rose*'s self-authorization is the key passage at the approximate midpoint of the conjoined *Rose* text (10495–678) in the speech that the Dieu d'Amors makes to his troops. Here the two French authors are named for the only time in the poem, and are presented as effecting a translatio, a genealogy, in terms of the composition of the text. Jean is presented as the continuator and completor of the romance begun and left unfinished by Guillaume:

> Vez ci Guillaume de Lorriz . . .
> E plus encor me deit servir,
> Car, pour ma grace deservir,

Deit il comencier le romant
Ou seront mis tuit mi comant. . . .
Ci se reposera Guillaume,
Li cui tombeaus seit pleins de baumes. . . .
Puis vendra Johans Chopinel. . . .
Me servira toute sa vie. . . .
Cist avra le romanz si chier
Qu'il le voudra tout parfenir . . .
Car, quant Guillaumes cessera,
Johans le continuera,
Emprès sa mort, que je ne mente,
Anz trespassez plus de quarante.
(10526; 10547–50; 10561–62; 10565;
10569; 10584–85; 10587–90)

(Here is Guillaume de Lorris. . . . He should serve me still more, for,
to merit my grace, he is to begin the romance in which all my commandments will be set down. . . . [Then] he Guillaume shall rest. May
his tomb be full of balm. . . . Then will come Jean Chopinel. . . . He
will serve me his whole life. . . . He will be so fond of the romance that
he will want to finish it right to the end . . . for when Guillaume shall
cease, more than forty years after his death—may I not lie—Jean will
continue it.)

At the same time, the two thirteenth-century French writers are presented as effecting a translatio by continuing the Latin elegiac tradition,
itself represented by a key literary genealogy (10507–25): Gallus, Catullus,
Tibullus, and Ovid.[19] Furthermore, this passage involves a rewriting of
Ovid's *Amores* 3.9, a lament on the death of Tibullus in which Ovid-author
speaks in the third person of the god of love's mourning for the deceased
Tibullus, here transformed into a first-person speech by Jean's god of love,
and leading to the prediction of Jean's own authorial mission. In addition,
the literary genealogy of Ovid's "autobiographical" *Tristia* 4.10 is here being
evoked and rewritten to include, and culminate in, Guillaume de Lorris
and Jean de Meun. At this structurally central point, then, Jean's *Rose* not
only cites Ovid as *auctor*, but explicitly presents Jean as Ovid's literary "de-

19. See Karl Uitti, "From *Clerc* to *Poète*: The Relevance of the *Roman de la Rose* to Machaut's World," *Annals of the New York Academy of Science* 314 (1978): 209–16.

scendant" by means of the *translatio* construct. The very heart of Jean's plotline deals explicitly with the issue of authorial identity by setting the poem's only instance of the authors' names, within a literary genealogy, a translatio.

Perhaps the most aggressive gesture made by the *Fiore* toward its French model text involves the fact that the parallel moment of authorial self-naming by Durante in sonnet 82 writes out any mention of his French authorial predecessors.[20] Indeed, the entire 183-line speech by the *Rose*'s god of love to his troops (the French poem's single most important staging of its authority as resulting from claims to cultural and textual genealogy) is reduced to the fourteen lines of this sonnet:

> Amor disse a' baroni: "I' v'ò mandato
> Perch'e' convien ch'i' aggia il vostro aiuto,
> Tanto che quel castel si' abattuto
> Che Gelosia di nuovo à già fondato.
> Onde ciascun di voi è mi' giurato:
> Sì vi richeggio che sia proveduto
> Per voi in tal maniera che tenuto
> Non sia più contra me, ma si' aterrato.
> *Ch'e' pur convien ch'i' soccorra Durante,*
> *Chéd i' gli vo' tener sua promessione,*
> *Ché troppo l'ò trovato fin amante.*
> Molto penò di tòrrelmi Ragione:
> Que' come saggio fu sì fermo e stante
> Che no-lle valse nulla su' sermone."
> (Emphasis added.)

(Love said to his barons: "I have sent for you because I must have your help so that the castle recently built by Jealousy may be conquered. Every one of you is sworn to my service: I therefore ask you that help be provided by you in such a way that it can no longer hold out against

---

20. Cf. also the *Fiore*'s other naming of "Ser Durante" in 202.14, which as Contini notes, does not correspond to any proper name in the model passage in the *Rose*, but rather to line 14816: "Mais il m'avint tout autrement." While the name "Durante" here designates (as it had in sonnet 82) the lover-protagonist, it *seems* to be used in the third person by the authorial voice, thus suggesting a separation between protagonist and author. Perhaps, however, "Ser Durante" is just a witty periphrasis for the *io* of 202.12.

me, but that it be demolished [that you help ensure that it no longer hold out against me, but that it be demolished]. *Now without fail I must help Durante, for I want to keep my promise to him, whom I have found to be such a superlative courtly lover.* Reason tried hard to take him away from me: he reacted as a wise man, so resolute and upright that her long speech was wasted on him.)

Most specifically, of course, (and as Contini has noted), Durante-Amante here refigures Guillaume-Amant in the model passage in the *Rose:*

> Si vous cri merci jointes paumes
> Que cist las doulereus Guillaumes,
> Qui si bien s'est vers mei portez
> Seit secouruz e confortez.
> (10657–60)

(And I beg your grace with joined palms that this poor wretched Guillaume, who has borne himself so well toward me, may be helped and comforted.)

But within this moment in the *Rose,* the dieu d'amors had presented Guillaume in a double context that the *Fiore* erases. First, there was Guillaume's status as fifth in a series of six love poets, extending back to Gallus and forward to Jean de Meun.[21] This key mimesis of literary genealogy disappears in the *Fiore,* whose first-person lover-protagonist is thus purposefully denuded of the line of literary ancestors by means of which the *Rose* depicts its authority, incorporating the figure of translatio into its plotline. At the same time, the *Fiore's* rewriting of this key passage from the *Rose* suppresses

---

21. David Wallace (*Chaucer,* p. 52) insightfully points out that this status of "sixth place in a confraternity which unites the enterprise of ancient and modern poets" itself became a powerful topos of authority qua literary genealogy, that is, as *translatio.* As Wallace notes, it is echoed in key passages in Dante (*Inferno* 4.79–102); in Boccaccio (*Filocolo* 5.97.4–6); and in Chaucer (*Troilus and Criseyde* 5.1786–92). To this impressive list could also be added the famous tombs of the great poets "en nombre jucques a six et non plus": Ovid, Guillaume de Machaut, Boccaccio, Jean de Meun, Petrarch, and Alain Chartier from René d'Anjou's *Livre du cuer d'amours espris* of 1457, ed. Susan Wharton (Paris: Union générale d'éditions, 1980). My point is that the *Fiore* constitutes a spectacular *exception* with regard to this powerful genealogical strategy: it writes out, it suppresses the names of its literary fathers (and of their named line) in favor of its own name, which stands "alone."

the model text's exaggerated distinction between protagonist and author, between Guillaume and Jean, in terms of translatio. It is important to remember in this context that Amors in the *Rose* makes a double request: that Guillaume be helped as lover (and perhaps implicitly as writer), and that Jean be helped explicitly and exclusively as writer. The *Fiore* reduces this to a single request by the *dio d'amore*, for a Durante-protagonist presented exclusively as lover, as *fin amante*. Or, better, collapses the two named authors of the *Rose* into a single figure, presumably bearing the Italian author's name, but functioning only as lover-protagonist.

Not only does the *Fiore* eliminate the *Rose's* elaborate self-authorization at this specific point in its narrative structure by means of references to and citations of Latin models which it is presented as continuing in the vernacular, by means of translatio, but, in addition, the Italian text—so clearly and visibly based on its French canonical model—strikingly omits to name that model (or its authors) at any point whatsoever. This is all the more striking in that the god of love's speech in the *Rose* also contains a new title for the work, the *Mirouer aus Amoureus* (10651).[22] If the *Rose* is the thirteenth-century French text par excellence which both incorporates and stages translatio constructs as part of its very textual status, the *Fiore* seems to place translatio into question. The visible and explicit translatio from Greece to Rome to France (a construct extending back to the very beginnings of French vernacular literature in the twelfth century, with the *romans d'antiquité* and Chrétien) cannot, it seems, be allowed in the Italian *Fiore's* representation of its relation to its French model, but is, rather, given an ambiguous, even questionable, status. The *Fiore* thus presents itself as an implicit continuation/rewriting of the *Roman de la Rose* which simultaneously and explicitly conceals its direct link to its French model, in the interest, I would suggest, of a newly emergent Italian claim to literary and linguistic primacy and authority that must, paradoxically, be based on a French vernacular model that is both evoked and denied. We have then in the *Fiore* a flagrantly ambivalent staging of the relation between the estab-

---

22. With its elimination of Guillaume's prologue, the *Fiore* also erases the textual moment at which the French model text first names itself. Thus both the "rose" as object of desire, and the *Roman de la Rose* as textual entity are transmuted by the Italian poem. Perhaps incidentally, the only other occasion at which the title *Roman de la Rose* appears in the French poem is in Genius's speech, which the *Fiore* also suppresses.

lished French and the newly emerging Italian literary, political, and cultural enterprise.[23] But this staging is implicit, and only emerges, paradoxically, from the strong intertextual presence of the *Rose*. In this sense, the *Fiore* may be said to eschew explicit theorizing about its own production and authority (as found in the *Rose*), and rather to function "exclusively," as it were, in terms of literary practice. Thus it simultaneously exploits the prestige of the *Rose* as model text and denies (or even deconstructs) the *Rose* as French authority. And in this way, the Italian *Fiore* aggressively appropriates the French *Rose* into a newly emerging Italian cultural context.

By way of conclusion, I would like to turn, in an overly brief and schematic way to be sure, to Dante's *Commedia* and its reaction to French culture. We must begin with the place of France in Dante's political and ecclesiastical ideology, where, in terms both of empire and of papacy, France is represented as a threat. In both cases this French threat is to Dante's vision of the legitimate, divinely ordained *centrality* of Italy in general and Rome in particular within the context of world history. For Dante, both the Roman Empire and the Roman papacy were consecrated by God.[24] France was "eccentric." It constituted a threat to the legitimate renewal and continuation of these two Roman institutions by attempting to substitute for them illegitimate alternative centers of political and ecclesiastical power. Dante's use of the translatio topos in these contexts definitively does not allow for post-Roman geographic change, for transfers of authority to a different place, only to a different time: from imperial and Petrine Rome, to contemporary Rome. These direct links in Dante's notion of *translatio imperii et ecclesiae* thus involve continuities in both time and space. While Rome has had predecessors in political and religious power, it cannot, for Dante, have successors.

Politically speaking, Paris is thus an eccentric, illegitimate substitute for Rome. A primary villain here is the French king Philip the Fair, who first opposed the election of Henry VII of Luxemburg to the imperial crown by unsuccessfully attempting to gain that office for his brother, Charles

23. See Zygmunt Baranski's essay, "The Ethics of Literature: The *Fiore* and Medieval Traditions of Rewriting," in Baranski and Boyde, *Context*, pp. 207–32.
24. For Dante's politics, see Charles Till Davis, *Dante and the Idea of Rome* (Oxford: Clarendon Press, 1957); and "Dante and the Empire" in *The Cambridge Companion to Dante*, ed. Rachel Jacoff (Cambridge: Cambridge University Press, 1993), pp. 67–79.

of Valois, in 1308. Philip's opposition to Henry continued after the latter entered Italy in 1310 to be crowned emperor at Rome (1312). Dante considered Henry VII to be the new and long-awaited Roman emperor (only the seventh one in Dante's world historical perspective), who would restore order and greatness to the wartorn Italy.[25] Henry's premature death in 1313 was the end of Dante's political project in any practical terms, and placed greater emphasis on perfidious French opposition to Henry, under the leadership of Philip the Fair. From Dante's point of view, all of this was directly tied to the second great French threat.

For in the ecclesiastical context, the eccentric, illegitimate Rome was Avignon. And the transfer of the papal seat from Rome to Avignon in 1309 was effected by Philip the Fair through Pope Clement V (r. 1305–14). Clement, himself a Gascon and former archbishop of Bordeaux who never set foot in Italy, was elected pope through the machinations of Philip, whose tool he became. The new pope was crowned at Lyons and ordered the Curia to join him in France. Because of Philip's power over him, Pope Clement secretly turned against Henry VII after having first supported his entry into Italy to be crowned emperor. The final denunciation of this treachery in the *Commedia* is made by Beatrice at the end of her last speech in the poem (*Paradiso* 30.142–48). In addition, the removal of the papacy from Rome to Avignon is figured as the seventh, the last, and greatest calamity to befall the Church in history, at the close of the pageant of the *carro* and its transformations in *Purgatorio* 32.148–60. The *puttana sciolta* (32.149) (ungirt harlot) represents the papacy, culminating in Clement V; and the *gigante* (32.152) (giant), the royal house of France, culminating in Philip the Fair. Their display of voluptuous affection (32.153) figures the corrupt alliances between the French kings and the papacy. The canto closes as the giant takes away the cart carrying the harlot until it is out of sight, thus figuring the ultimate calamity of the church, the displacement of the papal see to Avignon.[26]

In the ideological context of Dante's *Commedia*, France is thus a threat

25. See also Dante's three political *Epistolae* (5, 6, 7), and the *Monarchia*, in the excellent new edition and translation by Prue Shaw (Cambridge: Cambridge University Press, 1995), esp. "Introduction," pp. xiii–li.

26. Cf. the important article of Lino Pertile, "La puttana e il gigante (*Purgatorio* XXXII, 148–60)," *Seminario Dantesco Internazionale: Atti del primo convegno* (Florence: Le Lettere, 1994), pp. 243–72.

to the proper political and ecclesiastical centrality of Italy. A basic parallel exists with regard to Dante's reception and representation of French culture, that is, the French language and literary tradition. In the *Commedia*, there is virtually no French participation in the various translatio authorizations for Dante's project. The use of translatio to authorize the *Commedia* as a new (and unique) literary enterprise is found throughout the work. It is, indeed, fundamental to Dante's poetics at every level, beginning with the character Virgilio who guides Dante-protagonist through the first two thirds of his journey, and whose *Aeneid* is repeatedly staged as one of the *Commedia*'s master models. Similar use is made of the works of the other principal *auctores:* Ovid, Lucan, and Statius.

The direct line of translatio authorization in the *Commedia* runs from classical Latin to Dante's new Italian vernacular.[27] There is no "detour" to France; on the contrary. Dante does not represent himself and the innovative literary enterprise for which he makes the highest cultural claims as "depending" on a previously dominant France that is now surpassed. Rather, the French cultural achievement is basically passed over in silence, suppressed, as it were, as such. Or rather, it is simply not accorded the elaborate and explicit treatment reserved for Latin (and to some extent Greek) culture.[28]

Thus the *Commedia*'s few explicit evocations of what we might consider to be French cultural figures function, as it were, in isolation. They also demonstrate Dante's familiarity with French literature. On the one hand, there is Arthurian romance with its highly erotic content. In *Inferno*

27. For the importance to Dante's poetics in this context of the *translatio* from Greece to Rome to the *Commedia*, see Iannucci, *Dante e la Bella Scola*; and Brownlee, "Dante and the Classical Poets" in Jacoff, *The Cambridge Companion to Dante*, pp. 100–19.

28. For Dante's earlier notion of the subject matters appropriate to the literary medium of the French vernacular, see *De vulgari eloquentia:* "Allegat ergo pro se lingua oïl quod propter sui faciliorem ac delectabiliorem vulgaritatem quicquid redactum est sive inventum ad vulgare prosaycum, suum est: videlicet Biblia cum Troianorum Romanorumque gestibus compilata et Arturi regis ambages pulcerrime et quamplures alie ystorie ac doctrine" (Thus the language of oïl adduces on its own behalf the fact that, because of the greater facility and pleasing quality of its vernacular style, everything that is recounted or invented in vernacular prose belongs to it: such as compilations from the Bible and the histories of Troy and Rome, and the beautiful tales of King Arthur, and many other works of history and doctrine). Ed. and trans. Steven Botterill, *Dante: De vulgari eloquentia*, Cambridge Medieval Classics 5 (Cambridge: Cambridge University Press, 1996), pp. 22–23.

5, Tristan is evoked (5.67), and the Old French *Prose Lancelot* plays a key role, though the principal characters are Italian (Francesca and Paolo) and the figure of Dido dominates the canto in important ways. The end of this romance, with Mordred's treacherous murder of King Arthur, is mentioned by Camicione de' Pazzi (in Caina) in *Inferno* 32.61–62; in *Paradiso* 13–15, Beatrice's smile when Dante begins to speak to Cacciaguida is compared to the cough of warning to Guinevere by one of her ladies. On the other hand, there is the *matière de Roland*, which Dante tends to treat as *historia*. Ganelon is placed in the second division (Antenora) of the ninth circle, among the traitors to their country (*Inferno* 32.122); Roland and Charlemagne are placed among the crusaders in the fifth heaven (*Paradiso* 18.43); along with William and Renouard (*Paradiso* 18.46). There is also the comparison between Nembròt's horn and Roland's horn at the defeat at Roncesvalles (*Inferno* 31.16–18), and the all-important fact that Dante considers Charlemagne to be the last world-historical Roman emperor (*Paradiso* 6.96).

Dante's notion of translatio is not therefore the progression from Greece to Rome to the France of Chrétien de Troyes and the French literary tradition, but rather, from Greece to Rome to Italy, including, of course, from Dante's perspective, Provençal as part of the Romance vernacular lyric tradition on the basis of which he (in part) positions himself in the *Commedia*. There is, from Dante's point of view, no threat posed by Provençal to the centrality of Italian culture, either politically or literarily.[29]

It is in this overall context, I suggest, that we should view the *Commedia*'s reception of the *Rose*, its literary practice in this regard. For the *Roman de la Rose*, especially, I would argue, qua dominant, canonical French literary text, receives no "official" recognition in the *Commedia*.[30] There is no

29. From Dante's perspective, the relative dominance of lyric in the Provençal tradition is thus quite important; as is the absence, from this same perspective, of any dominant, canonical work in Provençal narrative verse. For Dante's representation of his genealogical relations to Provençal poets, see esp. Teodolinda Barolini, *Dante's Poets. Textuality and Truth in the "Comedy"* (Princeton, N.J.: Princeton University Press, 1984). Of particular importance are the figures of Sordello, Arnaut Daniel, and Folco.

30. There are various scholarly views on Dante's knowledge of the *Rose*, and where it starts to appear in the *Commedia*. See esp. Richards, *Dante and "Le Roman,"* pp. 85ff. My own preference is for the more recent positions that see traces of the *Rose* relatively early in the *Commedia*. In any case, even if the first reflection of the *Rose* in the *Commedia* occurs in the Earthly Paradise, I assume this results from Dante's authorial intentionality, rather than

programmatic presence of the French text, of the kind that characterizes Dante's mimetic treatment of all the texts, Latin and vernacular, that he presents as models or precursors. Indeed, this programmatic representation and rewriting of textual models is one of the *Commedia's* most striking and characteristic features. The *Rose,* by contrast, has a fragmentary, diffuse presence in the *Comedy.*[31] By implication, I would argue, what we have in the *Commedia's* response to the *Rose,* is a denial of the French work's canonical status, of its centrality. This epitomizes the Italian poem's reaction to and mimesis of French culture and power in general.

A telling example of this occurs in *Purgatorio* 28, where Dante enters the Earthly Paradise.[32] In the *Romance of the Rose,* we remember, when Amant first entered into his "Gardin," its beauty made him feel that he was "em paradis terrestre" (634). The sensual landscape of the Garden of Eden in the *Commedia* is a classic *locus amoenus* that recalls that of Guillaume de Lorris's *Rose,* especially with its evocation of birdsong (*Purgatorio* 28.14–18; cf. Guillaume de Lorris, *Rose,* 641–80). The pure stream issuing from a pure fountain recalls the Fountain of Narcissus in the *Rose* (and, indeed, the stream of Lethe will serve as the site for Dante's own Narcissistic drama in *Purgatorio* 30.76–99). The solitary *bella donna,* singing and gathering flowers, recalls the first human figure encountered in the *Rose's* garden: the sensual Oiseuse, wearing a "garland of fresh roses" (553) and carrying a mirror (555). Indeed, Dante's sexual reaction to his lady is more powerful and more violent than that of Amant in the *Rose.* On first seeing the beautiful Matelda, Dante is moved the way Pluto was just before he raped Proserpina; Matelda gazes at Dante erotically as Venus did when she first lusted after Adonis; Dante's desire to cross the river to Matelda is like Leander's desire to cross the Hellespont to his lover Hero.[33]

---

from his not having read the French text previously, which strikes me as circular reasoning. Would it be at all fruitful to speculate on the possibility that *Vita Nuova* 25, with its striking deconstruction of the personification of the God of Love, might (among other things of course) involve an early (and critical) Dantean response to the *Rose?*

31. For the best discussion to date of the relationship between the two great poems, see Richards, *Dante and "Le Roman,"* esp. chap. 3, "Textual Parallelism between the *Rose* and the *Commedia,"* pp. 71–105.

32. Cf. Richards's insightful consideration of the presence of the *Rose* in Dante's Earthly Paradise, beginning with the dream of Leah in *Purgatorio* 27.97–105, *Dante and "Le Roman,"* pp. 85–89.

33. For these Ovidian mythographic references, see Peter S. Hawkins, "Watching Matelda,"

All three of these models of intense sexual desire are, however, Ovidian. Indeed, Ovid also provides Dante with numerous models both for the *locus amoenus* and for the idyllic landscape of the golden age (esp. in *Metamorphoses* I). *Rose* reminiscences are staged haphazardly, as it were, in order to be displaced by a programmatic use of Ovid. A similar effect results from the contrast between the *Rose's* metaphoric use of "paradis terrestre," and Dante's claim to represent the literal, historical, geographically specific Earthly Paradise.

To the extent that the *Rose's* Garden is evoked as a model for Dante's Earthly Paradise, it is *preempted* by what Dante presents as the more powerful models with which he is directly and explicitly engaged: the Bible and the *auctores.*[34]

Indeed, the authority of the great Latin poets with regard to figuring or prefiguring the Christian Eden (which was, of course, unknown to them in any literal sense) is explicitly emphasized at the conclusion to *Purgatorio* 28, when Matelda says:

> Quelli ch'anticamente poetáro
> l'età dell'oro e suo stato felice,
> forse in Parnaso esto loco sognáro.
> (28.139–41)[35]

(Those who in ancient times made poetry about the golden age and of its happy state, perhaps were then on Parnassus dreaming of this place.)

In this context, which also links (directly and genealogically) Dante's literary activity to that of his Latin and biblical predecessors, the *Rose* is simply excluded. And this exclusion is all the more striking in *Purgatorio* 28 because of the canto's initial, and, in retrospect, apparently fragmentary or

―――――
in *The Poetry of Allusion. Virgil and Ovid in Dante's "Commedia,"* ed. Rachel Jacoff and Jeffrey Schnapp (Stanford, Calif.: Stanford University Press, 1991), pp. 185–95. See also Robert Hollander, *Allegory in Dante's "Commedia"* (Princeton, N.J.: Princeton University Press, 1969), pp. 154–58. For the canto as a whole, see Victoria Kirkham, *"Purgatory 28,"* in *Dante's Divine Comedy: Introductory Readings—Il Purgatorio,* ed. Tibor Wlassics, special issue of *Lectura Dantis* 12 (1993): 411–32. See also Kirkham, "Dante's Polysynchrony: A Perfectly Timed Entry into Eden," *Filologica e Critica* 20 (1995): 329–52.
34. Especially Ovid, but also the other classical poets. See, e.g., Iannucci, *Dante,* p. 28.
35. See Hawkins, "Watching Matelda," p. 184.

"casual" evocation of the *Rose*'s Jardin de Deduit. To the extent that the *Rose* has a textual presence in the *Commedia,* it is consistently put to one side, marginalized in favor of the Italocentric line of authoritative cultural descent, of which Dante presents his book both as a culmination and (more importantly) as a new beginning.

The claims that the *Divine Comedy* makes for itself are profoundly aggressive. It explicitly undertakes the creation of a new Italian literary vernacular, combining the authority of Latin (both classical and theological) with the vitality of living speech. In this endeavor, it strategically ignores the fact of French cultural primacy in the vernacular, claiming that it itself creates a new and superior Italian literary canon. Long before it is even finished, the *Divine Comedy* asserts its status both as a canonical and as a foundational work. With its successful completion, the *Commedia* both embodies and establishes the authoritative Italian language and literature whose creation was at the heart of the Dantean project from the beginning. With the completed *Commedia,* the new fact of (what presents itself as) an already "full-blown" Italian cultural tradition significantly challenges and modifies French cultural hegemony in the vernacular middle ages. This is, of course, most fully true in Italy itself. And in this sense, while Dante's literary practice and his sublime self-promotion can be seen as transforming the historicocultural givens of fourteenth-century Romance Europe in general and varied terms, they transform Italian literary and cultural politics in direct and specific ways. The *Commedia*'s strategic response to the fact of French hegemony as a cultural given in early fourteenth-century Italian literary contexts involves a powerful and complex strategy of decentering, of marginalizing France. In political, in ecclesiastical, and in literary terms, the very bases of French claims not just to superiority but even to legitimacy are relentlessly interrogated, subverted, attacked.

Hauntings:
The Materiality of Memory on
The Renaissance Stage

PETER STALLYBRASS

On the English Renaissance stage, clothing was often powerfully associated
with memory. In *King John,* Constance's grief for her son Arthur is physically located in the places that make present his absence: her grief "fils the
roome vp of my absent childe," "[l]ies in his bed," "[s]tuffes out his vacant
garments with his forme."[1] Indeed, "vacant garments" are often imagined
as retaining a person's "forme" in and of themselves. And the scattered body
of the dead is also present in the fragments that survive. As John Kerrigan
notes, Thomas Kyd's *The Spanish Tragedy* traces a scarf which Bel-Imperia
gives as a love token to Andrea. When Andrea is killed, his friend Horatio
takes the scarf in remembrance of him. Similarly, after Horatio is murdered, his father, Hieronimo, dips his son's handkerchief into his blood to
create a material memorial both of his life and of his death. And Antony
presents the dead emperor to the people by showing them his rent mantle,
"Our *Caesars* Vesture wounded."[2] In *Twelfth Night,* Viola memorializes the

I am particularly indebted to the work and comments of Ann Rosalind Jones, Margreta
de Grazia, and Phyllis Rackin, and to the suggestions of John Kerrigan, Laurie Maguire,
Michael Neill, and Stephen Orgel.

1. William Shakespeare, *The Life and Death of King John,* in Charlton Hinman's *The Norton
Facsimile: The First Folio of Shakespeare* (New York: Norton, 1968), 3.4.93–97 (TLN 1478–82).
All further quotations from Shakespeare, except for *Hamlet,* are from *The Norton Facsimile:
The First Folio of Shakespeare,* ed. Charlton Hinman (New York: Norton, 1968). They are
followed by act-scene-line numbers keyed to *The Riverside Shakespeare,* ed. G. Blakemore
Evans (Boston, Mass.: Houghton Mifflin, 1974) and by the "through line numbers" (TLN) of
Hinman's edition of the Folio.
2. Shakespeare, *Julius Caesar* 3.2.196 (TLN 1732). See John Kerrigan, "Hieronimo, Hamlet
and Remembrance," *Essays in Criticism* 31 (1981): 105–26.

brother she believes dead by having her clothes cut in imitation of his. The ghosts of the English Renaissance theater can be seen as the logical extension of the material remains (rings, scarves, handkerchiefs, jewels, shoes) that are so frequently staged. Ghosts testify simultaneously to death's undoing of the body and to the materiality of survival.

But why are these ghosts so precisely clothed and situated on the stage? It is, mundanely, so that they will be known. If a ghost says, above all, "[R]emember me," remembrance is materialized through the physical attributes that named the person when alive. And these attributes are above all *superficial:* they lie on the surface, they can be displayed to the eye (Andrugio's ghost is "displayed"). If a ghost is a mnemonic, the stage ghost is often remembered by what it wears, what is most visible and tactile—its clothes. Interiority is equally literalized, but in terms of unnaming. That is, if a later regime of individuality will try to trace its most fundamental forms in an interior subjectivity, the interiority of Renaissance tragedy is displayed in the fully material skull beneath the skin. And what characterizes the skull is anonymity. The body, given over to death, could be anyone's: the skull may be Alexander's or Yorick's or anyone's. Without a memorial or a gravestone or a gravedigger to tell you whose the skull was, you don't know. But if the depths of the body display only the workings of anonymous death, the surfaces of the body trace the insignia of identity.

The Materiality of Ghosts

In an aristocratic society the most privileged markings of identity are those of the knight, and they are to be found less within the body than in the heraldic signs that adorn it. Medieval and Renaissance tombs that display the armored body above and the cadaver below make explicit this relation between surface and depth. The surface (the armored body) is elaborately identified through complex heraldic devices; it is identified, of course, not as an "individual" but as a genealogical body, a body marked, on the shields that surround it, by its kinship connections. The cadaver beneath is unidentified, unidentifiable; it is simply food for worms, which are sometimes literally depicted eating away any unique characteristics, laying bare the anonymous bones. One recognizes Hamlet's father, in death as in life, by his armor. The Ghost wears, or we might almost say *is,* were it not for his raised visor, a suit of armor. Not any suit of armor but "the very Armor he had on" when he fought with Fortinbras.[3]

It is exactly such suits of armor that were transmitted as the markers and, indeed, creators of genealogy. In other words, the ghost of Hamlet's father, when it first appears, is uncanny less because of its spectral quality than because this suit of armor, which would, of course, have survived the father's death, moves, and because from this armor issues the father's voice. The Ghost in *Hamlet* thus activates a specific memory system: the transmission of property, including armor, as the material "[R]emember me's" that mark the heir as the living embodiment of his father, Hamlet as Hamlet. If the father dies, his material identity survives in the helm and crest, the target or shield, the coat of arms which heralds carried in front of the coffin at his funeral. The aristocratic funerals of Renaissance England testify to the attempt to make memory and inheritance two sides of the same coin. For the principal mourner had to be of the same sex and status as the deceased. Thus, for all the literary demands that the wife should grieve for her dead husband, widows were in reality completely marginalized within the social processes of mourning. As Clare Gittings notes, "[O]nly the eldest of any of the sons could act as mourner to a dead father." [4] And the rite of mourning was itself a ritual transmission of the father's armor to his son. At the church, the chief mourner gave money to the church, after which the coat of arms was carried to the altar and given to the church. The function of the chief mourner's financial offering was to ensure that the armor, now technically the church's, would be immediately handed back to him. Thus did the heir step into the shoes, uncomfortably metallic as they may have been, of his father.

Funerals, then, asserted the materiality of memory, and so equally did the aristocratic wills in which fathers bequeathed their armor to their sons. Such bequests remained a striking feature of aristocratic wills. They are, as one would expect, common enough in the Middle Ages. In 1368, Sir Michael

3. All quotations from *Hamlet,* unless otherwise noted, are from Q2 (*The Tragicall Historie of Hamlet, Prince of Denmarke* [London, 1604]) as reproduced in *Shakespeare's Plays in Quarto,* ed. Michael J. B. Allen and Kenneth Muir (Berkeley: University of California Press, 1981), 1.1.60 (TLN 76).
4. Clare Gittings, *Death, Burial and the Individual in Early Modern England* (Beckenham, England: Croom Helm, 1984), pp. 173, 175.

de Poynings left "to my heir," "all my armour"; in 1368, the Earl of Suffolk left "to William, my eldest son, my sword, which the King gave me in name of the Earldom"; in 1369, the Earl of Warwick gave "to Thomas, my son and heir, . . . the coat of mail sometime belonging to that famous Guy of Warwick, and . . . all my harness, weapons, and such like habiliments [to] be equally divided between my two sons Thomas and William."[5] But one equally finds precise instructions as to the disposition of armor in the sixteenth century. In his will, dated 16 January 1580, Wistan Browne left to his son and heir "my armour and weapons in Weald Hall and Rookewood Hall; all which I will shall remain in such studies, galleries and other rooms as they now be to the use of my son"; in 1579, Richard Cook left "[t]o my son Anthony my armour and weapons at Gidea Hall"; in 1578, Clement Sysley left to his son and heir, Thomas "my armour and furniture of armour, my guns, dags, pikes, bills, targets and crossbows, and they are to remain as standards and implements of household to him and his heirs forever at Eastbury."[6] In 1582, Robert Camocke left to his wife Mary "my new bible of the greatest volume for life, and my household stuff." But he explicitly excludes his armour "which I give to my son Thomas" and which is "to remain in my house to my heirs."[7] What is striking in these four sixteenth-century wills is the explicit attempt to prevent the armor from becoming a moveable, to ground it in a specific house, even in specific rooms. This is even more extreme in the will of Richard Kynwelmarshe: he leaves his armor not to a person but to a place: "to the manor [Newton Hall]."[8] Such wills make clear that the identity of the gentry is not the same as individuality. It is shaped from the outside by the value and the honors it can absorb into itself.

Armor was often a form of haunting, whether or not it was activated by a ghost. It remained as a memorial system within the house. In *2 Henry VI*, as Phyllis Rackin notes, Iden, having killed "that monstrous traitor" Jack Cade, transforms his deed "from a defense of private property to a heroic

---

5. Nicholas Harris Nicolas, *Testamenta Vetusta* (London: Nichols and Son, 1826), 1:73, 74, 79.
6. F. G. Emmison, *Elizabethan Life: Wills of Essex Gentry and Merchants* (Chelmsford, England: Essex County Council, 1978), pp. 64, 70, 180.
7. Emmison, *Elizabethan Life*, p. 175.
8. Emmison, *Elizabethan Life*, p. 221.

victory in defense of his king" by elevating his sword as "a historical monument":[9]

> Sword, I will hallow thee for this thy deede,
> And hang thee o're my Tombe, when I am dead.
> (4.10.67–68 [TLN 2972–73])

The material survival of armor asserts the continued presence of an absent body or line of bodies and of their martial status. Sometimes, the armor will be activated by, and in turn activate, another body — the father's heir, for instance. Sometimes, it was hung up in the church as a memorial. The helm of Sir Nichols Heron used to be above his monument in Croydon church until it was removed to the Museum of London, and the helm of Sir John St. John, who died in 1594, is still next to his tomb at Lydiard Tregoz in Wiltshire. Sir Roger Manwood's tomb in Saint Stephen's Canterbury is surmounted by a helm and crest, a pair of gauntlets, and a mourning sword, dating from his funeral in 1592. And the most complete remaining set of armor in a church dates from an even later period, hanging above Sir William Penn, who was buried in Saint Mary Redcliffe, Bristol, in 1670. "The coat, complete with tassels, is above the memorial, then, in order of ascendancy, the breast-plate with attached leg-guards, the helm and crest, and the painted wooden target behind which is tucked the sword." [10] Such displays of the armor of the dead were frequently planned in advance and set down in wills.

But although armor was a crucial memorial bequest of clothes amongst the aristocracy, the Ghost of Hamlet's father is unusual, if not unique, in returning in his armor. When the Renaissance stage ghost returned clothed, it had a striking range of clothes at its disposal, from the white surplice and cardinal's mitre of Calchas; to the leather cassock, boots, and cowl of Brachiano; to the armor, and later bedgown, of Hamlet's father. In the induction to *A Warning for Faire Women,* a play belonging to the King's Men and probably performed by them a year or so before *Hamlet,* Comedy mocks Tragedy, sneering that she stages ghosts with tattered outfits:

---

9. Phyllis Rackin, *Stages of History: Shakespeare's English Chronicles* (Ithaca, N.Y.: Cornell University Press, 1990), 212.

10. Julian Litten, *The English Way of Death: The Common Funeral since 1450* (London: Robert Hale, 1991), pp. 181, 184, 183.

[A] filthie whining ghost,
Lapt in some fowle sheete, or a leather pelch,
Comes skreaming like a pigge halfe stickt,
And cries *Vindicta*, reuenge, reuenge.[11]

A pelch or pilch was an outer garment made of skin, such a garment as Brachiano wears. The "fowle sheete," on the other hand, is related to the sheet that is the familiar garb of modern ghosts. Yet the sheet of the Renaissance ghost has nothing in common with the "spirit drapery" of a later age. It is as material as the Ghost's armor. But whereas armor displays the continuity of aristocratic identity, the sheet marks the dissolution of any identity. For the "sheet" is, of course, the winding sheet in which the dead body is buried. It is this winding sheet, or shrowd, that Andrugio imagines repossessing as he flees the coming day, and it is probably the remains of a winding sheet that scarcely conceal the naked body of the Ghost depicted in Stephen Batman's *Doom Warning Judgment* (1581).

John Donne strikingly displays his winding sheet in what was probably then, as now, the most famous English monument of the early seventeenth century. The monument portrays Donne, still in his winding sheet, standing up, although his knees are partially bent, as he rises out of the urn which symbolically contains his ashes. Isaac Walton gives a (disputed) account of the preparations for the memorial:

A Monument being resolved upon, Dr. Donne sent for a Carver to make for him in wood the figure of an vrn, giving him directions for the compass and height of it; and to bring with it a board of the just height of his body. These being got: then without delay a choice Painter was got to be in readiness to draw his Picture, which was taken as followeth: — Several Charcole-fires being first made in his large Study, he brought with him into that place his winding-sheet in his hand, and, having put off all his cloaths, had this sheet put on him, and so tyed with knots at his head and feet, and his hands so placed as dead bodies are usually fitted, to be shrowded and put into their Coffin, or grave. Upon this vrn he thus stood with his eyes shut, and with so much of the sheet turned aside as might shew his lean, pale, and death-like face, which was expressly turned toward the East, from whence he expected the second coming of his and our Saviour Jesus.

11. Anon., *A Warning for Faire Women* (London, 1599), sig. A2v.

In this posture he was drawn at his just height; and when the Picture was fully finished, he caused it to be set by his bedside, where it continued, and became his hourly object till his death: and it was then given to his dearest friend and Executor, Dr. Henry King . . . , who caused him to be thus carved in one entire piece of white Marble, as it now stands in that Church.[12]

The epitaph, which Donne wrote, further testifies to the significance of clothing, even in, or especially in, death: "DECANATU HUJUS ECCLESIAE INDUTUS XXVII. NOVEMBRIS, MDCXXI. EXUTUS MORTE ULTIMO DIE MARTII MDCXXXI" ("Having been invested [indutus] with the Deanery of this Church, November 27, 1621, he was stripped [exutus] of it by Death on the last day of March 1631").[13] Here, it is the disrobing of the body, its unnaming in death, which is staged. But this is done for the sake of a renaming—not by the final disappearance of clothes but by the taking on of new clothes. This process of rerobing is proclaimed in the epigraph attached to the engraving of Donne in his funeral shroud: "Corporis haec Animae sit Syndon, Syndon Jesu" ("[M]ay this shroud of the body be the shroud of the soul, the shroud of Jesu").[14] Donne strips himself of his clothes so that he will be re-membered in Christ's shroud. But in Saint Paul's Cathedral, it is his own material winding sheet that is remembered, the "fowle sheet" in which his face, the eyes still closed, appears—both the face of the dying Donne, just before his dissolution,[15] and the face that is turned toward the east, at the moment of rematerialization, the resurrection.

Donne's monument both reasserts the literalness of the sheet in which the dead body is bound and powerfully stages the antithesis of the armored

12. Izaak Walton, *The Lives of John Donne* . . . , ed. George Saintsbury (London: Oxford University Press, 1927), p. 78. For a sceptical reading of Walton's account, see Helen Gardner, "Dean Donne's Monument in St. Paul's," in *Evidence in Literary Scholarship*, ed. René Wellek and Alvaro Ribeiro (Oxford: Clarendon Press, 1979), pp. 29–44.
13. Edmund Gosse, *The Life and Letters of John Donne* (London, 1899), 2:282.
14. For the inscription and the problem of translating it, see John Donne, *Deaths Duell*, ed. Geoffrey Keynes (Boston: David Godine, 1973), 43–44. John Sparrow suggests a different translation: "This is my body's shroud, may my soul's shroud be that of Jesus." (Joe Farrell has independently communicated to me a similar translation.) Sparrow notes that Donne was familiar "with Alfonso Paleoti's treatise on the Sindon, or winding-sheet, of Christ preserved in Turin" (44). See also Catherine Creswell, "Reading Subjectivity: The Body, the Text, the Author in John Donne," Ph.D. diss., SUNY Buffalo, 1992, 109–10.
15. Or possibly after his dissolution (see Gardner, "Donne's Monument").

body. These two contradictory images (the armored body, the shrouded body) are brought together in the many two-decker monuments that present the armored, aristocratic body above, the anonymous, decaying cadaver below, body and winding sheet alike eaten by worms. In the body above, it is as if the armor that sheathes the body has also had the power to sheathe the face, which is preserved in stone, unreachable by death. But neither face nor body will live long in the tomb, as both the cadaver below and the gravedigger in *Hamlet* remind us. The armor alone will endure. This ironic relation of living armor to dead body is captured in the famous monument to Engelbert II of Nassau and his wife, Cimburga of Baden, begun in 1526. Below, husband and wife lie naked, in their winding sheets; above, the empty, separated parts of Engelbert's armor are displayed. Yet here, even though the armor is preserved, it no longer creates a whole body. Scattered, empty, it lives on in a twilight world, both deathless and dead.[16]

Ghosts of both the armored and the shrouded body are in fact present in the most influential of all ghost plays, the play which profoundly influenced Seneca and, through him, Renaissance drama: Euripides' *Hecuba*. From the perspective of Renaissance tragedy, a striking feature of Greek tragedy is the absence of staged ghosts. There are none in Sophocles, and Aeschylus has only the ghost of Darius in the *Persae* and of Clytemnestra in the *Eumenides*. But neither of these ghosts was as influential as the ghost of Polydorus, Hecuba's son, as he appears in the prologue to Euripides' play. Polydorus's ghost stands at the opposite extreme from Hamlet's. Polydorus has been murdered by his protector, Polymestor, and his body thrown into the sea:

> Here, pounded by the surf, my corpse still lies,
> carried up and down on the heaving swell of the sea,
> unburied and unmourned.[17]

16. See Ethan M. Kavaler, "Being the Count of Nassau: Refiguring Identity in Space, Time, and Stone," in *Beeld en Zelfbeeld in de Nederlandse Kunst, 1550–1750,* ed. Reindert Falkenburg, Jan de Jong, Herman Roodenburg, and Frits Scholten (Zwolle, The Netherlands: Waanders, 1995), 13–51. The device was copied by Maximilian Colt in the early seventeenth century for his monument to Sir Francis Vere, but Colt erases the absolute contrast by representing Vere below clothed.

17. Euripides, *Hecuba,* trans. William Arrowsmith, in *Euripides III, The Complete Greek Tragedies,* ed. David Grene and Richard Lattimore (Chicago: University of Chicago Press, 1958), lines 26–28.

Polydorus's body bears the marks of this death; as a corpse, he wears a gown (*peplos*), which, although he is described as a "naked corpse," is sufficient to identify him to Agamemnon as a Trojan ("[W]hat's that Trojan corpse beside the tents? / I can see from his *peplos* that he's not a Greek" [lines 734–35]). The crucial point, though, is that Polydorus's ghost appears to be marked by the ravages of death.[18] This is in striking contrast to the ghost of Achilles, which, although never physically staged, is seen by Polydorus "stalking on his tomb" (line 37). According to the Chorus, Achilles appears with "armor blazing" (line 111, literally, with "golden arms"). Polydorus, in other words, is materialized as a vulnerable body; Achilles is materialized "in his habit as he lived," the most heroic of warriors.

Both conceptions of the revenant are equally materialist and both emphasize the clothing of the body. But whereas in the ghost of Polydorus we are confronted with the corruptible body and the decaying shroud, in the ghost of Achilles we witness the splendid armor of the soldier in his prime. It is the corruptible body that Cornelia, in Kyd's *Cornelia,* sees in the ghost of her former husband:

> And loe (me thought) came glyding by my bed
> The ghost of *Pompey,* with a ghastly looke,
> All pale and brawne-falne, not in tryumph borne
> Amongst the conquering Romans, as he vs'de. . . .
> But all amaz'd, with fearefull, hollow eyes,
> Hys hayre and beard deform'd with blood and sweat,
> Casting a thyn course lynsel ore hys shoulders,
> That (torne in peeces) trayl'd vpon the ground;
> And (gnashing of his teeth) vnlockt his iawes,
> (Which slyghtly couer'd with a scarce-seene skyn).[19]

Like the ghost of Polydorus, Pompey's ghost undergoes the material corruption of the body: his skin is pale and scarcely covers his jaws; his flesh is falling away; his hair is "deform'd" by blood and sweat. Even the shroud

---

18. Similarly in *The Changeling,* Alonzo's Ghost displays his own maimed body; he appears to Deflores, *"shewing him the hand whose finger he had cut off."* Thomas Middleton and William Rowley, *The Changeling* (London, 1653), sig. F2, 4.1 S.D.

19. Thomas Kyd, *Cornelia,* in *The Works of Thomas Kyd,* ed. Frederick S. Boas (Oxford: Clarendon Press, 1955), 3.1.75–86.

("lynsel," from the French *linceul*, a winding sheet) has undergone decay and is "torne in peeces."

The Ghost in *Hamlet* is in striking contrast to Pompey's ghost. Like Achilles, it is unmarked by death. In his moment of death, the Ghost relates,

> [A] most instant tetter barkt about
> Most Lazerlike with vile and lothsome crust
> All my smooth body.
> (1.5.71–73 [TLN 756–58])

But when the Ghost returns he is "[a]rmed at poynt, exactly *Capapea* [F1: *Cap a Pe*]," "[f]rom top to toe," "from head to foot" "in compleat steele." [20] His "canoniz'd bones," having "burst their cerements," revisit the earth in their most martial guise (1.4.47–48 [TLN 632–33]). This Ghost looks "like the King," has a "faire and warlike forme," is "Maiesticall" (1.1.43, 47, 142 [TLN 55, 60, 142]). There is thus no sign of the corrupting and corrupted body, no mark of the agony of his murder. This ghostly body is in contrast not only to Pompey's ghost but to most descriptions of theatrical ghosts. In *2 Henry VI*, Warwick speaks of ghosts as being "[o]f ashy semblance, meager, pale, and bloodlesse"; and Reginald in Heywood's *The English Traveller* describes a murdered ghost as appearing with "His body gasht, and all orestruck with wounds." [21] But *Hamlet*'s Ghost's previously "smooth body" is not wounded but further smoothed and hardened into a carapace of "compleat steele," a carapace which, like Achilles' armor, bears his memory in a way that no mere body could do. The "mirror stage," Lacan writes, manufactures a "succession of phantasies that extends from a fragmented bodyimage to a form of its totality that I shall call orthopaedic—and, lastly, to the assumption of the armour of an alienating identity." [22] But "the armour of an alienating identity" was a perfectly normal feature of a knightly aristocracy. That is, its identity crucially depended upon what Derrida calls both "a prosthetic body" and "a technical body or an institutional body." [23]

20. 1.2.200 [TLN 391], 1.2.227 [TLN 423], 228 [TLN 424], 1.4.52 [TLN 637].

21. *The Second Part of Henry the Sixt*, in *The Norton Facsimile: The First Folio of Shakespeare* (New York: Norton, 1968), ed. Charlton Hinman, 3.2.161 (TLN 1866); Thomas Heywood, *The English Traveller* (London, 1633), sig. Ev.

22. Jacques Lacan, "The Mirror Stage as Formative of the Function of the I as Revealed in Psychoanalytic Experience," in *Écrits*, trans. Alan Sheridan (New York: Norton, 1977), p. 4.

23. Jacques Derrida, *Specters of Marx: The State of the Debt, the Work of Mourning, and the New International*, trans. Peggy Kamuf (New York: Routledge, 1994), pp. 126–27.

This prosthetic body is given shape by the work of the armorer and by the emblems of genealogical identity. Assuming armor, the Ghost erases the memory of his fragmented body. The body that confronts Hamlet is monumentalized. Clad in the "very Armor he had on" when he defeated Fortinbras, the Ghost is fixed in the habit of triumphalism, even as he tells of his own overthrow. The armor brings with it its own memory system; it is itself the alienated but material ghost of the royal body.

Armor and Alienation

Armor as a form of clothing is at the furthest remove from the pliancy and absorbancy of cloth. In the Renaissance, it was both a protective carapace and a worked and engraved mnemonic system, inscribing aristocratic genealogy. The fantasy of armor was that unlike cloth it would not decay. Moreover, armor, unless it is given by the gods, is imagined as both the work and the wear of men. If women spin thread and life alike, armor is forged, not spun. But one of the ironies of Renaissance armor is that it was always already belated. The more glorious its ceremonial forms, the more pointless its promise of material preservation in the age of gunpowder. Moreover, not only does armor rust, and therefore like cloth decay, but, like cloth, it is transferrable from body to body.

The alienability of armor is already inscribed in the fate of Achilles. In Euripides' *Hecuba*, as I noted above, Achilles appears in "golden arms." Like the Ghost of Hamlet, Achilles comes back in his most heroic guise. But if armor is seen as conferring heroic identity, it is also detachable. For all the fantasy that armor will confer absolute identity—name and fame—the fate of Achilles' armor is in fact to be alienated. In the *Iliad*, Achilles' first suit of armor was given by the gods to his father, Peleus, from whom he inherited it. It is thus both a mark of the blessings of the gods and of the assimilation of the son to the father. Yet in book 16, Patroclus becomes the *therapon* or symbolic substitute for his friend, and, as he takes Achilles' place, he takes his armor. Patroclus is wearing Achilles' armor when he is killed. And it is Achilles' armor that Hector takes by stripping Patroclus. At first, Hector puts the armor of his great enemy in a chariot to have it taken back to Troy. But then, changing his mind, he puts it on himself. As Gary Wills puts it:

> The whole matter of shifts in identity, whereby men kill themselves over and over, is worked out . . . through the passage of Achilles' first

set of armor . . . to Patroclus and then to Hector. . . . [T]he Achilles who goes out in his divinely supplied second armor already fights as a dead man: and when he confronts his own armor, now carried on Hector, he kills himself a second time.²⁴

Not only is Achilles dispossessed of his armor, but his power is temporarily transferred to Hector. Even as Zeus prophesies the death of Hector, he bends the armor to fit Hector, who, in turn, literally grows to fit the armor:

> he made fit his lim
> To those great armes, to fill which vp the Warre god entred him,
> Austere and terrible: his ioynts and every part extends
> With strength and fortitude. . . .
> . . . He so shin'd that all could thinke no lesse
> But he resembl'd euery way great-soul'd Aeacides [Achilles].²⁵

Insofar as Achilles is absorbed into his own armor, he is detachable from himself, able to enter into his friend Patroclus or to be entered by Hector.

The detachability of armor enables it to reach out beyond a single body and to take hold of other bodies. Its detachability is, for instance, what enables it to join father to son. But it is also that detachability that makes it alienable. The vision of Achilles in "golden arms," then, is a nostalgic myth that erases the passage of his armor from body to body. It is the literal transference of armor that Shakespeare dramatizes in *Troilus and Cressida*. In the final act of the play, a stage direction reads *"Enter one in armour"* (5.6.26 [TLN 3462]). But the "one" is never identified, or only as a "[m]ost putrified core" (5.8.1 [TLN 3497]), and his "goodly armour" is the cause of his death. Hector kills him so as to "be maister of it" (5.6.30 [TLN 3467]). And it is when Hector has unarmed, prior to his putting on of the anonymous knight's armor, that he is struck down by Achilles and his Myrmidons. Indeed, martial combat had the dispossession of armor written into it. In the *Iliad*, Hector, having defeated Patroclus, takes his armor; in *Troilus and Cressida*, Hector kills a

---

24. Gary Wills, "Homer Alive," *New York Review of Books* 39, no. 8 (April 23, 1992): 42. For our account of armor in Homer, and of its relevance to Shakespeare, I am indebted to John Parker.

25. *Chapman's Homer,* ed. Allardyce Nicoll, vol. 1, *The Iliad* (London: Routledge and Kegan Paul, 1957), 16.180–84.

man so as to possess his armor; in Kyd's *The Spanish Tragedy,* the armor of the defeated Balthazar is awarded to Horatio.[26]

Not only does armor change hands; for all its power to endure, it grows old, falls out of fashion, rusts. In fact, the hanging of real armor on the walls above tombs was becoming increasingly rare because it was an expensive "waste" and because the armor was liable to be stolen. Funeral armor was sometimes made of wood, and even when steel armor was used, it was often composed of mismatched and disposable parts from different periods.[27] And the professional theaters of Renaissance England played their own part in the transformations of the material ghosts of chivalry. Henry Peacham's drawing of *Titus Andronicus* shows six of the seven actors on stage wearing some kind of armor. The theater itself had become a collector and renter of armor, transforming the insignia of martial prowess into money-making display. But the theatrical stagings often suggested that armor was outmoded. One of Titus's sons, according to Martin Holmes, is wearing a "Gothic cuirass of about 1480, that had found its way eventually to a theatrical wardrobe." [28] *Hamlet* itself, for all the Ghost's armor, marks the outdatedness of this martial attire. If Old Hamlet fought in armor and with a sword, his son will fight without armor and with a rapier.[29] If clothes are often mocked for their fashionable innovations, armor is often suggestive of the antiquated. In *Measure for Measure,* Claudius talks of the unenforced laws as having "(like vn-scowr'd Armor) hung by th' wall" (1.2.167 [TLN 260]). In *Troilus and Cressida,* Ulysses argues that to rest on one's reputation is

> to hang
> Quite out of fashion, like a rustie male,
> In monumentall mockrie.
> (3.3.152 [TLN 2004–06])

26. Thomas Kyd, *The Spanish Tragedy,* in *The Works of Thomas Kyd,* ed. Frederick S. Boas (Oxford: Clarendon Press, 1955), 1.2.190.
27. See Nigel Llewellyn, *The Art of Death: Visual Culture in the English Death Ritual, c. 1500– c. 1800* (London: Reaktion Books, 1991), p. 68; Litten, *The English Way of Death,* pp. 176–81.
28. Martin Holmes, *Shakespeare and His Players* (London: John Murray, 1972), 152. I am indebted to Holmes's account of stage armor throughout this paragraph.
29. On the "unrecoverable heroic world" of sword-and-buckler and "the sequestration of violence to the bureaucratic state," see Sheldon P. Zittner, "Hamlet, Duellist," in *Hamlet: Critical Essays,* ed. Joseph G. Price (New York: Garland, 1986), pp. 123–43, esp. pp. 124–28.

The rusty chainmail is, at the same time, a hero whose time has gone by, an out-of-date male.

In *Pericles,* "rustie male" and "vn-scowr'd Armor" are literally staged. When Pericles has been washed ashore in a storm, bereft "of all his fortunes," the fishermen give him "a rusty Armour." [30] It is this rusty armor that enables Pericles to participate in the tournament that Simonides holds for his daughter Thaisa's birthday, and it is thus the precondition for his wooing and wedding of Thaisa. But the armor's decay marks him out to the spectators as "the meane Knight" (sig. C4v [2.2.58 S.D.]). Pericles armor is indeed the subject of mockery: the First Lord sneers that "by his rustie outside, he appeares, / To haue practis'd more the Whipstocke, then the Launce" (sig. C4v [2.2.49–50]); and the Third Lord jests that Pericles has "let his Armour rust" so that it will be scoured in the dust when he is dismounted (sig. C4v [2.2.53–54]). But Simonides rebukes them with a curiously garbled version of the conventional piety that the clothes are not the person:

> Opinion's but a foole, that makes vs scan
> The outward habit, by the inward man.
> (sig. C4v [2.2.55–56])

From Steevens onward, editors have emended the line to make it conform to the notion that we cannot judge inward "being" from outward "seeming." But we should note how distant this view is from Pericles' own. For it is the armor that is both the identifier of his status, however decayed, and, at the same time, the material mnemonic that joins him to his father. Having lost his armor along with all his other possessions in the storm, he says: "What I haue been, I haue forgot to know" (sig. C 2v [2.1.71]). Without the support of his material memory systems, he has no identity.

He is in fact rescued by the fishermen, one of whom clothes him ("I haue a Gowne heere, come put it on, keepe thee warme" [sig. C3 (2.1.78–79)]), thus conferring a new identity and set of obligations upon him. And it is the fishermen who draw out of the sea the armor with which Pericles will "repaire [him] selfe" (sig. C3v [2.1.121]). Not only does this armor enable him to participate in Simonides' tournament, it also repairs his memory and his name:

---

30. *Pericles, Prince of Tyre,* in *Shakespeare's Plays in Quarto,* ed. Allen and Muir, sig. C3 (2.1.118). All further references are in the text.

It was mine owne part of my heritage,
Which my dead Father did bequeath to me,
With this strict charge, euen as he left his life,
Keepe it my *Perycles*, it hath been a Shield
Twixt me and death. . . .
It kept where I kept, I so dearely lou'd it.
(sig. C3v [2.1.122–29])

As in so many aristocratic wills, as in the case of Achilles, Pericles' armor
has been transmitted to him by his father. For Pericles, indeed, the armor
comes to stand in for his father ("It kept where I kept, I so dearely lou'd
it"). But the armor is not clearly his. For it is through the fishermen's labor
that the armor is recovered and their labor entitles them to lay claim to it.
As the Second Fisherman says, "['T]was wee that made vp this Garment
through the rough seames of the Waters" (sig. C3v [2.1.147–49]). The language of the Second Fisherman recalls the language of tailoring, of those
artisanal rather than aristocratic labors through which the armor first came
into being. For it was craftsmen, not gods, who "made vp this Garment."
The fisherman thus opens up the question of ownership and entitlement.
Even Pericles is aware of the fishermen's entitlement and has to "begge" of
them "this [not "his"] Coate of worth" (sig. C3v [2.1.135]).

The scene is an extraordinary one in showing the prince as being literally "made vp" through the labors of the poor. The fishermen first clothe
Pericles and then restore his armor to him, and they also give up their own
clothes to prepare him for the tournament. For after the armor is given to
him, Pericles is still "vnprouided of a paire of Bases" (sig. C4 [2.1.159–60]).
"Bases" were the pleated skirts of velvet or rich brocade attached to the
doublet and reaching from the waist to the knee. And even these bases will
be provided by the fishermen. As the Second Fisherman says:

Wee'le sure prouide, thou shalt haue
My best Gowne to make thee a paire.
(sig. C4 [2.1.161–62])

When one recalls the extraordinarily high percentage of the wealth of the
poor that was stored in the few clothes that they possessed, one recognizes
that in giving away his "best Gowne," the fisherman is giving away much
of his wealth. The fisherman asks for a single thing in return for his gifts:
"I hope sir, if thou thriue, you'le remember from whence you had them"

(sig. C 3v [2.1.150–51]). Indebtedness will take the form of memory itself, the right of the fishermen to enter the social memory system, along with Pericles' father and Pericles himself.

But Pericles does not remember the fishermen. They disappear from the play, having given up their best clothes and their richest catch, never to be heard of again. It is the productions of armorers and, in *Pericles,* of fishermen that create the material supports of aristocratic memory. But as the aristocrats consume those productions, they also consume the memories of those who made them. The aristocrats are, in fact, the "rich Misers" whom the First Fisherman denounces; hoarding their own memories, they erase the remembrance of the poor. Like whales, "the great ones eate vp the little ones." For armor and clothes tell a history of their producers different from that of their consumers. As in the writing of history itself, it is the proud possessors who are commemorated. History, Sir Walter Ralegh wrote, "hath made us acquainted with our dead Ancestors; and, out of the depth and darkness of the earth, delivered us their memory and fame." [31] But whose memory and fame are rescued? As the prefatory letter to Edward Hall's *The Union of the Two Noble and Illustre Famelies of Lancastre & Yorke* puts it: "What diuersitie is betwene a noble prince and a poore begger . . . if after their death there be left of them no remembrance or token?" [32] The remembrances and tokens of the fishermen are taken by Pericles, but not so as to record their memory. As their possessions and labor are alienated from them, so is Pericles' memory of them. And yet, in the play itself, the fishermen's gifts of armor and clothes are staged as the material preconditions that haunt the story of "the meane Knight."

Hauntings

Who gets to be a ghost in the first place? Who gets to make the demand "Remember me"? Who gets to haunt? One of the strangest things about haunting is the word itself. It appears that the word was first used in rela-

31. Sir Walter Ralegh, *The History of the World* (London, 1677), "Preface," sig. Bv. I am indebted for this and the following quote to Rackin, *Stages of History,* pp. 3–5, and, more generally, to her fine account of the emergence of "history" at the expense of the dispossessed. See, in particular, chapters 1, 4, and 5.
32. Edward Hall, *The Union of the Two Noble and Illustre Famelies of Lancastre & Yorke* (London, 1548), sig. B1.

tion to ghosts in the drama of the 1590s. The OED (not, of course, that it is always reliable on these questions) gives *Midsummer Night's Dream* as the first occurrence of "haunt" to mean "to visit frequently or habitually with manifestations of [the] influence and presence" "of imaginary or spiritual beings, ghosts etc.": "O monstrous. O strange. We are haunted. Pray masters: fly masters: helpe."[33] When Oberon reiterates "haunted" a scene later, it is surely in the older sense of the word, although it will not be interpreted that way by most modern readers. Oberon says to Puck: "How now, mad spirit?/ What night rule now about this haunted grove?" (3.2.5). Oberon, the king of the fairies, is not worried about ghosts; rather, he is referring to the overpopulation of the grove by mortals. But the new sense of haunting in reference to spirits that *Midsummer Night's Dream* records seems above all to have emerged in the professional theater of the late sixteenth century. The next two references that the OED gives to this new sense are from *Richard II* ("Some haunted by the Ghosts they haue depos'd" [3.2.158]) and from Marston's *Antonio's Revenge* ("Bug-beares and spirits haunted him" [3.2]). Prior to the 1590s, the word simply meant to practice or to use habitually, to resort to a place habitually, to associate with someone habitually. ("Diuers and sundry goldes . . . yee may reduce into your vsuall money, such as you daily haunt [i. e. 'use']"; "I haue charg'd thee not to haunt about my doores"; "Their populous and great haunted cities"; "Africke hath euer beene the least knowen and haunted parte in the worlde.")

It is fascinating to note that as the theaters conjured up the hauntings of spirits, they were increasingly attacked as familiar "haunts" of ill resort. Gosson wrote in 1579 that "the abuse of such places [theaters] was so great, that for any chaste liuer to *haunt* them was a black swan, and a white crowe."[34] Similarly, William Prynne derides "play-*haunters* upon common playes and maskes in our publicke theatres," and Milton attacks the "Animadverter" as one who "*haunts* Playhouses and Bordelloes."[35] The theater itself ironically incorporated this sense of itself as a dangerous haunt.

33. *A Midsommer nights dreame* (London, 1600) in *Shakespeare's Plays in Quarto,* ed. Allen and Muir, sig. D2v, 3.1.107.
34. Stephen Gosson, *The Schoole of Abuse,* ed. Edward Arber (London, 1868), 30.
35. William Prynne, *Documents Relating to the Proceedings against William Prynne,* ed. Samuel Rawson Gardiner, Camden Society n.s. vol. 18 (1877), p. 49; John Milton, *Apology for Smectymnus,* in *The Complete Prose Works of John Milton,* ed. Don M. Wolfe et al. (New Haven, Conn.: Yale University Press, 1953), 1:886. See also Sir Henry Wotton's reference to "Haunters of theatres," *Reliquiae Wottonianae* (London, 1651), 84.

In *The Devil Is an Ass,* Merecraft tells Everill that he has been undone by "haunting / The *Globes,* and *Mermaides!*"[36] On the one hand, "haunting" seems to be one of those antithetical words that Freud analyzed in his essay on "The Uncanny." He noted there that the word *heimlich* could mean both "homely," "familiar," and exactly the opposite: "unhomely," "unfamiliar" — "haunted," one might say.[37] "Haunting" splits in antithetical directions: from an action that suggests familiarity and habit to an action that suggests profound disturbance and the shattering of habit; from the desire to repeat to terror at the unfamiliar ("flye masters: helpe"). But, on the other hand, these antithetical senses of "haunting" start to inhabit each other. For those who attacked the theaters saw them both as overpopular (like "populous and great haunted Cities") and as "Devil-haunted," that is, both as places of overfamiliarity and as the disruption of all familiarity.

I would note, though, that the haunting of ghosts emerges as part of a theatrical apparatus. That is, it is manifestly contrived: it requires the costumes, the trapdoors, the special effects of the new professional theater,[38] a theater which, as Steven Mullaney has argued, profoundly displaces the familiar *topoi* or places of the dominant culture. "Haunting" thus parallels the later "phantasmagoria," which, as Terry Castle has shown, is first used to describe the specters created by magic-lantern shows at the beginning of the nineteenth century.[39] In both cases, the uncanny is produced through spectacular technologies.[40] This sense of ghosts as theatrical productions is explicit in John Gee's critique of the "Apparitions of two new female Ghosts" in *New Shreds of the old Snare* (1624). Gee argues that Catholicism itself is merely an imitation of the theater, and an expensive one at

36. Ben Jonson, *The Devil Is an Ass,* in *Ben Jonson,* ed. C. H. Herford, Percy and Evelyn Simpson, vol. 6 (Oxford: Clarendon Press, 1954), 3.3.25–26.

37. Sigmund Freud, "The Uncanny," in *The Standard Edition of the Complete Psychological Works of Sigmund Freud,* ed. James Strachey (London: Hogarth Press, 1955), 17:218–52, especially pp. 220–26.

38. For a full account of the auditory and visual materialization of the "ghostly" by thunder and lightning, see Leslie Thomson, "The Meaning of *Thunder and Lightning:* Stage Directions and Audience Expectations," *Early Theatre* (forthcoming).

39. Terry Castle, "Phantasmagoria: Spectral Technology and the Metaphors of Modern Reverie," *Critical Inquiry* 15, no. 1 (1988): 26–51.

40. Stephen Greenblatt has written brilliantly about the Renaissance theater's ambivalent relation to magic and technology throughout his work. See in particular *Learning to Curse: Essays in Early Modern Culture* (New York: Routledge, 1990), pp. 161–63.

that: "The *Jesuites* being or having *Actors* of such dexteritie, I see no reason but that they should set up a company for themselves, which surely will put down The *Fortune, Red-bull, Cock-pit, & Globe.* . . . *[T]hey make their spectators pay to[o] deare for their Income.* Representations and apparitions from the dead might be seen farr cheaper at other Play-houses. As for example the Ghost in *Hamblet, Don Andreas Ghost* in *Hieronimo.*" [41] But if Renaissance ghosts are seen to emerge from the machinery of professional entertainment, their demand to be remembered depends upon their paradoxical claim that they have been displaced. Murdered and cast out from their homes (the places they haunted when alive), they return to reclaim what has been taken away from them, to reassert the property/propriety that the professional theaters dislocated for commercial gain. For within the staged fictions, ghosts produce terror so as to memorialize their rights to what they consider to be their own. As Jane Cooper asks in "Being Southern": "When is memory transforming? when, a form of real estate?" [42]

For something to be your own, you have to own it. And the question of ownership casts an unexpected light on the ghosts of the Renaissance theater: with important exceptions, these ghosts are materially and legally entitled, even though performed by actors who are tenuously entitled at best. Most stage ghosts have active stakes in inheritance, which is both about the ownership of the future and about the control of memory. Most of these ghosts are the revenants of men and of aristocratic men at that: Andrea in *The Spanish Tragedy;* Andrugio in *Antonio's Tragedy;* Hamlet in *Hamlet;* Banquo in *Macbeth;* Alonzo in *The Changeling;* Brachiano in *The White Devil.* They return to claim a future that they "properly" own and that has been taken away from them. There is nothing given about this predominance of male ghosts. Of Aeschylus's two ghosts, one was a woman: Clytemnestra. And Seneca's (or at least the pseudo-Seneca's) one nonprologue ghost was Agrippina in *Octavia.* But the Renaissance theaters did not, on the whole, follow this precedent.

More striking still is the fact that in the 1590s, there was a wave of female ghosts in narrative poetry. These ghosts stemmed from the extraordinary if belated influence of Thomas Churchyard's poem on Jane Shore, the mistress of Edward IV, printed in the 1563 edition of the *Mirror for Magistrates.* Jane Shore, though, is the antithesis of the "inheritance" ghosts of the

41. John Gee, *New Shreds of the old Snare* (London, 1624), pp. 17, 20.
42. Jane Cooper, *Green Notebook, Winter Road* (Gardiner, Me.: Tilbury House, 1994), p. 27.

Renaissance stage: not only was she a commoner, being a citizen's wife, but she was a woman. What did it mean to bring back such a person from the dead? What could be her claim to be remembered? When Samuel Daniel reused the form of the female complaint for *The Complaint of Rosamond* in 1592, it was self-consciously to memorialize the unremembered, to bring back to life a woman whose memory had been erased. Rosamond was, according to legend, the mistress of Henry II and, according to Daniel's poem, her tomb at Godstowe nunnery had been destroyed.[43] It is this very erasure of name and fame which raises the ghost of the dead woman, who appeals to the poet to be remembered, having been immured in a castle when alive and forgotten when dead. Daniel's poem was immensely popular and created a vogue for female complaints by women commoners: Thomas Lodge's Elstred, Anthony Shute's Jane Shore, ballads in Deloney's *Garland of Good Will* on Rosamund, Jane Shore, and Elstred, Churchyard's rewritten Jane Shore, all published or registered in 1593, and Michael Drayton's and Richard Barnfield's Matildas, both published in 1594.[44] At the very time when ghosts were stalking the professional stage, then, there was a vogue for the ghosts of women commoners in narrative poetry.

The revenge plays, though, usually turned their backs upon both the avenging Clytemnestra of Greek tragedy and the revenants of women commoners like Jane Shore. They more commonly staged the ghosts of the patriarchal father and the husband/lover. This father or husband, though maimed in death, returns to claim the inheritance of the future. Banquo's progeny will rule even "till the crack of doom." But Banquo's ghost is unique in this regard. No other revenge ghost so successfully restores his inheritance to its supposedly rightful owner. In *Antonio's Revenge*, Antonio, the most successful of stage revengers, is spurred on by the ghost of his father, but having achieved his ends, he refuses to take back the kingdom and, turning from his patrimony to mourn for his beloved Mellida, he withdraws to a monastery. In other words, he rejects rule, inheritance, and the control of the future in favor of private grief. Moreover, he memorializes

43. Samuel Daniel, "The Complaint of Rosamond" in ed. Alexander B. Grosart, *The Complete Works . . . of Samuel Daniel* (London: Hazell, Watson, and Viney, 1885), vol. 1, p. 112, lines 869–82; see also Hallett Smith, *Elizabethan Poetry: A Study in Conventions, Meaning, and Expression* (Cambridge, Mass.: Harvard University Press, 1952), p. 106.
44. Smith, *Elizabethan Poetry*, pp. 108–19.

not the father who demands to be remembered but "th'immortal fame of virgin faith" (5.3.178).

Nowhere is the demand for patriarchal remembrance more insistent and yet more thwarted than in *Hamlet*. The problems begin with how to name a ghost who claims paternal authority. To Marcellus, Barnardo, and Horatio, the Ghost is "it": "Speake to it *Horatio*"; "Marke it"; "It is offended." But to the son, the Ghost, because dressed in his father's armor, cannot be "it" although it is only questionably "he": "Ile *call* thee *Hamlet*, / King, Father, Royall Dane" (my emphasis).⁴⁵ And if Hamlet can ascribe the name "King" to this apparition, that appellation is given to Claudius alone in stage directions and speech prefixes alike. When he first enters in Q2, which is the only text in which the name "Claudius" occurs, the stage direction calls him "*Claudius, King of Denmarke*" (1.2 [TLN 176]), and although the first speech prefix reads "*Claud.*" (1.2.1 [TLN 179]), he is uniformly "*King*" thereafter. Old Hamlet, on the other hand, however physically present in his suit of armor, is never fully interpellated through his name (he is, simply, "Ghost") and never fully interpellates the son whom he haunts, despite having given Hamlet his name. As Janet Adelman notes, Hamlet's memory of his father is constantly subsumed by his disgust at his mother's remarriage.⁴⁶ The Ghost's constant demand that Hamlet should "remember" is equally constantly rewritten as a memory of the bed on which the king and queen, that is Claudius and Gertrude, lie. Hamlet's memory is thus of the physical displacement of his father's body by his uncle's.

But it is also a memory of the scandal of his mother still sleeping in his father's bed. For the rules of inheritance, in the England of the Globe theater, if not in the Denmark of Hamlet, increasingly laid down that the bed of the father should become the bed of the eldest son, as the armor of the father became the armor of the son. That is, while widows had, at least in the sixteenth century, usually been allowed bench right, or a third of the profits from their husband's estates for their own lifetime, they were commonly excluded from the house and from the bed which they had occupied with their husbands. As far as the goods of the house were concerned, widows could only officially claim "paraphernalia," which in

---

45. *Hamlet*, 1.1.45, 43, 50 (TLN 54, 55, 63), 1.4.44–45 (TLN 629–30).
46. Janet Adelman, *Suffocating Mothers: Fantasies of Maternal Origin in Shakespeare's Plays*, Hamlet *to* The Tempest (New York: Routledge, 1992), pp. 11–37.

common law was limited to their dress, jewels, and immediate personal belongings. And even these a widow could not legally bequeath without her husband's permission. They were officially hers only while she lived, to be returned after her death to the heir. The widow kept her clothes; the heir got the father's bed.

The significance of the bed lay partly in its literal cost. As Amy Louise Erikson observes, "of household items, the most valuable piece of furniture was the bed." In 1616, one Sussex yeoman unusually left his best featherbed with all its "appurtenances" to his wife, Agnes Mockford, but he did so only on the condition that she sign a "dede of release in the law of all hir dower" with the exception of £3 a year. The bed was thus thought to be equivalent in value to a dower. In analyzing the inventories of working people in the seventeenth century, Erikson notes that a cottage could be bought for the price of five to ten beds, whereas today a modest house would cost the price of at least eighty luxurious beds.[47] Of course, the aristocracy owned much more, and their beds accounted for a smaller proportion of their household valuables. Yet their beds were both extraordinarily costly and symbolically charged as the site of patrilineal inheritance.[48] As Sasha Roberts points out in an important article on English Renaissance beds, the inventories of Charles I's domestic goods in 1651 valued his Raphael cartoons as £300; his bed, with its rich furnishings, was valued at £1,000.[49] The economic value of the bed materialized its significance as a site of memory.

In *The Odyssey*, the connection between the bed and family "roots" is literalized: Odysseus carves his bed out of a rooted tree and his home is built around it. And the power of the bed as a materialization of the relation between husband and wife and as a site of crisis is worked out in *Othello*, as well as in other plays after 1600 that increasingly used the bed as an important theatrical prop.

47. Amy Louise Erikson, *Women and Property in Early Modern England* (London: Routledge, 1993), 65.

48. Jasper Griffin comments on the symbolic significance of Odysseus's bed: "The bed . . . turns into the vital key which allows husband and wife to find each other at last. Odysseus built it, as part of his house; unmoved and unrevealed to any outsiders, it embodies the solidity and wholeness of their union" (*Homer on Life and Death* [Oxford: Clarendon Press, 1980], 13).

49. Sasha Roberts, "Lying among the Classics: Ritual and Motif in Elite Elizabethan and Jacobean Beds," in *Albion's Classicism: The Visual Arts in Britain, 1550–1660*, ed. Lucy Gent (New Haven, Conn.: Yale University Press, 1995), p. 327.

The connection between the best bed and patrilineal inheritance is implied in Shakespeare's own will, which contains the famous phrase: "I gyve vnto my wief my second best bed with the furniture." The best bed, together with his sword, would have gone to his son Hamnet, if he had survived. Given the absence of a male heir, the bed, together with the Stratford house itself, went to his daughter, Susanna Hall and to "her heires for ever."[50] His dead son, Hamnet, is indirectly conjured up in the gift of 26s. 8d. to "Hamlett Sadler," the probable godfather of Hamnet, to buy a mourning ring. More striking and unusual is the emphatic expression of the intent to take back the property from the female heirs and give it to male heirs.[51] The will goes to extraordinary lengths to insist upon male inheritance. The majority of the property is to be left to Susanna Hall "for & during the terme of her naturall lief,"

& after her Deceas to the first sonne of her bodie lawfullie yssueing & to the heires Males of the bodie of the saied first Sonne lawfullie yssueing, & for defalt of such issue to the second Sonne of her bodie lawfullie issueing and (so [deleted]) to the heires Males of the bodie of the saied Second Sonne lawfullie yssueinge, & for defalt of such heires to the third Sonne of the bodie of the saied Susanna Lawfullie yssueing and of the heires Males of the bodie of the saied third sonne lawfullie yssueing, And for defalt of such issue the same soe to be & Remaine to the ffourth (sonne [deleted]) ffyfth sixte and Seaventh sonnes of her bodie lawfullie issueing one after Another & to the heires Males of the bodies of the said fourth fifth Sixte & Seaventh sonnes lawfullie yssueing, in such manner as yt ys before Lymitted to be & Remaine to the first second and third Sonns of her bodie and to the heires Males; And for defalt of such issue the said premisses to be & Remaine to my sayd Neece Hall & the heires males of her bodie Lawfullie yssueing, and for defalt of issue to my daughter Judith & the heires Males of her bodie lawfullie yssueing.[52]

50. E. K. Chambers, William Shakespeare: A Study of Facts and Problems (Oxford: Clarendon Press, 1930), 2: 170.
51. On the extent to which Shakespeare's will breaks with customary forms, see E. A. J. Honigman, "The Second-Best Bed," New York Review of Books 38, no. 18 (November 7, 1991): 27–30; and Richard Wilson, Will Power: Essays on Shakespearean Authority (London: Harvester Wheatsheaf, 1993), pp. 184–237. I am generally indebted to Wilson's suggestive account.
52. Chambers, William Shakespeare, 2:173.

There is a certain comedy to this document in which a man without lawful male heirs tried (unsuccessfully, as it turned out) to write male heirs into his future. Having failed of lawful male heirs himself, Shakespeare bequeathed his sword outside the family to his Stratford neighbor, Thomas Combe.[53] What is not at all comic about the will is the active dispossession of the wife, the second daughter and the grandaughters, along with second sons and any illegitimate children.[54] They are to have no part in the property, which (like the sword and the mourning ring) is a *memory system*—a mnemonic to attach father to eldest son, father to eldest son, even till the crack of doom. Cast out of the best bed and out of the house, the widow is detached from the place and the things in which her own memories are stored.

This situation is almost exactly reversed in *Hamlet*. Here, there is a male heir, but he does not inherit the best bed. There is a widow, but she is not cast out of the house; indeed, she continues to sleep in the best bed, as if in deliberate defiance of Ralegh's axiom: "If thy wife love again let her not enjoy her second love in the same bed wherein she loved thee."[55] The dead patriarch is left with the widow's lot: namely, his paraphernalia—a suit of armor and a nightgown. It is Gertrude who inherits and who thus remains at the center of the memory system from which widows were increasingly excluded.[56] The father's bed becomes that of the mother, the father's sheets those of the mother. This disposition of goods is in striking opposition to the patrilineal fantasy inscribed in Sir Thomas Hungerford's will, where

53. Chambers, *William Shakespeare*, 2:172.

54. Shakespeare's will is not normative. The rigorous enforcement of patrilineal inheritance seems to have been resisted by most working people in early modern England. While sons normally inherited land (with the exception of Yorkshire, where daughters also inherited), land itself was so frequently bought and sold that in Terling, Essex, of a sample of twenty-one freeholds, not a single one remained in the male line during the seventeenth century. Even if daughters did not usually inherit land, "their parents tended to compensate them with a substantially larger share of moveable goods than their brothers had, in order to approximately balance all children's shares of parental wealth." Erikson, *Women and Property*, pp. 66, 224.

55. Quoted in Wilson, *Will Power*, p. 210.

56. On the diminishing rights of widows to dower in the Renaissance, see Wilson, *Will Power*, pp. 209-10. But for a more detailed analysis of the complex legal situation, see Erikson, *Women and Property*, and Tim Stretton, *Women Waging Law in Elizabethan England* (Cambridge: Cambridge University Press, 1998).

his beds, "all wayes as long as the said beddes will endure," will "remayne from heire to heire in worship and memory of my lord, my father, Walter, Lord Hungerford, that first ordeyned them and paid for them." [57] In *Hamlet*, in a wonderful reversal of the customary rules of inheritance, the father is excluded. "Must I remember?" exclaims Hamlet. But what he has to remember is that the material bearers of the memory of his father are either disposed of (like Gertrude's mourning clothes) or in the hands of his mother (like his father's bed):

> Must I remember. . . .
> A little month or ere those shooes were old
> With which she followed my poore fathers bodie
> Like *Niobe* all teares. . . .
> She married, o most wicked speede; to post
> With such dexteritie to incestious sheets.
> (Q2, 1.2.147–57 [TLN 331–41])

It is Gertrude and Claudius who now possess (who *haunt* in its older sense of "habitually use," "habitually occupy") what the Ghost calls "the royall bed of Denmark" (1.5.82 [TLN 767]) [58] and what Hamlet, deprived of the idealized but thoroughly material memories of patriarchal inheritance, reimagines as "an inseemed bed" (3.4.92 [TLN 2469]) with "incestious sheets."

The more powerful the imagination of the queen's haunting of "the royall bed of Denmark," the less powerful the hauntings of the dead father. The Ghost enters for the last time at the moment when Hamlet, yet again, is magnifying his father at his uncle's expense. Claudius is, he declaims,

> A slaue that is not twentieth part the kyth
> Of your precedent Lord, a vice of Kings,
> A cut-purse of the Empire and the rule,
> That from a shelfe the precious Diadem stole
> And put it in his pocket.
> (Q2, 3.4.97–101 [TLN 2476–80])

57. Quoted in Roberts, "Lying among the Classics," 327.
58. The public significance of the "royall bed" is frequently noted in Shakespeare's plays. In *The Winter's Tale*, Dion recommends remarriage to Leontes "to blesse the Bed of Majesty again" (5.1.33 [TLN 2765]); in *Richard II*, Bolingbroke accuses Richard's favorites of breaking "the possession of a Royall Bed" (3.1.13 [TLN 1325]); in *Henry V*, Henry speaks of the king's "Bed Maiesticall" (4.1.267 [TLN 2117]).

But Hamlet's speech, while denigrating Claudius, dethrones his father. His father, the monarch, does not wear the crown: the crown simply sits on a shelf for any cutpurse to lift. "The precious Diadem" is the material sign both of Claudius's acquisition of the monarchy and, in his pocket, of his power to soil state and marriage bed through his marriage to the queen. The revenant father is thus stripped of armor, of crown, of wife, and finally of the monopoly of memory itself. Revenge takes place as if by accident, and in the absence of the Ghost. It is Gertrude, widow, wife, mother, queen, who remains to haunt Hamlet, to assert, against the monopoly of male inheritance, the material place of women in the system of memory.

In fact, the dislocation of paternal inheritance is prefigured by the failure of the son to resemble the father, despite the identity of name. This failure of resemblance is quite literal. The son wears an inky cloak and suit of solemn black at the beginning of the play, and he moves toward an increasingly unarmored state. He visually refuses his father's legacy: he does not do the very thing that an aristocratic funeral enacts—inherit his father's armor. Although Hamlet takes upon himself the Ghost's demand, although he re-iterates, and reverses, his father's conflict with Fortinbras, although he is buried as a soldier with "[t]he Souldiours Musicke, and the rites of Warre," he never becomes his armored father (5.2.399 [TLN 3900]).

It is as if the solidity of the armored father transforms his son into a ragged creature, like those ghosts who return from the grave maimed and wearing their winding-cloths. Indeed, the Ghost, clad "in compleat steele," seems to materialize at the expense of the dematerialization of his ob-servers, who are "distil'd / Almost to gelly" (1.2.205 [TLN 396]). Hamlet, "the glasse of fashion, and the mould of forme, / Th'obseru'd of all obseruers" (3.1.153–54 [TLN 1809–10]) is displaced by a pale figure clad only in his shirt. He appears to Ophelia

> with his doublet all vnbrac'd,
> No hat vpon his head, his stockins fouled,
> Vngartred, and down gyued to his ancle,
> Pale as his shirt, his knees knocking each other,
> And with a looke so pittious in purport
> As if he had been loosed out of hell
> To speake of horrors.
> (2.1.74–81 [TLN 973–80])

It is this image of Hamlet, stripped to his linen like madman or ghost, that stuck in the imagination of those who recalled the play: Hamlet less as a man of words than as an unclothed revenant. The hero of Anthony Scoloker's 1604 poem *Diaphantus,* for instance,

> Puts off his cloathes; his shirt he onely weares,
> Much like mad-*Hamlet.*[59]

In Dekker's appropriation of Hamlet as figure for a "counterfet mad man," the man's clothes are torn like a Bedlamite: "furious *Hamlet* woulde presently eyther breake loose like a Beare from the stake, or else so set his pawes on this dog that thus bayted him, that with tugging and tearing one anothers frockes off, they both looked like mad *Tom* of Bedlam."[60] When Hamlet returns from England, he writes to Claudius in a curiously ambiguous phrase that he is "set naked on your Kingdome" (4.7.43–44 [TLN 3054–55]). It seems, in other words, as if Hamlet gets ever more distant from the armor which his father wears, but ever more like a ghost as it was customarily imagined, "naked" and disheveled. At the same time, in putting an "antic disposition" on, Hamlet becomes the fool or court jester. And it is the court jester, Yorick, not his father, whom Hamlet most fondly recalls: "[H]e hath borne me on his backe a thousand times: And how abhorred in my Imagination is, my gorge rises at it. Heere hung those lipps, that I have kist I know not how oft" (5.1.185–89 [TLN 3374–76]). The lips that he has kissed: the lips not of the father but of the jester.

One of the striking features of Alleyn's inventory of the costumes of the Admiral's Men in 1598 is a list of "Antik sutes."[61] It is not entirely clear whether "antik" here means antique or belonging to the jester, since the two words were usually written alike. Perhaps "antik" means both, since the list includes both cloth of gold and of silver and "will somers cote."[62] If the suit had belonged to Will Summers, it was both "antique" and "antic," a memorial to the power of the fool to reach out with his mocking legacy into the present. Though Yorick is dead, his skull memorializes the legacy

59. Anthony Scoloker, *Diaphantus, or the Passions of Loue* (London, 1604), sig. E4v.
60. Thomas Dekker, *The Dead Tearme* (London, 1608), sig. G3.
61. *Henslowe's Diary,* ed. R. A. Foakes and R. T. Rickert (Cambridge: Cambridge University Press, 1961), p. 318.
62. Walter W. Greg, *Henslowe Papers* (London: A. H. Bullen), pp. 53, 54.

he leaves, a legacy which includes the "antic disposition" which Hamlet, his illegitimate heir, puts on. In striking contrast to *The Spanish Tragedy*, where the ghost returns gloatingly to conclude the plot, the Ghost of *Hamlet* simply disappears after act 3.[63] One might say that the ghost of the jester displaces the ghost of the soldier-king.

But if we are to believe the so-called bad Q1, the soldier-king had been displaced even before act 3. In the bedchamber scene, as Hamlet berates his mother, the stage direction reads "Enter the ghost in his night gowne" (3.4.101 [TLN 2482]). Nearly all editions delay this entry by a single line, the line where Hamlet says: "A King of shreds and patches" (3.4.102 [TLN 2483]). Moved to this position, the line can refer only to Claudius (especially if, as in many modern productions, the Ghost is still wearing armor). But in its earlier position in Q1, Q2, and F1 alike, the line seems to hover between the mock king who rules and the dead king who returns, no longer clad in complete steel, but in a robe of undress, a nightgown. "A King of shreds and patches": the father, like the son, *as* jester, denuded of his armor, yet still "my Father in his habite, as he liued" (3.4.135 [TLN 2518]). The bedchamber scene, in fact, suggests the unnaming and renaming of father and mother alike. Hamlet, the old King, returns for the last time, vulnerable now, no longer the warrior hero, as if the relative impermanence of cloth prefigures his own impermanence.

Yet when Hamlet fantasizes the transformation of his own body, it is not into steel. On the contrary, he wants his "too too sallied [F1, solid] flesh" to "melt / Thaw and resolue it selfe into a dewe" (1.2.129–30 [TLN 313–14]). Nor does he figure memory in terms of monumentalizing brass or stone but in terms of a commonplace book or the assumption of clothes. At the beginning of the play, it is true, Hamlet emphasizes the insufficiency of clothes as memory: they are "but the trappings and the suites of woe" (1.2.86 [TLN 267]). His claim, though, at least in Q2, is that it is not "alone" his incky cloake" or "customary suites of solembe blacke" that can "deuote" [F1, "denote"] him truly (1.2.77–78 [TLN 258–59]). Having cast off her mourning

---

63. The significance of the *absence* of the Ghost at the conclusion of the play struck Alexandre Dumas who, for his 1847 production, rewrote the final act with the Ghost at the center of the action. Having pronounced on the deaths of Laertes, Gertrude, and Claudius, his sentence to Hamlet is: "Tu vivras!" ["You will live!"]. Dumas's version thus works in the opposite direction from Shakespeare's, toward the reconciliation of father and son. See Romy Heylen, *Translation, Poetics, and the Stage: Six French Hamlets* (New York: Routledge, 1993), pp. 53–55.

clothes, Gertrude has ceased to devote herself to the memory of her dead husband. Retaining his mourning clothes, and thus refusing to celebrate the remarriage of his mother, Hamlet attempts to perpetuate his father's memory, even if his clothes alone are inadequate for the work of mourning. He reiterates the significance of clothing when, attacking the "frailty" of Gertrude, he claims that, between the funeral and the marriage, it has been

> A little month or ere those shooes were old
> With which she followed my poore fathers bodie.
> (1.2.1147–48 [TLN 331–32])

Taking off her mourning shoes, Gertrude takes her feet out of the past. She casts off Old Hamlet, just as she asks Hamlet to "cast [his] nighted colour off" (1.2.68 [TLN 248]). For the material memory of mourning devotes its wearer to the ghosts of the past.

And it is in terms of clothing that Hamlet demands of his mother that she remake herself:

> Assume a vertue if you haue it not,
> That monster custome, who all sence doth eate
> Of habits deuill, is angell yet in this
> That to the vse of actions faire and good,
> He likewise giues a frock or Liuery
> That aptly is put on.
> (3. 4. 160–65, TLN 2544–44 + 5)

Virtue is figured as a garment that can be put on; the more frequently put on, the more it will be a livery that will dedicate its wearer to "actions faire and good." The costume of custom habituates one to the habits (both dress and customary behavior) of good and evil alike.[64] And the clothing of habit "almost can change the stamp of nature" (3.4.168 [TLN 2546 + 1]). It is, Hamlet claims, Gertrude's ability to be permeated, like cloth, that can (almost) undo the "stamp" that Nature, like a seal or a press, has imprinted upon Gertrude's wax or paper.[65] Although here the livery of custom is opposed

64. Harold Jenkins notes of "habit" that "its original meaning, dress, was still the usual one; and indeed the passage beautifully illustrates how a word which at first referred to clothing can come to denote customary behaviour" (*Hamlet*, ed. Harold Jenkins, the Arden Shakespeare [London: Methuen, 1982], p. 521).

65. On memory, stamping and materiality, I am deeply indebted to Margreta de Grazia's unpublished paper, "Embodied Memory in *Hamlet*."

to the stamp of nature, Hamlet had previously envisaged "the stamp" of a defect as itself "Natures liuery" (1.4.31–32 [TLN 621 + 15–621 + 16]), as if clothes were themselves a seal that imprinted their wearer. While Hamlet imagines the body as stamped, Gertrude imagines her soul as dyed. Turning her eyes into her soul, Gertrude sees "such blacke and grained spots, / As will not leaue their Tinct" (F1, 3.4.90–91 [TLN 2466–67]).[66] "Tinct" is from the Latin *tingere,* to dye or stain. And the spots that Gertrude sees in F1 are both black and red, since the technical meaning of "grained" is dyed in scarlet.[67] The dyeing or imprinting of clothing, though, is not to be undone by the revelation of "naked" Truth, but by a new imprinting or permeation by it.

As Margreta de Grazia observes, *Hamlet* "is pervaded by images of permeable materials and matter, specifically textile materials and corporeal matter."[68] Old Hamlet's Ghost seems finally both too immaterial ("This bodilesse creation," Gertrude calls it [3.4.139 (TLN 2521)]) and too armored to be memorable. The heart can only be moved, Hamlet tells Gertrude,

> [i]f damned custome haue not brasd it so,
> That it be proofe and bulwark against sence.
> (3.4.37–38 [TLN 2419–20])

Covered with brass, the heart becomes "proofe" — that is, like proof armor, or armor of tested strength and quality. For the heart to be invulnerable, it must become as unbending as armor. Hamlet, though, invokes his mother's heart as "made of penitrable stuffe" (3.4.36 [TLN 2418]), made, that is, of material that can be stained.[69] In *Hamlet,* it is "penitrable stuffe," rather than the armored legacy of the father, that is the material of haunting.

---

66. Q2 reads here: "And there I see such blacke and greeued spots/ As will leaue there their tinc't." The curious opposition between "will not leaue" (F) and "will leaue" (Q2) is partially undone by the ambiguity of "leave," which, as Harold Jenkins observes, "means either cease, give up (F) or cause to remain behind (F)" (*Hamlet,* 324).

67. Scarlet was, by the late sixteenth century, made from cochineal beetles imported from Mexico. The beetles looked like, and were constantly mistaken for, seeds, hence the name "grain."

68. De Grazia, "Embodied Memory," 8.

69. "Stuff" could mean matter generally, but it was directly related to the Italian *stoffa,* a piece of rich textile fabric, and was frequently used in English both for the material for making garments and for a specific kind of woollen cloth. See the OED, heading 5.

INDEX

Augustine of Hippo (*continued*)
Remission of Sins, 20; *On Free Will,* 20;
On Holy Virginity, 31; *On Marriage and
Concupiscence,* 23–24, 32, 34; *On the Good
of Marriage,* 31, 34
Augustus (emperor), 88
Aurelianus, Celius, 170
Authority: cultural, 263–64, 279, 286;
female, 209, 225; patriarchal, 3, 13, 166,
201; transference of cultural, 263. *See
also* Translatio
autoeroticism: female, 183
Avenzoar, 247
Avicenna, 247; *Canon,* 126, 249; on men-
struation, 141
Avignon: transfer of the papal seat to, 281

Babayan, Kathryn, 167
Bale, John, 217–20, 225; protestant poetics
of, 219, 229
Ballaster, Ros, 193
Balsam, 250
Barker, Francis, 199
Barnes, Robert, 148
Barnfield, Richard, 306
Bartholin, Thomas, 109, 111, 120, 122, 137,
171–73, 176; *Anatomia reformata,* 127
Bateson, Gregory, 110
Beatrice, 281, 282
Behn, Aphra, 69, 194
Belli, Onorio, 249
Belon, Pierre, 250
Benedict XIV (pope). *See* Lambertini,
Prospero
Benivieni, Antonio, 115, 131
Bennett, Paula, 181
Benoît de St. Maure: *Roman de Troie,* 264
Bentley, Thomas, 228; *The Monument of
Matrons,* 225, 231
Bequest: ritual of, 208
Beza, Theodore, 228
Bhabha, Homi, 191
Birthmarks: and maternal imagination,
57–58

Bisexuality: Fliess on, 151
Bleeding, 100–104, 128–30, 134; artificial,
111
Blondel, James, 56
Blood, 2, 91–92; excess of, 133; fermenta-
tion of, 135–36; menstrual, 98–101, 143;
nobility of, 218; purity of, 9, 196, 199;
retention of, 139; therapeutic use of, 2,
120. *See also* Plethora
Bloodletting, 11, 138–39, 240, 243–47;
menstruation and, 139
Bloom, Harold, 3
Boiardo, Matteo Maria: *Orlando innamo-
rato,* 57
Boleyn, Ann, 212
Boose, Lynda, 71
Borch, Olaf: *The Wisdom of Hermes of the
Egyptians,* 260
Botany, 240, 250–51, 254
Boyle, Robert, 144
Bradamante, 46
Bradstreet, Anne, 195
Brown, Peter, 23
Burton, Richard: *A Thousand and One
Nights,* 178

Cady Stanton, Elizabeth, 18
Camilla, 72
Camocke, Robert, 290
Campanella, Tommaso, 49, 59, 63
Cancellar, John, 218–23, 228; *The Path of
Obedience,* 219
Cardano, Girolamo, 248, 255
Cardoso, Isaac: *Las excelencias de los
hebreos,* 120–22
Casaubon, Isaac, 258
Castillo y Solórzano, Alonso, 191
Castle, Terry, 304; *The Apparitional Lesbian,*
179–80
Castration, 88; symbolic, 74
Catherine de Medici, 221
Catherine of Aragon, 212
Catullus, 276
Cecil, William, 225

Celsus, 84, 89, 94–96, 100, 102–3, 247, 256
Cervantes, Miguel, 193
Chariclea, 67
Charles d'Anjou, 265
Charles de Valois, 281
Chartier, Roger: on privatization of
    reading, 203–4
Chiron the centaur, 241
Chojnacki, Stanley, 66
Christ: genealogy of, 18, 34; generation of,
    4–5, 17, 31, 33–39; and theory of virgin
    birth, 37–38
Churchyard, Thomas, 305–6
Cicero: De divinatione, 52
Cimburga of Baden: monument to, 294
Circumcision: female, 174. See also Clitori-
    dectomy
Class: genealogy of, 190–91
Clement of Alexandria: Stromateis, 241, 255
Clement V (pope), 281
Clitoridectomy, 65, 168, 174–75, 178
Clitoris, 8: anatomical illustration of, 172;
    colonialist discourse of, 180; as emblem
    of female erotic transgression, 169–70,
    173–74, 176; equation with the penis,
    153–55, 158, 180–82, 184–85; hypertrophy
    of, 167–75; and lesbianism, 154–56, 158,
    176, 181; of African women, 167–70; and
    orgasm, 158; rediscovery of, 156–58,
    169; and tribadism, 155, 173–77. See also
    clitoridectomy
Clorinda, 6, 43–46, 63, 68–77; armor of,
    77; baptism of, 6; martyrdom of, 6;
    masculine behaviour of, 75; as mon-
    strous daughter, 43, 47, 69, 75; and
    paternal authorization, 76; as Persian,
    76; as woman warrior, 45–46, 70
Clothing: associated with memory, 287,
    314–16; of ghosts, 288
Clytemnestra, 305–6
Coffee, 245
Colombo, Realdo, 8
Columella, 85–86
Combe, Thomas, 310

Community: bond of female, 207–8
Concupiscence, 25, 40
Conring, Hermann, 258–60
Continence. See Asceticism
Contini, Gianfranco, 272, 278
Cook, Richard, 290
Crisis: medical notion of, 100–101, 128, 138,
    141, 144–45
Crooke, Helkiah: Microcosmographia,
    169–72
Cruz, Sor Juana Inés de la, 195
Culpeper, Nicholas: Complete Midwife's
    Practice Enlarged, 172; Fourth Book of
    Practical Physick, 174
Cyprian, 19

Daniel, Samuel: The Complaint of Rosa-
    mond, 306
Dante Alighieri: Commedia, 12, 263, 280–86
D'Aquapendente, Fabrizzi, 122–23
David (biblical king), 222
De Grazia, Margreta, 316
Deiphobe (Cuman sibyl), 190
Dekker, Thomas, 313
Della Porta, Giambattista, 59
Della Terza, Dante, 68
Democritus, 84, 242, 256
Denham, Henry, 219, 225
Derrida, Jacques: on "prosthetic body,"
    296–97
De Wenckh, Johann Baptist, 109
Diderot, Denis: Dream of D'Alembert, 152
Dido, 282
Diodorus Siculus, 241
Dioscorides, 250–51, 256
Discharge: bodily, 136–38; as a pathologi-
    cal symptom, 144–45
Domenichini, Lodovico, 54
Donne, John: monument to, 292–93
Drayton, Michael, 306
Dudley, Robert, 220–23, 230

Eamon, William, 246
Eden, Garden of, 31

Effeminacy: bleeding and, 104–5, 118–19

Egypt: genealogy of medicine and 11, 235–61; and hypertrophy of the clitoris, 167–68

Ejaculation, 84, 94–95

Elizabeth I (queen), 10–11, 209–31; as Christ's spouse, 224–25, 227; and holy incest, 10, 227–29; as illegitimate daughter, 10, 213–14; as mother and spouse of England, 216; as translator of Marguerite de Navarre, 10, 210–11, 215; virginity of, 223, 228–29

Empedocles, 54

Empirics, 246–47

Engelbert II of Nassau: monument to, 294

Ephemerides medico-physicae, 115–18, 124, 142

Epicurus, 256

Erikson, Amy, 308

Essentialism: anatomical, 9, 170–71, 182, 186; and colonialism, 179, 182

Este (family), 47

Ethiopians, 28, 56; and Anabaptism, 5, 66; as demons, 66; as monstrous people, 43, 63–66, 72; wives, 71; women, 65

Eunuch, 1, 74, 102

Euripides: *Hecuba*, 294, 297

Eve, 26, 30–32, 35, 40

Falloppio, Gabriele, 8

Farnese (family), 251

Federman, Lillian, 174

Female body: dismemberment of, 199–200; and law of vital periodicity, 150; as paradigm of bodily processes, 8, 149–50; as site of presumed pathologies, 43; as therapeutic model, 138, 141

Femininity: domestication of, 68; as masquerade, 198; orthodox, 70

Ficino, Marsilio, 2, 54, 258

Fioravanti, Leonardo, 246

Il Fiore, 12, 263, 272–80

Fisher-Homberger, Esther: *Krankheit Frau*, 142

Fleming, John, 273

Fliess, Wilhelm, 150

Foucault, Michel, 42, 157, 159, 193

Fracastoro, 255

Franck, Georg, 122–23

Freind, John, 141; *Emmenologia*, 133

French: cultural hegemony of, 12, 262–86

Freud, Sigmund, 41, 71, 75, 151; on the clitoris, 153–55; on lesbian identity, 156, 177, 179–80, 185; *The Uncanny*, 304

Fuss, Diana, 182

Galen, 5, 36, 48, 85–88, 94, 99–100, 103, 126, 131, 141, 235, 245–52, 256; *De sectis*, 124; *De venae sectione adversus Erasistratum*, 138; *On Hygiene*, 82, 107

Gallagher, Catherine, 194

Gallop, Jane, 182–83

Gallus, 276

Garrick, David, 126

Gee, John: *New Shreds of the old Snare*, 304

Gender relations: abusive, 9, 190–93, 196–99; and marriage, 199–200; struggle for epistemological authority and, 193

Genealogy: incestuous, 209, 231; literary, 3–4, 9, 90, 262–63, 273, 276–78, 286

Generation: of Christ, 4–5, 17, 31, 33–39; masculinity and, 84, 105; maternal imagination and, 54–61; of monsters, 49–61, 85; paternal primacy in, 1, 71; role of women in, 5, 48–63; spontaneous, 4

George, Saint, 5, 43–45, 66–68, 72, 74; as patriarchal father, 70

Getto, Giovanni, 70

Ghiselin de Busbecq, Ogier, 162, 164, 178

Ghost: in armor, 291–92, 299, 312–16; female, 305; of Hamlet's father, 12, 291, 313–16; haunting of, 302–4, 316; paternal inheritance and, 13, 305, 312; of the patriarchal father, 305; in Renaissance theater, 288–89, 302–3, 305; winding sheet and, 13, 292–94

Gittings, Clare, 289

Glover, Thomas, 164
Goldberg, Jonathan, 168
Gonorrhea, 65
Gosson, Stephen, 303
Grey Dudley, Jane, 225
Grosz, Elizabeth, 196
Guanierio, Antonio, 51
Guilandinus, Melchior, 11, 237–40, 243, 248–54; *Papyrus*, 240, 252

Hackett, Helen, 229
Hagendorn, Ehrenfried, 116
Hall, Edward, 302
Hallet, Judith, 176
Hamlet, 12, 288–91, 294, 287, 312–16
Harem, 162–67; associated with nunnery, 163
Haunting, 302–4; of the dead father, 311, 316. *See also* Ghost
Headlam Wells, Robin, 229
Hector, 297–98
Hegel, Friedrich: *Philosophy of the Mind*, 57
Heirloom, 210, 215
Heliodorus; *Aethiopica*, 67–68
Helvidius, 33
Hemorrhoids: 116–17, 119, 121, 127–28; functional equivalence between menstruation and, 7, 111–13, 118, 124–26; salutary character of, 125–26
Henry VII of Luxemburg, 280–81
Henry VIII, 212, 223
Heraclitus, 256
Herdt, Gilbert: *Rituals of Manhood*, 110
Hermaphroditism, 7, 119; pseudo-, 149
Hermes Trismegistus, 11, 235, 241, 257–60
Hermetica, 258
Heron, Sir Nichols: tomb of, 291
Heywood, Thomas: *The English Traveller*, 296
Hippo Regius, 23
Hippocrates, 117, 133–34, 241–42, 247, 256–57; *Epidemics*, 100
Hippocratics, 99–100

Hoffmann, Friedric, 144
Holmes, Martin, 299
Homer, 253
Homoeroticism, 8, 200–203
Homosexuality, 155, 204; female, 162, 166–70, 176–77, 180–81, 183; Foucault on, 159. *See also* Lesbianism; Tribadism
Huarte, Juan, 56
Huet, Marie-Hélène, 62
Hulme, Peter, 156
Humors: retention of, 137. *See also* Obstruction sickness
Hungerford, Sir Thomas, 310–11

Iliad, 297–98
Imagination: maternal, 13–14, 43, 54–63; paternal, 48, 58
Incest: as enabling condition for female agency, 10–11, 210, 214, 231; holy, 210–12, 218–19, 227–29
Infanticide, 51
Inheritance: of the father's bed, 307–11; in *Hamlet*, 311; memory and, 289, 305; patrilinear, 308–11; rules of, 307–8, 311
Insemination, 83, 86, 97
Intercourse, 83–86, 89, 105; Celsus on, 95
Irigaray, Luce, 181; *This Sex Which Is Not One*, 182–83
Isidore of Seville, 52; *Ethymologiae*, 48, 63
Isomorphism, 157–58

Jed, Stephanie, 194–95
Jerome, 31–33
Jews: accused of infanticide, 120; and male menstruation, 120–23
Jonson, Ben: *The Devil Is an Ass*, 304
Joseph (Jesus' father), 5, 32–36
Journal des savants, 115
Julian of Eclanum, 4, 18–40; *To Turbantius*, 24

Kahn, Victoria, 193
Kaminsky, Amy Katz, 198
Keller, Eve, 169

Kerrigan, John, 287
King, 150
Klein, Lisa M., 215
Kristeva, Julia, 76
Kyd, Thomas: *Cornelia*, 295; *The Spanish Tragedy*, 287, 299, 305, 314

Labor pain, 30
Lacan, Jacques, 70, 296; *The Meaning of the Phallus*, 76
Laguna, Andrés, 113–14, 119, 122–23
Laius, 3
Lambertini, Prospero (cardinal), 145
Lange, Johann, 242–43, 254, 260
Laqueur, Thomas, 8, 112, 153, 157–59, 177–78
Latifau, Pére, 56
Latini, Brunetto: *Il tesoretto*, 12, 263–72
Le Clerc, Daniel, 257, 260
Lecat, Nicolas, 57
Lennio, Levino, 2
Leo Africanus, 168–72; *The History and Description of Africa*, 165
Leonardo da Vinci: *Quaderni d'anatomia*, 49
Lesbianism, 7–8, 69, 160, 177, 179, 186, 191, 200; colonial discourse of, 180; as a pathology, 156, 186
Leucippus, 256
Lipen, Martin: *Bibliotheca realis medica*
Lipenius. See Lipen, Martin
Locus amoenus, 12, 263, 267, 284–85
Lorris, Guillaume de: *Roman de la Rose*, 12, 267–68, 271, 273–79, 283–84
Lucan, 282
Lucretius: *De rerum naturae*, 48
Lusitanus, Amatus, 115, 123, 125, 131, 137
Lusitanus, Zacutus, 122–23
Lust, 26–27. *See also* Concupiscence

MacCaffrey, Wallace, 213
Madellén, Maria Caro de, 191
Magic: Jewish, 243; natural, 11, 242–43, 254, 260–61

Male body: as a paradigm of sexual difference, 112; as standard of bodily processes, 152; superiority of, 134–35
Mamelukes, 247
Manfred (king of Sicily), 264–65
Manicheanism, 19–20, 23–24, 32, 34–35
Manuli, Paola, 142
Manwood, Sir Roger: tomb of, 291
Marguerite de Navarre: on the biblical story of Miriam, 216; *Heptameron*, 197; *Mirror of the Sinful Soul*, 10, 209; trope of incest in, 210–16
Marinello, Giovanni, 60
Marriage, 31–35, 40, 199; criticism of Christian, 9, 200–201
Martial, 176
Masculinity, 2, 81–83; contradictions of, 7, 83, 105–8; efficiency of, 102; insemination and, 85–86, 105; sexual asceticism and, 7, 88, 90, 97; upper-class control of, 7, 106–8
Matelda, 284
Maternity: as a masquerade, 61
Mattioli, Pietro Andrea, 251
McClure, Peter, 229
Mead, Margaret, 110
Medicine: Arabic, 247, 254, 259; Egyptian origins of, 11, 235–61; Greek origins of, 11, 241–42; Paracelsian, 236, 258–59
Melanchton, Philip, 53
Menstruation, 2–3, 83; anti-Jewish bias and, 120–23; and birth defects, 50; as brand of women's physical inferiority, 142–43; as a divine punishment, 123–24, 143; ectopic, 148; effeminacy and, 118–19; and epileptic crisis, 145; female, 97–101, 134, 149; fertility and, 119; iatrochemical theory of, 135; longevity and, 115, 119, 141; male, 7–8, 101–5, 109–52; as a marker of sex difference, 149; ovular theory of, 146; as a pathology, 146–47; Plutarch on, 98; suppression of, 132; therapeutic value of, 141–42; unusual pathways of, 132–36, 144, 147–48; vicari-

CONTRIBUTORS NOTES

KEVIN BROWNLEE is professor of French and Italian at the University of Pennsylvania. He is the author of *Poetic Identity in Guillaume de Machaut* and coeditor of *Rethinking the Romance of the Rose: Text, Image, Reception; Discourses of Authority in Medieval and Renaissance Literature; The New Medievalism;* and *Romance: Generic Transformation from Chrétien de Troyes to Cervantes.*

MARINA SCORDILIS BROWNLEE is the Class of 1963 College of Women Professor of Romance Languages at the University of Pennsylvania. Among her books are *The Poetics of Literary Theory: Lope and Cervantes, The Status of the Reading Subject in the "Libro de buen amor," The Severed Word: Ovid's "Heroides" and the "Novela Sentimental,"* and *The Cultural Labyrinth of María de Zayas.*

ELIZABETH A. CLARK is John Carlisle Kilgo Professor of Religion at Duke University. As a scholar of early Christian history and texts, she has written on women, sexuality, asceticism, heresy and orthodoxy, and Biblical interpretation in the Early Christian era. Among her recent books are *The Origenist Controversy: The Cultural Construction of an Early Christian Debate* and *Reading Renunciation: Asceticism and Scripture in Early Christianity.* She is currently at work on a book on the intersections of history and theory in early Christian studies.

VALERIA FINUCCI teaches Italian at Duke University. She is the author of *The Lady Vanishes: Subjectivity and Representation in Castiglione and Ariosto;* edited Moderata Fonte's *Tredici canti del Floridoro* and *Renaissance Transactions: Ariosto and Tasso;* and coedited *Desire in the Renaissance: Psychoanalysis and Literature.* A recently completed manuscript, *The Politics of the Body in the Italian Renaissance,* explores the construction of the castrated, improper, hermaphroditic and idealized body in the literature and culture of early modern Italy.

DALE B. MARTIN, Professor of Religious Studies at Yale University, specializes in New Testament studies and the social history of early Christianity. His publications include *Slavery as Salvation: The Metaphor of Slavery in Pauline Christianity* and *The Corinthian Body*. He also works on issues of gender, sexuality, and cultural studies of the Greco-Roman world. A recently completed manuscript, *Grand Optimal Illusion: The Ancient Scientific Invention of Superstition,* provides an ideological analysis of ancient medical, scientific, and popular materials on disease and healing.

GIANNA POMATA teaches History of Science at the University of Bologna, Italy. She is the author of *La promessa di guarigione: medici e curatori* (1994, English: *Contracting a Cure: Patients, Healers and the Law in Early Modern Bologna,* 1998), of *Un tribunale dei malati* (1983), and coedited *Ragnatele di rapporti* (1988).

MAUREEN QUILLIGAN is R. Florence Brinkley Professor of English at Duke University. Author of a number of books on allegory and epic, she is currently at work on two books about female authority in the Renaissance: *Incest and Agency* and *When Women Ruled the World: The Glorious Sixteenth Century.*

NANCY G. SIRAISI is professor of History at Hunter College and the Graduate Center of the City University of New York. She is the author of various studies of medieval and Renaissance medical learning and practice in their intellectual and social contexts.

PETER STALLYBRASS teaches English and Comparative Literature at the University of Pennsylvania, where he also directs the seminar on the History of Material Texts. With Allon White, he wrote *The Politics and Poetics of Transgression,* and he co-edited *Staging the Renaissance: Studies in Elizabethan and Jacobean Drama, Subject and Object in Renaissance Culture,* and *Language Machines: Technologies of Literary and Cultural Production.* His most recent books are *O Casaco de Marx: Roupas, Memória, Dor,* and, with Ann Rosalind Jones, *Renaissance Clothing and the Materials of Memory.*

VALERIE TRAUB teaches English and Women's Studies at the University of Michigan. She is the author of *Desire and Anxiety: Circulation of Sexuality in Shakespearean Drama,* as well as of numerous essays on gender, sexuality, and homoeroticism in early modern England.

Library of Congress Cataloging-in-Publication Data

Generation and degeneration : tropes of reproduction in
literature and history from antiquity to early modern
Europe / edited by Valeria Finucci and Kevin Brownlee.

Includes bibliographical references and index.

ISBN 0-8223-2655-8 (cloth : alk. paper) —
ISBN 0-8223-2644-2 (pbk. : alk. paper)

1. Sex role—History.   2. Sex role in literature.
3. Human reproduction—Social aspects.   4. Human
reproduction in literature.   5. Genealogy (Philosophy)
6. Genealogy in literature.   7. Patrilineal kinship.
I. Finucci, Valeria.   II. Brownlee, Kevin.

HQ1075 .G4674 2001   305.3'09—dc21   00-045185